The Reformation was, in many ways, an experiment in conversion. English Protestant writers and preachers urged conversion from popery to the Gospel, from idolatry to the true worship of God, while Catholic polemicists persuaded people away from heresy to truth, from the schismatic Church of England to unity with Rome.

Much work on this period has attempted to measure the speed and success of changes in religion. Did England become a Protestant nation? How well did the regime reform the Church along Protestant lines? How effectively did Catholic activists obstruct the Protestant programme? However, Michael Questier's meticulous study of conversion is the first to concentrate on this phenomenon from the perspective of individual converts, people who alternated between conformity to and rejection of the pattern of worship established by law. In the process it suggests that some of the current notions about Protestantisation are simplistic. By discovering how people were exhorted to change religion, how they experienced conversion and how they faced demands for Protestant conformity, Michael Questier develops a fresh perspective on the nature of the English Reformation.

Cambridge Studies in Early Modern British History

CONVERSION, POLITICS AND RELIGION IN ENGLAND, 1580–1625

Cambridge Studies in Early Modern British History

Series editors

ANTHONY FLETCHER
Professor of History, University of Essex

JOHN GUY
Professor of Modern History, University of St Andrews

and JOHN MORRILL
Reader in Early Modern History, University of Cambridge, and Fellow and Tutor of Selwyn College

This is a series of monographs and studies covering many aspects of the history of the British Isles between the late fifteenth and the early eighteenth century. It includes the work of established scholars and pioneering work by a new generation of scholars. It includes both reviews and revisions of major topics and books, which open up new historical terrain or which reveal startling new perspectives on familiar subjects. All the volumes set detailed research into our broader perspectives and the books are intended for the use of students as well as of their teachers.

For a list of titles in the series, see end of book.

CONVERSION, POLITICS AND RELIGION IN ENGLAND, 1580–1625

MICHAEL C. QUESTIER

CAMBRIDGE
UNIVERSITY PRESS

Published by the Press Syndicate of the University of Cambridge
The Pitt Building, Trumpington Street, Cambridge CB2 1RP
40 West 20th Street, New York, NY 10011-4211, USA
10 Stamford Road, Oakleigh, Melbourne 3166, Australia

First published 1996

Printed in Great Britain by Redwood Books, Kennet Way, Trowbridge, Wilts

A catalogue record for this book is available from the British Library

Library of Congress cataloguing in publication data
Questier, Michael C.
Conversion, politics, and religion in England, 1580–1625 /
Michael C. Questier.
p.   cm. – (Cambridge studies in early modern British history)
Includes bibliographical references and index.
ISBN 0 521 44214 1
1. England – Church history – 16th century.   2. England – Church
History – 17th century.   3. Great Britain – History, Elizabeth,
1558–1603.   4. Great Britain – History – James I, 1603–1625.
5. Conversion.   6. Anglican converts – England – History.
7. Catholic converts – England – History.   8. Reformation – England.
I. Title.   II. Series.
BR755/Q47   1996   95–47280
274.2'06–dc20   CIP

ISBN 0 521 44214 1 hardback

WD

CONTENTS

ACKNOWLEDGMENTS

When I started research as a postgraduate, and surveyed the bleak horizons of an apparently most hostile academic environment, my experience, probably the same as that of many others, was that the prefaces of academic books which rendered such unrestrained gratitude to so many people for their selfless assistance were no reflection of reality. But academic research in the end always means reliance on the goodwill of others. I would like to express my thanks towards a number of individuals from whose advice and criticism I have greatly benefited. To the following in particular am I indebted: Peter Lake, Kenneth Fincham, Andrew Foster and Anthony Milton for explaining the nature of the field to me in the first place, and for incredible generosity with their time and their unpublished research; to the late John Aveling for making available to me his extraordinary notes on the proceedings of the high commission at York; to Robert Dodaro for advice on style and help on the seventeenth-century use of patristic sources; to Simon Healy of the History of Parliament trust; and to Michael Hawkins, my indefatigable doctoral supervisor; also to Antony Allison, Michael Bowman, Geoffrey Holt, David Katz, Roy Kendall, Thomas McCoog, Gregory Randolph, and to my doctoral examiners John Bossy, William Lamont and Nicholas Tyacke, and William Davies and Pauline Leng at Cambridge University Press. I have been assisted by the staffs of the libraries and record offices where I have worked, and most notably by Ian Dickie of Westminster Cathedral Archives. The staff of Sussex University Library were highly efficient, particularly the late Mrs Audrey Taylor who provided copies of microfilms. I am grateful also to the British Academy for its support over the years, and in particular for its flexibility in allowing me to move from one institution to another in order to facilitate research.

I firmly believe that this is not just the 'book of the thesis' (my doctoral research dissertation at the University of Sussex) but has gone some considerable way beyond the dissertation on which it is based. The dissertation dealt with conversion principally by tracing people who altered their ecclesiastical allegiance. Towards the end of writing the dissertation it was starting to dawn on me that in the late sixteenth and early seventeenth centuries conversion was a very large part of contemporary religious experience. It impinged heavily on theological discourse, the relationship between the Church and the State, and the enforcement of conformity and uniformity. In some sense the Reformation can be described as an experiment in conversion. The present volume is not, of course, a new history of the Reformation. It explores the connection between politics and religion in contemporary experience of conversion. But it argues that a study of people who consciously changed their religious orientation so that they became either Romanist or Protestant throws light on the nature of the English Reformation more generally.

My greatest debt is still unquestionably to my parents for making sure that I was never in debt. (How many of the sixteenth- and seventeenth-century clerics in this volume would have been grateful for patronage such as theirs!) To them, whether they are interested by it or not, in gratitude this book is dedicated.

NOTE ON THE TEXT

In the text dates are given Old Style but the year is taken to begin on 1 January. The place of publication of the printed works cited is London unless otherwise stated. Original punctuation, capitalisation and spelling has been retained in all quotations from contemporary manuscripts and printed works (with contractions silently expanded) and in citations of printed works, though i is transposed to j, and u to v.

ABBREVIATIONS

AAW	Archives of the Archdiocese of Westminster
Add.	Additional Manuscripts
Anstruther	G. Anstruther, *The Seminary Priests* (4 vols., Ware and Great Wakering, 1968–77)
APC	*Acts of the Privy Council of England*, ed. J. R. Dasent *et al.* (46 vols., 1890–1964)
ARSJ	Archivum Romanum Societatis Jesu (Society of Jesus, Archives)
Bodl.	Bodleian Library, Oxford
Borders	*Calendar of Letters and Papers relating to the Affairs of the Borders of England and Scotland* (2 vols. for 1560–1603) ed. J. Bain (Edinburgh, 1894–6)
BI	Borthwick Institute, York
BIHR	*Bulletin of the Institute of Historical Research*
BL	British Library
CCSL	*Corpus Christianorum, Series Latina*
CRS	Catholic Record Society
CRS 2	*Miscellanea II* (CRS 2, 1906)
CRS 3	*Miscellanea III* (CRS 3, 1906)
CRS 4	*Miscellanea IV* (CRS 4, 1907)
CRS 5	J. H. Pollen (ed.), *Unpublished Documents relating to the English Martyrs*, I, 1584–1603 (CRS 5, 1908)
CRS 9	*Miscellanea VII* (CRS 9, 1911)
CRS 10–11	E. H. Burton and T. L. Williams (eds.), *The Douay College Diaries* (CRS 10–11, 1911)
CRS 18	M. M. C. Calthrop (ed.), *Recusant Roll No. 1, 1592–3* (CRS 18, 1916)
CRS 30	E. Henson (ed.), *Registers of the English College at Valladolid 1589–1862* (CRS 30, 1930)
CRS 39	L. Hicks (ed.), *Letters and Memorials of Father Robert Persons, SJ*, I, (CRS 39, 1942)

CRS 41	L. Hicks (ed.), *Letters of Thomas Fitzherbert 1608–1610* (CRS 41, 1948)
CRS 51	P. Renold (ed.), *The Wisbech Stirs (1595–1598)* (CRS 51, 1958)
CRS 52	A. G. Petti (ed.), *The Letters and Despatches of Richard Verstegan (c. 1550–1640)* (CRS 52, 1959)
CRS 53	C. Talbot (ed.), *Miscellanea* (CRS 53, 1961)
CRS 54–5	A. Kenny (ed.), *The Responsa Scholarum of the English College, Rome* (2 vols., CRS 54–5, 1962–3)
CRS 56	E. E. Reynolds (ed.), *Miscellanea* (CRS 56, 1964)
CRS 57	H. Bowler (ed.), *Recusant Roll No. 2 (1593–1594)* (CRS 57, 1965)
CRS 60	A. G. Petti (ed.), *Recusant Documents from the Ellesmere Manuscripts* (CRS 60, 1968)
CRS 61	H. Bowler (ed.), *Recusant Roll No. 3 (1594–1595) and Recusant Roll No. 4 (1595–1596)* (CRS 61, 1970)
CRS 64/68	A. J. Loomie (ed.), *Spain and the Jacobean Catholics* (2 vols., CRS 64, 68, 1973, 1978)
CRS 67	P. J. Holmes (ed.), *Elizabethan Casuistry* (CRS 67, 1981)
CRS 71	H. Bowler and T. J. McCann (eds.), *Recusants in the Exchequer Pipe Rolls 1581–1592* (CRS 71, 1986)
CRS 73	M. Murphy (ed.), *St Gregory's College, Seville, 1592–1767* (CRS 73, 1992)
CSEL	*Corpus Scriptorum Ecclesiasticorum Latinorum*
CSPD	*Calendar of State Papers, Domestic Series* (12 vols. for 1547–1625), ed. R. Lemon and M. A. E. Green (1856–72)
CSPV	*Calendar of State Papers, Venetian Series* (11 vols. for 1581–1625) ed. H. F. Brown and A. B. Hinds (1894–1912)
CU Libr.	Cambridge University Library
DNB	*Dictionary of National Biography*
EHR	*English Historical Review*
Foley	H. Foley, *Records of the English Province of the Society of Jesus* (7 vols., 1875–83)
Harl.	Harleian Manuscripts
HMC	Historical Manuscripts Commission
HMC Downshire MSS	*Report on the Manuscripts of the Marquess of Downshire*, ed. E. K. Purnell *et al.*, (5 vols., HMC, 1924–8)

HMC Rutland MSS	*The Manuscripts of his Grace the Duke of Rutland*, ed. H. C. Maxwell Lyte (4 vols., 1888–1905)
HMC Salisbury MSS	*Calendar of the Manuscripts of the Most Honourable the Marquess of Salisbury*, ed. M. S. Giuseppi *et al.* (24 vols., HMC, 1888–1976)
HJ	*Historical Journal*
HR	*Historical Research*
JBS	*Journal of British Studies*
JEH	*Journal of Ecclesiastical History*
Lansd.	Lansdowne Manuscripts
LPL	Lambeth Palace Library
n.p.	no place (of publication)
PL	*Patrologia Cursus Completus . . . Series (Latina) Prima*, ed. J.-P. Migne (221 vols., Paris, 1844–64)
P&P	*Past and Present*
PRO	Public Record Office
Rawl.	Rawlinson Manuscripts
RH	*Recusant History*
TD	M. A. Tierney, *Dodd's Church History of England* (5 vols., 1839–43)
WSRO	West Sussex Record Office

1

Introduction

Why offer to the press yet another book about politics and religion in early modern England? Considering the current flood of published material on the dissensions within the English Church before the Civil War, one might well admit, with John Hacket, that 'the easie Dispatch of so many Sheets in a day . . . hath found the World a great deal more Work then needs'.[1] My defence for adding to these torrents of paper is that this monograph is not another general review of the quarrels between Catholics and Protestants in late-sixteenth- and early seventeenth-century England. But its central topic – conversion to and from the Church of Rome – does, I hope, allow for a revision of aspects of the historiography of those quarrels, and principally in that vexed question of the course and intensity of the later English Reformation. Historians have recognised that there was considerable flux in religious opinion and practice during this period but they have notoriously disagreed about the speed and efficiency with which Protestant religion was accepted and enforced. There is little meeting of minds between those who see the triumph of novelty and reform and those who perceive insuperable obstacles to it, a mixture of Romishness and die-hard opposition to anything new.

Deciphering the course of the English Reformation has always entailed determining whether, primarily, politicians exploited Reformed ideas to achieve their political aims, or whether an irrepressible wash of novel, humanist, Protestant theological discourse exploited, and even sometimes determined, the ebb and flow of political conflict. I suggest that the perennial debate over the chains of causation in Reformation history can be extended by trying to determine what made a person think he had become either a Protestant or a Catholic, and also what the aims were of the manipulative controllers who sought to induce change of religion in him. This is not to pretend that a study of individual converts allows anything so precise as an accurate geographical or chronological record of the flux in

---

[1] John Hacket, *Scrinia Reserata* (1693), I, 1.

1

Protestant and Catholic allegiances. (Conversion does not generally lend itself to quantitative analysis.) But, even if the Protestant Reformation in England cannot be described as a series of individual conversions, an analysis of individual uncertainty and resolution of doubt may affect the way we think about central questions in Reformation studies.

On its own it might not seem very remarkable that, once the battle lines were drawn, a decision to become a Catholic or a Protestant in England should always be partly a matter of politics and partly a matter of religion, and that, try as they might, people could not consciously adhere to the Roman or the English Church without having an eye constantly to both sorts of motive. It is a commonplace in all ecclesiastical history that doctrinal beliefs have the capacity to engender factional allegiances which have a political character. In that the Church is an institution in which power is exercised by some over others, an organised form of ecclesiastical society as well as a religious concept, it has political characteristics, and the things which it does (even the way that it expresses doctrine) are affected by political considerations. In addition, because religious opinion affects the way that people behave, those who exercise authority on behalf of the State cannot ignore people's opinions about religion. In late-sixteenth- and early seventeenth-century England, attitudes to Rome incorporated not just a series of doctrines about grace but also a view of the relationship between the Church and the State. None of this is very surprising. But it is quite another thing to define exactly how politics and religion commingled in ecclesiastical flux. Conversion is an ideal topic for this type of study because it is drawn out of a matrix of political and religious factors. Consequently conversion is a key to unlocking the nature of religious allegiance in this period. It may be no great insight to perceive that, when people wavered between Roman and Protestant allegiances in England, the rationality of following their own best material interests could be disrupted by anxieties about right and principled belief and conduct just as easily as the purity of their faith and its observance could be clouded by the need to look to their temporal well-being. Still a view of the tensions plaguing the mind of the man who found himself engaged by politico-ecclesiastical questions allows us to think beyond the rigid and stultifying classifications of people based just on their outward behaviour (for example, whether they conformed to the observance of the religion established by law). Not everyone who acted outwardly in a similar way shared identical thought patterns. What are we to make of people who do not really fit into the pigeonhole categories of 'recusant' or 'conformist'? How do we interpret the motivation of the dutiful conforming 'church papist' who, when not under the watchful gaze of the State, suddenly exhibited an enthusiasm for religious ideas of which the State did not approve? More particularly, what of the moderate 'Church of England man' who suddenly adopted explicit Romish opinions, or the rigid Protestant enthusiast who exchanged his Protestant doctrinal enthusiasms for precisely the ones which before he claimed most fervently to reject?

It might be thought that, when political and religious motives mixed, one would naturally subordinate the other almost into extinction. How could the purity of religious motivation (the persuasions based on theological discourse leading towards the regulation of a man's life and faith) autonomously coexist with political motivations (e.g., preservation of estates, career and self against the State's potentially violent intolerance of religious deviance) to believe and practice one thing rather than another? If a man's religious affections happened to coincide with the dictates of the regime, he was fortunate in not having to wrestle with conscience over his external religious profession. But, if a conflict did occur, then historians have tended to assume that he had to take the difficult path of principled resistance (and take the consequences) or cynically make a political accommodation with authority. Thus we see the historiographical fragmentation of the religious and ecclesiastical spectrum into zealots and conformists, and notably the Romish recusant Catholics separated out from the church papists or schismatics, the lukewarm ones who would, if necessary, be circumcised at Constantinople 'with a mentall reservation'.[2]

But this study argues that when political and religious motives were both engaged in the mind of the individual convert they were maintained in a constant tension; they do not fuse, nor is one subordinated to the other. This approach to the paradoxes of politico-religious conflict allows us to determine the nature of ecclesiastical allegiance in a more sophisticated way than by saying merely that a certain person changed his religion because either his patron went to the wall, or he became alienated, wanted a better clerical job, more money, felt persecuted, had a mid-life crisis, or redefined his opinions about the doctrine of predestination. We can thus describe how different elements of political and religious motivation combined with each other and acted out of their separate spheres to influence individuals who were not securely anchored in their religion. In addition, since conversion was recognised as having a continuing quality as well as being a one-off event, its study can tell us not just about the nature of the initial decision to change religion, but, more generally, what it meant to be a Roman Catholic or a Protestant in England during this period.

It is common knowledge that in theology, conversion refers primarily to the way in which sinful man is made regenerate by grace. Nevertheless, the

---

[2] BL, Harl. MS 1221, fo. 65ᵛ.

theology of conversion raises certain imperatives about the sort of Church to which the regenerate man should adhere. This promotes a second type of conversion, namely between ecclesiastical institutions, which takes on a political character. The question of whether a man thinks that he has converted to the true Church, true faith or more generally to true religion raises the question of what he thinks about the conversion of others. The state of other people's religion affects his perception of the structure and regulation and government of the Church to which he and they both think they belong. After the break with Rome, a welter of contradictory philo-sophical views about central Christian tenets engaged with a series of political conflicts so that, for some, the alignment of true faith and Church with institutional faith and Church became exceptionally intense. The association of the two meant that alteration of opinions about the one naturally tended to promote alteration of opinions about the other. It was virtually impossible for people in this period to explain one aspect of change in religious opinion or practice without referring to the other sorts of conversion with which they were familiar: a man's fluctuation between Rome and the Church of England must affect his standing in grace just as deterioration (or amelioration) in his life and 'conversation' could be attributed to his consorting with (or rejection of) the errors and workmen of Romish popery or Protestant heresy.

This study therefore operates on two levels. First, it explores aspects of individual conversion between Roman Catholicism and Protestantism in England in the later Elizabethan and Jacobean periods. On a second level it tries to relate individual alterations of opinion to some of the larger questions about the later English Reformation. It seems fairly clear to historians that at some point in Elizabeth's reign England became a Protestant country, but the debate about Protestantisation has more than occasionally been bedevilled by imprecision as to what it meant for England (or Englishmen) to be Protestant. This book, while not pretending to be a revision of everything which English Reformation historians have said, aims, by studying the microcosm of conversion, to reflect on the ways in which England could be said to have become Protestant.

THE POLITICS OF CONVERSION, 1580–1625

In one sense, of course, the issue was decided by the end of the 1580s. A forcible change of national religion with foreign military assistance was now no longer possible (assuming that it ever had been). English Catholics started to accept minority status. Rome imposed a severe definition of what it meant to be a Roman Catholic in England. The political conflict between the Churches was clarified and intensified, and alteration of a man's religious allegiance became an extreme step. Did the extremism of Romanist politics, its scheming and flirtations with resistance theory, drive a wedge between religious and political Romanism? Outside the propaganda about popery and the threat from Rome, we might think, people would have made decisions about what they really believed in matters of faith in one part of their minds, and dealt with the aspect of religion which touched on allegiance to institutional Churches in another part entirely.

But large numbers of people were compelled to think about which Church they really belonged to precisely because faith was inextricably connected with the fact of the royal supremacy and the challenge to it which definitions of papal primacy seemed to imply. As Edmund Bunny wrote in reply to Robert Persons, English Romanism was proving a tough nut to crack because

> no man . . . can be of that profession [Roman Catholicism], unlesse hee bee under that governement too. Could their Church, and court [of Rome] be sundred; could their religion and regiment be parted . . . then indeed I think that (with many) much might be done; but when as these go so close togither, than no man can professe the one, but that he must be under the other, that goeth . . . somwhat hard with many, that otherwise would finde no scruple at al.[3]

Undoubtedly many people would have liked politics and religion kept apart. Those Catholic clerics who saw their best interests served by a termination of the more ambitious plans for a Catholic succession wanted to sever the connection between their clerical affiliation and their political allegiance.[4] Thomas Wright, a Jesuit who left the order in 1593 on political grounds, seemed to think that just because he was a loyalist the English regime would allow him to follow his conscience in matters of religion.[5] The Lancashire gentleman John Ashton in 1605 said under examination that his conscience would not allow him to conform to the established religion but he acknowledged in his conscience the lawfulness of the royal supremacy.[6] Towards the end of this period we find people like Richard Montagu speculating on the separation of the Church of Rome from the Court of Rome.[7] But such accommodations flew in the face of most contemporary experience. Movement in one sphere meant movement in the other. John Racster expressed a truism when he wrote that 'the change of Common-wealths . . .

---

[3] Edmund Bunny, *A Booke of Christian Exercise* (1585), sig. Yviir.
[4] A. Pritchard, *Catholic Loyalism in Elizabethan England* (1979), 198; AAW, A VII, 444–5.
[5] BL, Lansd. MS 109, fo. 48r.
[6] J. Tait (ed.), *Lancashire Quarter Session Records* (Chetham Society, new series, 77, Manchester, 1917), 282–3.
[7] Bodl., Rawl. MS D 1331, fo. 152v. When toleration came, temporarily, in August 1622, its basis was the suspension of penalties against Catholics in 'any point of recusancy which concerns religion only, and not matter of State', *CSPD 1619–23*, 436.

especially . . . beginneth with the change of religion', and that alterations of government are generally preceded by notorious heresy or schism.[8] Virtually all Protestant polemicists treated the Catholics' toleration petitions in 1603 as an attempt to bring about a change of religion which would snowball into a subversion of the commonwealth.[9] When Archbishop Marc'Antonio de Dominis asserted to Bishop Richard Neile in 1622 that Rome was a true Church (thus justifying his decision to return to full communion with it) Neile did not deny it but said that 'the toleration of two Religions would bee a certaine cause of a combustion in the Church; and subversion of the whole State'.[10] Conversely, political alteration was seen to cause religious change. In 1607 William Bedell reported from Venice how disappointing it was that the Venetian State and the papacy had reached a compromise over their political quarrels. Nevertheless, Bedell thought that the Pope's power 'ys irrecoverablie broken heere, and long yt will not be ere some change [of religion] follow'.[11] The English in Venice had reluctantly decided 'that to propound . . . [Protestant religion] in it owne naked simplici[ty] to men . . . blinded with superstition . . . were but to expose it to contempt'. Bedell believed, however, that the 'same men [who would ridicule Protestant doctrine] read gladly discourses of pollicy, so . . . [if] under that name [re]ligion could be conveied it were like to find much better entertainement'.[12] Thomas Harding, the polemical writer who abandoned his Protestantism after Mary's accession, thanked God 'who used the chaunge of the time, as an occasion and meane, whereby to chaunge . . . [him] unto the better'. By 'the new condition of the time' he was 'compelled to seeke the truth which before . . . [he] knew not, and willingly to holde that, which before . . . [he] refused'.[13] God could bring divine order out of human disorder.

Politics, though, was a two-edged sword. God did not always choose to correct human political errors and vice. The existence of a Protestant regime

---

[8] John Racster, *A Booke of the Seven Planets* (1598), sig. A2ᵛ.

[9] Gabriel Powel, *The Catholikes Supplication* (1603), 27, 29; P. Milward, *Religious Controversies of the Jacobean Age* (1978), 72–6; HMC *Salisbury MSS* XV, 283; C. Russell, 'The Parliamentary Career of John Pym, 1621–1629', in C. Russell, *Unrevolutionary England, 1603–1642* (1990), 205–28, at p. 216, citing Pym's fears that papists having gained a toleration will progressively seek equality and then superiority, 'and after superiority they will seek the subversion of that religion which is contrary to theirs'.

[10] Richard Neile, *M. Ant. de Dnis. Archbishop of Spalato, his Shiftings in Religion* (1624), 10–11.

[11] BL, Lansd. MS 90, fo. 108ᵛ.

[12] BL, Lansd. MS 90, fo. 136ᵛ. This thinking lay behind the presentation of James I's *Premonition* (condemning the papal deposing power) to the authorities in Venice, L. P. Smith (ed.), *The Life and Letters of Sir Henry Wotton* (2 vols., Oxford, 1907), I, 100–7.

[13] J. E. Booty, *John Jewel as Apologist of the Church of England* (1963), 74.

and even relative political security for its Church did not preclude the dangers of subversive popish alterations, as Protestant commentators who doubted England's elect status sometimes opined. At a deeper level, political forms and structures were no guarantee of any sort of religious stability and purity. True religion was always endangered by the corruption and decay of its external expression. The royal chaplain Benjamin Carier saw religion corrupted by politics: 'those points of doctrine wherin wee are made to be at warrs with the church of Rome . . . argue the Corruptions of that state, from whence they come'. In his view 'the contradiction of doctrine hath followed the alteration of state, and not the alteration of state bin grounded uppon any truth of doctrine'. In Humphrey Leech's opinion, the rule in England was 'pipe state; and dance Churche', and 'religion must have no coate otherwise, then measure is taken by the State'.[14] Matthew Sutcliffe would have agreed with Carier, though from a different perspective. Among the motives which Sutcliffe identified as inducing 'so many to like their [Roman] religion' were 'Fire and Sword' and tyrannicide.[15] William Bradshaw thought that conversion to true profession of Protestant religion was within the realm of grace but could be hindered by unfavourable political circumstances. Political uncertainty over religion assisted the Romanists greatly. The secular authorities must assist grace by dashing the political aspirations of the papist 'of state' who adheres to his Romanist profession because he conceives 'great brittlement and uncertaintie in the course of this present government which he supposeth cannot longe last'. By strict enforcement of the law such a person might be compelled to become a Protestant 'of state'. Political Protestantism could then create a holding area out of which Protestants of religion might be drawn by grace.[16] For all these writers, movement in one sphere, political or religious, engendered movement in the other.

One might still enquire whether this mattered very much if England's Protestant polity was so firmly secured, particularly after the principal elements of Catholic resistance had petered out in the early 1590s. Undoubtedly, the actual number of people who, after a period of uncertainty, positively affirmed that Rome was the safe way to salvation, and then signalled it unequivocally by going abroad or refusing to attend church, was relatively small (considered in relation to the total number affected by contemporary religious issues). But this is to miss the significance of

---

[14] Benjamin Carier, *A Treatise* (Brussels, 1614), 34; Humphrey Leech, *A Triumph of Truth* (Douai, 1609), 102; cf. James Sharpe, *The Triall of the Protestant Private Spirit* (St Omer, 1630), 271.
[15] Matthew Sutcliffe, *The Examination and Confutation of a certain scurrilous Treatise entituled, The Survey of the newe Religion* (1606), 28.
[16] William Bradshaw, *Humble Motives* (n.p., 1601), 10–15.

conversion. If conversion were just a matter of expressing allegiance to a political position, then defections to and from Roman Catholicism would be of little interest historically since there is no evidence that numerical fluctuation of itself was ever sufficiently great to make much difference.[17] But, even in pure politics, it was clear enough that activism rather than a democratic counting process was what mattered. As Sir Robert Cotton remarked, 'to what purpose serves it to muster the names of the Protestants, or to vaunt them to be ten for one of the Roman Faction? as if bare figures of numeration could prevaile against an united party'.[18] When an individual converted to Rome, he demonstrated the existence of a hidden fund of latent popery about which Protestants had every reason to be anxious. Paradoxically, most conversions from Rome also emphasised the instability of the religious settlement since they dressed up the providential Protestant homecoming in the language of escape from almost certain spiritual death and the alluring attractiveness to the majority of idolatry and superstition. Virtually all conversions, therefore, were a visible index of man's general tendency to stagger in religion. This was certainly not limited to the comparatively small number of overt and outrageous rejections of one or other Church which hit the headlines in this period (though such changes were thought, according to a religious domino theory of conversion and apostasy, to induce a cascade of further alterations in faith and allegiance).[19] Whether the total number of Catholics was increasing or decreasing was far less important than whether the increase or decrease occurred through the mechanism of change of religion. Contemporaries were acutely aware of this. When, in the first

[17] The problem of counting converts is an intractable one. John Bossy has made an impressive effort to estimate numbers of Catholics in England during this period, J. Bossy, *The English Catholic Community, 1570–1850* (1975), chapter 8. But this is a different exercise from measuring flux in religion to and from Rome. A manifest difficulty is that the records of changes of religion are even more patchy than the evidence of how many English people during this period could be described as Catholics or papists. It is, of course, possible to count people who abandoned the Church of England by becoming recusants, or conformed to the established Church by abandoning recusancy. (Such records confirm contemporary comment that at times when the regime took severe measures against papistry many more people would conform than at times when the State took a more relaxed view, and that when the regime looked set to tolerate Romishness, the number of persons prepared to consider themselves as in some way Catholic shot up.) But the records of conformity and nonconformity in religion were usually generated for bureaucratic purposes and so do not give a full account of how many people altered their religion in defiance of or obedience to the State. In consequence I have largely shied away from making bold statements about numbers of converts because such figures more often provide information about the system which recorded them than about national trends in conformity.

[18] James Howell (ed.), *Cottoni Posthuma* (1651), 114–15.

[19] Contemporaries frequently saw notorious conversions as indicators that other individuals would do the like, N. McClure (ed.), *The Letters of John Chamberlain* (2 vols., Philadelphia, 1939), I, 483; CRS 68, 14; CRS 64, 36; G. Wickes, 'Henry Constable, Poet and Courtier, 1562–1613', *Biographical Studies* 2 (1953–4), 272–300, at p. 290.

decade of the seventeenth century, the Venetians quarrelled with the papacy
the excited English diplomatic party in Venice attempted to convert specific
Venetians and to create separate Protestant congregations there.[20] In part
this was because anti-papal foreign Catholics were useful for the polemic
they could write against papal authority.[21] But the Venice phenomenon had
a theological significance as well. One mark of the true Church which
all contemporaries recognised was that it must continually increase. The
Venetian quarrel with the papacy, and individual rejections of Rome
associated with it, suggested to Protestants that the Church of Rome was in
decline, and therefore not the true Church which it claimed to be.[22] Many
Protestants thought that the notorious Archbishop de Dominis's severance
of links with Rome and arrival in England (by way of Venice) in 1616
was a sign of Rome's inevitable decline, God's apocalyptic decrees against
Babylon. Thomas Goad saw that God had 'raysed Wickleff from their
Schooles, John Husse from their Pulpits, Martin Luther from their
Cloysters, and now Mark Antonie [de Dominis] from their Arch-episcopall
Chaire', and 'nowe Dalmatia [which de Dominis deserted] looking over the
Venetian Gulffe, assureth Italie that her next Advertiser shall bee within her
bowels'.[23]

This perception of conversion suggests to us that it is a misreading to see
the English Reformation just as a struggle between two tightly consolidated
blocs, Roman and Protestant, facing each other across a deserted religious
no-man's-land with a few isolated and lack-lustre nonentities risking
the shell-fire in order to move backwards and forwards between the two
positions. Institutional transfer of loyalties was a reflection of other aspects
of conversion which can be seen only in the shallowest sense as the product
just of institutional strife.

In the chapters which follow I propose to explore conversion as an
historical phenomenon in this period. First, why did people change their
religion? The polemical books, the manuals of controversy, contain almost
every possible argument which was ever used to urge contemporaries to

---

20 N. Malcolm, *De Dominis (1560–1624)* (1984), viii–ix, 37–8; Smith, *Life*, I, 90–1, 94, 116,
161–2, II, 148–9, 178–9; T. W. Jones (ed.), *A True Relation of the Life and Death of
William Bedell* (Camden Society, second series, 4, 1872), 105–6; BL, Lansd. MS 90,
nos. 54, 66; *HMC Salisbury MSS* XIX, 71–2; *CSPV 1607–10*, 270.

21 CRS 68, 11–12.

22 The contemporary annotator of the Bodleian Library's copy (Antiq.e.E.1608.8) of Anthony
Wotton, *A Trial of the Romish Clergies Title to the Church* (1608), 290, a tract written in
answer to John Percy, *A Treatise of Faith* (n.p., 1605), remarked that the Church of Rome
could not be the true Church because 'she hath decreased within these 200 yeeres I thincke
well nighe the one halfe of that she was'.

23 Marc'Antonio de Dominis, ed. and transl. Thomas Goad, *A Declaration of the Reasons*
(Edinburgh, 1617), 3–4.

think about change of religious allegiance. But as the second chapter argues, the essence of conversion does not lie in polemical texts, even though all contemporaries recognised that the changes of allegiance which polemicists dwelt on were a central element of true conversion. In chapter 3 I suggest that changing allegiances can be elucidated only through a reconstruction of what individuals did rather than what rival polemicists told them to do. There was a potentially radical division between the intellectual perceptions of religious division thrown at people and the way in which they actually experienced conversion between antagonistic expressions of Christianity. Of course, even without the hectoring of the clerical controversialists, the waverers still found that the aspects of religious faith which they regarded as changeable had a tendency to be battered into politically articulated forms and that their changes of religion tended to be subject to the quasi-political discipline of polemical ideas. If, as all the handbooks of practical religion told them, the pursuit of true faith meant a personal experience and outward effectual signification of conversion and repentance, this had to be given formal expression through the liturgy and sacraments of a true and particular institutional Church. This outward profession of conversion was vulnerable to a politicising of religion, even to the extent of virtually identifying either the Church of Rome or the Church of England with the practice of true religion. Still, conversion extended beyond mere allegiance to institutional Churches, and, so chapter 4 argues, changes of religion to and from Rome did not occur along a simple spectrum of obedience, at one end an acknowledgement of papal primacy, at the other a genuflection to a royal one. The second half of the book unravels contemporary attitudes towards practical proselytisation. The major player was the State which could not ignore the fact that people's innermost religious beliefs were in some ways connected with their political obedience. But how far could the State demand that people resolve the tension between religion and politics so as to conform according to law? Failure to enforce conformity was surely the result of inherent structural weaknesses in the early modern State rather than of any failure of nerve or intention on the part of the regime? But, chapters 5 and 6 contend, while the regime could quite effectively prevail upon individuals to conform very thoroughly, this was not the same as persuading all towards a profession of a single version of true religion. Tensions between the requirements of politicians and churchmen explain better than pure provincial localism or bungling officialdom the slow and uncertain spread of English Protestantism, or at least the ease with which its dispersal could be resisted. Chapter 7 suggests that the clerics on both sides who used their rhetorical gifts to influence potential converts did not always think just to instil a politico-ecclesiastical obedience in new proselytes. Instead they experimented with conversion in a way which transcended politico-ecclesiastical boundaries. This approach to conversion, it is suggested, will perhaps alter the way we discuss Catholicisation and Protestantisation, and the nature, speed and success of the Reformation in England.

2

Conversion and polemical theology

On what grounds did people change religion? Conversion to and from Rome was discussed almost exclusively in doctrinal and, indeed, polemical terms. Few were so cynical as to suggest that a man's beliefs should automatically follow his best temporal interests. To change religion a man needed to persuade himself (or be persuaded by others) that one or other side could claim to be in some sense the true religion. Contemporaries could not, apparently, envisage such truth except in the phraseology of the sharp doctrinal oppositions with which they filled their books of polemical theology. Conversion, we are frequently told, came through a decision that the side previously favoured had lost its doctrinal charms under the scrutiny of rival polemicists. Common sense, therefore, might suggest to us that contemporary books of controversial theology are the first place we should look to establish a model of religious flux. Trite and opinionated as they seem outside the context of contemporary disputes, they nevertheless set out with absolute and bigoted clarity the reasons for belonging to one side or the other. The whole course of the Reformation, readers were told, could be understood by referring to the diametrically opposed Roman and Protestant doctrines of faith, assurance, perseverance, election and predestination, and the Church, underwritten by disagreement about the relative weight of authority in Scripture and the Church's tradition. There were many other motives to consider one's allegiance, but all ultimately turned on the question of who professed the true religion, the only certain path to salvation.

The purpose of this chapter is to discuss the arguments put forward polemically for changing religion and to indicate the potential and also the limitations of controversial theology in this sphere. The writers claimed that truth could be grasped in its entirety through their swift and mechanistic tractate summaries of the deepest puzzles of Christian soteriology, but did polemic really provide an adequate basis on which to change religion? Did it summarise, for contemporaries, the complex siren calls of antagonistic ecclesiastical structures?

12

THE BATTLE OF THE BOOKS

Initially there is bound to be a suspicion that what was said in polemic was simply the concern of a small professional clerical elite – an in-house debate which was completely alien to those without an extensive background reading in patristic literature and scholastic texts as well as a solid understanding of the forms of rhetorical and logical argument. John Aveling suggested that even the most basic exposition of Catholic objections to Protestant doctrines of grace, and the crudest invocation of the names of early Church heresies with which to characterise those doctrines, were far too complex for the average reader.[1] The modern historian wonders how dramatic these books would have appeared even to a theologically literate person. They seem turgid and it is hard to believe that their reasoning could have been thought decisive. To every polemical argument there is an equally good counter-argument. For every 'clear' proof for a particular doctrine from a patristic text, every opponent is able quite easily to bring a diametrically opposed citation, frequently from the same patristic work, often from the same chapter. As William Barlow said (citing Ecclesiastes 12: 12), 'There is no End of making many books . . . especially if they be Bookes of Encounter.'[2] John Brereley wrote in one of his prefaces that he published 'not from any great hope to perswade', and others like Humphrey Leech doubted the power of the written word compared with spoken disputation.[3] The speed with which some tracts were assembled suggests that their writers were offering merely standard responses to equally standard assertions.[4]

Yet polemic was more suited to persuasion than this and had a wider audience than clerics and scholars. Controversial books were not published just to reinforce the morale of the writers' co-religionists (though there was evidently a purpose in some of them to prevent waverers falling away). They were designed to be widely available, immediately comprehensible and were

---

[1] J. C. H. Aveling, *Catholic Recusancy in the City of York 1558–1791* (CRS monograph 2, 1970), 74; J. C. H. Aveling, *The Handle and the Axe* (1976), 51; cf. more generally, George Gifford, *A Dialogue betweene a Papist and a Protestant* (1599), sig. A2^r; D. Nugent, *Ecumenism in the Age of the Reformation* (Cambridge, Massachusetts, 1974), 32.

[2] William Barlow, *An Answer to a Catholike English-Man* (1609), 1.

[3] John Brereley (*vere* James Anderton), *Sainct Austines Religion* (n.p., 1620), sig. C^v; Humphrey Leech, *A Triumph of Truth* (Douai, 1609), sig. †3^r.

[4] John White, *A Defence of the Way to the True Church* (1614), sig. **6^r, says that this massive work was completed only eighteen months after he received John Percy's *Reply made unto Mr. Anthony Wotton and Mr. John White* (St Omer, 1612) to which it is a reply. Aveling argues that the use of texts was dominated by the keeping of 'indexed commonplace books of quotations', and a highly uncritical approach, J. C. H. Aveling, 'The English Clergy, Catholic and Protestant, in the 16th and 17th Centuries', in J. C. H. Aveling, D. M. Loades, H. R. McAdoo and W. Haase, *Rome and the Anglicans* (Berlin, 1982), 131.

meant to tap into established forms of persuasion and argument. Some of the tracts produced by clerical writers dealt with straight political questions (though with reference to religion): allegiance, resistance, the succession and so on. Their significance was obvious. They could not be ignored except by those who had no interest in politics at all. But the production of straight theological vernacular tracts in quite considerable numbers indicates that a sufficiently wide audience did exist to create a market for them as well.[5] Even if each individual reader was not passionately concerned with the finer points of exegesis, the theological doctrines in the tracts were politicised and thus attracted the attention of people who otherwise might have been little interested by them.[6] The theological basis for papal primacy was of more than academic concern when the views of Catholics about the papal deposing power were dangerously vague.[7] Furious arguments about the interpretation of Augustine ensued when Catholic laymen imprisoned in York Castle were forced in 1599–1600 to listen to a series of puritan sermons preached for their benefit.[8] John Good, MP for Camelford in James I's first parliament, resorted to Augustine's complete works to sort out religious doubts (prompted in part by a political row in the House of Commons over his opposition to prominent puritans there).[9] Barbara Donagan has shown that dispute in this period based on patristic citations was quite within laymen's capacity, though they might find clerical dialectical disquisition on it boring.[10] Richard Woodcock complained that

---

[5] J. Ellul, *Propaganda* (New York, 1969), 49, argues that propaganda is effective (and, therefore, marketable) only when it is aimed first at a collective prior 'center of interest'. Cf. J. Solé, *Le Débat entre Protestants et Catholiques Français de 1598 à 1685* (4 vols., Lille, 1985), I, 153.

[6] Cf. Solé, *Débat*, I, 145–6; William Allen, *An Apologie and True Declaration of the Institution and Endevours of the two English Colleges* (Rheims, 1581), fo. 27ᵛ: 'even the very severitie of the lawes made against the Catholikes . . . and the popular pulpit-mens perpetual balling . . . against the Pope, caused many one that otherwise should never have heard or thought of him, to enquire what the Pope is' and consequently they saw 'that there lay some great moment in these causes of religion'.

[7] For the patristic debate about primacy at the trial of John Bodey and John Slade, J. H. Pollen, *Acts of English Martyrs* (1891), 51–2.

[8] BL, Add. MS 34250, fo. 6ʳ⁻ᵛ.

[9] BL, Lansd. MS 776, fos. 13ʳ, 33ʳ⁻ᵛ. Good had been to university but only to do the arts course, J. Foster, *Alumni Oxonienses: The Members of the University of Oxford, 1500–1714* (4 vols., 1891–2), II, 581.

[10] B. Donagan, 'The York House Conference Revisited: Laymen, Calvinism and Arminianism', *HR* 64 (1991), 312–30, at pp. 317–18; William Stillington, in York Castle, told Sir Thomas Cecil that he was unlearned and not able 'Logicallie to dispute . . . Controversies' yet he was able to 'alledge aucthorities both of Scriptures and doctours for the chieffe poyntes of our Faith', BL, Add. MS 34250, fo. 63ᵛ. Lay people as well as clerics used tracts to proselytise, M. O'Dwyer, 'Catholic Recusants in Essex c.1580 to c.1600' (MA thesis, London, 1960), 47; PRO, SP 12/192/52.i; BL, Lansd. MS 50, no. 76; cf. PRO, SP 12/193/18, fo. 30ᵛ; AAW, Anglia IX, no. 68; John Swynnerton, *A Christian Love-Letter* (1606), sig. Bʳ; CRS 54, 233.

'every child and audacious woman' among the papists presumed 'to speake Fathers and Doctors'.[11]

The writers were sensitive to the requirements, tastes and aptitudes of readers. They tried to adapt the length and format of their works to attract non-specialists. For example, some abandoned the standard lengthy lists of patristic authorities and took instead the shorter route of citing as proofs for their own opinions the texts of their opponents (or those who could be regarded as adherents of the opponents' side).[12] The long-running polemical debates between English Catholics and Protestants in the 1560s, fired by John Jewel's challenge issued at Paul's Cross on 26 November 1559, were exceptionally unwieldy and tedious (mainly because the protagonists thought it necessary to reply on every controverted point), but this style was not universally maintained.[13] Outside of the individual duels between clerics like William Perkins and William Bishop, or John Percy, Anthony Wotton and John White, some controversial writers distilled their persuasions by reducing the disputed issues into essential summaries, manuals of controversies which lay out in short but numerous sections the differences between Catholics and Protestants.[14]

---

[11] Richard Woodcock, *A Godly and Learned Answer* (1608), sig. A3^r.

[12] Controversialists have always manipulated the ambiguities and contradictions among the statements of their enemies, but some of the polemicists in this period, especially Thomas Bell, John White, John Brereley, Richard Broughton and George Fisher, employed this technique systematically, Thomas Bell, *Thomas Bels Motives* (Cambridge, 1593), sig. ¶2^r: God, said Bell, inclined his heart to 'peruse more seriously, some learned papists'; this was the basis on which he then wrote his polemic, BL, Lansd. MS 75, fo. 40^r; John White, *The Way to the True Church* (1616), sig. c8^{r-v}; John Brereley (*vere* James Anderton), *The Apologie of the Romane Church* (n.p., 1604); idem, *The Protestants Apologie for the Roman Church* (St Omer, 1608); cf. William Wright, *A Treatise of the Church* (St Omer, 1616), 45, which cites *The Protestants Apologie* as if it were a Protestant book; Richard Broughton, *The First Part of Protestants Proofes* (n.p., 1607); idem, *Protestants Demonstrations* (Douai, 1615); idem, *A Booke Intituled: The English Protestants Recantation* (Douai, 1617); George Fisher, *The Bishop of London his Legacy* (St Omer, 1623), viii, says 'the acknowledgments of Protestants in poynts controverted, prevent, that we need not to recurre (through a long and wearisome enquiry) to Scriptures, Fathers, or Historyes'. Richard Verstegan also contemplated writing in this style, CRS 52, 142. Cf. A. Milton, *Catholic and Reformed* (Cambridge, 1995), 233.

[13] M. C. Questier, 'The Phenomenon of Conversion: Change of Religion to and from Catholicism in England, 1580–1625' (DPhil. thesis, Sussex, 1991), 41–2.

[14] For Catholic instances, Richard Smith, *The Prudentiall Ballance of Religion* (St Omer, 1609); Anthony Champney, *A Manual of Controversies* (Paris, 1614); cf. AAW, A XIII, 489; Edward Weston, *The Trial of Christian Truth* (Douai, 1614); C. W., *A Summarie of Controversies* (n.p., 1616); James Gordon, *A Summary of Controversies* (n.p., 1618); John Pickford, *The Safegarde from Ship-wracke* (Douai, 1618); Richard Smith, *A Conference of the Catholike and Protestant Doctrine with the Expresse words of Holie Scripture* (Douai, 1631). Longer tracts like Thomas Worthington, *An Anker of Christian Doctrine* (Douai, 1622) or Lawrence Anderton, *The Triple Cord* (St Omer, 1634) are more akin to reference works than manuals but fulfil a similar function. William Perkins's *A Reformed Catholike* (Cambridge, 1598) has a 'manual' form, and in 1612 one of the functions of the

Although Barbara Donagan suggests that what laymen could not take was argument about argument (i.e. subjection to the science of scholastic reasoning),[15] polemicists thought that, in reasonably simplified form, techniques of logical argument were an aid to persuasion. William Fulke said that 'the truth of argumentes is best discerned when it is brought into the judgement of Logicke', and Anthony Wotton provided short guides to syllogistic disputation in the texts of his polemical tracts.[16] John Percy's popular and effective tracts relied heavily on techniques of syllogistic debate. When Percy engaged in somewhat rowdy semi-public disputations with Protestant clerics the debate proceeded according to 'logic-form'.[17] 'Logic-form' was simply an effort to regulate and schematise the way in which the mind was thought to contend over any disputed polemical point.[18] Syllogistic or not, several tracts were the product of actual confrontations between belligerent Catholics and clerics of the established Church. They did not originate exclusively in ivory towers.[19] There was a clear connection

English writers at the newly founded Collège d'Arras in Paris (several of whom wrote the above-cited works) was to produce 'a breife and pithye Enchyridion of Controversies like to that of Parkins', AAW, OB III. ii, fo. 430ᵛ; cf. Queen's College MS 284, fo. 206ᵛ, for Sir John Warner's choice of reading in the early 1660s to resolve his intellectual difficulties. John Morgan argues that a like simplification of abstruse points of divinity was performed by godly preachers in English pulpits, J. Morgan, *Godly Learning* (Cambridge, 1986), 128–9, 135. Thomas Worthington thought it was possible to cut down the verbiage by attacking only the first part of an opponent's work 'seeing that divers authours do commonly fortify and strengthen the first part of their wrytings, with more forcible proofes and authorities then the latter part' in order to 'invade the judgment of the reader' more quickly, because 'many do peruse the beginninges of bookes, who through a werisome carelesnes do never reade the latter parte of them' (Thomas Worthington, *Whyte Dyed Black* (n.p., 1615), epistle dedicatory, sig. A6ᵛ–7ʳ), even though Worthington's instances of John White's 'impertinences' seem to be drawn from all parts of White's *The Way to the True Church*. Francis Bunny also thought long treatises were unlikely to be read, Francis Bunny, *A Short Answer to the Reasons* (1595), published with his *Truth and Falshood* (1595), sig. Ccᵛ.

15 Donagan, 'York House Conference', 318; cf. Quirinus Breen, 'John Calvin and the Rhetorical Tradition', *Church History* 26 (1957), 3–21, at p. 14.

16 William Fulke, *A Retentive, to stay good Christians, in true Faith and Religion, against the Motives of Richard Bristow* (1580), sig. ¶iiiʳ; Anthony Wotton, *A Trial of the Romish Clergies Title to the Church* (1608), sig. A3ʳ–4ʳ; cf. *idem, Runne from Rome* (1624), 2–4, 6; cf. *Keepe your Text* (n.p., 1619), 4–5, 6–7.

17 Daniel Featley, *The Fisher Catched in his owne Net* (1623); BL, Add. MS 28640, fo. 113ʳ; Sylvester Norris, *A True Report of the Private Colloquy betweene M. Smith, aliâs Norrice, and M. Walker* (St Omer, 1624); George Walker, *The Summe of a Disputation* (1624), sigs. A3ʳ, C2ᵛ–3ʳ; cf. *idem, Fishers Folly Unfolded* (1624).

18 L. S. Stebbing, *A Modern Introduction to Logic* (New York, 1961), 84. Ramist logic was arguably an attempt to construct a system which reflected the 'basic structures of human rationality', P. Lake, *Moderate Puritans and the Elizabethan Church* (Cambridge, 1982), 101.

19 Robert Crowley, *An Aunswer to sixe Reasons, that Thomas Pownde . . . required to be aunswered* (1581), sig. Aiiʳ; Woodcock, *Godly and Learned Answer*, sig. A3ʳ; G. Ornsby (ed.), *The Correspondence of John Cosin* (2 vols., Surtees Society, 52, 55, 1869, 1872), I,

between printed tracts and the type of arguments which were employed when individual proselytisers tried to draw people to profess the religion of one Church or the other. John Percy's published works were derived from manuscript tracts written for precisely this purpose.[20] Even at a less intellectually refined level, for example when Protestant preachers castigated the catch-all of popery, the doctrines which they thought contributed to the more general and everyday popish sins of lust, idolatry and epicureanism were essentially the same as the doctrinal errors analysed by the higher-flown tract literature – papal primacy, implicit faith, transubstantiation, auricular popish confession and so on.

Contemporaries were in no doubt therefore that tracts really did exert persuasion to change religion. If writers were unwilling to allow that their enemies' books changed men's minds through any intrinsic virtue in their arguments they still conceded that leaving a tract unanswered was as good as admitting defeat.[21] They believed that defections from their own side would occur if opponents' major works went without a reply. Bishop Tobias Mathew in 1597 called for a prohibition of the circulation of 'up-market' Catholic books which had no official Protestant answer attached to them: 'it is incredible what decay the contrary custom hath bred in religion'.[22] William Bedell observed morosely in March 1605 that Robert Persons's massive reply to John Foxe, *A Treatise of the Three Conversions of England*, went unanswered.[23] Richard Woodcock wrote that even the delay in copying out his manuscript reply to a papist who had challenged him allowed his opponent to brag that the reasons for the truth of the

---

32–3. See also the genesis of Richard Bristow, *A Briefe Treatise of diverse plaine and sure Wayes to finde out the Truthe* (Antwerp, 1574), and *idem, Demaundes to bee proponed of Catholickes to the Heretickes* (Antwerp, 1576), William Fulke, *Two Treatises* (1577), sig. *iii^v–4^r.

[20] White, *Way*, sig. d7^v: the copy of Percy's *Treatise of Faith* (n.p., 1605) which White answered was a manuscript one, and the basis of White's reply was the arguments which he had already used in refuting it verbally; cf. BL, Harl. MS 360, fo. 29^r. See also T. H. Wadkins, 'The Percy–"Fisher" Controversies and the Ecclesiastical Politics of Jacobean Anti-Catholicism, 1622–1625', *Church History* 57 (1988), 153–69, at p. 156; Questier, 'Phenomenon', 37–8, 71–2, 299.

[21] Robert Persons, *The First Booke of the Christian Exercise* (Rouen, 1582), 2; CRS 52, 86. When William Stillington in York Castle found that he could not adequately answer the points made by Alexander Cooke in his sermon there in early 1600 (and was taunted on this ground by Sir Thomas Cecil), he obtained a copy of the sermon and sent it out of the prison to 'gett [it] answered', BL, Add. MS 34250, fo. 25^r.

[22] *HMC Salisbury MSS* VII, 453 (for which reference I am grateful to Anthony Milton). Bishop Curteys had shown a similar concern in 1577, W. P. M. Kennedy (ed.), *Elizabethan Episcopal Administration* (3 vols., Alcuin Club, 25–7, 1924), II, 51. John Dove said, however, that recusant Catholics were 'contented to give more mony for the Rhemish Testament alone, then for the same booke with Doctor Fulkes answer joyned with it', John Dove, *A Persuasion to the English Recusants* (1603), 7.

[23] Bodl., Tanner MS 75, fo. 132^r–v.

Roman Catholic religion which he had delivered to Woodcock 'could not be answered'.[24] Equally the writers said that if their own books were allowed to stand unchallenged this was a polemical victory irrespective of the book's subject matter.[25] Thomas Bell claimed that the papists' 'silence in not answering my . . . bookes, hath reclaimed many a man from their popish faction'.[26] A frenzy of reply and counter-reply developed in the debate over the Jacobean oath of allegiance, and Catholic clergy in England pleaded with their agent in Rome to ensure that adequate replies were solicited from Bellarmine to the English defenders of the oath.[27] Both sides thought that ideally there should be a systematic answering machine to deal with their opponents' tracts. Chelsea College and the Collège d'Arras in Paris were set up for this reason.[28]

This account of polemic as persuader could still leave us thinking that the books were nothing more than a series of political slogans. On this reading the labels 'Catholic' and 'Protestant' were mere party tags. Changes of religion, justified by passing references to the latest polemical text, would have had no necessary connection with religion at all. But though the theology was politicised in a way which was utterly alien to non-partisan exegesis, a closer reading of what polemicists said shows that the theology of polemical debate is not merely for show. Polemic politicises theological ideas in order to represent a division into parties between which the reader *must* choose. The writer thus exerts a persuasive effect on the reader which is not derived purely from the writer's philosophical acumen. (Though, as Donagan indicates, argument about 'consequents' and 'antecedents' might well fatigue the layman, the level of logical sophistication in the polemical tracts was relatively low.)[29] Syllogistic reasoning deals in the comparison of

24 Woodcock, *Godly and Learned Answer*, sig. A3^r. For similar cases, Crowley, *Aunswer*, sig. Aiii^r; Robert Abbot, *A Mirrour of Popish Subtilties* (1594), sig. *^{v}.

25 F. Edwards (ed.), *The Elizabethan Jesuits* (1981), 308–9. Walter Montagu pointed out that there had never been a Protestant answer to the book on which he based his conversion, Bodl., Rawl. MS D 853, fo. 166^v.

26 Thomas Bell, *The Downefall of Poperie* (1604), sig. Aii^v. John Copley said that one of his relatives had promised to become a Catholic if he could see Perkins's *Reformed Catholike* 'well answered and confuted', John Copley, *Doctrinall and Morall Observations* (1612), 19–20.

27 AAW, A IX, 395, X, 486 (John Jackson's message to the secular clergy's agent in Rome that answers are expected by the English Catholics to Lancelot Andrewes's *Tortura Torti* (1609) and Thomas Preston's *Apologia Cardinalis Bellarmini* (1611), 'or els it wyll . . . leave diverse staggering at the least'); TD IV, clxxiii.

28 PRO, SP 14/54/91, fos. 134^r–5^r, SP 14/36/8; CRS 41, 52; Milton, *Catholic and Reformed*, 32–4; A. C. F. Beales, *Education under Penalty* (1963), 191–2.

29 Donagan, 'York House Conference', 318. There is a general tendency to resort merely to accusations of the logical fallacy *petitio principii* (begging the question), engendering a perpetual redefinition of terms, Featley, *Fisher*, 14; O. N., *An Apology of English Arminianisme* (St Omer, 1634), 41; Stebbing, *Modern Introduction*, 216, 219. The

propositions rather than their substance; logical proof depends on first principles but cannot itself prove them.[30] Though writers were unlikely to persuade the reader just because they alleged proofs in a more scholarly way than their opponents, what polemicists did with the theological propositions at their disposal was crucial.

Of course, Catholic and Protestant polemicists did not try to bring over the hostile reader by attempts to present an impartial or even a particularly deep or sophisticated opinion about matters in dispute. Pure academic discussion might allow a reader to think that right was not all on one side. So they manipulated the doctrines which they dealt with in the text in order to construct a case which was strategically even if not academically superior to their opponents'. If done carefully this could leave the opponent in difficulties when he made his (perhaps doctrinally quite satisfactory) reply. Academic sophistication did not necessarily add bite to a polemical attack. Certainly the mere bringing in of increasingly heavy weights of citations was unlikely to offer the basis for any final decision by the undecided reader. Nor was the endless enumeration of individual doctrines sufficient to persuade. To argue about hundreds of specific single issues (e.g. the Real Presence in the eucharist) was tedious and, as far as one can tell, often fruitless. What was really required was to establish a general way of thinking about controverted polemical questions to which the reader might refer the various disputed elements which he subsequently encountered. As Thomas Clarke wrote, 'every error and controversie doth minister sufficient matter for . . . many sermons'; what is required is a rule of faith, a politicising of doctrine, which will govern attitudes to all questions in dispute.[31] This was the principal drawback of the massive 'Challenge' controversy in the 1560s and 1570s. Some Catholics at the time thought it was a success and, later on, both Protestants and Catholics still believed the major tracts produced as a result of Jewel's challenge could induce changes of religion.[32] But

sterility of the exchanges between John Percy, Sylvester Norris and their various Protestant adversaries in London in the early 1620s demonstrates that a resort to 'logic-form', on its own, was no guarantee of effective debate, Featley, *Fisher*, 8, 15; Norris, *True Report*; Walker, *Summe*, sigs. E^{r-v}, C2^v–3^r, and *passim*; *idem*, *Fishers Folly*, 9–10; Questier, 'Phenomenon', 38–9.

30 J. H. Newman, ed. I. T. Ker, *An Essay in Aid of a Grammar of Assent* (Oxford, 1985), xvii–xviii.

31 Thomas Clarke, *The Recantation of Thomas Clarke* (1594), sig. A3^v, A6^v–7^r.

32 Edmund Campion, *Campian Englished: Or a Translation of the Ten Reasons* (n.p., 1632), 106–7; Robert Persons, ed. E. Gee, *The Jesuit's Memorial, for the Intended Reformation of England* (1690), 41; R. Peters, 'Some Catholic Opinions of King James VI and I', *RH* 10 (1968–9), 292–303, at p. 294; Francis Walsingham, *A Search Made into Matters of Religion* (St Omer, 1609), 50, 128, 195, 234–5; Smith, *Life*, I, 90, 417; CRS 54, 202; K. C. Fincham (ed.), *Visitation Articles and Injunctions of the Early Stuart Church*, I (Church of England Record Society, Woodbridge, Suffolk, 1994), 96–7; BL, Lansd. MS 776, fo. 16^v;

though the 'Challenge' appealed to a standard topic (the perennial question of the connection between Scripture and tradition in deciding how to interpret Scripture authoritatively) it was a flawed debate because it persistently degenerated into rival claims about who could interpret the Early Church writers more accurately. The 'Challenge' works are more like the proceedings of an exegetes' convention than the record of the political claims of two opposed ecclesiastical titans.[33]

Post-'Challenge' polemicists tried to frame their use of controversial theology so that it would change the opinion and allegiance of an initially hostile reader. Basically, the more astute writers in this period worked in the same way when they attacked the theology of the opposing side. First, they wilfully attributed to opponents definitions of concepts held in common (e.g. faith, assurance, perseverance and so on) which those opponents did not accept. They then proceeded to attack their enemies' doctrinal statements (e.g. about the place of faith, assurance and perseverance in the process of justification) as if they did accept such definitions.[34] Thus it made them seem inconsistent, untrustworthy and mendacious. To be persuasive, however, a polemical writer had to do slightly more than this (since his enemy would always retaliate in an identical fashion and produce a mirror

---

John Harding, *A Recantation Sermon* (1620), 4. Richard Cholmeley was purchasing books by the 'Challenge' writers Thomas Dorman and Thomas Heskins as late as January 1618, 'The Memorandum Book of Richard Cholmeley of Brandsby 1602–1623', *North Yorkshire County Record Office Publications* 44 (1988), 151.

[33] The Catholic writers staked everything on the inextricable linking of Scripture to tradition which was not a crucial or necessary element of exegesis for Protestants anyway, Walsingham, *Search* (1609), 168, 197, 430; Francis Savage, *A Conference betwixt a Mother a devout Recusant, and her Sonne a zealous Protestant* (Cambridge, 1600), 15. Catholic and Protestant 'rules' for determining the Fathers' authority were almost identical, cf. John Strype, *The Life and Acts of John Whitgift* (3 vols., Oxford, 1822), I, 197–8; Daniel Featley, *Cygnea Cantio* (1629), 30–2; Hugh-Paulin de Cressy, *Exomologesis* (Paris, 1653), 69; A. H. Mathew (ed.), *A True Historical Relation of the Conversion of Sir Tobie Matthew* (1904), 28. But it was inevitable that the Protestant concept of scriptural primacy should relegate the importance of the Church Fathers, J. E. Booty, *John Jewel as Apologist of the Church of England* (1963), 137–41; P. Hughes, *Theology of the English Reformers* (1965), 33; P. Collinson, *A Mirror of Elizabethan Puritanism: The Life and Letters of 'Godly Master Dering'*, Friends of Dr Williams's Library Seventeenth Lecture 1963 (1964), 5. The logical conclusion of Protestant polemic in this vein was that the Fathers had frequently been in error and were no reliable authority at all, Thomas Bell, *The Golden Ballance of Tryall* (1603), fo. 1ᵛ; White, *Way*, 325, 327; cf. George Webbe, *Catalogus Protestantium* (1624), sigs. I2ᵛ (arguing that even if manifest corruptions did not openly appear in the first 600 years, the 'Mysterie of Iniquitie', an entire principle of corruption, was at work in the Church during that time), K3ʳ; cf. at the extreme, John Keltridge, *Two Godlie and learned Sermons* (1581), sig. Hiiᵛ, 'the Fathers have beene faithlesse, and have sinned: the Scriptures are sacred, and no filthinesse hath beene found in them'; cf. M. Maclure, *The Paul's Cross Sermons 1534–1642* (Toronto, 1958), 215.

[34] Thus Matthew Kellison, *A Survey of the New Religion* (Douai, 1605), 276–7, attacks a parody of the Protestant concept of assurance by assuming that Calvin held a Roman doctrine of faith.

image of any hostile tract). If the first rule of polemic is that the issue in dispute must be one of central importance (which, arguably, much of the 'Challenge' debate was not), the second is that the writer should make central an issue which his enemy has no wish to use (because it creates dissension in his own ranks).[35] Sir Dudley Carleton wrote from Venice in April 1614 to his cousin George Carleton. He had received the latter's *Consensus Ecclesiae Catholicae contra Tridentinos* which was naturally of interest to the anti-papal Venetians. But said Dudley Carleton, 'to deale playnely with you, all men heer do not so well allow of your providence in some poyntes, as of your ingenuitie in all'. In some things George Carleton had taken a line which, though not doctrinally wrong, was polemically inconvenient. Catholic controversial writing constantly emphasised the authority of traditions within the Church. George Carleton was curtly informed that 'you allow of some traditions, whereof your self discover the danger, in that you doe *"fenestram aperire Pontifici figmentis"*, but you shew no meanes how to shut this window agayne, and therefore we were best content our selves with the light we have from the sufficiencie of the scriptures'.[36] It was necessary for a writer to locate an issue on which he and his opponents were utterly divided but on which his opponents found it difficult to agree among themselves so that they could not produce so easily a coherent equal and opposite reply to what he had said. At the York House Conference Lord Say and Sele warned that Richard Montagu's prevarications would allow the papists to 'take advantage against us out of his wordes' while Hugh Paulin de Cressy said that Romanist disputes afforded 'answers and objections to Protestants against Catholiques'.[37] In consequence good polemicists tried to concentrate on areas where they saw their opponents divided on matters of principle and denied that apparent divisions over doctrine in their own ranks were fundamental.[38]

---

[35] Catholics concentrated on Protestant opinions over Christ's descent into Hell because it was an article of the Creed which was variously interpreted by Protestants, D. D. Wallace, 'Puritan and Anglican: The Interpretation of Christ's Descent into Hell in Elizabethan Theology', *Archiv für Reformationsgeschichte* 69 (1978), 248–86; Bodl., Rawl. MS C 167, fos. 17r–23r; BL, Lansd. MS 776, fo. 38v.

[36] PRO, SP 14/77/9, fo. 14r.

[37] Bodl., Tanner MS 303, fo. 36v; Cressy, *Exomologesis*, 72.

[38] William Rainolds, *A Refutation of Sundry Reprehensions* (Paris, 1583), sig. b3v, b4r, b6v, b8v–cr; Wotton, *Trial*, 317–19; Bunny, *Truth*, sig. Cc7v–8r; Richard Sheldon, *The First Sermon of R. Sheldon Priest, after his Conversion from the Romish Church* (1612), 62; for concentration on Bellarmine as an anti–papist, Bunny, *Truth*, sig. Cc5r–v; Francis Dillingham, *A Disswasive from Poperie* (Cambridge, 1599), sig. A5r–v; Thomas Bell, *A Christian Dialogue* (1609), 102; Joseph Hall, *The Works of Joseph Hall* (1634), 296; White, *Way*, 155, 169, arguing that all papists disagreed with each other at all times; cf. Thomas Morton, *A Catholike Appeale* (1609), 209–10. Robert Persons, *The Warn-word* (Antwerp, 1602), fos. 51v, 57v, 96v–98r, pointed to differences between Sir Francis Hastings and Matthew Sutcliffe over puritanism, an issue in which Catholics saw promising

Finally, to persuade his audience that his Church has a monopoly of truth, the polemical writer must frame his argument around the selected topic so that it reflects on and directs all polemical argument generally, and avoids the 'single-issue' nature of the 'Challenge', and the need to commence argument *ab initio* on every single disputed point. Doctrine must be subjected to a quasi-political form of discipline. In the conclusion of his tract against Marc'Antonio de Dominis, John Sweet considered (in a passage sufficiently significant to be worth quoting in full) the principal ways to convince a reader of the truth of the Roman religion:

Such reasons as may induce a man to be of any Religion, are of two sorts. For either they prove every point of Religion in particuler to be true, or else they open, and declare the evidence of certaine generall principles, which being once received, draw after them the consent of the mind to all those thinges in speciall, which are taught or practised in that Religion. Unto the first kind do belong all those books, which treat of particuler Controversyes, as of the Masse; of prayer for the dead; of prayer to Saints; Purgatory; and the like, which indeed to a man that hath but little will, or little leasure to read, is a wearisome course, and tedious way to tryall. Unto the other doth belong those shorter discourses which some have tearmed motives,

i.e. which constitute a general reason to change religion.[39] John Copley, in his tract describing his conversion, enumerated many motives for abjuring Rome, but the general motive to change which made them effectual could be traced to Christ and the effects of grace which led him to reject all Rome's

Protestant divisions, CRS 52, 134 (Verstegan's comments on the appearance of Richard Bancroft's *Survay of the Pretended Holy Discipline*). Francis Walsingham played on the differences over attitudes to the Church of Rome among moderate and puritan Protestants, Walsingham, *Search* (1609), 39–40; see also Leech, *Triumph*, 89–90. French polemicists employed the same tactic, Solé, *Débat*, I, 440. Protestants had a target to aim at in the way that some Catholic polemicists, notably Stapleton, handled theories of faith, Daniel Price, *The Defence of Truth* (Oxford, 1610), 22; White, *Way*, 27, 41; G. H. Tavard, *Holy Writ or Holy Church* (1959), 5, 25; A. McGrath, *The Intellectual Origins of the European Reformation* (Oxford, 1987), 140–1; and more obviously over the papal deposing power, as demonstrated by the disputes between Persons and Richard Smith over Smith's book, *An Answer to Thomas Bels late Challeng* (Douai, 1605), CRS 41, 122–3, and in the general controversy over the Jacobean oath of allegiance. During the Appellant controversy, astute Protestant writers like Thomas Bell exploited the factional divisions among the Catholic clergy and gave them a doctrinal twist, Bell, *Christian Dialogue*, 6–7; *idem, The Anatomie of Popish Tyrannie* (1603), 5, 19–20 (playing also on the fact that the Jesuit Thomas Lister had castigated the refractory secular priests as 'schismatics'); cf. Andrew Willet, *An Antilogie or Counterplea* (1603), 13–14; AAW, OB III. ii, fo. 338ʳ; J. H. Pollen, *The Institution of the Archpriest Blackwell* (1916), 39–40; P. Milward, *Religious Controversies of the Elizabethan Age* (1977), 111, 124–6.

39   John Sweet, *Monsigr Fate Voi* (St Omer, 1617), 153. Other writers said the same, e.g. Bristow, *Briefe Treatise*, fo. 2ʳ⁻ᵛ; *idem, A Reply to Fulke* (Louvain, 1580), sig. Aʳ; John Percy, *A Treatise of Faith* (St Omer, 1614), sig. A4ʳ⁻ᵛ; Bunny, *Truth*, sig. Ee7ᵛ; Bodl., Jones MS 53, fo. 235ʳ⁻ᵛ; cf. Barbarini's instructions to the legate Panzani, Joseph Berington (ed.), *The Memoirs of Gregorio Panzani* (Birmingham, 1793), 241.

individual errors. He cites by way of analogy the phenomenon of the loadstone in Augustine's *De Civitate Dei*: 'a Loadstone of so great power and efficacie, that it drew manie Rings unto it, which were one of them behinde the other, placed farre off asunder; first one, then that drew the other, the third the fourth, and so consequently all the rest, untill that at length by the secret vertue of the Stone, after an invisible manner adjoyning the Rings together . . . [an] . . . entire Chaine was made of them'. In his case, Christ was the persuasive loadstone that worked to draw together in his mind the individual reasons or motives for leaving Rome (the Mass, transubstantiation, pardons, indulgences and clerical marriage) which his tract sets out.[40] This, then, might appear to be the way that polemic worked best to persuade people to change religion, and, indeed, the way that conversion between the Churches occurred in this period – through the polemical clarification of disputed doctrinal issues.

THE CHURCH IN CONTEMPORARY POLEMIC

If we accept that the source of virtually all Reformation doctrinal controversy was a disagreement about the way that grace was allotted to men before time and is afterwards distributed in the world, then the polemic which most nearly expressed this in such a way as to indicate that grace is found exclusively in the polemicist's own concept of the true Church was likely to be the most direct and effective. If polemic were written convincingly along these lines, then all other controversial endeavour would become merely automatic and supplementary. The theological definition of the Church became the single most important authority to which doctrinal disagreement could be referred. Furious arguments about the true Church were accompanied by polemic about obedience to an ecclesiastical structure which faithfully represented it. All demands in controversial theology that people should change from one side to the other stand or fall ultimately by an exposition of the Church. So English polemicists (particularly after *c.* 1575) discoursed hard about the nature of the Church and its authority.[41]

All controversial writers acknowledged that the true Church had a series of distinguishing characteristics. In some sense it could be said to be not just one, holy, catholic and apostolic but also visible, infallible, universal and so

---

[40] Copley, *Doctrinall and Morall Observations*, 232–3; *De Civitate Dei* xxi, 4, CCSL, XLVIII, 763; cf. Bunny, *Truth*, sig. Ee7ᵛ.

[41] This was something which the 'Challenge' writers had omitted to do. Not that they necessarily held opinions about the Church which were different from those of later writers, but they did not make them explicit in their polemic, Booty, *John Jewel*, 134–5.

on.[42] But Catholics and Protestants understood in different ways the true Church which possessed these characteristics. What they tried to do was to express them so as to point the undecided man towards a particular expression of the true Church on earth. Roman Catholic polemic stressed heavily the connection between characteristics such as inerrancy in the true Church and in the institutional Church. (The lesson to be drawn from this was that the Protestant separation made them schismatics and worse.) Protestant polemic emphasised the potential weakness of this connection. Their assertion of jurisdictional independence therefore was not a schismatic act. It was always finally an argument about defining where the true Church is located and how its essence is transmitted through time. The French Protestant Philippe de Mornay was ready to acknowledge the marks attributed to the Church in Romanist polemic but 'the question', he said, 'is . . . of the puritie of the Church'. Antiquity, a characteristic frequently alleged by papists (because to establish the continuous existence of the Church of Rome, Catholics thought, demonstrated its inerrancy), is not a guarantee of the integrity of the institution even if it is proof for continuous succession.[43] This was the reason that Protestants stressed the force of Scripture against tradition. In Reformed thinking Scripture is a figure for pure doctrine, not a physical series of authoritative texts (though Roman polemicists always pretended not to understand this);[44] and tradition for Protestants is always a series of human accretions (separate from revelation). The visible Church, repository for those traditions, might go astray, but God's promises to his Elect, and their scripturally based redemptive faith, would not be affected.

So, in conformity with these rules of polemic, the writers set down a general motive to convert to their own Church by dwelling on the nature of the true Church. To persuade the hostile opponent or the uncommitted waverer that they might communicate with the true Church through one

---

[42] A. Milton, 'The Church of England, Rome, and the True Church: The Demise of a Jacobean Consensus', in K. C. Fincham (ed.), *The Early Stuart Church, 1603–1642* (1993), 187–210, at pp. 188–91 (my debt to Anthony Milton in the following paragraphs is obvious); Philip de Mornay, *A Notable Treatise of the Church* (1579), sigs. Evi^v, Diii^v; Bunny, *Truth*, sig. Cc6^r; Wotton, *Trial*, 259.

[43] Mornay, *Notable Treatise*, sigs. Diii^r–v^r, Eii^r–v; Walker, *Summe*, sig. B2^v. John White argued that the four principal marks of the Church were 'Qualities abiding in the Church, and certaine adjuncts belonging thereunto: but [they are] not . . . the markes whereby to finde it', thus denying the significance which a Roman polemicist would want to foist upon them, White, *Way*, 135. George Abbot told puritans in the Goldsmiths' Company that their banner depicting St Dunstan was not superstitious because Dunstan was his predecessor and his values were much to be admired (AAW, A XI, 23), but he would not define the true Church by reference to succession, George Abbot, *The Reasons which Doctour Hill hath Brought* (Oxford, 1604), 35; cf. Savage, *Conference*, 71; Sutcliffe, *Examination*, 6.

[44] Humphrey Leech, *Dutifull and Respective Considerations* (St Omer, 1609), 84–8.

rather than another particular expression of it on earth, the writers all constructed somewhat extreme models of the Church. Catholics appear to say that the outward continuous earthly structure of the institutional Church (by definition in communion with Rome because continuous) is necessarily coterminous with the true indefectible Church. Protestants, by contrast, appear to say that the outward structure of the institutional Church has a natural tendency towards total corruption (though they might differ about the extent and certainty of that tendency).[45] The logical conclusion of the Protestant polemical line of argument which wanted to associate hostility to Rome with the natural errancy of human institutions and particular Churches was to identify Rome with the apocalyptic Babylon in the book of Revelation.[46] Although Reformers might well think that institutional particular Churches had characteristics which they saw as belonging properly to the true Church, Protestants who wanted to argue for radical separation from Rome had to say that in principle there must exist the possibility of a total and complete division between these two concepts of the Church. On earth the true Church might exist only in the body of the Elect, the saving remnant. In this sense it would be so separate from the structures of the institutional Church that for all intents and purposes it might be said to be 'invisible'.[47]

This difference of opinion over the nature of the Church informs many other arguments which were put forward by writers to discredit their opponents and to persuade people that they ought to change their religion. In particular, material was drawn from the area where Scripture was thought to be in conflict with tradition. The arguments over the authority of the early Church Fathers were not an early modern exercise in source criticism but a comment on the Church which guaranteed their veracity. The Catholic polemical tendency to imply that the Church precedes Scripture is simply another expression of the Roman understanding of the connection between the true Church and the visible Church.[48] When Protestants claim

[45] Milton, 'Church', 190; Mornay, *Notable Treatise*, sig. Dviiᵛ–viiiʳ.
[46] Richard Finch, *The Knowledge or Appearance of the Church* (1590), sig. B2ʳ⁻ᵛ; P. Lake, 'The Significance of the Elizabethan Identification of the Pope as Antichrist', *JEH* 31 (1980), 161–78.
[47] Some Protestants argued that, in practice, this had taken place when, before the Reformation, the Church had been obscured by the 'mists of Popery', Milton, 'Church', 189–91.
[48] Benjamin Carier, *A Copy of a Letter* (n.p., 1615), 4; Leech, *Dutifull and Respective Considerations*, 84, 106; Thomas Vane, *A Lost Sheep Returned Home* (Paris, 1649), 23–5. The same thinking lies behind the tendency in Catholic polemic to associate the infallible judgment residing in the papacy with the inerrancy of the true Church, Brereley, *Sainct Austines Religion*, 39–40, 50; R. Dodaro and M. C. Questier, 'Strategies in Jacobean Polemic: The Use and Abuse of St Augustine in English Theological Controversy', *JEH* 44 (1993), 432–49, at pp. 444–5. To Protestants, Catholics appeared to associate the true Church with the Church's governors, Mornay, *Notable Treatise*, sig. Miiiᵛ–iiiiʳ; Abbot, *Reasons*, 26.

that the Fathers cannot be trusted because they were frequently in error (and that Scripture entirely precedes tradition) it is not because, as Catholics alleged, they just rejected texts which seemed to affirm a line which they found distasteful. It was because any concession that patristic writings were an independent source of authority pointed to an infallibility in the institutional Church which must have therefore the power to decide which of the patristic texts are to be credited as expressing orthodox doctrine.[49] Argument over what Augustine thought was a dispute more about the nature of the Church than the integrity of his complete works. A Protestant like William Crompton who might speculate on the potential defectibility of the entire institutional Church could nevertheless base every single argument for it on Augustine.[50] Both sides were prepared to distort the meaning of the patristic and other sources on which they relied. (The writers probably consoled themselves with the thought that a more balanced exposition of their sources of authority would actually hinder the wavering reader from arriving at a final decision about which Church possessed a monopoly of truth.) On the question of the infallibility of the Church, for example, Catholics tended to misinterpret what Augustine had said in a different polemical context over key scriptural texts like Ephesians 4: 5 and 5: 27.[51] The promising language in some of Augustine's works about persecution dimming the light of the Church allowed Protestants to claim that Augustine sets down 'in . . . manifest termes' that 'in the time of persecution the Church shall not appeare' (because limited to the body of the Elect).[52] This is not exactly what Augustine meant in his quarrels with the Donatists about the true Church.[53] Catholic polemic which argues from Augustine that the true Church cannot be other than continuously visible in its institutional form is also misleading.[54]

To coax the non-aligned into an unambiguous profession of Romanism, Catholics said that scriptural and patristic sources showed that the true Church was continuously visible. For it to be continuously visible there must necessarily have been an unbroken succession of pastors from Christ to the present day. Only the Roman Church could point to a visible succession of such pastors and 'professors' of its doctrines in every age of the Church since

[49] BL, Lansd. MS 776, fo. 39ᵛ; Finch, *Knowledge*, sig. Gᵛ: the Church of Christ should accept only a perfect rule of faith 'in stead whereof Antichristes generation hath many bookes and rules, as holy decrees and decretals, fathers, counsels, holy doctors'; White, *Defence*, 285–6.
[50] William Crompton, *Saint Austins Summes* (1625); P. Lake, 'Calvinism and the English Church, 1570–1635', *P&P* 114 (1987), 32–76, at pp. 62–3.
[51] Brereley, *Sainct Austines Religion*, 39–40; *Contra Cresconium* I, 28, 33, *CSEL* LII, 352; *ep.* liv, 5, *CSEL* XXXIV/2, 165; *De Baptismo* VII, 53, *CSEL* LI, 359.
[52] Crompton, *Saint Austins Summes*, 59–60; Mornay, *Notable Treatise*, sig. Bvʳ–viᵛ.
[53] Dodaro and Questier, 'Strategies', 443–4.
[54] Dodaro and Questier, 'Strategies', 442–3.

its foundation. Rome's teaching authority was therefore guaranteed not by its conformity to Scripture (a precarious point to argue with a Protestant) but by its continuous visibility.[55] Even patristic works are cited not because they themselves are authentic independent sources but because their content shows their writers to have been in conformity with the present Roman Church.[56]

This was rapidly translated into a series of debating points which came to typify the Catholic polemic of this period. It was unnecessary, Catholics claimed, to enquire endlessly into the doctrinal veracity of what the Roman Church said. That would be an uncertain way to faith, quite impossible for the unlearned, and confusing even for the educated. All that was necessary for the undecided man was to determine a continuous institutional visible profession of the faith back to the foundation of the Church and then he could be secure in the knowledge that this was the true profession of the Christian religion.[57] The way to do this was to take the marks or character-istics which all agreed belonged to the true Church and test which of the competing institutional Churches could claim them.[58] This, in fact, was the application of the 'general motives' principle (enunciated by John Sweet) to the problem of persuading people to accept Rome's authority. Instead of wracking one's brain over each element of doctrine (transubstantiation etc.) individually, the recognition of the true Church by its characteristics is the pathway to certainty about all doctrine. Thus Sweet writes 'for the Catholike party' such persuasions are 'seen in such as have handled the notes of the Church, in "Campian his ten Reasons", in . . . [Robert Persons's]

---

[55] Leech, *Dutifull and Respective Considerations*, 44–5.

[56] Theophilus Higgons, *The First Motive of T. H. Maister of Arts, and lately Minister, to suspect the Integrity of his Religion* (Douai, 1609), 25; Anthony Clarke, *The Defence of the Honor of God* (Paris (imprint false, printed secretly in England), 1621), chapter 3; Tobias Mathew jnr, *The Confessions* (St Omer, 1620), sig. a4r; Edward Weston, *The Repaire of Honour* (Bruges (imprint false, printed at St Omer), 1624), 11–14; Matthew Sutcliffe, *The Unmasking of a Masse-monger* (1626), sig. A2v, 39–40; BL, Lansd. MS 776, fos. 32v, 33v. Protestants argued that patristic writers were members of their Church, but they put a different polemical slant on the Church's visibility, Alexander Cooke, *Saint Austins Religion* (1625).

[57] John Percy, *A Catalogue of divers visible Professors* (St Omer, 1614), sig. A2r; Robert Persons, *A Treatise of Three Conversions* (3 vols., n.p., 1603–4), I, 631; Walsingham, *Search* (1609), 481–2; Percy, *Reply*, 5; N. N., *An Epistle of a Catholike Young Gentleman* (Douai (imprint false, printed secretly in England), 1623), 14–32.

[58] Percy, *Treatise* (1614); *idem, Reply; idem, Catalogue*; P. Milward, *Religious Controversies of the Jacobean Age* (1978), 216–27; William Wright, *A Discovery of Certaine Notorious Shifts, Evasions, and Untruthes uttered by M. John White Minister* (St Omer, 1614); *idem, Treatise*; Worthington, *Whyte*; Clarke, *Defence*; Sylvester Norris, *The Guide of Faith* (St Omer, 1621); *idem, An Appendix to the Antidote* (St Omer, 1621); Bodl., Rawl. MS D 853, fos. 20r–1r, 22r–v, Bodl., Jones MS 53, fos. 221v–2r, all following the line of argument in William Allen's 'articles' which emerged in print in Bristow's *Briefe Treatise* and *Demaundes*.

booke of the "Three Conversions of England", in [Richard] Bristow, and others'.[59] These Catholic polemicists had translated the speculative theological ideas about the integrity of the Church's structure into an affirmation of Roman authority. In the debate held in June 1623 between John Percy, John Sweet, Daniel Featley and Francis White in the house of Sir Humphrey Lynde, the subject for dispute was the central one of visibility and succession. As Percy and Featley were hammering out the finer points of visibility, Lynde (perhaps unaware of its significance) interrupted and said 'prove me but this one point out of Saint Augustine, namely, Transubstantiation . . . and I will promise you to go to Masse'. Sweet coldly cut him off with the words, 'that is not now to the question'. In a controversy about the Church, transubstantiation was a relatively trivial matter.[60]

The Church's characteristics were not individual points for debate, though a polemicist sometimes selected a specific mark for polemical treatment. Evidence that the Roman Church possessed one such characteristic (in the Roman sense) was evidence that it possessed all.[61] When Roman polemicists argued that the true Church must enjoy a continuous visible expression upon earth, contention about which ecclesiastical institutions could claim to represent the true Church developed into an argument about the general historical nature of the Church. Church history is frequently thought to have been exclusively the province of John Foxe and his demonstrations of an invisible Protestant Church of the Elect existing before the Reformation. But Catholics also translated polemic about the Church into historical discourse.[62] Richard Smith wrote that 'the questions of Doctrine are innumerable, but the questions of Fact, few', and 'there are few questions of doctrine of that nature, that all other controversies of faith depend upon them; but the most questions of Fact are such, as if they be well decided, al other Controversies of religion are at an end'.[63] History allowed

---

[59] Sweet, *Monsigr Fate Voi*, 153–4.
[60] Featley, *Fisher*, 10.
[61] Cf. Bunny, *Truth*, sig. Cc5ʳ. Percy followed Bellarmine in his emphasis that '[only] two things are required in every sufficient marke; the first is, that it be not common to many, but proper, and only agreeing to the thing, wherof it is a marke'; and the second requirement is that 'it be more apparent, and easy to be knowne, then the thing [of which it is a mark]', Percy, *Treatise* (1614), 74–5; see also Persons, *Treatise of Three Conversions*, I, 654; Sweet, *Monsigr Fate Voi*, 154. Romanist concentration on the marks of the Church seems to come partly from Gregory of Valentia and very heavily from Bellarmine's controversial writings, *Disputationes . . . de Controversiis Christianae Fidei, Adversus Huius Temporis Haereticos*, the purpose of which was to act as a manual for polemical engagement with Protestants, R. C. Bald, *John Donne* (Oxford, 1970), 69; Wotton, *Trial*, 221; Wadkins, 'Percy–"Fisher" Controversies', 156.
[62] Weston, *Repaire*, 7–8.
[63] Richard Smith, *Of the Author and Substance of the Protestant Church and Religion* (St Omer, 1621), sig. *2ᵛ; cf. Campion, *Campian Englished*, 117. This was an entirely different exercise from the historical source criticism of e.g. Protestant polemicists like John

Catholic writers to Romanise the past and to align Rome's continuous historical visibility with an unbroken doctrinal profession which was guaranteed by its continuity through all centuries as much as by its substance. Robert Persons's *Treatise of Three Conversions* Romanised the history of the English Church in reply to Protestant writers like John Bale, Matthew Parker and Foxe, and later Matthew Sutcliffe, who saw the Saxon period as having a plethora of satisfyingly proto-Protestant 'professors'.[64]

So, Catholics perennially put the historical question to the Protestants, 'Where was your Church before Luther?' They thought that insistence upon visible aspects or marks of the Church, for tactical and doctrinal reasons, gave them a vast polemical advantage. Some Protestant writers appeared to concede that this Catholic line of argument was effective in the sense that it was polemically (if not doctrinally) sound: Robert Crowley noted that an emphasis on the principal marks of the Church was the papists' most usual way of perverting the queen's subjects. John White observed that 'in all my acquaintance with persons affected to Popery' (in his own county of Lancashire) 'they object nothing against us more willingly' than visible succession. Robert Finch complained of the papists 'in whose mouth is ever Church, Church'. Robert Townson in a sermon in November 1602 pointed out that 'the papistes have a trick of appropriatinge the name of the church to themselves onely', though he was content to remark that 'as they reade the Church, it is theirs dead sure'. George Carleton prefaced a simplified version of his *Consensus Ecclesiae* by saying that since its appearance he has seen 'divers bookes' (evidently referring to those by people like John Percy) 'written in English to seduce the simple that cannot judge, insinuating to them faire pretences of a shewe of the Church: Which shewe of the Church is the thing that carrieth away many that cannot judge between trueths and shewes'. John Gee said that this polemical line, though nothing new in itself,

Cameron and Jean Daillé, Solé, *Débat*, I, 80–1, II, 573–4; B. G. Armstrong, *Calvinism and the Amyraut Heresy* (1969), 9–10, 12–13; J.-R. Armogathe, 'De l'Art de Penser comme Art de Persuader', in *La Conversion au XVIIᵉ Siècle* (Centre Méridional de Rencontres sur le XVIIe Siècle, Marseille, 1982), 29–41, at p. 29. Initial English polemical lack of interest in historiography, commented on by Edmund Bolton, was made up for by Robert Persons, AAW, A XIII, 669; Persons, *Treatise of Three Conversions*, written in reply to points made by Sir Francis Hastings, *An Apologie or Defence of the Watch-word* (1600), 191–3; Robert Persons, *An Answere to the Fifth Part of Reportes* (St Omer, 1606); Questier, 'Phenomenon', 62–4. French Catholic polemicists used history against French Protestants in the same way as English Catholic polemicists, Solé, *Débat*, II, 629–30. A survey of all relevant Church history was arguably as tedious as a survey of the patristic literary corpus, Bodl., Rawl. MS D 853, fo. 156ᵛ.

64 H. A. MacDougall, *Racial Myth in English History* (Hanover, New Hampshire, 1982), 32, 35–9, 40; cf. Matthew Sutcliffe, *The Subversion of Robert Parsons* (1606), chapters 1–3; Bell, *Christian Dialogue*, 98.

had been intensified by Catholic clerics (like plagues of frogs and locusts) in James's reign. They have 'beene croaking and throtling out this harsh note and noyse to every Protestant passenger, "Where was your Church before Luther?", and they think 'to choake us with this Question'.[65]

Many people were pleased to record that they converted to Rome when they accepted the Roman case on the structure of the visible Church.[66] As the earl of Manchester's reply to Sir Walter Montagu's reasons for his conversion said, 'presently upon one poore prejudice, of Invisibility . . . you swallow all other scruples'.[67] Certainly Catholics thought that the quasi-physical representation of their case through an historical exposition of their visible Church was most effective. Richard Smith cited Isaac Casaubon to say that 'to insinuate into the mind of the Reader any opinion now in controversie, Baronius historyes are of greater force, then Bellarmines desputes'.[68]

It would be a mistake, though, to assume that, simply because one side said that its case was proved by a particular line of argument, the reasons which it advanced to prove such a line would have been automatically convincing to the confused and wavering reader. The observations of writers like Sweet and Percy that their opponents cannot assemble a case to answer on the subject of the Church are merely polemical taunts. Protestant writers would not have dissented from Theophilus Higgons's opinion that 'the Church it selfe . . . [is] the highest sphere in the great world of theological controversies'. They were as ready to dispute about the Church as

---

65 Robert Crowley, *A breefe Discourse, concerning those foure usuall Notes, whereby Christes Catholique Church is knowen* (1581), sig. Aiiii[r]; White, *Way*, 337; Finch, *Knowledge*, sig. B[r]; R. P. Sorlien (ed.), *The Diary of John Manningham* (Hanover, New Hampshire, 1976), 144; George Carleton, *Directions to Know the True Church* (1615), sig. A4[v]–5[r]; Webbe, *Catalogus*, sig. ¶[v].

66 E.g. Theophilus Higgons, *The Apology of Theophilus Higgons lately Minister, now Catholique* (Rouen, 1609), 25; BL, Lansd. MS 776, fos. 35[v]–7[r]; Queen's College MS 284, fos. 206[v]–7[r]. Virtually no convert to Rome in this period omits the visibility issue among his recorded motives.

67 Bodl., Rawl. MS D 853, fo. 156[r].

68 Smith, *Author*, sig. *4[r]; Solé, *Débat*, II, 532, 546–52; cf. Edmund Bolton's point about the persuasiveness of arguments respectively from theology and the arts, AAW, A XIII, 669. Walter Montagu based his account of his conversion squarely on Smith's distinction between history and school-disputes over divinity, Bodl., Rawl. MS D 853, fos. 153[r], 166[v]. Converts like Theophilus Higgons accepted Roman doctrinal tenets on the basis of historical evidence (taken, in Higgons's case, from Persons's *Treatise of Three Conversions*), Higgons, *First Motive*, 20. The historical points which Benjamin Carier made against the break with Rome are evidently drawn out of Nicholas Sander, *Doctissimi Viri Nicolai Sanderi, de Origine ac Progressu Schismatis Anglicani, Liber* (Rheims, 1585), Carier, *A Treatise* (Brussels, 1614), 11, 38; George Hakewill, *An Answere to a Treatise Written by Dr Carier* (1616), sig. B2[r]; cf. Carier, *Copy*, 6; cf. also CRS 54, 150, 233; BL, Lansd. MS 776, fo. 30[v].

any other topic.[69] In polemic Protestants countered Romanists by arguing
that the true Church is invisible. Yet this does not mean that they were
conceding simplistic Romanist charges that they imagined God's Church
might fall irredeemably into corruption. They mean that its earthly structure
lacks the integrity that could guarantee it from becoming entirely invisible
to the non-Elect.[70] Reformed Protestants held a different concept of election
from Roman Catholics. In Reformed Protestant thought the Elect cannot
tumble from grace. Whatever spiritual disasters they may experience, they
cannot fall finally and totally from their elect status. So it follows that the
true Church cannot permanently be hidden from them, or they from each
other. This aspect of their experience of grace is personal to them. It does
not come through the Church and its sacraments and institutional structure.
God's promises to his Elect will not fail if the Church falls into decay. For
the Reprobate (in whatever manner their reprobation is thought to depend
on the will of God), the Church cannot assist to reverse God's decrees in
their unfortunate cases. Sometimes the true Church *may* be entirely hidden
from them.[71] Roman Catholics, who think differently about the way saving
grace is allotted to men, and see justifying as well as sanctifying elements of
grace within the institutional Church militant, cannot conceive of the
defectibility of that Church in the same manner.[72]

This meant that Protestants had perfectly adequate replies to every
Catholic polemical point about the Church. Employing their Reformed
concept of election, all they had to do was to reduce the extent to which
the true Church's characteristics could be envisaged as necessarily institutionally visible, and emphasise how far the Church's marks could exist
independently of its physical structure.[73] The unity which Roman polemicists described by reference to communion of particular Churches with
Rome Protestants located in consent over fundamental points of doctrine,
itself a sign of the invisible mystical unity of the church militant. The true
Church on earth represented in its institutions is only visible, infallible, holy
and so on, 'according unto the relation and dependance which it hath upon
the Triumphant Church, and the assistance which it hath from Christ, his

---

69 Theophilus Higgons, *A Sermon preached at Pauls Crosse* (1611), 44; see also *idem*,
   Apology, 25; White, *Way*, sig. a2ʳ⁻ᵛ; BL, Lansd. MS 776, fos. 18ᵛ–19ʳ; Sorlien, *Diary*,
   143–4.
70 Abbot, *Reasons*, 26; Wotton, *Trial*, 215; White, *Way*, 85–9; cf. White, *Defence*, 285,
   stressing that the Elect themselves do not at all times perceive the authority of the Scriptures
   because their authority can be discerned only through the operation of grace, not the mere
   status of election.
71 Finch, *Knowledge*, sig. F2ʳ: 'if it be dim and hid, it is hid unto them that perish: but unto
   the children of light it is manifest inough'; White, *Way*, 91.
72 Leech, *Dutifull and Respective Considerations*, 109–10.
73 Milton, 'Church', 191.

Prophets and Apostles, upon whose doctrine and Scriptures it doth wholly cast it selfe'.[74] Protestants like Francis Bunny said that in determining the true Church 'there ought to be no quaestion at al among us: but only, of the members therof, who they are, that more truly answer unto their calling', a consideration of visibility but locating the visible nature of the Church by reference to the activity of grace within the members of the Church.[75] In reply to the Catholic accusation exemplified in Walter Montagu's and John Good's criticism of John White that Protestants create a paradox by claiming a continued succession 'though not visible to the World', Protestants merely replied that the more the papists emphasised the integrity of the institutional visible Church the more they obscured the true Church.[76] In fact, if the integrity of the Church is to be measured by reference to Christ and Scripture then the allegations that the genesis of Protestantism is a recent historical phenomenon and that the Protestant Church lacks unity are quite irrelevant. As Sutcliffe replied to Kellison, 'Luther is not our founder, nor any of late time', and Francis Bunny rejected the Catholic use of 'reprochfull names of "Lutherans, Zwinglians, Calvinistes, Bezites", and such like' because 'we holde not any of these, no nor of them all, but as they holde of Christ'.[77] Protestants defined the Church as both visible and invisible, the multitude and the Elect, but they still thought that the true and the false Churches should not be confused with ecclesiastical structures. Thus Robert Finch, like so many other Protestants, challenged the papists to 'shewe unto us plainely in simple wordes, what Church they doe speake of, whether of the Church of Christ, or else of the Church of Antichrist'.[78] In such a scheme, Protestants had an equally serviceable model for persuading the reader to abandon one particular Church for another (even if they could not relate its terms to institutions in quite the way that Catholics did).[79] They simply argued

---

[74] Mornay, *Notable Treatise*, sigs. Dviii^r–Eiiii^r; Bunny, *Truth*, sig. Cc6^r, Cc7^v; Abbot, *Reasons*, 25–6; Walker, *Summe*, sig. B4^r.

[75] Bunny, *Treatise*, 108.

[76] Bodl., Rawl. MS D 853, fo. 154^r; BL, Lansd. MS 776, fo. 22^v; Abbot, *Reasons*, 31, 35–6.

[77] Sutcliffe, *Examination*, 39; Bunny, *Truth*, sig. Cc7^v; Bodl., Rawl. MS D 853, fo. 156^v.

[78] Finch, *Knowledge*, sig. B2^r; Theophilus Higgons, *Mystical Babylon* (1624), sig. ¶4^v.

[79] The effectiveness of the Protestant equal and opposite case on the Church is demonstrated by Persons's decision to answer in full the tract written by the otherwise rather insignificant renegade John Nichols who had used long passages from Mornay. John Nichols, *A Declaration of the Recantation of John Nichols* (1581), sigs. Cv^v–Diii^v, Dv^v–vii^r employs passages from Mornay, *Notable Treatise*, sigs. Diii^r–vii^r, E^v–ii^r. After these direct transcriptions Nichols follows Mornay's series of ideas. Persons noted that Mornay's book was proving influential in England, Robert Persons, *A Discoverie of J. Nichols* (1581), sig. Iv^v. Sir Anthony Hungerford claimed to have been converted in part by reading Mornay, Anthony Hungerford, *The Advise* (1639), 61.

that people should avoid the Roman Church by considering the nature of the true Church and the extent to which the Roman Church fell short of it.

Protestants therefore did not have to avoid the topics which might be thought to focus attention inevitably on visible aspects of authority – for example the papacy. For Roman Catholics, the significance of the Petrine texts was that they guaranteed the inerrancy of the Roman Church's earthly structure. The standard Protestant reply (based on patristic texts) was that of Matthew Sutcliffe: when Augustine spoke of 'the Rock, against which the proud gates of Hell cannot prevaile', he 'understandeth S. Peters Confession and Doctrine, and not the succession of Popes'; a spiritual not a physical succession.[80] The citations from Augustine which Protestant writers struck upon were frequently apposite. Andrew Willet and William Crompton could emphasise the 'invisible' elements of the petrine texts out of Augustine's works, notably *De Utilitate Credendi*, *Contra Litteras Petiliani* and *Retractationes*. Even if they did not grasp the exact significance which Augustine attributed to the fifth-century papacy, they could show that it was not the one Roman polemicists drew out of his works.[81]

Of course, the mere fact that the rival polemical arsenals were equally matched did not prevent the occasional hint of a tactical victory by one or other side. On the subject of visible succession within the Church, Protestants might sometimes leave themselves open to attack. Their lingering desire to demonstrate that they too could show an historical line of 'professors' of Protestant opinions sometimes put them in a dilemma as to whether they should deny the importance of succession altogether or qualify the papists' account of it. Both these difficulties seem to have beset Daniel Featley when he publicly took on John Percy in June 1623. Featley's own narrative suggests that the debate did not go as well as he might have liked. Percy syllogistically linked outward and spiritual succession, and when Featley tried to turn the argument so as to concentrate on the characteristics of an invisible Church, and thus avoid Percy's challenge to name some Protestant 'professors' in every age since the foundation of the Church, sections of the audience started to heckle him, chanting 'names, names, names'.[82] Featley was simply stating the line subscribed to by most

---

[80] Sutcliffe, *Unmasking*, 49.
[81] Crompton, *Saint Austins Summes*, 63, 67; *Retractationes* I, 21, CCSL LVII, 62; *De Utilitate Credendi*, 17, CSEL XXV, 45; Crompton, *Saint Austins Summes*, 66; Andrew Willet, *Synopsis Papismi* (1600), 133, 146; *Contra Litteras Petiliani* LI, 118, CSEL LII, 88; Dodaro and Questier, 'Strategies', 439–41. Cf. Crompton's similar exploitation of other Augustinian passages, *Saint Austins Summes*, 61–2, 65; *Enarrat. in Ps. CVIII* I, CCSL L, 1585; *Tractatus in Epistulam Johannis* X, 1, PL XXXV, 2054.
[82] Featley, *Fisher*, 11–13.

Protestants of a 'leftish' inclination in the English Church.[83] And Protestants were convinced that Featley had been victorious. It was Percy who was doing the evading since he 'neither could denie that Christ and his Apostles taught the same faith and doctrine, which the Protestants now professe, nor would abide the triall by it, but fled from that to the practise of ensuing times'.[84] But, Catholics seem to have been aware, certainly in the later part of James's reign, that they had found a potential polemical dilemma for Protestants in their disagreements over the Church as a theological concept. The definition of the true Church was inextricably bound up with Protestants' self-definition against Rome. Disagreement over that self-definition started to create serious divisions in the Jacobean Church. Arguments about the characteristics of the visible and invisible expressions of the Church had always been a shorthand device for debate about the structure and regulation of particular Churches. Some Protestants' positive emphasis on certain institutional elements of the Church, its sacraments and orders, was automatically expressed in definitions of the positive aspects of visibility which were unpalatable to other Protestants. As Anthony Milton has shown, there may have been a satisfactory agreement among moderate Calvinists like Richard Field and John Prideaux that visibility and invisibility were simply two aspects of the same Church. But the 'relative invisibility' to which moderate Calvinists subscribed arguably left them open to attack. If they conceded that the Church as an institution *had* to play some part in salvation, they were liable to be accused, as they were by Catholics, of ambiguity and evasion over the authority which could be accorded to an institutional particular Church. Apparently irreconcilable statements about the defectibility of the Church, and differences over who might be claimed from history as Protestant 'professors', then appeared to be evidence of perversity among Protestants.[85] There was a polemical inconsistency, even if not a logical one, in Featley's tactics of arguing on the one hand that Protestants did not need to show a formal succession of 'professors' and on the other that he could prove them to have existed in every age since the foundation of the Church.[86] He would probably have done better to avoid Percy's bait and take instead Wotton's more relaxed line: 'they bid us shew a beadroll of their names that were professours of our faith; what if we cannot? there may be a Catalogue, though we cannot shew it'; or alternatively the position taken by Richard Sheldon – to concede that

---

[83] Thomas Bell, *The Survey of Popery* (1596), 193; *idem, Christian Dialogue*, 66–7, 99–100; Savage, *Conference*, 62, 66, 70–1; Willet, *Synopsis Papismi*, 69.

[84] Webbe, *Catalogus*, 87; T. Birch (ed.), *The Court and Times of James the First* (2 vols., 1848), II, 408–9; cf. Thomas Bedford, *Luthers Predecessours* (1624).

[85] Wright, *Treatise*, 48; Milton, 'Church', *passim*.

[86] White, *Way*, 338–9, conceded the uncertainty of Protestantism's historical record.

Rome (only) had been continuously visible but this was irrelevant (since continuous institutional visibility was not an aspect of the true Church).[87]

It was considerably easier for a Catholic than for a Protestant to insist that an individual ought to belong to an institutional Church since Catholics connected membership of it with election and grace in a way that Reformed Protestant doctrine did not allow.[88] It is certainly possible to show that many of the motives which Catholic converts expressed, both in print and privately, for changing their religion to conform with that of Rome were closely connected with polemic. More often than not a convert will expatiate on his new perception of the form of the Church and refer, implicitly or explicitly, to the arguments over visibility. Thus Humphrey Leech, Theophilus Higgons and Benjamin Carier all attacked the faulty disciplinary structure of the Church of England – a sure sign that it did not possess all the outward visible marks of a true Church.[89] James Wadsworth snr and Francis Walsingham argued that certainty and security in religion were impossible among the fractured Protestant congregations.[90] Such converts follow the logic of polemic and emphasise the precedence of the Church's authority over that of Scripture.[91]

Yet even if in places it is possible to show that polemically one side had weaknesses, in the end that side could always find similar targets to shoot back at. Examples of clear polemical victories and defeats are few and far between. The impression is that reasons for changing religion which are phrased by reference to polemic are simply *ex post facto* rationalisations of whatever it was that really induced the conversion. Furthermore, it is arguable that the very characteristics which made polemic persuasive (as I have outlined them) were also its limitations. This was not just because polemic was so self-evidently a distortion both of the sources alleged for the arguments put forward and of the position of the other side. It was because

---

[87] Wotton, *Runne*, sig. L^v; cf. White, *Way*, 338, 394, 403 (arguing that it is not necessary to show any external succession at all; proof that there were any Protestants before Luther is enough); Richard Sheldon, *The Motives of Richard Sheldon Pr.* (1612), sig. Dd4^v; cf. White, *Defence*, 350. Before 1623 Featley was apparently more wary of Jesuit challenges to debate about the Church, George Roberts (ed.), *Diary of Walter Yonge* (Camden Society, first series, 41, 1848), 63.

[88] Mornay, *Notable Treatise*, sig. D^r. It was harder also for Protestant writers to persuade Catholic recusants that they must attend churches than for Catholics to argue that they must not.

[89] Higgons, *First Motive*, 21 (though the passage he cites from St Jerome could easily be employed in a diametrically opposed sense, cf. Wotton, *Trial*, 171); Leech, *Triumph*, 93; cf. Leech, *Dutifull and Respective Considerations*, 44–54; Carier, *Treatise*, 10; Balliol College MS 270, pp. 153–63. Carier among others located the substance of the Church in institutional forms in a way that was unthinkable for Reformed Protestants, Carier, *Copy*, 6.

[90] William Bedell, *The Copies of Certaine Letters* (1624), 4; Walsingham, *Search* (1609), 55.

[91] Carier, *Copy*, 4–5; cf. Vane, *Lost Sheep*, 23–5; N. N., *Epistle*, 12–13.

the way in which polemicists argued about the nature of the Church itself shows that there was no sufficient ground within their tracts for making up one's mind about the Church to which one should belong, or rather, no basis for deciding that one must, at peril of losing eternal life, adhere to one particular Church and reject another. This is not because the tracts failed to address the problem of ecclesiastical allegiance. They did, and polemicists could subtly combine political and religious considerations to persuade people to convert from one Church to the other. But an examination of what the controversialists said should have told an interested party in the sixteenth century what it tells us now: that there is no such thing, fundamentally, in polemic (on this issue of the Church and virtually all related matters) as absolute right and wrong. Polemical formulae do not provide the basis for conversion to and from Rome in the way that polemicists said they did.[92] In fact, the politicised nature of the doctrinal debate did not allow the protagonists to express fully what they meant by conversion when they exhorted the uncommitted or hostile reader to adhere to their Church (even though such a change they would have considered as an integral part of true conversion). Or rather, their insistence on one particular reading of conversion meant concealing the elements of it which both sides held in common (though seen from different perspectives). Their agenda – that their readers had to decide between Roman and Protestant versions of the true Church – meant that they had to restrict artificially the full sense of what it means to belong to 'the Church'. Ultimately their books give only a veiled impression of why it is important to adhere to one or other institutional Church, and they necessarily produced only a parody even of the things which they genuinely thought erroneous in their opponents' position. This, rather than incompetence, prejudice or fraud, was the source of the complaints by polemicists like Theophilus Higgons that their opponents use patristic sources to 'make their conclusions against some doctrine, which is not particularly handled by the Fathers in those places, whence they assume such proofes', or William Rainolds that in his 'adversaries doctrine' there was 'no kind of stay or assurance, no maner of certaintie or steadfastnes', 'no order or forme to conclude and resolve of any thing'.[93]

So the books were by themselves no adequate reason to convert. Anyone who did change his Church simply because of the doctrinal reasons presented by the polemicists did so on the basis of word-games and literary sleight of hand. It is possible that there were many who did look to the polemicists to confirm their opinions at times of uncertainty and even to justify a renunciation of one or other Church. Polemical reading might

---

[92] *New Catholic Encyclopaedia* (17 vols., Washington, 1967–78), III, 691.
[93] Higgons, *First Motive*, 114; Rainolds, *Refutation*, sig. a4r–5r.

actually trigger the doubts which led to a conversion. Still, in the accounts left by those who made a serious business of conversion, the statements that the careful reading of polemical books had changed their religion are slightly too uniform and trite to be convincing; or rather, if taken at face value, they are likely to mislead. Though leading clerical intellectuals wrote these polemical tracts it is scarcely credible that the intellectuals who converted should automatically have fallen into line behind such simplistic formulations. The emotional and spiritual forces unleashed by the doubts which many converts said they had experienced could hardly be satisfied by polemical books even though, after conversion, the convert might express his new perception of true religion by reference to polemical categories. Of course, there were many who claimed to have converted after going back to the patristic texts to examine them for themselves.[94] But even these texts were then immediately interpreted in the light of contemporary polemical attitudes. The tracts did, admittedly, deal with all the elements of what contemporaries said was true conversion: not just movement between the rival Churches but also the nature of sin, the process of regeneration, the mysteries of election, the terrors of predestination, the consolations of assurance and the necessity of perseverance. But all of these fell very quickly into a disciplined political line behind Roman or Protestant claims to truth. The reader was invited to associate true conversion in all its aspects with movement to and from Rome. Such extreme mental regimentation was not the sum total of contemporary conversion experience. Polemical books did not contain the essence of conversion.

That this is so can be demonstrated by a book – Robert Persons's *Christian Directory*. Despite its outwardly non-controversial character it was recognised as a solver of confessional doubt. People who were perplexed about the doctrinal division between the Churches and read this book seem often to have resolved their difficulties through reading it. And yet this work was capable of obviating doctrinal doubt altogether. In the preface to the first edition of 1582 Persons states that the 'principall cause and reason' for publication was 'to the ende our countrye men might have some one sufficient direction for matters of life and spirit, among so manye bookes of controversies as have ben writen, and are in writinge dailye. The whiche bookes, albeit in thes our troublesome and quarrelous times be

---

[94] J. C. H. Aveling, *Northern Catholics* (1966), 29; Robert Persons, 'Of the Life and Martyrdom of Father Edmond Campian', *Letters and Notices* 11 (1876–7), 219–42, 308–39 and 12 (1878), 1–68, in vol. 11 at p. 227; CRS 54, 215; Walsingham *Search* (1609), 229–30; Higgons, *First Motive*, sig. †7ʳ; CRS 54, 229; BL, Lansd. MS 776, fos. 19ᵛ–33ᵛ; Foley VII, 1113–14; Cressy, *Exomologesis*, 74–5: Cressy relied not 'upon a few select passages and Texts pick'd out by late Controvertists, but by observing the maine designe and intention of those Fathers'.

necessarie for defence of our faithe, againste so many seditious innovations . . . yet helpe they litle oftentymes to good lyfe, but rather do fill the heades of men with a spirite of contradiction and contention'.[95] The book was aimed at Protestants as much as Catholics. A spy reported in 1584 that Catholics were distributing it to Protestants, and that it (and the Rheims New Testament) 'are as much sought for, of the protestanttes as papistes'.[96] George Birkhead, the future archpriest, wrote in August 1584 that 'both because its matter was new to us and also on account of its special object, viz., the reformation of a sinful life', it 'has borne immense fruit; the number of conversions of heretics to the faith by reading it can scarcely be believed'.[97] Thomas Worthington said in 1601 that by it not only were 'innumerable Catholiques' confirmed but also 'Schismatikes and Heretikes continually converted'.[98] Protestant editions of it were published, shorn of its Roman terminology.[99]

Why should a book which refrained, except in the preface, from attacking the opposing religion and Church have been so effective in making people change their religion to Rome? Obviously its Roman terminology might make people think that Rome must be a true Church if it promoted the exercise of a godly life. Lawrence Caddey's printed recantation which appeared in 1583 claimed that Protestants 'cannot abide' books of 'contemplation, meditation, and instruction of Christian life and manners', because they know that 'devout praier onely, penaunce and amendement of life, will easily bring men from their pretended Religion, in which no such devotions are found'.[100] But in the case of the *Christian Directory* this would be to put a purely polemical slant on a motive to change religion which cannot be explained in such terms. The *Christian Directory* transcended standard polemic altogether as well as cutting through the verbiage of ordinary controversial discourse. There is no doubt that it was intended to convince the reader that Roman Catholicism was orthodox Christian faith. But it took John Sweet's 'general motives' a step

---

[95] Persons, *First Booke*, 2.

[96] PRO, SP 12/168/31, fo. 75ʳ; cf. *CSPD Addenda 1580–1625*, 112; PRO, SP 14/95/24.i, fo. 72ʳ. The aim of the proselytiser was to induce the sudden moment of illumination which could then be capitalised on doctrinally. This would appear to be the way William Rainolds's *Refutation* was used as well, CRS 54, 2; Mathew, *True Historical Relation*, 24.

[97] CRS 4, 153, 155.

[98] Thomas Worthington, *A Relation of Sixtene Martyrs* (Douai, 1601), 73.

[99] The Yorkshire puritan minister Edmund Bunny produced expurgated editions from 1584 onwards. Persons wrote a savage reply in the preface to the republished and expanded version of 1585, *A Christian Directorie Guiding Men to their Salvation* (Rouen, 1585); cf. PRO, SP 12/194/13, fo. 33ʳ.

[100] William Allen, *A True Report of the late Apprehension and Imprisonnement of John Nicols* (Rheims, 1583), fos. 20ᵛ–1ʳ. Caddey was referring not to Persons's work but to that of Luis of Granada.

further by abandoning polemic as the principal means of persuasion. William Fitch, who became a Capuchin, began his conversion which ended in the Roman Church by reading the Protestant version of Persons's *Christian Directory*. It seems from his account of his spiritual transformation that the essence of the change was achieved before he even considered the polemical arguments about which institutional Church he should embrace.[101]

In a very real sense, then, neither the mechanism nor the essence of conversion was contained in the polemic by which Rome and the Protestants appear to have set out the corpus of reasons for belonging to their Churches. Polemical reasoning is not really the key to understanding why people became Catholics or Protestants. Conversions were the culminations of a range of experiences as wide as the number of causes which unsettled the minds of contemporaries in religion. Even a man's vaguest discomfort with his ecclesiastical setting could not be adequately explained by looking in the neatly set-out sections of the polemical tracts. From the basest motive of temporal well-being and security through to the principled pondering of which Church was doctrinally sound, and finally the explosive spiritual experience of evangelical conversion which seemed to transcend polemical bickering altogether, the polemical books could point to the issues which might absorb the mind of a man who decided to express his uncertainties and final resolutions in religion through movement between the institutional Churches of England and Rome. But by themselves the polemical tracts were not it. Conversion surged through a realm of experience in which the books of controversial theology were a pale reflection of the sum total of contemporary understanding of change of religion. For this reason also, to talk about the advent of Protestantism after the collapse of the Marian restoration or the English struggle between Reformed Religion and Counter-Reformation Catholicism purely in terms of a polemical set of hatreds, tends to obscure how the country became, or failed to become, Protestant. Even though Protestant evangelisation proceeded on the back of an anti-Roman polemic (and, vice versa, Catholic conservative activism defined itself by a loathing of Reformed theology), it is still not adequate to say that people became Catholics or Protestants simply by defining their beliefs solely against a range of doctrinal opposites put about by polemical rivals. The Reformation, contemporaries thought, advanced largely through conversion, but conversion, they knew, was not limited merely to an exchange of opinions.

---

[101] Jacques Brousse, *The Life of the Reverend Fa. Angel of Joyeuse* (Douai, 1623), sig. Bb5ᵛ–6ᵛ.

3

The experience of change of religion

If good cause for conversion to and from the Church of Rome could not be found in the polemical books of theology, on what grounds, then, did people change religion? Contemporaries were still absolutely certain that conversion as an expression of grace could be understood entirely within a conscious rejection of the structure and ministrations of one Church for those of another. The kaleidoscopic entirety of conversion experience – intellectual satisfaction with a newly discovered doctrinal synthesis, liberation from a disappointing ecclesiastical or political environment, the sensation of God's judgments for sin, the salve of the Gospel after the hammer of the law, the agonies and ecstasies of repentance – all could be comprehended within the rejection or embrace of the Church of Rome. Of course, conversion in the realm of grace was not itself dependent on an exchange of ecclesiastical allegiance, or even an awareness of the polemical issues involved. Conversion reliant on the activity of grace – in regeneration, repentance and sanctification – is at the centre of all Christian life, and thus a necessity for all the Church's members.[1] This was the common currency of vast swathes of sermons, all the literature about affliction and consolation, the *ars moriendi* genre and so on. Perhaps the majority never did consider the perennial problem of division in the institutional Church. But conversion to and from Rome was not just an isolated and eccentric sense of changing religion. Though many sermons and tracts on repentance and grace deliberately shied away from cavils and disputes, the rejection of Rome or of Protestant heresy could be interpreted as part of a more general conversion process, a resolution against sin and ungodliness. Popery and heresy were seen to contain a wider principle of corruption than merely a faulty style of exegesis. So the politicising of conversion in this way – the general agreement that it could be perceived through ecclesiastical rivalry and the example of some individuals rejecting one Church and embracing another – is clearly a key to understanding the processes of the Reformation more

---

[1] J. Morgan, *Godly Learning* (Cambridge, 1986), 31; Stephen Denison, *The New Creature* (1619), 52.

generally. The motives which contemporaries could allege for ecclesiastical conversion are a guide to the intersection between the general issues of Reformation religion and the war between the Churches. This certainly takes us beyond the artificial categories of religion in the polemical books which we saw in the previous chapter. Movement between the Churches cannot be understood just as the function of an academic debate.

In this chapter I wish to look at what converts actually did when they changed religion and how they explained it to a sometimes incredulous public. Their difficulty was that kicking over the traces could so easily be interpreted as a cynical exploitation of the division between the Churches for personal gain and, especially, as a means of starting afresh politically. As George Birkhead, the superior of the Catholic secular clergy between 1608 and 1614, wrote (when faced with his priests' indiscipline over the Jacobean oath of allegiance) 'yf any be once discontented and cannot have his will, he presently beginneth to imagin his flight to the enemie'.[2] It might seem odd, therefore, that people should ground their experience of change of religion so firmly within the vitriol of ecclesiastical conflict. Surely it would have made more sense as a public relations exercise to mumble irenic sweet-nothings about true religion and to say that they had converted to the truth by abandoning former prejudices and hatreds. This might at least have protected them from some of the more vicious character assassinations which they suffered from those they were leaving behind. Yet they, and particularly the clerical converts on whom this chapter largely focuses, almost automatically interpreted their changes of religion within a scheme of conflict and division. By referring to the clerical waverers' largely polemical tractate justifications for what they did and the hostile response which they often elicited, I want to show how even the wider experience of conversion could be assimilated almost completely into the factional divisions among English clergy. Conversion (when perceived as an impulse towards and under grace) might appear distorted by the historian who locates it within obsessive politicised divisions. Indeed, as the next chapter seeks to show, it did not inevitably and slavishly follow the logic of overt political oppositions. But, to understand the contemporary experience of it, it is necessary to explain why people elucidated and expounded it through reference to ecclesiastical conflict.

CLERICAL PROSPECTS AND ECCLESIASTICAL POLITICS

To contemporary eyes the most visible instances of conversion were the high profile declarations by intellectuals and politicians, especially clerical ones,

---

[2] AAW, A XI, 63.

that they were leaving their Church and cleaving to another. At a time when so much discourse about political instability referred to changeability in ecclesiastical affairs these inconstant people seemed to represent not just the way the political wind was blowing but more generally how religious reform and reaction were underwritten, promoted or undermined by political forces.

To what extent was ecclesiastical conversion simply a feature of the economics of clerical employment? Much noted by contemporaries were the career problems which had apparently instigated the journey of dissatisfied clerics out of one Church and into another.[3] Sir Edward Hoby accused the notoriously unstable Theophilus Higgons of changing religion out of ambition. His disease was that of Arius whose 'emptie stomacke being disappointed of the fat Bishopricke, after which he did long gape, sent up such foggie mysts of discontentment into his daseled head . . . [that he became a heretic]'.[4] John Meredyth poured scorn on those 'Ambitious Spirits', who like Arius, impatient of the advancement of persons more worthy then themselves, perfidiously flye to the Tents of Antechrist'. In that Archbishop Marc'Antonio de Dominis was ever a convert at all he provided plenty of material for Protestant disdain. Only unworthy, unspiritual motives could cause apostasy, and de Dominis had plenty of those.[5] Such charges were levelled also against people like the former godly Protestant clerics Theodore Price and James Wadsworth.[6] Benjamin Carier, a royal

---

[3] Both theological and psychological theories of conversion state, from different perspectives, that change of religion may be caused in some sense by external as well as internal factors, S. de Sanctis, *Religious Conversion* (1927), 40–1 ('as in every psychic process, the initial stimulus is to be sought outside consciousness', though 'without the interior elaboration of the stimulus . . . the process would never develop'); cf. *New Catholic Encyclopaedia* (17 vols., Washington, 1967–78), IV, 288; A. H. Mathew (ed.), *A True Historical Relation of the Conversion of Sir Tobie Matthew* (1904), 164–5; Richard Baxter, *Directions and Persuasions to a Sound Conversion* (1683), 437.

[4] Sir Edward Hoby, *A Letter to Mr. T. H. Late Minister* (1609), 10; cf. Thomas Morton, *A Direct Answer unto the Scandalous Exceptions, which Theophilus Higgons hath lately objected against D. Morton* (1609), 3; Theophilus Higgons, *The Apology of Theophilus Higgons lately Minister, now Catholique* (Rouen, 1609), 8–10, 12, 19. It was alleged that Richard Sheldon had changed religion out of 'wante', AAW, A XI, 79, a credible allegation in that funds for the relief of imprisoned priests were not forthcoming for those like Sheldon who took the Jacobean oath of allegiance, AAW, A X, 45.

[5] John Meredyth, *The Sinne of Blasphemie* (1622), 46; N. Malcolm, *De Dominis (1560–1624)* (1984), *passim*.

[6] William Prynne, *The Popish Royall Favourite* (1643), 70; T. Birch (ed.), *The Court and Times of Charles I* (2 vols., 1848), II, 21; John Hacket, *Scrinia Reserata* (1693), I, 207; E. Sawyer (ed.), *Memorials of Affairs of State* (3 vols., 1725), II, 136; cf. B. Camm, 'An Apostate at St Omers, 1618–1622', *The Month* 94 (1899), 163–70, at p. 165. Rumours of this kind circulated about Andrew Downes, Regius Professor of Greek at Cambridge, one of the translators of the King James bible, L. P. Smith (ed.), *The Life and Letters of Sir Henry Wotton* (2 vols., Oxford, 1907), II, 169–70; PRO, SP 14/40/1; CU Libr., MS Mm 1 44, p. 215. Downes may have had Catholic sympathies already, since he was approached

chaplain (likened to Arius by Thomas Goad), had experienced enough setbacks at Cambridge, at Court and in his search for benefices, to give George Hakewill the opportunity to make taunts of this nature.[7] Sir Julius Caesar's brother Henry had simply gone off to be ordained in the Roman Church after he lost his living at Lostwithiel.[8] Leonard Rountree the unreliable seminary priest was observed to waver between the Churches of England and Rome for material reasons.[9] The initial motivation for the notorious John Gee (a poorly beneficed curate in Winwick parish) to start associating with Catholics was his desire to supplant the wealthy rector of Winwick, Josiah Horne.[10]

Protestants certainly thought that Catholic proselytisers deliberately exploited English clerics' career difficulties to attract them to Rome, and adequately maintained them when they converted.[11] There seems to have

by Sir Thomas Tresham to suggest a suitable tutor for his son, BL, Add. MS 39828, fo. 143ʳ. John Bossy speculates that Henry Constable's change of religion was caused principally by the obstruction to his career at the English Court after he published *Examen Pacifique*, J. Bossy, 'A Propos of Henry Constable', *RH* 6 (1961–2), 228–37, at p. 234. John Good MP said that he was accused of converting with the hope of political preferment, BL, Lansd. MS 776, fo. 10ᵛ.

[7] Marc'Antonio de Dominis, ed. and transl. Thomas Goad, *A Declaration of the Reasons* (Edinburgh, 1617), 3; *CSPD 1601–3*, 287–9, 292; *HMC Salisbury MSS* XVI, 348–9; PRO, SP 46/63/11 (I am grateful to Kenneth Fincham for this reference); M. Pattison, *Isaac Casaubon* (1875), 311; CRS 68, 14; George Hakewill, *An Answere to a Treatise Written by Dr Carier* (1616), sig. d4ʳ⁻ᵛ.

[8] PRO, SP 12/173/61, SP 12/176/46; SO 3/1, February 1593. L. M. Hill, however, thinks it likely that he was ordained abroad merely as an infiltrator to spy on English Catholic exiles, L. M. Hill, *Bench and Bureaucracy* (Cambridge, 1988), 96.

[9] *CSPD 1611–18*, 390.

[10] M. C. Questier, 'John Gee, Archbishop Abbot, and the Use of Converts from Rome in Jacobean Anti-Catholicism', *RH* 24 (1993), 347–60, at pp. 347–8.

[11] Francis Dillingham, *A Disswasive from Poperie* (Cambridge, 1599), sig. A3ʳ; E. Cardwell (ed.), *Documentary Annals* (2 vols., Oxford, 1839), II, 25. William Allen had tried to allure unhappy prospective clerics to the Rheims seminary by claiming that 'we have mo disputations, lessons, conferences, examinations . . . in our two Colleges, then are in their two Universities [Oxford and Cambridge] conteining neere . . . 30 goodly Colleges', William Allen, *An Apologie and True Declaration of the Institution and Endevours of the two English Colleges* (Rheims, 1581), fos. 67ᵛ–8ʳ, 22ᵛ. Forty-one of those who replied to the questions put to them when they entered the seminary at Rome between 1598 and 1640 mentioned that they had had an inadequate education in England. Thirty-two of them had previously been, according to their own account, out of communion with Rome, CRS 54–5. The Walsingham lectureship was established in Oxford in 1586 partly in order to compete with Rheims, C. Dent, *Protestant Reformers in Elizabethan Oxford* (Oxford, 1983), 148. Protestant polemicists said Roman proselytisers tempted their dupes in the English universities to go to Rome or Spain 'where they shall (say they) bee had in great estimation, and come to greater preferment than ever they shall in England attaine unto', Lewis Owen, *The Running Register* (1626), 4; John Gee, *The Foot out of the Snare* (fourth edition, 1624), sig. L4ʳ⁻ᵛ; *idem*, *Hold Fast* (1624), 33. For the method of interpreting and analysing the data from the seminaries at Rome and Valladolid during this period, M. C. Questier, 'The Phenomenon of Conversion: Change of Religion to and from Catholicism in England, 1580–1625' (DPhil. thesis, Sussex, 1991), 311–13.

been a certain amount of truth in this. Even if Mark Curtis's original thesis about a dissatisfied clerical underclass is now open to question, it is certainly true that exterior considerations of career and patronage were always present in decisions to change religion.[12] When the papist George Brome wanted to persuade the Oxfordshire minister Hugh Davies to convert to Rome he told him that when he returned to England and ministered to Catholics he should 'lacke neither golde nor Silver', and urged him to consider 'the contemptible state of [Protestant] mynisters at this daie'.[13] Edward Bennett, the secular priest, thought in September 1613 that an enhancement of Douai's status would attract to it English Protestant academics. John Jackson wrote to Thomas More (the English secular clergy's agent in Rome) in March 1612 that though men should not look principally for preferment when considering whether to alter religion, 'yet it wear fit to give it. We can not looke to have them saincts at the first.' Converts should be tempted from the opposing side as far as material resources allowed.[14] Temptation explained to Catholics why their own people left them. Francis Walsingham said of those like Anthony Tyrrell, Francis Shaw, Richard Sheldon and John Copley (who all married soon after their defections) that they 'fell . . . principally upon these motyves of good fellowship, good cheare, loose life and women'.[15] Catholics noted more particularly the maintenance which their renegades could expect in the Church of England. John Jackson thought that 'if these that come to us from them had the like or halfe the like countenance and favour shewed them that owrs which fall have at their hands', Theophilus Higgons (who abandoned his recently adopted Roman profession in 1610) 'had never return'd to scandalize religion as he did'. In similar vein the archpriest, George Birkhead, wrote to More about the renegade Peter Chambers. Anthony

---

12 M. H. Curtis, 'The Alienated Intellectuals of Early Stuart England', *P&P* 23 (1962), 25–43; I. Green, 'Career Prospects and Clerical Conformity in the Early Stuart Church', *P&P* 90 (1981), 71–115.

13 PRO, SP 12/192/52.i, fo. 83ʳ. Robert Atkins renewed these persuasions after Davies lost his living in the established Church, PRO, SP 12/193/13, fo. 30ʳ, SP 12/193/19, fo. 32ᵛ.

14 AAW, A XII, 357, XI, 122, cf. XII, 421. The archpriest Birkhead told the Roman agent to obtain for Carier every possible support lest 'he fall againe as diverse have don', AAW, A XII, 461. Catholics were keen also to recover by temporal temptations those who had deserted them. Humphrey Ely, the secular priest, tried to induce his nephew the renegade Anthony Major to retire abroad where Ely would find him a living, CRS 51, 276. The Jesuits had recovered Anthony Rouse by 1613, Francis Walsingham, *A Search Made into Matters of Religion* (second edition, St Omer, 1615), 355; *HMC Downshire MSS* IV, 458; AAW, A XII, 425.

15 Walsingham, *Search* (1615), 354–5; AAW, A XI, 3, 64, XII, 125; John Copley, *Doctrinall and Morall Observations* (1612), 6. There were suspicions that William Warmington, 'too much addicted to the feminine sexe' according to William Rayner, would do the same, AAW, A XI, 215; cf. T. H. Clancy, 'Priestly Perseverance in the Old Society of Jesus: The Case of England', *RH* 19 (1988–9), 286–312, at p. 293, concerning Anthony Pole.

Champney, another leading secular priest, lamented in October 1613 that 'the heretikes are so readie to entertayne our runegates and . . . we are so could to receave suche as seeke the harbour of godes churche'.[16] The regime in England showed at least a fitful concern with ensuring that, even when Catholic clerics had been compelled by force of law to change religion, there were adequate material rewards to prevent their defection the moment opportunity offered.[17] Archbishop Whitgift exhorted the bishops in December 1593 'to move the better and wealthier sorte of the clergie . . . to yelde some contribution' towards the relief of ex-seminary priests who are 'altogether destitute of maintenance, and driven to great extremitie through the same . . . a great temptation for them to revolt, and a discouragement for others to followe their example of conversion, and a slander to the state'.[18] In August 1600 the Council wrote to Matthew Hutton that he should receive into his own household the seminary priest James Bowland who had recently renounced Rome and 'bestowe upon him some such spirytuall living as may be in your . . . guyfte', which will refute the 'scandall . . . currant amongst them that when any of their sorte do reforme themselves there is no care had at all to provide for them'. In this way others might be brought to 'lyke conformyty'.[19] Though there is no record that Bowland acquired a benefice most other clerical converts who abandoned Rome, people like Anthony Tyrrell, William Tedder, Thomas Bell, Ralph Ithell, Thomas Simpson, John Copley, Theophilus Higgons, John and Henry Salkeld, John Gee and Richard Carpenter, eventually received a living or maintenance of some kind.[20] William Alabaster and Richard Sheldon became royal chaplains. Alabaster, in fact, did extremely well out of his change of religion as did the ex-Jesuit Christopher Perkins (after initial difficulties in the 1590s).[21] Apprehended priests were occasionally offered

---

16 AAW, A XI, 122, IX, 82, XII, 421. In about 1611 John Jackson wrote to More concerning William Alabaster that 'surely it is pittie that wee have noe more care of keeping such men', AAW, A X, 485.

17 CRS 4, 8; BL, Lansd. MS 982, fo. 35r; cf. Thomas Clarke, *The Recantation of Thomas Clarke* (1594), sig. Bvᵛ.

18 D. Wilkins, *Concilia* (4 vols., 1733–7), IV, 345–6; for money collected in the London diocese, Bodl., Tanner MS 77, fo. 60r.

19 *APC XXX*, 601.

20 Questier, 'Phenomenon', 173; Thomas Bell, *The Jesuites Antepast* (1608), 231; Higgons's rectory of Little Comberton was apparently promised to him in return for his forthcoming recantation, AAW, A IX, 395, X, 395; Sheldon obtained his reward almost immediately after he changed sides, Foley V, 854; Richard Carpenter got his benefice at Poling in Sussex after he preached his recantation sermon, LPL, Carte Antique et Miscellanee MS 943, p. 729.

21 G. M. Story and H. Gardner (eds.), *The Sonnets of William Alabaster* (1959), xx–xxi; AAW, A XII, 521; PRO, SO 3/1, December 1591; P. W. Hasler (ed.), *The House of Commons 1558–1603* (3 vols., 1981), III, 175–6; *CSPD 1591–4*, 247–8; *CSPD 1595–7*, 117, 130, 159 (though it could be argued that Perkins's ultimate good fortune was not directly the result of his conversion but of subsequent government service).

livings in the Church of England if they would abjure Roman religion.[22] Protestants were equally keen to attract those who left them back again in spite of professions by people like Joseph Hall and George Abbot that waverers were of no value to the English Church.[23] There is evidence from several sources that Benjamin Carier, the renegade royal chaplain, was offered a substantial reward to come home, possibly the see of Lincoln, made vacant by the death of William Barlow in September 1613.[24]

Of course, Romanist clergy who converted in England before being ordained abroad were less likely to have been influenced primarily by career considerations so early on, but it is possible that lack of secular financial prospects at home induced them to go abroad. Forty-six of the seminarists at Rome mentioned that they or their families had suffered financial adversity. Fifteen of them had previously been Protestants and some of these remarked on dissipated or lost inheritances.[25] Robert Venner, the convert seminary priest, said that he had first gone abroad in 1605 'for want of maintenance' in England.[26] The seminarist John Campion said his conversion process was commenced in part by family quarrels and the unlikelihood of any material support from that quarter.[27] Some of the convert seminarists referred to dissatisfaction at their employment in commerce or the professions.[28]

Casting off one set of loyalties made the search for a new set a pressing matter. Robin Clifton argues that the 'motives' tracts of renegade Catholic clerics were written principally to attain 'respectability and new patronage'.[29] Their stereotyped professions of Protestantism do suggest that they were parroting standard Protestant views of Rome to secure their absorption into the national Church and to obtain a satisfactory standard of living within it. Anthony Tyrrell, William Tedder, Thomas Bell and Thomas

---

[22] Foley IV, 499; J. Morris (ed.), *The Troubles of our Catholic Forefathers* (3 vols., 1872–7), II, 70.

[23] Joseph Hall, *The Works of Joseph Hall* (1634), 312; *HMC Downshire MSS* IV, 332; for the efforts to recover Wadsworth by subterfuge, Sawyer, *Memorials*, II, 109–10.

[24] AAW, A XII, 421, 467; C. Dodd, *The Church History of England* (3 vols., Brussels (imprint false, printed at Wolverhampton), 1737–42), II, 511; Foley VII, 1054; K. C. Fincham, *Prelate as Pastor* (Oxford, 1990), 29–30.

[25] CRS 54–5, *passim*. Sir Herbert Croft who changed religion and took up a monastic existence at St Gregory's, Douai, in 1617, was thought to have been escaping debt, *CSPD 1611–18*, 488; N. McClure (ed.), *The Letters of John Chamberlain* (2 vols., Philadelphia, 1939), II, 76–7, 105–6: John Chamberlain remarked 'desperation hath made more monckes then him'; though cf. W. J. Tighe, 'Herbert Croft's Repulse', *BIHR* 58 (1985), 106–9. William Lord Roos was in deep financial trouble before he went abroad and converted, *CSPD 1611–18*, 488.

[26] PRO, SP 14/49/72, fo. 113ʳ.

[27] Stonyhurst, Collectanea C, fo. 199ᵛ.   [28] CRS 54, 108, 140, 192.

[29] R. Clifton, 'Fear of Popery', in C. Russell (ed.), *The Origins of the English Civil War* (1973), 144–67, at p. 148.

Clarke had or sought patronage from Whitgift. Archbishop Bancroft made use of various renegades including Bell, Ralph Ithell, John Scudamore and Christopher Perkins.[30] Moreover, there was usually a clear link between the views of the ecclesiastical patron and those expressed by his renegade client. In the 1580s John Nichols (who had temporarily enlisted at the seminary in Rome) had been defended in print by Dudley Fenner, a leading light in the anti-subscription campaign. (Nichols's *Declaration* was based in part on Philippe de Mornay's work translated by John Field.) Nichols had clearly looked for maintenance to some of the more radical puritans. This may be the reason he was in disgrace by 1583.[31] Sheldon and Higgons, who expressed their conversions from Rome apocalyptically, were both patronised by the Calvinist bishop James Montagu.[32] Archbishop George Abbot made a point of recruiting ex-Catholic clergy who would propagate his anti-Romish political line. Sheldon said that Abbot obtained and made public the manuscript of his tract on the Jacobean oath of allegiance.[33] John Scudamore was retained in Abbot's household after Bancroft's death. In 1612 John Copley attended on Abbot following his surprise conformity and was soon collated by Abbot to the vicarage of Bethersden (and in 1616 received from Abbot the rectory of Pluckley).[34] The ex-Jesuit John Salkeld, despite his irenic veneer, was a real find for Abbot because he was capable of effective anti-Romanist preaching and he was prepared to go into print. Edward Bennett reported to Rome that Salkeld 'puts devises in Canter[bury's] head to tak all the preste[s] in England'.[35] The Jesuit-hating priest Anthony Clarke found refuge with Abbot by early 1614.[36] Abbot, it seems, may have employed the renegade Leonard Rountree in an attempt to get Benjamin Carier to come back to England.[37] Sir Thomas Lake wrote in

[30] Anthony Tyrrell, *A Fruitfull Sermon* (1589), sig. Aii^{r-v}; Clarke, *Recantation*, sig. A2^r; Thomas Bell, *The Survey of Popery* (1596), sig. A2^v–3^r; PRO, SP 12/223/110, fo. 180^r; Anstruther I, 185–6, 305; J. P. Sommerville, 'Jacobean Political Thought and the Controversy over the Oath of Allegiance' (Ph.D thesis, Cambridge, 1981), 15–16; Francis Walsingham, *A Search Made into Matters of Religion* (St Omer, 1609), 42, 46; Mathew, *True Historical Relation*, 70.

[31] Dudley Fenner, *An Answere unto the Confutation of John Nichols his Recantation* (1583); P. Collinson, *The Elizabethan Puritan Movement* (Oxford, 1967), 254, 266.

[32] Theophilus Higgons, *Mystical Babylon* (1624), sig. A^{r-v}; AAW, A XI, 122.

[33] AAW, A X, 91.

[34] AAW, A XI, 83; R. C. Christie, (ed.), *Letters of Sir Thomas Copley* (1897), xlvi–vii.

[35] AAW, A XII, 376.

[36] Anstruther I, 76; HMC *Downshire MSS* IV, 240, 292, 330; AAW, A XII, 486.

[37] AAW, OB I. i, fo. 63^{r-v}. Abbot also required that Rountree should 'write in some breife maner such a comprehension of the reasons both of my departure and returne as he might shewe it to the king'. Abbot had said that 'a quarter of a sheet' would suffice, but, when Rountree returned, Abbot 'craved more, to wit the conferences I had had all in very good order', which kept Rountree occupied for another three weeks. Abbot was enthusiastic that he should preach a recantation sermon in York Minster, PRO, SP 14/88/53.i.

January 1614 that Abbot 'hath of our own cuntry men manie proselytes wherein he much glorieth'.[38] Abbot was interested also in foreign clerical converts, even the rather unsatisfactory ex-Carmelites whom Sir Dudley Carleton sent to him from Venice in 1612 and, later on, Marc'Antonio de Dominis.[39] The Protestant clerical conversion tracts of the early 1620s seem to have been produced with Archbishop Abbot in mind.[40] All those whose conversions he superintended decried Rome as the apocalyptic Babylon and dwelt lovingly on its inane superstitions. The archbishop's opinions may have been dictating theirs. Those who did not follow his line were given short shrift. De Dominis was the most prominent of those whom he took against. The two Venetian ex-Carmelites, who had publicly renounced popery at the Italian Church in London in June 1612, infuriated Abbot when they changed their minds about their new ecclesiastical setting.[41]

Even more blatant than change of religion with the aim of securing a new patronage base was 'conversion' with the intention of selling information about Catholics to the authorities. Though most renegade Catholics at some point betrayed Romanists,[42] those like the early Jacobean Catholic defectors

38 PRO, SP 14/76/9.
39 Questier, 'Phenomenon', 199–200; HMC *Downshire MSS* IV, 331.
40 E.g. Christopher Musgrave, *Musgraves Motives* (1621) is dedicated to Abbot (though Musgrave had converted in 1608), CSPD 1603–10, 431. Ferdinand Texeda's *Texeda Retextus* (1623) was apparently sponsored by Daniel Featley; the preface appears in Featley's letter-book, Bodl., Rawl. MS D 47, fos. 32ᵛ–3ʳ (though Texeda was employed by John Williams, bishop of Lincoln, CRS 68, 185; Hacket, *Scrinia*, I, 126; Texeda's *Scrutamini Scripturas* (1624) is dedicated to Williams). Abbot's chaplains, Goad and Featley, cooperated in stage-managing the conversion of John Gee in 1624 and in the production of his *Foot out of the Snare*, Questier, 'John Gee', 347–8.
41 Questier, 'Phenomenon', 199; PRO, SP 14/76/9.i, SP 14/76/18, 48.
42 Renegades were among the few people able to testify to a priest's Roman clerical status and ordination, CRS 5, 168; CRS 30, 36; A. J. Loomie, 'Spain and the English Catholic Exiles 1580–1604' (Ph.D thesis, London, 1957), 273, 316–21; AAW, A X, 57, XII, 426. Thomas Bell gave a 'who's who' of Lancashire Catholicism to the authorities, HMC *Salisbury MSS* IV, 240–2; AAW, A IV, no. 38, Anglia IX, no. 41; F. X. Walker, 'The Implementation of the Elizabethan Statutes against Recusants 1581–1603' (Ph.D thesis, London, 1961), 319–21. According to Philip Woodward (*The Dolefull Knell, of Thomas Bell* (Rouen (imprint false, printed at Douai), 1607), 390), in Lancashire, armed with a commission, Bell 'searched divers houses in the night time'. Thomas Clarke, John Sacheverell, William Tedder, William Hardesty and Anthony Major all contributed to the arrest of at least one priest each, Anstruther I–II, *passim*; Saint Alban's College, Valladolid, Series II, leg. 1. Francis Shaw and (probably) George Snape informed against Catholics, CRS 60, 68–9. Robert Gray OFM was said in July 1615 to have given information about the secular clergy to John King and George Abbot, and in December 1616 the seculars thought that Gray had 'done much harme', AAW, A XIV, 435, XV, 495. Sheldon, Copley and Rountree said they would not lay information against priests, Richard Sheldon, *The Motives of Richard Sheldon Pr.* (1612), sig. *3ʳ⁻ᵛ; Copley, *Doctrinall and Morall Observations*, sig. ¶4ʳ⁻ᵛ; AAW, A XI, 239, OB I. i, fo. 63ʳ, though Copley was not averse to informing against lay Catholics later on, AAW, A XII, 341; CSPD 1611–18, 186; and Rountree likewise, so the secular clergy thought, AAW, A XII, 425.

Anthony Rouse and William Atkinson actually made a living by raking off profits from anti-Catholic and anti-recusant statutory penalties.[43]

FACTION

Converts' strenuous denials that they had exchanged religious allegiances for profit and that there were none so pure as they might seem like special pleading.[44] Their self-interest might suggest that there was no religious substance in the well-known instances of ecclesiastical conversion. Nevertheless, careerism by itself is not usually a sufficient explanation for alterations of allegiance and opinion. Many of those who changed religion had not gone unrewarded in the Church which they left behind. Benjamin Carier's motives were so complex that, although he did his best to pick up the occasional pension abroad after he abandoned the Church of England, it is a mistake to see him changing religion to improve the balance of his annual expenditure and income.[45] In the case of someone like Theodore Price, William Laud's friend, conversion came too late to have been instigated exclusively by career motives (though he was undoubtedly a dissatisfied man).[46] Noel Malcolm has argued that even the temporal woes and undoubted cupidity of Archbishop de Dominis were not the real motor for his various changes of religion.[47] How, then, are we to explain the mixed motivation of prominent converts? In particular, how did broadly political motives twist around religious ones sufficiently to give impetus to a man to say that he no longer believed as he did before? The clearest evidence lies in the factional divisions which affected both Churches. For example, prominent Catholic renegades' renunciations of the Roman Church were heavily influenced by the in-fighting within their own ranks over issues

---

[43] Anstruther I, 13, 295, II, 326; 'Annual Letters of the Vice-Province of England' (for 1619), *Letters and Notices* 11 (1876–7), 273–88, at p. 274; PRO, Stac. Proc. 8/15/8; AAW, A X, 117, 429, XII, 425; HMC *Salisbury MSS* XII, 228–9, 265, XV, 348–9; P. Caraman (ed.), *John Gerard* (1951), 102–3, 141–3, 166, 236, 245; Foley I, 25, 27–9; PRO, SP 14/4/74, 14/57/1; cf. George Roberts (ed.), *Diary of Walter Yonge* (Camden Society, first series, 41, 1848), 18.

[44] *The Recantations as they were severallie pronounced by Wylliam Tedder and Anthony Tyrrell* (1588), 38; Clarke, *Recantation*, sig. A5r–v; Theophilus Higgons, *A Sermon Preached at Pauls Cross* (1611), 48; Sheldon, *Motives*, sig. *3r; Copley, *Doctrinall and Morall Observations*, 6, 14.

[45] M. C. Questier, 'Crypto-Catholicism, Anti-Calvinism and Conversion at the Jacobean Court: The Enigma of Benjamin Carier', *JEH* 47 (1996), 45–64.

[46] For Price, see A. Milton, *Catholic and Reformed* (Cambridge, 1995), 370.

[47] Malcolm, *De Dominis*, 27, and *passim*. James Wadsworth snr got a smaller Spanish pension than his sceptical ex-employer Sir Charles Cornwallis thought, Sawyer, *Memorials*, II, 136; Magdalen College MS 281, no. 22. The seminarist John Gross failed to obtain the college post in Cambridge to which he aspired but claimed that he had already become a Catholic before this career setback, CRS 54, 132–3.

of doctrine and religious practice. Several had clearly fallen foul of their opponents over the problem in England of occasional conformity by beleaguered lay Catholics. (In practice all Catholic clerical groups were prepared to make allowances over strict recusancy. But there were bitter disagreements about the application of casuistical rules to such cases.)[48] The notable renegade Thomas Bell was attacked by Henry Garnet in two anti-conformity tracts published in late 1592/early 1593 at which time Bell was forced out of the Catholic clerical structure which he had done so much to create.[49] In print Garnet claimed that 'there is not one Catholike Preist in England, who differeth from the rest of his brethren' (over the question of occasional conformity) except Bell, but he admitted privately that there were others, many of whom also found themselves compelled into changes of religion by their impossible ecclesiastical position.[50] The pro-occasional conformity view had first been expressed polemically in a manuscript treatise by Alban Langdale which circulated in 1580. (Robert Persons had replied to it in his *Brief Discours* of that year.)[51] Robert Gray who conformed temporarily in 1593 and then finally before 1614 had a copy of Langdale's book on him when he was arrested in late 1593 (according to Richard Topcliffe, Langdale's own copy).[52] William Hart, executed at York in March 1583 (but seemingly tractable at one time), may have held Bell's views on occasional conformity. Hart had been one of Bell's principal associates and was one of the three seminary priests who attended Bell in the infamous celebration of high Mass in York Castle in July 1582.[53] Others who abandoned Rome at the same time as Bell, e.g. William Hardesty, evidently had close links with him and may have shared his opinions.[54] Robert Fisher, the somewhat inept courier for the appellant clergy, had (apparently) expressed contempt for the strict seminarist line on recusancy before he finally declared himself a Protestant.[55] The ex-Jesuit Thomas

---

[48] A. Walsham, *Church Papists* (1993), 56–60; Thomas Bell, *The Anatomie of Popish Tyrannie* (1603), 5.

[49] Questier, 'Phenomenon', 158–60; Henry Garnet, *An Apology against the Defence of Schisme* (n.p., 1593); *idem*, *A Treatise of Christian Renunciation* (n.p., 1593); A. F. Allison, 'The Writings of Fr Henry Garnet, SJ (1555–1606)', *Biographical Studies* 1 (1951–2), 7–21, at pp. 11–12; CRS 52, 79.

[50] Garnet, *Apology*, 12. For an exposition of Bell's ideas concerning occasional conformity, P. J. Holmes *Resistance and Compromise* (Cambridge, 1982), 95–8; CRS 51, 203.

[51] CRS 2, 28, 178–80.

[52] *CSPD 1591–4*, 378–80; Anstruther I, 135–6; *CSPD 1611–18*, 260; AAW, A XI, 295, 403, 557, XII, 103–4, 109, 125 (showing that Gray was being ostracised – the archpriest suspects 'he will fynd verie little interteinment in this land'), 145, 253, XIII, 34, 89, XIV, 383, 435–6, 475, 535. The complexities of the occasional conformist position are suggested by Gray's rebuke to Lord Montague for attending Protestant service, R. B. Manning, *Religion and Society in Elizabethan Sussex* (Leicester, 1969), 160–1.

[53] Morris, *Troubles*, III, 427; Anstruther I, 155.

[54] BL, Lansd. MS 75, fo. 42ʳ.   [55] AAW, OB III. ii, fo. 340ᵛ.

Wright held suspect views about the possibility of attending Protestant sermons, and Miles Dawson, another prominent 'apostate' in the North in the early 1590s had known Wright well.[56] Although there were evidently several priests in the North who dissented from the strict Roman line on recusancy, Bell, their natural leader, was unable to pull them together into a coherent party. Consequently many of them were forced to secede altogether. Conversion on matters of religious principle could, therefore, be catalysed by factional struggle. As Wright told Henry Garnet in 1596, men were likely to be alienated when they laboured to do good and received in return 'nothing but infamy and detractions'. Evil speeches and 'undiscreet proceedings' had been the 'ruin of many' and 'a cause of many Protestants'.[57]

Other disputes which generated friction among the Roman clergy also persuaded some of them to become Protestants. During the quarrels between seculars and Jesuits over the regulation of the Roman clergy in England some people were so alienated that they renounced Rome.[58] The superiors of the English College in Rome were concerned that if they expelled students involved in the anti-Jesuit agitation there in 1594–7 they would apostatise.[59] The factional basis for what Roman Catholics termed 'apostasy' was created almost immediately after the death of Mary Stuart. Divisions over the succession mapped onto quarrels about ecclesiastical organisation (expressed most virulently in the 'appellant' controversies over the archpriest regime). It has generally been thought that Robert Persons was grossly unfair when he attacked appellants and apostates in the same breath (though he was not the only one who voiced these accusations).[60] The appellant dispute was, of course, a quarrel over

---

56 Foley IV, 372–3; T. A. Stroud, 'Father Thomas Wright: A Test Case for Toleration', *Biographical Studies* 1 (1951–2), 189–219, at p. 207; J. C. H. Aveling, *Catholic Recusancy in the City of York 1558–1791* (CRS monograph 2, 1970), 72.

57 Stonyhurst, Anglia II, no. 20.

58 For example, Ralph Ithell and Robert Fisher, CRS 51, 318, 323–4, 329–30, 281.

59 M. E. Williams, *The Venerable English College, Rome* (1979), 19. Dissent tended to filter away into the division between Rome and Douai, Williams, *Venerable English College*, 20–1, 24.

60 Robert Persons, *A Briefe Apologie* (Antwerp, 1601), sig. Dd6ʳ, compares Thomas Bluet's negotiations with the Council to the machinations of Tyrrell and Bell; T. G. Law, *The Archpriest Controversy* (2 vols., Camden Society, second series, 56, 58, 1896, 1898), II, 13; cf. Robert Persons, *A Manifestation* (Antwerp, 1602), fo. 105ᵛ; Martin Array (the archpriest's proctor in Rome during the appeal) and the Jesuits in England made similar allegations about the connection between appellant sympathies and apostasy, Law, *Archpriest Controversy*, I, 122; CRS 51, 202–3; LPL, Fairhurst MS 2006, fo. 178ʳ; and such opinions were echoed among the English Catholic laity, CRS 51, 83. The anti-Jesuit party retaliated by claiming that the real lapses among English Catholic priests had been all on the Jesuit side, AAW, A V, 260; Anthony Copley, *Another Letter of Mr A. C. to his dis-jesuited Kinseman* (1602), 26–7.

secular politics and ecclesiastical jurisdiction, not religious belief. Moreover, it contained, in itself, no sufficient ground for leaving the Church of Rome. The basic appellant political position was a combination of rejecting Jesuit-led extremist plans for the succession to Elizabeth, hatred of the archpriest clerical regime which the Jesuits were thought to control, and a general belief that there should be a partial separation between religion and politics in England.[61] But, though the evidence is often patchy, there *was* a connection between appellant activity, general anti-Jesuit animus among the seculars and adoption of Protestant opinions. Aside from those like Ralph Ithell and Robert Fisher (whose cases are unusual since the pressure to apostatise came from the hostility of their own anti-Jesuit party), Francis Shaw who abjured Rome in 1593 had travelled around Europe with the anti-Jesuit Jonas Meredith. Shaw also knew James Younger, and was taken to see him in prison just before Younger turned government informant.[62] Younger, like Meredith, was part of the clerical group which was anti-Spanish in orientation, or rather, opposed the pro-Spanish succession policy followed by many English Catholic clergy under Jesuit direction.[63] William Watson, the most violent of the appellants, conformed briefly (to the extent of attending Protestant service in Bridewell) and caused embarrassment to his clerical friends.[64] William Atkinson, the future priest-hunter and ecclesiastical commission pursuivant, was involved in the opposition to the archpriest.[65] Mark Penkevell apostatised in late 1604. His brother was an enemy of the Jesuits and this may have influenced him.[66] The renegade Anthony Rouse had fallen out with John Gerard SJ.[67] Although the unstable John Scudamore had no clear appellant connections, his political orientation was anti-Spanish and anti-Jesuit; he was expelled from the

[61] A. Pritchard, *Catholic Loyalism in Elizabethan England* (1979), 167–70. Most Protestant polemicists professed to see the 'schism' among the Catholic clergy as a tactical ploy to make at least one Catholic clerical faction acceptable to the State, P. Milward, *Religious Controversies of the Elizabethan Age* (1977), 124–5; cf. George Abbot, *The Reasons which Doctour Hill hath Brought* (Oxford, 1604), 6–7; William Bradshaw, *Humble Motives* (n.p., 1601), 29, 34; *An Antiquodlibet* (Middelburg, 1602), 51; C. Cross (ed.), *The Letters of Sir Francis Hastings, 1544–1609* (Frome, 1969), 103. Francis Barnaby, the appellant, virtually surrendered his Catholic clerical identity, but there is no conclusive proof that he ever apostatised, LPL, Fairhurst MS 2006, fo. 191ʳ; PRO, SO 3/2, December 1604; AAW, A XI, 345.

[62] CRS 5, 307; Anstruther I, 227; CRS 52, 58; Anstruther I, 306.

[63] PRO, SP 12/238/181.

[64] Copley, *Another Letter*, 32–3; cf. Law, *Archpriest Controversy*, I, 218.

[65] Foley I, 25.

[66] *HMC Salisbury MSS* XI, 150; *CSPD 1601–3*, 199.

[67] Rouse signed the appeal drawn up at Paris in May 1603, Anstruther I, 295 (though Anstruther questions the reliability of the signatures on this document); Bell, *Anatomie*, 130; LPL, Fairhurst MS 2014, fo. 95ʳ.

seminary at Rome in 1595 and finally changed religion in 1606.[68] Several converts from Rome alleged in their published motives that these inter-Catholic disputes persuaded them that Rome was not the true Church.[69]

Even if appellant politicking was too short-lived to generate a stream of rejections of the Church of Rome, the Catholic political tradition which the appellants exploited certainly had the capacity to do this. Though Robert Persons attacked the appellants as schismatics and heretics, what he was really aiming at was the anti-Jesuit group, extant since the early 1580s, around Owen Lewis, ultimately bishop of Cassano (seen by some as the 'opposition' candidate for the spiritual control of disestablished English Catholicism after Cardinal Allen's death). Lewis was a shadowy figure but the apostasies of those like John Nichols, Thomas Bell, William Tedder and others, said Persons, were signs of God's judgments against those who 'at the first erection of the Romayne Colledge and some yeares after, upon separation there begun by Doctor Lewis and his followers' campaigned against the Jesuits. In Persons's opinion 'the Spirite of this faction' was 'opposite to the trew Spirite of Religion and favorable to Apostasie'.[70] The faction's connection with apostasy continued long after the appellant dispute was itself concluded. The prominent renegade Richard Sheldon had friends among those who looked to Owen Lewis for leadership and the unreliable John Scudamore had also been closely connected with him.[71] In this sense it is possible to say that many defections from the ranks of the English Catholic clergy involved serious ideological conflict over what form Romanism in England should take and who should lead it.

Factional strife also accelerated notorious Protestant conversions to Rome. Humphrey Leech is a well-known instance of a convert among the proto-Arminian group of clerics in the early Jacobean Church. His quarrel with the ecclesiastical authorities in Oxford seems to demonstrate that he regarded himself as one of a number (including, he said, John Buckeridge and John Howson) who held similar opinions about grace.[72] A sermon which he preached in 1607 appeared to challenge orthodox Calvinist ideas

---

68 *HMC Salisbury MSS* V, 446: Scudamore told the musician John Dowland in late 1595 that he was opposed to those 'who are of the Spanish faction' and that 'to defend my country against the Spaniards I would come into England and bear a pike on my shoulders'. A cousin of Scudamore was involved in the Bye Plot, *HMC Salisbury MSS* XV, 210, 213–14; PRO, SP 14/2/84, SP 14/3/6.

69 E.g. Henry Yaxley, *Morbus et Antidotus* (1630), 2.

70 CRS 2, 203, 209; cf. *Recantations*, 9.

71 Sheldon, *Motives*, sig. ¶ʳ; Anstruther I, 256, for Sheldon's association with Sylvester Norris, a Lewis protégé; *HMC Salisbury MSS* V, 447.

72 For Howson's sympathies with Carier, N. Cranfield and K. C. Fincham (eds.), 'John Howson's Answers . . . ', *Camden Miscellany* XXIX (Camden Society, fourth series, 34, 1987), 319–41, at pp. 335–6.

about election and supererogation. Leonard Hutton, the pro-vice-chancellor, threatened to send him before the Calvinist bishop of London, Thomas Ravis. The assault was renewed on him in 1608 by Sebastian Benefield. This led Leech to expound a third and violently outspoken version of his original sermon on 27 June 1608. There followed a confrontation between Leech and the Calvinist vice-chancellor, John King. Leech was suspended from preaching for a year. If he did have sympathisers, they did not then come forward to support him. Deserted by his Protestant friends, he had failed to secure a slot for himself among the doctrinal factions in the English Church, and his attempt to challenge an academic Calvinist consensus had come to nothing. Alienated and infuriated, he transferred his allegiance to the Church of Rome and went abroad.[73]

CONVERSION AND THEOLOGY

Still, theology was not just the plaything of politics. Even the factional projection of latent religious differences into conversion does not really explain why people changed from one profession of faith to another, or, at least, it explains it on only one level. Political quarrels may sometimes have provided a mechanism for alteration of ecclesiastical allegiance; they were not themselves the cause. For we know that political affiliation had no necessary connection with religion.[74] There were some complete cynics for whom a change of ecclesiastical setting had no doctrinal ramifications at all. Christopher Perkins was one of these. Despite his secession from the Society of Jesus and his apparent conformity to the religion established by law in England, he informed Sir Francis Walsingham in May 1589 that he did not approve of it. He was saying Mass (when occasion offered) as late as 1594. He told Tobias Mathew jnr (as he tried to get him to recant his newly adopted Roman opinions) that he regarded it as 'foolery' to suffer for one

---

[73] Humphrey Leech, *A Triumph of Truth* (Douai, 1609), *passim*; A. Davidson, 'Roman Catholicism in Oxfordshire from the Late Elizabethan Period to the Civil War *c.* 1580–1640' (Ph.D thesis, Bristol, 1970), 482–90; C. Dent, 'Protestants in Elizabethan Oxford' (DPhil. thesis, Oxford, 1980), 407–22; N. Tyacke, *Anti-Calvinists* (Oxford, 1990), 62–4; CRS 54, 215; Questier, 'Phenomenon', 120–1.

[74] With the exception of a brief period in the years 1586–8 Catholic clerics could compromise their principles (even to the extent of partial conformity) without publicly or finally abjuring Roman Catholicism, F. Edwards (ed.), *The Elizabethan Jesuits* (1981), 172, 169; CRS 60, 19–20; Aveling, *Northern Catholics*, 137–8; CRS 5, 26, 28–9; PRO, SP 12/178/57.iii, fo. 124^v; Anstruther I, 328; PRO, SP 12/195/72, fo. 131^r; CRS 4, 79; *HMC Rutland MSS* I, 161. For rare instances where conversion was associated by the authorities directly with political loyalty, Questier, 'Phenomenon', 146; Anstruther I, 8–9; P. L. Hughes and J. F. Larkin, *Tudor Royal Proclamations* (2 vols., New Haven, 1964, 1969), II, 520.

side or the other.[75] Among other defectors, one discerns a puzzling fluidity of religious opinion which seems politically unregimented. William Alabaster's long-running doctrinal conflicts with both Churches generally failed to coincide with his professions of institutional allegiance to one side or the other. (His account of the way in which he came to accept that Rome was a true Church would have been anathema to a Catholic polemicist.) The man responsible for his conversion was the ex-Jesuit Thomas Wright whose political loyalist stance confused his own series of allegiances. Some of this evidently rubbed off on Alabaster. His return to England in 1599 and decision to supply information to the authorities about belligerent Catholic political plans did not coincide with a surrender of Catholic opinions and he started to proselytise actively. His Catholic loyalties began to unravel again in Rome (after he became embroiled in English clerical disputes there in 1609 and was imprisoned by the Inquisition when his book *Apparatus in Revelationem Jesu Christi* was declared heretical). But when, thoroughly disenchanted, he was released and he returned to England, he declared himself Catholic still. He finally rejected Rome at least two years later – a thoroughly confusing spectacle for Protestants like John Chamberlain who preferred to see less ambiguous evidence of ecclesiastical affiliation from those who claimed to find the Church of Rome distasteful.[76] Like Alabaster, Marc'Antonio de Dominis drove to distraction all those who thought that his apparent shifts from one Church to another were good propaganda for their respective polemical and political lines. De Dominis had his own, vaguely ecumenical, programme. He refused to cooperate completely with anyone, either in England or on the Continent.[77] In the high commission hearing in April 1622 to ascertain his reasons for wanting to leave England and its established Church, George Abbot asked him in bewilderment, 'How then is Rome, that was then Babylon, when yow came hither, now become Sion?' De Dominis replied that his occasional anti-Romish tracts (written *populariter non dogmatice*) should not be confused with his serious works (the books of the *Ecclesiastical Republic*) in which he 'did more resolutely

---

[75] *HMC Salisbury MSS* III, 411; CRS 52, 211; Mathew, *True Historical Relation*, 72.

[76] Story and Gardner, *Sonnets*, xii, xvii–xviii, xix–xxi; R. V. Caro, 'William Alabaster: Rhetor, Meditator, Devotional Poet', *RH* 19 (1988), 62–79, 155–70, at pp. 64–7; CRS 54, 3; CRS 10, 43; Foley I, 620–1; CRS 41, 123; Copley, *Doctrinall and Morall Observations*, 103–4; AAW, A IX, 279, X, 41, 61, 91, 97, 485; CU Libr., MS Mm 1 45, p. 186; McClure, *Letters*, I, 568; cf. *HMC Salisbury MSS* XXI, 237. In December 1606 Thomas Worthington reported that Alabaster's 'vere countenance is abstract', PRO, SP 77/8, fo. 200ʳ. Alabaster simply refused to heed Robert Persons's warnings in 1607 that his *Apparatus* was likely to attract censure 'as a thing . . . subject to misconstruction', Stonyhurst, Collectanea P I, fo. 340ʳ.

[77] Malcolm, *De Dominis*, ix–x; *CSPV 1621–3*, 63.

and expressly sett downe his judgement'.[78] The view abroad after he left England in 1622 was soon that 'the man was neither Catholicke nor Protestant, for whiles he fondly laboured to make one Church of all, himselfe followed none'.[79] John Donne was loftily detached in his religious opinions until he finally took holy orders in the Church of England.[80] William Chillingworth in the 1620s and 1630s was perceived to be 'doubting between both communions' and the long process by which he finally conceded the authority of the established Church in England owed more to his own scruples than to any lack of employment.[81] The fluctuating opinions of priests like Francis Shaw, George Smith and Thomas Clarke show that they too were not primarily political animals.[82] Anthony Tyrrell was imprisoned for his religion in 1574, 1581, 1586 and 1588. He changed religion in 1586, 1587 (twice), 1588 (twice) and 1605.[83] Superficially his many alterations, allied with multiple denunciations of Catholics (mainly the Babington Plot conspirators), appear determined by political events. But each occasion of change was accompanied by perfectly plausible theological explanations of why he was still moving between particular expressions of the true Church and how he perceived himself on each occasion to be subject to the operations of grace.[84] Admittedly this was one way of defusing the accusations of inconsistency which were levelled at every convert.[85] Tyrrell's repeated changes of allegiance and his chronic malleability did preserve him from the full rigour of the law in England, but his constant inconstancy, which he explained by reference to conversion, could not reasonably have been to his temporal advantage. Anthony Rouse was similarly complex. Before his apostasy he had been an enthusiastic Catholic cleric. His conversion appears to have been accompanied by signs of a

---

[78] Bodl., Tanner MS 73A, fo. 138ʳ; cf. Marc'Antonio de Dominis, *M. Antonius de Dominis Archbishop of Spalato, Declares the Cause of his Returne* (St Omer, 1623), 20–1.

[79] AAW, A XVIII, 429.

[80] D. Flynn, 'Donne's Catholicism', *RH* 13 (1975–6), 1–17, 178–95, at pp. 1, 6, 178–9, 185–6, 190; *idem*, 'Irony in Donne's *Biathanatos* and *Pseudo-Martyr*', *RH* 12 (1973–4), 49–69, at pp. 56–7; cf. R. C. Bald, *John Donne* (Oxford, 1970), 232–3.

[81] R. R. Orr, *Reason and Authority* (Oxford, 1967), 30, and *passim*; Davidson, 'Roman Catholicism', 516–24; cf. Milton, *Catholic and Reformed*, 233–4.

[82] AAW, A IX, no. 115; *The Copies of certaine Discourses* (Rouen (imprint false, printed in London), 1601), 60–1; AAW, A X, 465.

[83] A. Kenny, 'A Martyr Manqué: The Early Life of Anthony Tyrrell', *Clergy Review* 42 (1957), 651–8; C. Devlin, 'An Unwilling Apostate: The Case of Anthony Tyrrell', *The Month* new series 6 (1951), 346–58.

[84] Questier, 'Phenomenon', 152–5; BL, Lansd. MS 51, no. 66; Morris, *Troubles*, II, 411–18, 433–43; *Recantations*, 32–3, 34–5, 40; Tyrrell, *Fruitfull Sermon*, sig. Biiᵛ.

[85] Cf. Higgons, *Sermon*, 43; Gee, *Hold Fast*, 21; Robert Persons, *A Discoverie of J. Nichols* (1581), sig. Bvʳ, 'a double or triple tonged man [referring to John Nichols] after so many recantations, will not be verie certaine in all his promises' and the most recent 'renegation' carries any credit only 'because it is the last, and so wil remayne untill he make another'.

profound mental upheaval.[86] His changes of allegiance sat rather uneasily with what really concerned him, a love–hate relationship with the ideals of the Society of Jesus.[87]

Conversion to and from Rome could thus follow a politically unscripted path. Motivation to and from Catholicism did not always come neatly politically packaged. Theophilus Higgons said that he left his papist friends in France before he had definitely decided to resume a place in the English Church.[88] Benjamin Carier's polemical declaration of his conversion to Rome makes extraordinarily disparaging remarks about English recusant Catholics. (His opinion of the idiot 'multitude' on 'both sides' evidently includes the English nonconformist Catholics as well as the unthinking Protestant opponents of Rome.)[89]

If the converts' doctrinal accounts of their changes in religion were not merely cosmetic we need to explain more fully how their theology of conversion coincided with their fluctuation between institutional Churches. There are two possible approaches towards their composite motivation. The first assumes that the converts of the late sixteenth and early seventeenth centuries were in a similar case to that of the politicians Quentin Skinner had in mind when dealing with the opposition politics of the 1720s. He argued that the fact or probability of a politician's insincerity should not negate all investigation into the source of his views. A man's motives are more than '*ex post facto* rationalizations' of his political manoeuvres. The early modern converts were inevitably faced with charges of inconsistency. Because the late-sixteenth- and early-seventeenth-century renegades were also 'engaged in a *prima facie* unjustifiable course of action' they, like Lord Bolingbroke in the 1720s, had to 'exhibit a plausible relationship between some . . . principle and their actual course of . . . action'.[90] A Skinner-type analysis of the converts' stated motivation reveals the public ideological basis for their conversions (even if this is not the same as showing what their exact reason for changing religion may have been). The second reading of conversion

[86] Anstruther I, 295–6; TD V, xii; *HMC Salisbury MSS* XI, 363–4. In about August 1600 Rouse wrote to William Waad 'signifying the tediousnes of mynde' which he endured 'by imprisonement', which, he told Waad in August 1601, 'is now much more encreased, and doth in deed . . . marvelously disquiet me', LPL, Fairhurst MS 2014, fo. 133ʳ; Sheldon, *Motives*, sig. *3ʳ; LPL, Fairhurst MS 2014, fo. 134ʳ.

[87] William Watson, *A Decacordon of Ten Quodlibeticall Questions* (1602), 90, for his animosity against John Gerard. In 1613 he returned to the Jesuits at Louvain, Anstruther I, 296; Caraman, *John Gerard*, 25, 220–1; AAW, A XII, 425; *HMC Downshire MSS* IV, 458.

[88] Higgons, *Sermon*, 48; Foley VII, 1014.

[89] B. Carier, *A Treatise* (Brussels, 1614), 37; Hakewill, *Answere*, 173; cf. A. Milton, 'The Laudians and the Church of Rome c. 1625–1640' (Ph.D thesis, Cambridge, 1989), 151–2.

[90] Q. Skinner, 'The Principles and Practice of Opposition: The Case of Bolingbroke versus Walpole' in N. McKendrick (ed.), *Historical Perspectives* (1974), 93–128 at pp. 94, 100–101, 103, 110, 111.

as an amalgam of politics and religion tries to show that conversions in religion, authentic experiences of grace, could be politicised without being entirely under the regime of politics. Or rather, that the correspondence between the wide spectrum of conversion experience and the range of evil things which Romanists and Protestants detected in each other's religion meant it was possible for change of religion to fall into politically comprehensible patterns of division between the Churches without ever being simply a branch of contemporary ecclesiastical politics.

CONVERSION IN RELIGION

Why should not just the doctrines of conversion but also the spiritual experiences associated with it have lent themselves so readily to politicised polemical separation between Romanists and Protestants? In Judaeo-Christian thought conversion comprises both an inward and an outward alteration. Inward renewal under the influence of grace requires the setting aside of former standards of behaviour and sometimes the adoption of different standards of religious belief and activity. However, these two aspects of conversion take many forms. In Owen Brandon's succinct words, conversion may be from 'irreligion to religion; or from one religion to another; or from one denomination to another; or from one theological position to another; or from a second-hand to a first-hand experience of religion' (sometimes described as evangelical conversion).[91] But these types of conversion are usually not conveniently segregated. While an individual's 'conversion' can mean anything from an explosive evangelical sensation to a quiet, cold intellectual modification of ideas, it frequently includes both. Conversion, then, refers first to the efficacious moment in the process generally described as justification. Though the word itself signifies merely a turning, in Christian theology it indicates initially the point at which man enters into a new relationship with Christ through the action of the Holy Spirit (mediated through the Church), and then subsequently embarks on a pilgrimage in grace.

Conversion was polemicised because people did not attribute the same significance to conversion's separate stages.[92] Naturally, for a Reformed

---

[91] O. Brandon, *Christianity from Within* (1965), 24; *A Catholic Dictionary of Theology* (3 vols., 1962–71), II, 125–7; *New Catholic Encyclopaedia*, IV, 289; A. Richardson and J. Bowden (eds.), *The Westminster Dictionary of Christian Theology* (Philadelphia, 1983), 123–4.

[92] C. L. Cohen, *God's Caress* (New York, 1986), 75, n. 2, 104–5; John Dove, *The Conversion of Salomon* (1613), 3; Denison, *New Creature*, 55–66; John Traske, *The Power of Preaching* (1623), 39–44; C. E. Hambrick-Stowe, *The Practice of Piety* (North Carolina, 1982), ix, 76–7; J. S. McGee, *The Godly Man in Stuart England* (1976), 55–6; *New Catholic Encyclopaedia* IV, 288; J. von Rohr, 'Covenant and Assurance in Early English

Protestant who gasped at the overwhelming power of grace and the relative powerlessness of man's will, conversion is effectual at the moment when the elect man is initially made just. There were many patristic texts which pointed to the weakness of the human will and the essential gratuitousness of grace and salvation as well as the complete sufficiency of Christ's atonement for sin. If man's will responds passively to grace and does not actively cooperate with it then it is logical to see conversion as taking place effectually at the regenerative instant when grace is grasped through faith.[93] Conversion is focused heavily, therefore, on vocation, the calling of the Elect who are then incapable of falling finally and totally from grace.[94] Though, after their conversion, they have the capacity to perform good works, their justification does not rely in any sense on meritorious acts. Even if the will may be said to cooperate with grace after the initial conversion this is not of its own volition. Grace remains in control though in different forms (preventing, working and co-working grace).[95]

But an equally powerful patristic and subsequent tradition stressed a relative freedom of the will assisted by grace and this dictated a different perception of conversion. For Catholics (and some Protestants who did not sympathise with a severe Reformed view of grace and sin), the elements of conversion which Reformed Protestants regarded as efficacious in the first moment of grace extended into the process which is frequently described as sanctification (when the will actively cooperates with grace after their initial encounter). So the Romanist–Protestant divisions over conversion were caused by placing a slightly stronger emphasis on aspects of grace which opponents would not want to stress quite so much.[96]

Clerical opponents played down the subtleties and highlighted the contrasts between themselves about the nature of conversion, as if different degrees of grace were pegged to different doctrinal beliefs. And this polemical tendency filtered through from doctrinal theory into the wider

---

Puritanism', *Church History* 34 (1965), 195–203, at pp. 195–6. For stages in preparation and conversion, Baxter, *Directions*, 401–3; Mathew, *True Historical Relation*, 39; Morgan, *Godly Learning*, 28–30.

[93] Denison, *New Creature*, 53; Matthew Sutcliffe, *The Examination and Confutation of a certain scurrilous Treatise entituled, The Survey of the newe Religion* (1606), sig. C4r; Thomas Morton, *A Catholike Appeale* (1609), 209–12.

[94] D. D. Wallace, *Puritans and Predestination* (North Carolina, 1982), 49.

[95] J. von Rohr, *The Covenant of Grace in Puritan Thought* (Atlanta, Georgia, 1986), 147; Higgons, *Mystical Babylon*, sig. S4v; Thomas Abernethie, *Abjuration of Poperie* (Edinburgh, 1638), 21; Bodl., Rawl. MS D 399, fo. 203r.

[96] J. S. McGee similarly discerns the opposition between those he terms 'Anglicans' and 'Puritans' as one of emphasis, McGee, *Godly Man*, 57, 64; *idem*, 'Conversion and the Imitation of Christ in Anglican and Puritan Writing', *JBS* 15 (1976), 21–39, at pp. 22–3; *New Catholic Encyclopaedia*, VIII, 90–1, suggesting that the difference lies in theological method and an opposition between nominalist and realist perceptions of grace.

understanding of conversion – the experience of grace and the practice of a Christian life. Catholic concepts of justification and the possibility of falling from grace (anathema to Reformed Protestants) meant that the substance of conversion was thrown forward into the process generally described as sanctification. Thus Romanists reduced the emphasis (which was so important to the Reformed Protestant mentality) on the suddenness and sufficiency of the initial effectual inspiration of grace. Catholics perceived regeneration to be completed at baptism but saw evangelical conversion as an intensification of the Christian life in which not all are expected to achieve a uniform degree of saving grace, something which the pessimistic Reformed view of human nature deemed necessary for all the Elect. For Catholics, evangelical conversion finds its highest expression in the life of the religious (requiring the pursuit of 'evangelical counsels' of voluntary poverty, chastity and obedience). Before the Reformation, *conversio* was particularly associated with entry into a religious order; monastic observance is a *conversatio* commenced by a *conversio*.[97] Though Protestants did not expect all to accomplish the same virtuosity in sanctification (and accused Catholics of demanding precisely this in their emphasis on the counsels of perfection), their tendency was to see saving grace as a single standard necessary for all who are to be saved. Consequently, for them, baptism only commences the regeneration process; regeneration is completed by conversion, properly understood as a new spiritual birth.[98] In a sense Protestants took conversion out of the monastery, in Charles Cohen's words 'from a small circle of professional discussants', and brought it into the world.[99]

Protestants (and particularly puritans) meditated on the relationship between *conversio* and *conversatio*; together they formed the 'process by which saints prepared for and progressively came into union with Christ'.[100]

---

[97] Of course, the evangelical counsels of perfection, the mechanism of Catholic evangelical conversion, were not tied strictly to those in a monastic profession which required also a vow of stability. The 'religious' life in the Roman sense of conversion does not necessarily imply retirement into a monastery or convent (though this is how it may be expressed).

[98] M. J. Harran, *Luther on Conversion* (1983), 23; J. Baillie, *Baptism and Conversion* (1964), 14; Cohen, *God's Caress*, 6; John Denison, *The Sinne against the Holy Ghost Plainly Described* (1611), 40; Denison, *New Creature*, 52; Baxter, *Directions*, sig. A2r–v; Bodl., Rawl. MS D 399, fo. 203r–v. Sir Edward Hoby, who sponsored Theophilus Higgons's reconversion and obtained subsequently a benefice for him, (reportedly) compared the spiritual rebirth of Higgons with the birth of his own son on the same day as Higgons's recantation. The seminary priest Edward Bennett drew polemically a parallel between the ensuing almost immediate death of Hoby's son and what he must have considered Higgons's spiritual death, PRO, SO 3/5, July 1611; *HMC Rutland MSS* I, 424; AAW, A X, 61, 395–6; Birch, *Court and Times of James the First*, I, 111; McClure, *Letters*, I, 306.

[99] Cohen, *God's Caress*, 6.

[100] Hambrick-Stowe, *Practice*, 200–2.

Man's duty of action within the covenant is to 'obey God's commandments in his life and conversation'.[101] Repentance, which is synonymous with conversion in puritan thought, operates in two senses. On the one hand it was a condition of entering the covenant, but in a second sense it was an evangelical continuing quality which led to a conscious attempt at amendment of life. But while both Catholics and Protestants could envisage different degrees of grace during men's progression in it,[102] Protestants found utterly unacceptable the regimentation of grace in Catholic formulae which refused to associate saving grace exclusively with the Elect and also seemed to push it unnecessarily into vows in religion (e.g. of obedience, poverty and chastity). In Francis Bunny's words, those who have experienced 'regeneration and new birth' will inevitably 'increase and growe (although not all nor at all times alike) in Holinesse'.[103]

Thus was it possible for contemporaries to draw parallels between evangelical turning in religion and movement between rival Churches – even seeing one as a function of the other. Conversion was an aspect of justification, and justification was universally understood as occurring within the confines and through the ministry of the Church.[104] It was inevitable that, in circumstances of doctrinal and jurisdictional division, conversion between bitterly opposed ecclesiastical bodies should be associated with movement in grace, and, conversely, that conversion to the true Church could be equated also with flux between separate particular Churches. John Good wrote that 'the practice of life and conversation, is comonly answerable to the rules of doctrine and religion, which yf sincere and spirituall, brings foorth good fruites, yf corrupt and carnall, correspondent effectes. Upon which grownd it hath bene generally observed, that when any one hath bene converted from any secte to [the Roman] Catholike Religion, he hath become more vertous and regulate, then before', and in reverse, 'when any hath bene falen from the Catholike faith to any secte he hath become more vicious and dissolute'.[105]

---

101 Von Rohr, *Covenant*, 6–7; cf. Hambrick-Stowe, *Practice*, 198–200.
102 Von Rohr, *Covenant*, 73; Denison, *New Creature*, 55–68; Stephen Egerton, *A Briefe Method of Catechizing* (1631), 9; Edward Elton, *A Forme of Catechising* (1634), sig. D3ʳ⁻ᵛ.
103 Francis Bunny, *Truth and Falshood* (1595), sig. Dd3ᵛ. The Elizabethan Homilies of 1563 attacked Roman devotional tenets and in particular the 'three chief principal points, which they called the three essentials (or three chief foundations) of religion, that is to say, obedience, chastity and wilful poverty', P. F. Jensen, 'The Life of Faith in the Teaching of Elizabethan Protestants' (DPhil. thesis, Oxford, 1979), 86.
104 Brandon, *Christianity*, 77; *New Catholic Encyclopaedia*, IV, 289.
105 BL, Lansd. MS 776, fo. 42ᵛ; cf. N. N., *An Epistle of a Catholike Young Gentleman* (Douai (imprint false, printed secretly in England), 1623), 7, 36, where the author says his conversion to Roman Catholicism commenced with a consideration of his misspent youth and that he had led an 'exorbitant and irregular life'.

Were these polemical expressions of the nature of conversion just a distraction from the profounder realities of spiritual experience and pastoral direction in this period?[106] Evangelical conversion did not positively require an ecclesiastical reorientation to express it (and movement between Churches might have no evangelical significance whatsoever), but the divisions in ecclesiastical allegiance between Rome and the Church of England, artificial as they appear theologically, were forms through which conversion by grace might readily be expressed, propagated and understood. Opposing ecclesiastical structures were thought by their enemies to err fundamentally rather than in doctrinal minutiae. They propped up not just error but also vice. Since they tempted man not only towards unbelief but even unrestrained carnal lusts and the reign of sin over the faculties of man's nature, the abandonment of a false Church could easily be equated with progress in grace. John Dove argued that conversion signified not just regeneration ('when a man is effectually called and converted to the Faith') but also 'repentance of them which have fallen away from the truth of Religion to Heresie, or Idolatrie' (as well as 'from vertue to sinne'), 'and afterward turne back againe unto God'.[107] John Copley interpreted his 'true and unfaigned conversion from the superstitious, idolatrous, and hereticall religion of the Romane Church' as a sign of the evangelical working of grace upon him 'contrarie unto common course and order'.[108] Rejection of Rome was not just a withdrawal of allegiance from an ecclesiastical institution but a rejection of the mystery of iniquity, a coming out of Babylon. Revelation 18: 4 where God calls his Elect out of Babylon was the prefatory citation or central text of most of the tracts of this period in which English Protestant converts explained how they had abandoned the Church of Rome. The Elect might exist within Rome but their effectual conversion induces them to depart from it.[109] This was not mere vitriol. If the Church of Rome could be

---

[106] P. Dumonceux, 'Conversion, Convertir, Etude Comparative d'après les Lexicographes du XVIIᵉ Siècle', in *La Conversion au XVIIᵉ Siècle* (Marseille, 1982), 7–15, at p. 9.

[107] Dove, *Conversion*, 3.

[108] Copley, *Doctrinall and Morall Observations*, 1, 4.

[109] Clarke, *Recantation*, sig. Bvʳ; Sheldon, *Motives*, sig. *ʳ; James Ussher, *A Briefe Declaration of the Universalitie of the Church of Christ* (1624), 47; Higgons, *Mystical Babylon, passim*, in which tract Higgons followed on logically from his *Sermon* of 1611 when he dealt briefly with the subject of 'spirituall Babilon', Higgons, *Sermon*, 42; Richard Sheldon, *A Sermon Preached at Paules Crosse* (1625), 46, saying that many papists in the Roman Church are 'not of the Popish Church' because they are 'ignorant of the altitudes of the Beast, or not obstinately wedded thereunto' and so are 'in the way of salvation'; Thomas Gage, *The Tyranny of Satan* (1642), 24; cf. John Swynnerton, *A Christian Love-Letter* (1606), sig. Lᵛ; Andrew Ramsay, *A Warning to Come out of Babylon* (Edinburgh, 1638), 9, asserting that the Reformation itself was a conversion in this sense. In answer to the question 'where was your Church before Luther?' Ramsay replies 'where they [were] who came out of Babel . . . before their coming out of Babel'.

all but identified with the spiritual Babylon of Revelation, then not only did conversion necessitate exit from Babylon but leaving Babylon/Rome was as close an institutional expression of true evangelical conversion as a Reformed Protestant could imagine.[110] Just as the reformed institutional Church through its relative purity might approximate to the true Church, so the Church of Rome in its absolute corruption might be associated almost exclusively with the false Church of Antichrist.[111] In such a model Protestants had a mirror image of the Roman polemical insistence (based on a different concept of the operation of grace) that true conversion was possible by adhering to the visible institutional Church represented by Rome. Neither side thought that a change between institutional Churches, even though it incorporated a surrender of false doctrines, was adequate if it was not accompanied by effectual motions of grace. Thus when the Capuchin Francis Nugent disputed with a company of English Protestant actors who arrived in Cologne they immediately yielded to the doctrinal truth of his persuasions, but they 'felt themselves so drie and tough harted that they knew not how to passe from the bewitching Babilonical Harlot to their true Mother, the Catholick Church'. Nugent preached to them about hardness of heart and redemption through grace, whereupon they were moved by grace and 'all reconciled and became sound Catholickes'.[112]

The theological conflict between Catholics and Protestants over how conversion was experienced actually lent itself to a reading of effectual conversion in terms of changing religion between institutional Churches. Central Reformation controversies generally took the form of disputes about how grace filtered from its source to its final destination. These disputes were the successors to patristic and mediaeval arguments about the extent to which man merited grace, prepared for it before conversion and cooperated with it after conversion. Contemporaries saw different aspects of conversion distributed in man between his will and his intellect. Protestants understood the will to be captive and absolutely subject to sin, and thus subject to the intellect in the conversion process. By contrast, Catholics emphasised the relative freedom of the will and allowed it a more active role in conversion. Both sides automatically resorted to a scholastic model of human nature around which to organise their theology of religious change. The art of defining regeneration lay in distributing its effects between the reason, the will and the affections, the three faculties in the possession of the soul. All three, it was agreed, were caught up in the radical changes brought

---

110 Richard Finch, *The Knowledge or Appearance of the Church* (1590), sig. B^r–B2^v.
111 Philip de Mornay, *A Notable Treatise of the Church* (1579), sig. Xii^r, Xiiii^v.
112 BL, Harl. MS 3888, fo. 50^r; cf. William Hinde, *A Faithfull Remonstrance* (1641), 15–17.

about in man's nature by conversion.[113] Humphrey Leech argued that the integrity of the Roman Church was sufficiently established by the spectacle of God enlightening 'the understanding [of so many converts], as in the middest and thickest of the darknes of heresy, to shew them the Catholicke Truth and Church, as also to frame their wills, and inflame their affections, to yield all obedience therunto'.[114] Robert Persons could envisage the affections (subject to a right orientation) as 'the key of all the rest to open the gate to true faith and beleefe'.[115]

What Catholics were certain of was that effectual conversion could not be limited to the intellect. (Protestants, they claimed, erroneously confined conversion, the effectual reception of grace, to an intellectual perception.) Though an inward acceptance that Rome has a monopoly of truth and is the only conduit of saving faith constitutes part of true conversion (for someone who stands outside the Roman communion), mere assent to all the doctrines of faith taught by that Church is insufficient. In this sense the exercise of the will in conversion takes precedence logically over the exercise of the mind. Whether true conversion was described by reference to movement into communion with Rome (to profit from its monopoly of grace) or the operation of grace itself, the will was the mechanism by which this was achieved. 'Wee find daily by experience', wrote Persons, 'that our will draweth after it our judgement; and as she is affected or dissaffected, so goeth our judgment and understanding also'.[116] As we noted in chapter 2, many people seem to have attributed to the reading of polemical books their changes of religion from the English to the Roman Church. Often they say that they were converted to a 'schismatic' position from their former 'heretical' one by reading and accepting controversial renderings of Catholic doctrine, but that a further stage was required which could come about only by exercise of the will. In Ralph Green's case, even after earnest prayer, and the use of books of controversy, 'many doubts or difficulties seemed to remain, which hindered . . . [his] conversion'. Henry Chadderton read and re-read Richard Bristow's *Briefe Treatise*, and 'became convinced of the truth of the Catholic faith, and was ready to argue upon it with any Protestant, but not to embrace it'. Henry Lanman perused the books of the

---

113 O. C. Watkins, *The Puritan Experience* (1972), 6. For a more developed account of the faculties contained in the vegetable, sensible and rational parts of the soul, Morgan, *Godly Learning*, 46; William Whately, *The New Birth* (1618), 69; Lancelot Andrewes, *XCVI Sermons* (1629), 207; cf. Sir Kenelm Digby, *A Conference* (Paris, 1638), 7–8.

114 Humphrey Leech, *Dutifull and Respective Considerations* (St Omer, 1609), 73; cf. Digby, *Conference*, 7: the soul (employing both the understanding and the will) seeks and investigates what is true and good, and then 'according to the judgement it maketh of it, the will followeth and with affections graspeth at it'.

115 Robert Persons, *A Treatise of Three Conversions* (3 vols., n.p., 1603–4), I, sig. ***6ᵛ.

116 Persons, *Treatise*, I, sig. ***6ᵛ.

'Challenge' stalwarts John Rastell and Thomas Harding but this 'produced no other effect' than to draw him 'a little from attending the churches of the Protestants'. Three years were spent in 'turning over many books of controversy'.[117] The difficulties in conversion experienced by converts to Rome are all described as an excessive reliance on the intellect, the erroneous belief that God's grace could be appropriated merely by thinking about faith. Like Henry Lanman, Francis Walsingham wrote that after extensive reading of Catholic and Protestant polemical tracts he was still 'fearfull to make any change in Religion for many respects'. He felt 'such a warre betweene . . . [his] understanding, will, and affection', the constituent parts of his nature, 'as . . . [he] could not tell . . . what to do'.[118] Likewise Tobias Mathew jnr's conversion was delayed when he conferred with Robert Persons in Rome in 1606. Persons 'did work so powerfully . . . upon my understanding . . . that, if I had not wilfully drawn the curtain between it and my will . . . I am half persuaded that perhaps I might have departed from thence . . . a true Catholic'.[119] John Good deferred his final conversion 'under a coulorable pretence of more knowledge, to infect me with curiositye stiring up a continuall desier to be alwaies . . . serchinge more fully to informe my understandinge; when in . . . truth the fault was not so much therin, as in my depraved and corrupted will, that could indure no reformation'.[120] Robert Persons stated it as a general principle that intellectual persuasion (in the form of disputation)

as it is a fit meanes to styrre up mans understandinge to attend the truth, by layinge forth the difficultyes on both sides; so is yt not alwayes sufficient to resolve his judgement, for that yt moveth more doubts than he can aunswere or dissolve. And this happeneth not only in unlearned people, which by no meanes can descerne which party hath the better, when both parts are learned and alleage arguments for themselves, in matters above their capacity, but even the most learned also, yf they have no other meanes of resolution then arguing to and from by disputation, are brought many-times to be more doubtfull therby then before.[121]

This was the problem with polemical persuasion. Resolution in conversion, these Catholics thought, took place principally in the will, something which philosophical debate about election and predestination did

---

117 Foley III, 179–80, 547, I, 175–6; cf. CRS 54, 128.
118 Walsingham, *Search* (1609), 473; cf. Jacques Brousse, *The Life of the Reverend Fa. Angel of Joyeuse* (Douai, 1623), sig. Cc4ᵛ–5ᵛ; Mathew, *True Historical Relation*, 39–40.
119 Mathew, *True Historical Relation*, 33.
120 BL, Lansd. MS 776, fo. 13ʳ.
121 Robert Persons, *A Review of Ten Publike Disputations* (St Omer, 1604), 19–20; Walsingham, *Search* (1609), 481–2, in which Persons probably collaborated (cf. John White, *A Defence of the Way to the True Church* (1614), 87), makes an almost identical point; cf. James Wadsworth snr, *The Contrition of a Protestant Preacher* (St Omer, 1615), preface, sig. Bᵛ–3ʳ.

not properly address. The Catholic friends of Francis Walsingham and William Fitch informed them that it was fruitless to expect to resolve their difficulties by continuous reading.[122]

Protestant expositions of the way in which they passed out of the Church of Rome by the promptings of grace seem to be very different. Admittedly, Protestants also said that a mere intellectual appreciation of points in dispute was no adequate basis for conversion.[123] Reason was not capable of conversion unassisted. Although at one point the seminarist John Nichols described his decision to become a Protestant as a decision to allow 'reason to rule . . . [his] will', he says nevertheless that the human faculty of rational decision-making by itself is an inadequate way of resolving religious doubt. He ignored conscience while he was at Rome because he still relied on his own unaided reason.[124] Reason is corrupt as well. For puritans, as Watkins says, there was nothing in man which was itself capable of conversion: 'reason, as the king of the faculties, should be in control, acting with the will to rule the affections; but in fallen man both the will and the affections are in revolt, while reason itself is imperfect'. Conversion came about by a 'simultaneous seizure' of all man's faculties by grace. As Richard Sibbes commented, God 'not only enlightens the understanding, but infuseth grace into the will and affections, into the whole inward man'.[125] Thus the convert Theophilus Higgons followed William Perkins and stressed that before the onset of grace, man is 'dead in the habit, and custome of sinne', dead in his 'faculties and powers' as much as in his 'Will, which is the Queene-regent of the soule; dead in the Understanding which is her Counsellor . . . dead in the Affections, which are her messengers'.[126] Still, Protestant emphasis on the passivity of the will in the moments of the onset of grace tended to play up the part of the understanding in the regeneration of the whole man. Protestant converts from Rome in this period virtually all subscribed to an orthodox Reformed process of preparation of the heart for conversion.[127]

[122] Walsingham, *Search* (1609), 481; Brousse, *Life*, sigs. Bb8ᵛ–Ccʳ.
[123] Francis Savage, *A Conference betwixt a Mother a devout Recusant, and her Sonne a zealous Protestant* (Cambridge, 1600), 90, where the convert is thoroughly persuaded in points of Protestant doctrine but cannot abandon recusancy.
[124] John Nichols, *A Declaration of the Recantation of John Nichols* (1581), sig. Bvᵛ, Biiiiᵛ.
[125] Morgan, *Godly Learning*, 43, 47, 54; Samuel Smith, *The Admirable Convert* (1632), 154–5; Watkins, *Puritan Experience*, 6; Richard Sibbes, ed. A. B. Grosart, *The Complete Works of Richard Sibbes* (7 vols., Edinburgh, 1862–4), VI, 525; cf. C. L. Cohen, 'Two Biblical Models of Conversion: An Example of Puritan Hermeneutics', *Church History* 57 (1988), 182–96, at p. 188.
[126] Higgons, *Sermon*, 18.
[127] Cohen, *God's Caress*, 77–8, 80; cf. N. Pettit, *The Heart Prepared* (New Haven, 1966), 64. Ferdinand Texeda's account of conflict of conscience, reason and will says his preparation for conversion lasted two years, *Texeda Retextus*, 32; cf. Nichols, *Declaration*, sig. Biiiiᵛ; Clarke, *Recantation*, sig. Bvʳ; Copley, *Doctrinall and Morall Observations*, 10; Sibbes,

The will is involved in preparatory struggle between flesh and spirit, but (though Continental Lutherans argued about the role of the will in preparation) the orthodox Calvinist and Reformed position was that the will is in no sense an efficient cause of conversion. Man's will is free only in 'things civill and indifferent'. Even after conversion, a man, says Stephen Denison, has a freed will only 'in some measure'. After effectual conversion, the will is free from the debilitating effects of sin but it still responds to rather than cooperates actively with grace. It is not in man's power to repent; such an opinion is Pelagian.[128] In the work of conversion 'we were passive, not active . . . and so passive, that there was nothing in us, to concurre with God. It was not a slumber . . . it was death.'[129] While grace comes in stages, the first where grace works alone and the second where the will (still in subjection) is active, Higgons stresses that 'it is the first . . . not the second, by which we are saved'.[130] 'Touching the beginning of our regeneration', wrote John White, 'what time we rise up from sinne, and enter into our first conversion, we say, that our will could no way dispose it selfe . . . whereby it might be made capable of grace; so when grace first enters it is meerly passive, till grace have renewed it', and at that moment when 'the Spirit of God . . . first layes hold, and sets upon our will to convert it, it findes nothing therein to helpe his grace in the conversion; but in order of working, first, grace gives life and qualitie to the dead will, and then being renewed it wils the conversion, and becometh the voluntarie instrument of God, both to apprehend his grace offered, and to worke forward with it', but 'not by it[s] owne naturall strength'. White likens conversion to the action of pen upon paper, God's pen upon the paper of humanity. The paper 'receives the inke passively, and brings nothing of it[s] owne to the writing . . . but being written [on] it becometh an instrument of the writing'.[131] Hence, Protestant conversions are portrayed as taking place effectually in the mind. John von Rohr comments that while there were divines like Beza who made faith almost exclusively a function of the mind, and others like Ames who were disturbingly voluntarist, the commonest

Complete Works, VI, 522. Virtually all Catholic renegades say that they had for some time previously doubted the truth of Rome's doctrinal assertions, John Nicholas y Sacharles, *The Reformed Spaniard* (1623), sig. A3r; *Recantations*, 7 (Tedder says he was 'alwaies distracted in minde with doubts of the greatest points of that Religion'), 46; Bell, *Survey*, 112; Higgons, *Sermon*, 42; Anthony Hungerford, *The Advise* (1639), 7.

128 Perkins, *Reformed Catholike*, 11–27; Denison, *New Creature*, 13–14; Sutcliffe, *Examination*, sigs. C4r–Dr; idem, *Unmasking*, 34; B. Citron, *New Birth* (Edinburgh, 1951), 110–18.

129 Higgons, *Sermon*, 19; cf. William Perkins, *A Reformed Catholike* (Cambridge, 1598), 17–18.

130 Higgons, *Sermon*, 20.

131 John White, *The Way to the True Church* (1616), 283.

position was an intermediate one which affirmed 'a significant place for both intellect and will in faith's act'. But even within this intermediate view, von Rohr says, 'despite the duality of emphasis, there was often a tendency to give the intellect a position higher than the will'. In general, such 'Puritan theologians saw the will as following the commendations of the intellect.'[132] This was certainly the case in the tracts of the converts who needed to counteract the Romish bias against the intellect in describing change of religion. Thus Richard Sheldon wrote that 'it was . . . the right hand of the Lord which did touch my understanding: and as hee thus wrought in my understanding, so hee did also internally, and immanentlie (as me thought) move my will'. John Copley alleged that his will was restricted by an 'extra-ordinarie heavinesse' for many respects and conversion came only through the force of scriptural and patristic passages on his mind.[133]

The division between the primacy of the will in Catholic conversions and the priority of the understanding and passivity of the will in Protestant ones mapped onto other polemical divisions, notably the quarrels over the relative authority of Scripture and the Church. Protestants insisted on the primacy of Scripture and the approach to faith by the Word (and particularly the Word preached). This, though, was not because Scripture was chronologically prior or its texts purer than the patristic and other authorities which Romanists pointed to for resolution of doubt. It was because Scripture (as pure Revelation) worked man's initial conversion with no exercise of his will, though he might have undergone already an extensive period of preparation. Scripture was the channel through which grace was transmitted infallibly to the Elect. Tradition, liable to corruption because not divine in origin, was not.[134] Romanists tended to see in conversion a decision to belong to 'the Church' (the guardian of revelation through its tradition) and interpreted this as an exercise of the will. Protestants saw conversion *sola Scriptura* as taking place in the mind with no accompanying action of the will. Possibly the most contested patristic text of this period was Augustine's reference to his own conversion where he says that he would not have believed the Scriptures if it had not been for the authority of the Church: 'ego vero evangelio non crederem nisi me catholicae ecclesiae conmoveret auctoritas'. Though Augustine is making a point irrelevant to the Reformation disputes over authority (in fact, he is

---

[132] Von Rohr, *Covenant*, 68–71; Sibbes, *Complete Works*, VI, 525, arguing that 'whatsoever is in the will and affections comes through the understanding'; Cohen, *God's Caress*, 97; for the Salmurian variation on Calvinist orthodoxy in this sphere of the relationship between the will and the intellect, B. G. Armstrong, *Calvinism and the Amyraut Heresy* (Madison, 1969), 63–4.

[133] Sheldon, *Motives*, sig. ¶4ᵛ; Copley, *Doctrinall and Morall Observations*, 9, 11.

[134] Thomas Bell, *Thomas Bels Motives* (Cambridge, 1593), 138; Hungerford, *Advise*, 6–7.

saying that he would reject both Gospels and Church if his Manichean opponents could prove their founder to have been one of Christ's apostles), Catholics argued that it proved that Church 'tradition' preceded Scripture, while Protestants argued that while 'the Church must of necessity propose things credible', 'Scripture it selfe convinces', and that Augustine's statement has no respect to time past; the authority of the Church mattered to Augustine only until he embraced the Scriptures, at which point his effectual conversion was located.[135]

Thus the experience of conversion, of life as well as doctrine, could be made sense of, could actually be intensified, by thinking of it in the terms of current ecclesiastical rivalry. This perception of how a man changes religion also allows us to reinterpret the positions (so frequently misread by historians) which contemporaries saw themselves as moving between as they were touched or after they had been abandoned by grace. As is well known, Catholics distinguished between degrees of separation from the institutional Church of Rome, principally between heresy and schism. Technically schism is a breach of ecclesiastical unity while heresy is an error in faith. Historians have tended to assume that by a 'schismatic' contemporary English Romanists meant simply a person whose views were Catholic but who conformed to the State Church's outward requirements, while a heretic was someone whose views were clearly anti-Romanist. This reading fails to recognise that there are several planes in the complex matrix of conversion to which 'schism' and 'heresy' refer. It risks interpreting these terms as expressions solely of politico-ecclesiastical allegiance, something which contemporary use of these words makes clear was not the case.

In Roman parlance, individuals are converted from heresy and reconciled from schism, but reconciliation is always required for full communion with Rome.[136] Church thinking distinguishes between mixed and pure schism. Pure schism is encountered but seldom. Generally it is derived from a heresy or is subsequently combined with one.[137] Thus conversion to Rome puts

---

[135] John Brereley (*vere* James Anderton), *Sainct Austines Religion* (n.p., 1620), sig. L^v; Patrick Anderson, *The Ground of the Catholike and Roman Religion* (St Omer, 1623), 85; William Crompton, *Saint Austins Summes* (1625), 38–9; Mornay, *Notable Treatise*, sig. Gvii^r; Anthony Wotton, *A Trial of the Romish Clergies Title to the Church* (1608), 238–40; White, *Way*, 120–1, 81; *Contra Epistulam Manichaei* 5, *CSEL* XXV, 197; also the debate over *Contra Cresconium* 2. 21, 26, *CSEL* LII, 385, Augustine's statement that Christ (taken by Protestants as a figure for Scripture) precedes the Church; Crompton, *Saint Austins Summes*, 38; Mornay, *Notable Treatise*, sig. Fiii^r.

[136] The canonical penalties are the same for schism and heresy since a schismatic is judged to be an exterior heretic.

[137] *New Catholic Encyclopaedia*, XII, 1130 (arguing that Augustine, in his polemic against the Donatists, reduced the distinction between schism and heresy to one of degree rather than order); Gregory Martin, *A Treatise of Schisme* (Douai (imprint false, printed in London), 1578), sig. **iiii$^{r–v}$; cf. Thomas Hide, *A Consolatorie Epistle* (Louvain (imprint false,

an emphasis on an exercise of the will (by a positive decision to repair the schismatic breach even after the individual has come to a right faith). A Protestant who embraces Rome tends to describe conversion as consisting of two clear stages, first an abandonment of heresy and then a positive choice to join the Church of Rome (thus purging his schismatic state).[138]

Admittedly, Protestants followed the same patristic sources as Catholics on the subject of schism and heresy. Nevertheless, they associated schism less closely with the institutional Church (because they did not link grace so precisely to the Church's visible structure). The institutional element of schism was played down. In Mornay's words 'the Romanists are Schismatikes, and not they which separate themselves from them', and 'the Communion of the Church doeth not consist in a locall union, neyther the separation, in removing of places'.[139] For a Protestant the effectual element of conversion was the rejection of heresy (or rather of popery and idolatry), just as faith rather than the will was the motor for change.

APOSTASY

These binary divisions over the nature of conversion were mirrored in the Catholic and Protestant divergence over the reverse process of 'apostasy'. The strict canonical meaning of apostasy is the defection of the baptised from the Christian faith.[140] It is not the same as heresy (the rejection of individual truths) or simply moving between particular Churches. Converts in this period tend to be called apostates by those they are leaving behind because the polemical tendency is for the controversial writer to identify as closely as possible the institutional structure to which he belongs with the true Church, visible and invisible. Consequently someone who leaves an ecclesiastical institution may be presumed by its members to be falling from faith as well.[141] Protestants saw the sin of blasphemy against the Spirit as a final apostasy, to be distinguished from a more temporary kind committed by merely associating with Rome. The purpose of John Meredyth's tract, *The Sinne of Blasphemie against the Holy Ghost* with its 'admonition to all

---

printed at East Ham), 1580), sig. Cviv–viir; William Fulke, *A Confutation of a Popishe and sclaunderous Libelle* (1571), fo. 7r; J. G. Goodwine, *The Reception of Converts* (Canon Law Studies no. 198, Washington, 1944), 128–34; Garnet, *Apology*, 69: 'even as the inwarde dissenting from trew faith is either inward infidelity, Apostasy, or heresie: so the outward shew of a false faith, or denying the trew faith, is called exteriour infidelity, or exterior heresy and apostasy', cf. *ibid.*, 82–3, though the Church is prepared to distinguish between schismatic states depending on the causes which have induced them, *ibid.*, 89–108; cf. CRS 67, 20.

[138] CRS 54–5, *passim.*   [139] Mornay, *Notable Treatise*, sig. Xv, Xiiiiv.
[140] *Catholic Dictionary*, I, 122; Goodwine, *Reception*, 126.
[141] Martin, *Treatise*, sig. Gviiiv.

Revolting Apostataes annexed', is to 'search into that fearefull Sinne of Apostacy, that those who repute it a small matter, to depart from the Truth of the Gospell, to the Tents of Antechrist, may consider the danger, and retire before they fall into that Sinne against the Holy Ghost, which is Irrecoverable'. Meredyth will not say that reconciliation to Rome is itself apostasy but, in that the Church of Rome may be envisaged apocalyptically, they are in danger of it: 'I say not, that such [who convert to Rome] commit that Sinne . . . but this Christ saith; "Hee that is not with mee, is against me."' John Denison wrote in exactly the same terms about those who 'send away Religion for a time, thinking to take it up againe at their pleasure' and urges 'those who are wandring' to 'returne with speede to the bosome of their mother, who hath not lost the bowels of compassion, except they have lost all sense of grace'.[142]

In that Catholics envisaged conversion as an exercise of the will and a sanctifying process, those who abandoned their monastic vocation could also be described as apostatising.[143] By contrast, those who abandoned Catholicism sometimes describe themselves as having tried and cast away Catholic monastic or regular lifestyles.[144] Robert Persons remarked that John Sacheverell's conversion to Protestantism was immediately

---

[142] Meredyth, *Sinne*, sig. A^r, A4^r, 47; Denison, *Sinne*, 56–7. Denison's sermon, *The Sinne against the Holy Ghost Plainly Described*, was preached at Paul's Cross six weeks after Higgons appeared there in order to recant. Denison took advantage of the recent changes of religion of Higgons and others to drive home the point of his sermon, *ibid.*, 57. Higgons had concentrated on a Catholic exposition of this aspect of sin in his tract explaining his conversion to Catholicism and demonstrating the existence of Purgatory, *First Motive*; cf. Bell, *Survey*, 299; Bedell, *Copies*, 2, 33. The certificate of absolution which William Alabaster received from George Abbot described Alabaster as 'vero errore deductus in Apostasiam et verae Religionis defectum lapsus quae ex fide Ecclesiae Anglicanae recte tenuisti', CU Libr., MS Mm 1 45, p. 186; cf. Sheldon, *Motives*, sig. Ee2^r, which insists that true apostasy from the faith is not really to do with secession from institutional Churches at all.

[143] Clancy, 'Priestly Perseverance', 286; cf. Persons, *A Briefe Censure*, sig. Evii^v, citing Augustine to the effect that there are none worse than those who have abandoned their monastic profession; cf. *idem*, *A Temperate Ward-Word* (Antwerp, 1599), 62–3, remarking that those who have left the Society 'often times become the greatest opposites of all others', and interpreting this in soteriological terms as apostasy: they are those who 'went from them and were not of them', the Johannine allusion which Protestants in particular used to refer to the reprobate, 1 John 2: 19. He thought that 'fall from religion' (i.e. the profession of the religious orders) is 'the next stepp to plaine apostasy and falling from the faieth of Christe', Saint Alban's College, Valladolid, Series II, leg. 2.

[144] John Nichols in his *Declaration*, sig. Bv^r, describes how 'unwisely . . . [he] slept . . . upon hard boards . . . scourged . . . [him] selfe with whipcordes' and fasted twice weekly. Many of those whom George Abbot tried to recruit for propaganda purposes had a monastic or regular background, notably Griffin Floyd, Leonard Rountree, Ferdinand Texeda, Christopher Musgrave and the friars whom Carleton sent to Abbot from Venice. Texeda suggests that his former Catholic regular lifestyle was inadequate as a means to defeat the world, the flesh and the Devil, *Texeda Retextus*, 32.

accompanied not only by becoming a 'minister' and a taker of priests but 'of late for the upshott of all hee hath marryed a publique queane, the widow of one Luke Hutton hanged a little before for thefte and murder'.[145]

Initial corruption in the will and the affections were the cause, potentially, of both a total loss of faith and of moral degradation. A spiralling fall from grace might induce a fall from the certainty and security of a true particular Church. When Theophilus Higgons returned to the Church of England he claimed that, before he converted to Rome, his temporal difficulties, though severe, 'did not prevaile in . . . [him] unto any mutation of my faith' but eventually '(the inferiour parts of . . . [his] soule rebelling against the superiour) . . . [his] earthly, darke affections . . . did, interpose themselves to eclipse the light' of his understanding.[146] Catholics likewise saw one fall succeeding another after initial moral defences were broken down by the commencement of doctrinal deviance. Lord Sanquhair, condemned in mid-1612 for murdering a fencing master, and executed in the palace yard at Westminster, 'professed himself to die a Catholique, and desired to be prayed for, and that he was so educated [i.e. as a Catholic], but thes nyne yeares he had not performed the dutie of a Cath[olique] in any sort, and therfor god did permitt him to fall into divers wickednesses, and if he had continued a Cath[olique] he had never consented to the murther', and he 'dyed verie penitent'.[147] The renegade seminarist Peter Chambers who abandoned his Catholic clerical orders in December 1608 was subsequently convicted of and hanged for sodomy. The archpriest reported that he 'protested at his death that he was never infected with that abominable synne untill he joyned with them [the Protestants]'.[148] When John Sacheverell came to London (apparently after flight from Viterbo in Italy and the regulation of the Order of Preachers) and seemed on the verge of abjuring Rome, it was noted not only that he was lukewarm in his Catholicism but also, ominously, that he was seen 'often at the play-house'.[149]

Roman and Protestant division over grace in conversion was nowhere more clearly indicated than in their reading of those who passed between them. The standard scriptural image for those who abandon faith, institutionally and evangelically, is the man possessed by the unclean spirit

---

[145] CRS 51, 252; Saint Alban's College, Valladolid, Series II, leg. 1; Luke Hutton, *Luke Huttons Lamentation* (1596). For Luke Hutton, kin to Archbishop Matthew Hutton, see Sir John Harington, *A Briefe View of the State of the Church of England* (1653), 192; D. Marcombe, 'The Dean and Chapter of Durham, 1558–1603' (Ph.D thesis, Durham, 1973), 41–2.

[146] Higgons, *Sermon*, 43; *Recantations*, 30–1.

[147] AAW, A XI, 291, 565; McClure, *Letters*, I, 364.

[148] Anstruther II, 51; AAW, A IX, 82; cf. Foley IV, 240.   [149] CRS 51, 252.

and the seven devils of Matthew 12: 43–5.[150] Anthony Tyrrell, following his second change of religion in 1588 (expounded in a Paul's Cross sermon of December of that year), needed to explain why he had previously reverted to popery. He referred to that verse and said of the 'Lybels and writings' that he had 'made in . . . [the Pope's] defence' that they came from 'that foule spirit which first was throwne out, and beeing returned againe, he brought seaven worse then him selfe to hold more sure possession'.[151] In a subsequent sermon of 13 July 1589 he took up this image again. One possible interpretation is that a defector from true religion is worse off than the man without any religion, 'for of an infidell there remaineth some hope that he may be converted and beleeve, but of an apostate, or an obstinate heretike there is scarse anie hope at all'. But, of course, this would hardly be favourable to him. Tyrrell wants to claim his place as one of the Elect who cannot fall totally and finally from grace. He says therefore that the 'litterall sence' of these verses is that the Devil may return to the convert only if the convert returns finally and irremediably to sin [i.e. falls totally and finally]: 'so soone as it pleaseth the Lord to cal us by his grace unto repentance . . . he must depart away from us'.[152] Thus Tyrrell plays down the significance of moving between particular Churches (something which he did rather a lot) and emphasises the primacy of motions of grace. Romanists who put more stress on the significance of adhering to the institutional structures of the visible Church chose to interpret those like Tyrrell who fell away from them less charitably.[153] Catholics subscribed to different models of perseverance and assurance. Godly activity was necessary by man's own efforts in order to ensure that the house had God in possession when the unclean spirit and his seven devilish companions returned. A Protestant naturally would argue that the efficient cause of godliness following conversion was the efficacy of God's decree which led to

---

[150] 'When the unclean spirit is gone out of a man, he walketh through dry places, seeking rest, and findeth none. Then he saith, I will return into my house from whence I came out; and when he is come, he findeth it empty, swept and garnished. Then goeth he, and taketh with himself seven other spirits more wicked than himself, and they enter in and dwell there: and the last state of that man is worse than the first'; cf. Luke 11: 24–6.

[151] *Recantations*, 34–5.

[152] Tyrrell, *Fruitfull Sermon*, sig. Bii^v, Bvii^v. He used a similar schema to explain his previous conversion to Catholicism, Morris, *Troubles*, II, 476.

[153] Richard Smith, *An Answer to Thomas Bels late Challeng* (Douai, 1605), sig. c8^r. Henry Garnet suggested that Thomas Bell's ungodly behaviour in countenancing occasional conformity meant that good Catholics ignored him 'least perhaps the ministeriall spirite of pride, which must needes have bene once in him' before he converted to the Church of Rome in the 1570s 'should returning unto his former house make the last things worse then the former', *Apology*, 12. See also CRS 4, 31, Persons's application of Matthew 12: 43–5 to Robert Alfield; Martin, *Treatise*, sigs. Gviii^v–H^r.

the unclean spirit's unceremonious exit in the first place. Subsequent godly behaviour was merely the result of 'assistant grace'.[154]

The two types of conversion, between states of life and between Churches, are inextricably connected because, all agreed, only in the true Church (however defined) could grace be effectually exercised. 'Heresy and bad life, doe goe together' was a general truism.[155] Both aspects of conversion are rooted in grace. In practice many of those who converted to Catholicism relied on a Catholic evangelical model of conversion to express their polemical rejection of Protestantism. A number of the seminarists at Rome said that the desire to embrace monastic ideals – to go from the precepts (of the law) to the counsels (of perfection) – was a motive for exchanging the Church of England for the Church of Rome.[156]

Although the binary divisions between Catholics and Protestants in polemic were artificial, doctrinal differences over the nature of conversion allowed religious forms of change to flow in and out of political ones, and political forms of change were used to express those which are more usually thought to transcend politico-ecclesiastical divisions. Progress in grace, God's work in the world, could be represented most graphically (and even experienced) in terms of the war between the Churches. Regeneration through grace could be aligned with peregrination between Churches, politics and religion moving together.

Nevertheless, it is extremely misleading to see the ecclesiastical divisions between Catholics and Protestants *predetermining* how converts converted, as if grace in conversion could be expressed *only* through established forms and structures. This chapter has emphasised one side of the politics/religion coin to show that movement between the Churches of England and Rome could combine with a range of concepts of religious conversion familiar to contemporaries. The political, theological, polemical, intellectual, emotional and psychological elements inevitably became associated with each other. But the historian should not imagine that the cloying banalities

---

[154] Higgons, *Mysticall Babylon*, sig. S4ᵛ.

[155] Brousse, *Life*, sig. Aa6ᵛ. Thomas Wright divided the chapters of his book *Certaine Articles or Forcible Reasons* (Antwerp (imprint false, printed secretly in England), 1600) into two groups – those which concerned faith and those which concerned 'good life'. Articles like 'Protestants make God the Author of sin' and 'faith once had may be lost' (standard polemical topics) are found under the second, not the first, heading.

[156] Humphrey Leech, in the account of his conversion which he gave at the Roman seminary, stressed not so much his objections to Calvinist predestination, for which he is frequently noted, but his opposition to the Jovinian heresy as manifested in the Church of England, i.e. the rejection of the Catholic regular way of perfection, CRS 54, 216; cf. Leech, *Triumph*, 100; also CRS 54, 88, 175; cf. Theophilus Higgons, *Try before you Trust* (Douai, 1609), 63–6; for similar evidence in the cases of Francis Walsingham, Benjamin Carier and Sir Herbert Croft, Walsingham, *Search* (1609), 160–1; Balliol College MS 270, p. 160; Izaak Walton, *Reliquiae Wottoniae* (1685), sig. d5ᵛ.

of the philosophical polemical system which underpinned movement to and from Rome dictated exactly how people redefined their allegiances. Conversion in religion, the affective subject of so much Reformation literature and preaching, did not fit neatly into the politico-ecclesiastical conflict between the Churches. The next chapter shows why contemporary conversions were not preordained by a political agenda. Conversion is as much a declaration of freedom from institutions as a pledge of allegiance to them. Thus may we comprehend some of the more glaring anomalies and paradoxes in contemporaries' changes of religion – why, for example, some people moved between Churches on several occasions; why there seem to be so many connections between the religious state at which Catholic and Protestant converts aimed (despite the enmity of the institutional Churches in which they wished to experience it); why extremists on one side adopted equally extreme positions on the other; and, most of all, why the more extreme the change, the less, in a sense, the convert's conversion between Churches seems to be a change at all. The more intense the experience of conversion, the more keenly that dilemmas over grace and repentance were felt and the starker the difference between the hope of heaven and the threat of damnation, the less did changes of religion obey the logic of the strict doctrinal formulae which appear on the pages of the polemical tracts.

✦ 4 ✦

Change of religion and the end of polemic

DIVISION AND CONSENSUS

The previous chapter suggested that divisions over the workings of grace in conversion arose initially out of differences of emphasis within the regenerative scheme in Christian soteriology. Warring clerics politicised their expression of these subtle variations in thought. So successfully did they do this that it was easy for those who thought they were subject to the motions of grace to interpret their experience of it in terms of the conflict between the Churches. The glaring inadequacies of doctrinal controversy which we have discussed in chapter 2 did not prevent them from construing the Church's mediation of grace from God to man as a battle between the Gospel and popery, or between the Roman Church and Protestant heresy. Nor did contemporaries believe that the philosophical constructs which they used to describe conversion were artificial, or that the vitriolic ensuing quarrels between Romanists and Protestants had no substance. Even if they must have known that polemic did not fairly represent their opponent's position, rival churchmen did not think their enemies were any the less wrong. The logical end of Romanist thinking about different degrees of grace seemed to a Reformed Protestant to slander the majesty and sovereignty of God and the sufficiency of Christ's atonement for the Elect. As already remarked, the highest expression of evangelical conversion, an active seeking of assurance, in the Roman tradition was the following of a regular life, the transcending of the precepts of the Law by following the counsels of perfection. Entry into the religious life, monastic or otherwise, was the negation of all the principal Protestant tenets concerning conversion.[1] Protestants abominated the Catholic monastic orders. Timothy

---

[1] Robert Persons complained of Edmund Bunny's edition of his *Christian Directory* that 'wher I saie out of holie scripture, "here hence doe proceede al those large promises, to virginitie, chastitie, voluntarie povertie, &c." he maketh me saie; "hence doe proceede thos promises to mortification and newnes of life" ', Persons, *A Christian Directorie Guiding Men to their Salvation* (Rouen, 1585), fo. 11ʳ.

Rogers mocked the 'monastical lives' required by Romish 'necessarie perfection'. What perfection was it when 'reasonable creatures' were 'immured within the walls of a Cloyster . . . like a company of bruit beasts or swine shut up in a stye a fatting'?[2] Polemical opponents argued hotly about whether Augustine, after his conversion, became a monk. In Matthew Sutcliffe's words, 'it is most untrue, that he vowed Chastitie, or other Monkish Vowes'. Sutcliffe scorned Tobias Mathew jnr's claims to this effect (on the grounds, for example, that Augustine 'read Scriptures, which Monkes use not much to doe now'). William Crompton, by contrast, was prepared to admit the institution of monasticism in the early Church; but he denied the motivation which Catholic polemicists attached to it. Catholics badly misrepresented the theological significance of what Augustine did when he appeared to retire from the world: 'to the ancient Monks, things of indifferencie, as of . . . apparell, and other Ceremonies, were left as indifferent'. Augustine would condemn the monastic practices of modern times.[3] But Catholics imagined that the Protestant scheme of grace made God an unreasonable tyrant, saving and condemning men without respect to their works. In Catholic polemic, the Protestants' God became the 'author of sin', a predestinarian monster whose decrees of election and reprobation turned men into puppets, deprived of any trace of freedom of the will. Doctrinal divisions were thought to express irreconcilably two different approaches to grace, and neither side could accept that the other represented a tolerable, let alone a safe, way to salvation.

So, the ecclesiastical destination of the convert could never be an extraneous matter. The doctrine and structure of the Church to which he finally decided to adhere were never *just* a convenient rationalisation of his reorientation after the event. But that did not necessarily mean that the effectual motive to change was inspired directly and exclusively by the structure or doctrines of that Church. Even though conversion could be dramatised by polemic so that it seemed to obey the rules laid down in Roman or Protestant schemes of salvation, the experience of conversion did not always follow an ecclesiastically disciplined path. Oppositional doctrinal formulae always supplied the vocabulary for converts' explanations of why they kicked over the traces. Yet underneath the institutional superstructures of conversion created by Catholics and Protestants to make people believe that grace was channelled exclusively through their concept of a Church, there were substructures of religious change to which converts

---

[2] Timothy Rogers, *The Roman-Catharist* (1621), 28–30.
[3] Matthew Sutcliffe, *The Unmasking of a Masse-monger* (1626), 41; William Crompton, *Saint Austins Summes* (1625), 2; cf. the Catholic perception of Augustine's monasticism, BL, Lansd. MS 776, fo. 33ᵛ; Francis Walsingham, *A Search Made into Matters of Religion* (second edition, St Omer, 1615), 340–3.

who travelled in both directions subscribed equally. This is more than saying just that both sides connected affiliation to their own Church with justification, or that to live a good life required a right faith and the two could not be separated. Nor was it a matter of converts looking to fuzziness around the edges of rival doctrinal definitions to justify their removal from one Church to another (though some scholars have indeed argued that lines of division between different shades of doctrinal opinion had a tendency to dissolve and so there might be ideologically a measure of consensus among those who technically disagreed with each other's doctrinal formulations).[4] Evangelicals did not irenically recognise good qualities in all who probed the theology of repentance and the life of faith, or think that ecclesiastical quarrels could be quietly forgotten by the godly because all good men were of one religion. People with godly aspirations did not move around between Churches in their experience of grace just because they perceived that there were inconsistencies in the doctrinal formulae which those Churches produced (so they could comfortably ignore theological divisions and concentrate on enjoying a cocktail of doctrines held in common). Those who did drift between Churches without any reference to politicised doctrinal divisions – the uncommitted, fellow-travellers, occasional conformists and so on – were not converts except in a very superficial sense. Still, we know that, particularly in the cases of the self-consciously evangelical, the motions which persuaded an individual to convert in the sense of responding to grace were not identical to or coterminous with the ones which told him that he should leave one Church and adhere to another.[5] If this is so, then it helps

---

[4] E.g. P. F. Jensen has suggested that puritan pietistic focus upon the necessity of good works allowed the development 'at the heart of Protestant theology [of] a doctrine which, while not being identical with Catholic teaching on grace, was akin to it', and that a concern with the gaining of assurance meant orthodox Calvinist concepts of the link between faith and assurance started to lose ground among Protestants (and thus that Catholic and Protestant ideas moved closer together), Jensen, 'The Life of Faith in the Teaching of Elizabethan Protestants' (DPhil. thesis, Oxford, 1979), 224, 211. See also the modern academic debate as to whether the efficacious stage of Protestant conversion was shifted by English Calvinists following the revisionist line of Theodore Beza (e.g. R. T. Kendall, *Calvin and English Calvinism to 1649* (Oxford, 1979), 35, arguing that 'Calvin insists we cannot truly repent until we are first assured of God's grace. Beza delays assurance until the "effects" are there'; cf. N. Pettit, *The Heart Prepared* (New Haven, 1966), 17; C. L. Cohen, *God's Caress* (New York, 1986), 9–11, nn. 15, 17; for the opposite line, J. von Rohr, *The Covenant of Grace in Puritan Thought* (Atlanta, Georgia, 1986), 26, 31, 68, 89–90; P. Lake, *Moderate Puritans and the Elizabethan Church* (Cambridge, 1982), 98–9, 218–19; Lake accepts that second-generation Calvinists may have adopted formulae defining reprobation of which Calvin would not have approved but rejects the idea that Calvinist definitions of the order of faith and repentance were reversed.

[5] An institutional change could spark an evangelical one, or an evangelical twinge might lead the convert to look for a purer institutional Church in which to experience his conversion. Henry Lanman came across an edition of the Jesuit Jerome Platus's book on the virtues of the religious life after he had become a recusant and had been reconciled to Rome, CRS 54,

us to make sense of the somewhat chaotic and unregimented nature of conversion in this period, and to explain why some people's rigid godly principles could be combined with an infinite ecclesiastical malleability.

Perhaps the best way to explain this is to show that the more intensely a change of religion was experienced the less likely it was that its stages would conform to the way in which contemporaries would expect to rationalise it afterwards. As we have seen, conversion had two principal strands – an institutional one (in which an unsettled man might consider which of the rival Churches merited his allegiance) and an evangelical one (in which he pondered the mystery of grace and his standing in it). If a man inclined to think more deeply about the first then the issue of whose established ecclesiastical hierarchy and structures were most satisfactory would principally occupy his mind. He would be drawn more readily to think of conversion between rival establishments. But if the issues of grace absorbed his mind and he began to see conversion, even in the leaving of one Church for another, principally as an evangelical expression of repentance for sin and assurance of election, then the experience of conversion would not focus so clearly on establishment matters. There was no confessional monopoly on the evangelical contemplation of sin and corruption, the absolute impossibility of man's capacity to redeem himself by his own efforts, total reliance on grace at all stages of conversion, and the constant need to assure oneself of the possibility of salvation and one's status within the covenant. The man who was most exercised by these things would tend to see the divisions among Christian professors to lie between people who disagreed over man's potential to escape from sin and the extent of his natural depravity. For him this would set the parameters for conversion more soundly than the formal, even cold, codifications of scholastic arguments about such topics written by professional disputants.

So – we might not expect a person of Protestant puritan sympathies to have gone off and become a monk or clerk in a Catholic religious order, or, in reverse, a Catholic evangelical to have abandoned the religious order to which he belonged and transfer to a Church where all such things were abominated. But in practice this was precisely what did happen. Converts to Rome who progressed subsequently to the religious orders (or to an association with them) very frequently said that there had been strongly Protestant elements in their past, reformed tenets which they or members of

---

88; cf. the English edition of Platus, *The Happines of a Religious State* (Rouen, 1632). The seminarist Nicholas Hart's conversion from an 'immoral' life came after he had abandoned his schismatic state, Foley I, 167. Robert Persons said his failing in England had been to compromise with the regime (even though not in heart); he corrected this by renouncing vanity and the world at a stage when he would still probably have been described in a Catholic seminary abroad as '*schismaticus*', CRS 2, 19.

their families had held, notably (in the case of the Jesuits) in the families of
Robert Persons, Henry FitzSimon and Edward Walpole.[6] George Gilbert, so
close to Campion and Persons, was described by Henry More as having an
earnest nature which 'inclined him . . . to Puritanism', confirmed in him by
daily resort to the sermons of Edward Dering.[7] One wonders too about the
Jesuit-inclined Tobias Mathew jnr and his religious inheritance in the house
of his father, the archbishop.[8] Others who had connections with the Jesuits
displayed similar tendencies. Theophilus Higgons may have had puritan
inclinations before he converted to Rome. Sir Edward Hoby, his ecclesiastical 'minder', alleged that at Oxford Higgons had been violently anti-
popish and in his London lectureship had made hostile comments about
episcopacy.[9] Certainly there is no evidence of any irenic trait before he
became a Catholic under Jesuit auspices. Richard Etkins, who travelled to
Douai to try to recover Higgons, had been Higgons's friend at Christ Church
and held very Calvinist opinions.[10] And when Higgons changed back again
he asserted a thoroughly puritan theology of grace and an apocalyptic view
of Rome. James Wadsworth snr, the chaplain who accompanied Sir Charles
Cornwallis on his embassy to Spain, made contact with the Jesuits there.[11]
Formerly he had been at Emmanuel College, Cambridge, and was taught by
Perkins. He was a friend of William Bedell and Joseph Hall. Izaak Walton
remarked that 'of the three . . . [Wadsworth] was formerly observ'd to be the
most averse to that Religion that calls it self Catholick'.[12] His conversion to
Catholicism was followed about ten years later by a published tract which
concentrated on sin and repentance and excludes almost all references to
confessional division. It contains meditations on Psalm fifty, and
Wadsworth says that he planned to publish meditations on all the peni-
tential psalms. (This psalm, David's repentance, was a standard scriptural

---

[6] CRS 2, 38, 40; E. Hogan (ed.), *Words of Comfort* (Dublin, 1881), 201–2; F. Edwards (ed.),
The Elizabethan Jesuits (1981), 255.
[7] R. Simpson, *Edmund Campion* (1896), 173.
[8] Cf. *CSPD 1595–7*, 168 (Dudley Carleton's interesting account of extreme friction in the
Mathew household).
[9] Sir Edward Hoby, *A Letter to Mr T. H. Late Minister* (1609), 12–13. The replies which
Theophilus Higgons, *The Apology of Theophilus Higgons lately Minister, now Catholique*
(Rouen, 1609), 2–5 makes to Hoby's accusations are elusive rather than a straight denial.
[10] Hoby, *Letter*, 16–17; Higgons, *Apology*, 29; Foley VII, 1151; Christ Church College MS
xii. b. 49, fos. 14ᵛ, 16ʳ, 30ᵛ, MS xii. b. 48, fo. 71ᵛ (showing, apparently, a link between
Higgons, Etkins and Ferdinando Moorecroft, who collected stipends for each other when
they were absent and, in the same circumstances, for others who were evidently mutual
friends); Etkins and Higgons were both chaplains to the Calvinist bishop Thomas Ravis;
N. Tyacke, *Anti-Calvinists* (Oxford, 1990), 73.
[11] B. Camm, 'An Apostate at St Omers, 1618–1622', *The Month* 94 (1899), 163–70, at
pp. 164–5.
[12] Izaak Walton, *Reliquiae Wottoniae* (1685), sig. d5ᵛ.

focus for puritan conversion thought.)[13] Augustine Baker, before his conversion, had puritan evangelical sympathies and they remained evident in his subsequent Catholicism when he joined the Order of St Benedict.[14] Robert Venner, a seminarist at Rome who became a Benedictine in 1614 had been converted in France but had previously held Romish religion in 'great detestation'.[15] Leonard Rountree who converted backwards and forwards several times had considered entry into both the Society of Jesus and the Order of St Benedict.[16] Daniel Price, in his reply to Humphrey Leech, implied that Leech had a certain amount of nerve to label his opponents at Oxford puritans, and that 'the Church of Englande never had any so Puritannical' as people like Leech who judge themselves to be 'celestiall men . . . excelling, surmounting, transcending in perfection'.[17] It is perhaps significant that in the account of his conversion to Catholicism which he gave to the authorities at the English College in Rome Leech (already Jesuit-minded) said, in classic puritan phraseology, that he had heard a voice calling on him to depart from Babylon: 'exito exito a babilonica ista Heretica Anglicana congregatione quoties te vocavero'.[18] John Gennings, who changed religion in the early 1590s, claimed that he had been of a puritan disposition. His account of his evangelical change of religion may be read as a response to standard puritan exhortations to search for signs of election. In 1616 he became a Franciscan.[19] The Jesuits Charles Yelverton and Francis Walsingham stressed how far they had formerly been in

---

[13] C. L. Cohen, 'Two Biblical Models of Conversion: An Example of Puritan Hermeneutics', *Church History* 57 (1988), 182–96 at pp. 191–5; Wadsworth portrays himself as the Prodigal, who, for the puritan, 'epitomised the person in preparation', James Wadsworth snr, *The Contrition of a Protestant Preacher* (St Omer, 1615), sig. B3ʳ; Cohen, *God's Caress*, 78; John Good likened himself to the Prodigal, BL, Lansd. MS 776, fo. 47ᵛ.

[14] T. H. Clancy, 'Papist–Protestant–Puritan: English Religious Taxonomy 1565–1665', *RH* 13 (1975–6), 227–53, at p. 252, n. 128.

[15] Anstruther II, 328; PRO, SP 14/49/72, fo. 113ʳ.

[16] Anstruther II, 273; AAW, A XII, 425, 461.

[17] Daniel Price, *The Defence of Truth* (Oxford, 1610), 39. Among Leech's friends was Richard Kilby who preached a strongly Protestant funeral sermon for Thomas Holland in 1613, Richard Kilby, *A Sermon* (Oxford, 1613); *DNB*, *sub* Kilby, Richard; cf. Price, *Defence*, 87–8. Leech was a friend also of Theophilus Higgons while they were both at Christ Church, Higgons, *Apology*, 53. When Higgons returned to England and recanted at Paul's Cross, Francis Hore wrote from Venice to the secular clergy's agent in Rome that 'Mr Higgins (our Oxford minister) you may please to tell Mr Leech is fallen back againe', AAW, A X, 78. Leech appears to have been part of a circle of latent evangelicals in Oxford which included the schoolmaster Richard Ireland, and possibly also the royal chaplain Benjamin Carier, Anstruther II, 167; Hoby, *Letter*, sig. Q3ᵛ; Christ Church College MS xii. b. 48, fo. 15ʳ (showing that Higgons collected Richard Ireland's stipend for him); M. C. Questier, 'Crypto-Catholicism, Anti-Calvinism and Conversion at the Jacobean Court: The Enigma of Benjamin Carier', *JEH* 47 (1996), 45–64, at pp. 60–1.

[18] Price, *Defence*, 103; CRS 54, 213.

[19] Anstruther I, 128–9; John Gennings, *The Life and Death of Mr Edmund Geninges* (St Omer, 1614).

sympathy with a Calvinist theology of grace. They had read the *Institutes of the Christian Religion* and Walsingham had even consumed the writings of John Napier. In Yelverton's case, 'a book on the Contempt of the World' came to his notice and he 'began to be very ill at ease' with himself 'on the subject of overcoming ourselves by chastity, poverty and obedience'. Walsingham does not say specifically that evangelical concerns instigated his conversion to Rome. He says merely that he was thrown off balance by reading Persons's *Defence of the Censure*. But Persons's book contains extensive passages on the Catholic interpretation of evangelical perfection.[20]

Those Catholic renegades who continued their clerical careers in the Church of England stressed how evangelically zealous they had previously been as Romanists. Their zeal had merely been misdirected. Thomas Bell had been a Catholic fanatic, a preacher and proselytiser in the North for ten years before he changed sides.[21] Richard Sheldon had spent his time 'earnestlie labouring, by preaching, exhorting, writing, early and late, to draw all to a zealous profession of all doctrines' of the Roman Church.[22] John Copley claimed that he had been an active proselytiser before he recanted his Catholicism.[23] Bell's *Christian Dialogue* is dedicated to his 'approved good friends', leading Yorkshire puritan gentry Sir Stephen Procter, Sir Timothy Whittingham, Sir Timothy Hutton and the exchequer official Sir Vincent Skinner. Among his patrons he numbered Bishop Tobias Mathew.[24] He joined with the Yorkshire puritan clerical establishment to preach to a reluctant recusant audience in York Castle in 1600.[25] Other

---

[20] Foley I, 145; Francis Walsingham, *A Search Made into Matters of Religion* (St Omer, 1609), sig. **3ʳ⁻ᵛ; Robert Persons, *A Defence of the Censure* (Rouen, 1582), sigs. C7ᵛ–D5ʳ, Fʳ, pages to which Walsingham specifically refers, Walsingham, *Search* (1609), 13–14, 18.

[21] CRS 56, xxiii; PRO, SP 12/215/79; AAW, A IV, 453. Before his conversion to Catholicism in the 1570s he was equally enthusiastic, T. F. Knox (ed.), *The First and Second Diaries of the English College, Douay* (1878), 100–1; J. C. H. Aveling, *Northern Catholics* (1966), 28–9; *idem, Catholic Recusancy in the City of York 1558–1791* (CRS monograph 2, 1970), 43–4, 62; Richard Smith, replying to Thomas Bell's *The Downefall of Popery* (1604), said that 'no water . . . waxeth so could, as that which hath bene once hot: no enemies become so cruel to a common wealth, as Rebels who have bene once subject', Richard Smith, *An Answer to Thomas Bels late Challeng* (Douai, 1605), sig. c7ᵛ.

[22] Richard Sheldon, *The Motives of Richard Sheldon Pr.* (1612), sig. ¶4ʳ.

[23] John Copley, *Doctrinall and Morall Observations* (1612), 16, 18–19.

[24] Thomas Bell, *A Christian Dialogue* (1609), sig. A3ʳ; *idem, The Survey of Popery* (1596), sig. A3ʳ; *idem, The Catholique Triumph* (1610), sig. A3ʳ. He was not just roped in as a propagandist; he was keen to preach from the very first, AAW, A IV, 431. The earl of Huntingdon wanted Bell to remain in the North 'where the harvest is great, and the workmen few', John Strype, *Annals of the Reformation* (4 vols., Oxford, 1824), IV, 210–11.

[25] BL, Add. MS 34250, fo. 67ʳ. Some of Bell's citations and ideas about abandoning Rome are close to those which appear in Francis Bunny's *A Short Answer to the Reasons* (1595) (the appendix to *Truth and Falshood* (1595)). For their respective treatments of conscience,

renegade Catholics, like Thomas Clarke, William Hardesty and Miles Dawson also proselytised among the northern Romanists.[26] Catholics said that John Copley, after his conversion, started trying privately to persuade Catholics away from Rome.[27] Moderate Protestants noted how converts from among the evangelicals on each side (whom they disliked equally) tended to assume a similar position when they converted to the other Church. Laud observed that evangelical zeal allowed extremists, puritans and Jesuits, to cross from one extreme to the other: 'many rigid professors have turned Roman Catholics, and in that turn have been more Jesuited than any other', while on the other hand 'such Romanists as have changed from them have for the most part quite leaped over the mean, and been as rigid the other way as extremity itself'.[28] Richard Montagu, in similar vein, said that 'many, once Puritans, turne often Papists. And no marvell: for fleeting is commonly from one extreme unto another. Men of moving, violent, Quick-silver, Gun-powder spirits, can never rely upon middling courses, but runne . . . on headlong into extremes'.[29] In Thomas Abernethie, a Scot who abandoned the Society of Jesus in the 1630s, Laud and Montagu would seem to have had a point. In his recantation sermon he said it was natural for him to transfer straight from the Society to the Kirk. It makes a refreshing change, he says, since it distinguishes him from 'those who are converted, and come out of the Romish church' but 'use commonly to take them to a church, which endeavours to draw Protestants and papists to a conformitie, selecting out the best of both; because not in extremitie, but

---

Thomas Bell, *Thomas Bels Motives* (Cambridge, 1593), 9; Bunny, *Truth*, sig. Aa8ʳ, and, on the point of instructing the conscience, Bunny's admonitions are similar to those of another northern renegade, Thomas Clarke, Bunny, *Truth*, sig. Aa7ᵛ; Thomas Clarke, *The Recantation of Thomas Clarke* (1594), sig. A6ᵛ. Bell's polemical strategy, his conscious effort (his 'wonted manner') to use Romish authors to show how Catholicism is divided against itself, and his incessant repetition and self-quotation, is designed to persuade, not to alienate, M. C. Questier, 'The Phenomenon of Conversion: Change of Religion to and from Catholicism in England, 1580–1625' (DPhil. thesis, Sussex, 1991), 167–8; Bell, *Christian Dialogue*, 55; Philip Woodward, *Bels Trial Examined* (Rouen (imprint false, printed at Douai), 1608), sig. a4ᵛ–6ʳ. Bell stressed the practical value of repetition in any attempt to get unwelcome ideas into stubborn recusants' heads, Bell, *Christian Dialogue*, 98–102. Nevertheless, his tracts dwell little on the apocalyptic nature of Rome and concentrate instead on repelling the absurd accretions such as belief in Purgatory, a technique subscribed to by Thomas Clarke, who must have known Bell and converted at about the same time, Clarke, *Recantation*, sigs. A6ᵛ, Cviᵛ; cf. Thomas Bell, *The Golden Ballance of Tryall* (1603), fos. 29ᵛ–30ʳ (though Clarke did represent himself as departing from Babylon, Clarke, *Recantation*, sig. Bvʳ) and Bell's sermon in York Castle in 1600 was described as 'reasonable sober' which certainly distinguished it from some of the other puritan sermons delivered there, BL, Add. MS 34250, fo. 67ʳ.

26　Foley III, 762, 767–8; *HMC Salisbury MSS* VI, 339, VII, 404.
27　AAW, A XI, 23.
28　William Laud, ed. J. Bliss and W. Scott, *Works* (7 vols., Oxford, 1847–60), II, p. xv.
29　Richard Montagu, *Appello Caesarem* (1625), 112.

in mediocritie consisteth vertue', something which Abernethie utterly denies.[30]

In overtly evangelical changes of religion the intense focus on experience, the searching of the soul to see if one could be assured of saving grace, might prompt a temporary disengagement from polemical expressions of conversion. There was a common element in all evangelical conversion which contemporaries called 'resolution' (even if converts would afterwards describe their experience by reference to opposing doctrines of grace, and sometimes convey the intensity of their turning in religion by the most savage denunciations of confessional error). Roman and Protestant polemical disagreement about grace and conversion focused on philosophical quibbles over the extent of the will's independence and vitality. But Roman and Protestant evangelicals were both passionately concerned with the will's response to grace (in whatever way it was thought to be initiated). For both, effectual conversion is stimulated by arousing the will's 'resolution' to throw off the shackles of sin, even though they might disagree fiercely about the precise definition of how the will is made regenerate by grace. John Good saw his corrupt will could not prevent him from continuous lapses from communion with the Roman Church: 'what with the motives of my depraved will, prone to sensuality, suggestinge the facility of the solifidian way to salvation . . . I quickly fell back againe to the Doktrin and practise of the new Evangelicall libertie'. When by the illumination of God's spirit he is at last delivered from his doubts about which is the true Church 'ther wanted nothinge for my finall conversion, but to rectifie my depraved will'.[31] But actual rectification of the depraved will was something which happened outside the crude barbarity of ecclesiastical name-calling. It is significant that Richard Sheldon's polemical ridicule of John Gennings's martyrological life of Edmund Gennings deliberately does not mention the final chapter in which John Gennings describes his own entirely 'puritan' Catholic conversion experience.[32]

This was also the sensation of those who cited Robert Persons's *Christian Directory* (mentioned at the end of chapter 2 as a central conversion text) as the instigator of their changes of religion to Rome. The principal conversion which this book promoted (like the intense religious experience in the first week of Loyola's Spiritual Exercises to which the *Christian Directory* is

---

[30] Thomas Abernethie, *Abjuration of Popery* (Edinburgh, 1638), 35, 37; C.M. Hibbard, *Charles I and the Popish Plot* (North Carolina, 1983), 110, 113–14.

[31] BL, Lansd. MS 776, fos. 12^{r-v}, 46^r.

[32] Gennings, *Life*, 98–101; Richard Sheldon, *A Survey of the Miracles of the Church of Rome, proving them to be Antichristian* (1616); he must have recognised Gennings's model of resolution as authentic even if he could not subscribe to the chain of causation which Gennings adduced.

closely related) was not provoked by the book's Romanist phraseology.[33] It was designed to stir up the will. William Fitch's conversion (culminating in entry to the Capuchin order) commenced before he considered Roman Catholic doctrines, in fact when he read the puritan Edmund Bunny's Protestant expurgated edition of Persons's book.[34] He saw it as triggering within him a conversion which was purely evangelical though he described its later stages in standard Roman polemical terms.[35] The book's resolving tendency was as effectual for Richard Baxter as it was for William Fitch.[36] Neither the *Christian Directory* nor the Spiritual Exercises persuaded people to abandon doctrinal Protestantism by suggesting that the Roman Church propagated a superior spirituality. But the conversion which they promoted might be given expression subsequently by a decision to change one ecclesiastical setting for another as a considered response to the experience of grace. People might be subject to such motions only after they had become unsure about the integrity of the Church to which they belonged, but, in an important sense, security in one's ecclesiastical allegiance was possible only after one had grasped the knowledge of one's election and had experienced the comfortable resolving sensation of assurance. Francis Walsingham, as he drew towards the end of his fruitless polemical odyssey, said to his Catholic contact (evidently a Jesuit) that 'having setled now my mind [i.e. intellectually], I felt a good desire also in myself to accommodate my life for the time to come to a more diligent observation of Gods commandements', and the man points him in the direction of the first eight to ten days of the Spiritual Exercises with their 'purifying meditations on the malice of sin and the sufferings of hell', and also the 'necessity and sweetness of turning from one's old ways and attitudes'. The purpose of the Exercises is to dispose the soul so as to rid itself of its disordered affections. Walsingham felt complete confusion disrupting his affections as well as his will and intellect. His reading of polemical tracts has already convinced him (if he needed it) of the truth of Roman Catholic doctrine. But it leaves him unresolved. His evangelical conversion (which

---

33 Cf. J. W. O'Malley, *The First Jesuits* (Cambridge, Massachusetts, 1993), 38, 42. For the source material and construction of Robert Persons's *Christian Directory*, and for its relationship to the Spiritual Exercises, see V. Houliston, 'Why Robert Persons would not be Pacified', in T. M. McCoog and J. A. Munitiz (eds.), *The Reckoned Expense: Edmund Campion and the Early English Jesuits* (1996).

34 Jacques Brousse, *The Life of the Reverend Fa. Angel of Joyeuse* (Douai, 1623), sig. Bb2ᵛ–3ʳ.

35 Cf. CRS 54, 11, 139–40, 150, 198, 207, 234; BL, Lansd. MS 72, fo. 122ʳ (for the effect of chapter 7 in part II); cf. Foley I, 215–16.

36 Richard Baxter, *Directions and Persuasions to a Sound Conversion* (1683), 400. Baxter experienced grace through reading a Protestant edition of Persons's book, H. C. White, *English Devotional Literature [Prose] 1600–1640* (New York, 1966), 143.

confirms his suspicions that Rome is doctrinally sound) is not itself the product of intellectual enquiry but an active rousing of his will towards resolution. His re-orientation of self led him eventually to join the Society, a renunciation of the world to follow the evangelical counsels of perfection in a religious order.[37]

Theophilus Higgons's conversion tract, *The First Motive*, is an attack on three leading Protestant polemicists, Humphrey, Field and Morton, and is based on the principal scriptural and patristic texts from which the existence of Purgatory may be elicited.[38] On the surface the tract appears to state merely that Higgons accepts the infallible Church of Rome's teaching of this particular doctrine. But, in fact, it is an evangelical statement about sin and repentance, falling from and recovery of grace. Before he went abroad he had written a tract in which he explored the relationship between the concepts of mortal and venial sin (though in a mainly anti-Roman formulation).[39] His conversions backwards and forwards between the Churches occurred as the emphases on different elements of justification shifted about in his mind and promoted different models of assurance. If sin can be classified as venial and mortal then not only is the concept of Purgatory allowable but Catholic statements about the way grace is distributed in the world must also be true. (Protestant perceptions of freewill and sin do not permit the Roman distinction between degrees of sin.)[40] Higgons's tract proceeds to an attack on Protestants for their heretical rejection of Roman attitudes to assurance and the counsels of perfection, and, like Humphrey Leech (Higgons's friend), equates Protestant doctrine

---

[37] Walsingham, *Search* (1609), 505–7; cf. R. V. Caro, 'William Alabaster: Rhetor, Meditator, Devotional Poet', *RH* 19 (1988), 67–79, 155–70, at p. 66; G. M. Story and H. Gardner (eds.), *The Sonnets of William Alabaster* (1959), xvi; Questier, 'Phenomenon', 105–6; cf. J. de Guibert, *The Jesuits: Their Spiritual Doctrine and Practice* (St Louis, 1972), 124, 129–30, 532, describing the place of the counsels of perfection in the making of the Exercises (in which is provided 'a method for finding and embracing God's will, either in the choice of a state of life or in the manner of reforming and ordering one's life'); O'Malley, *First Jesuits*, 37, 39; Caro, 'William Alabaster', 164.

[38] E.g., Matthew 12: 32, and the Dialogues of Pope Gregory the Great (a recusant edition of which appeared in 1608).

[39] Hoby, *Letter*, 17, which tract on sin, Hoby says, was 'flat against the principles of that [Roman] profession'; Theophilus Higgons, *A Briefe Consideration of Mans Iniquitie, and Gods Justice* (1608).

[40] Bell, *Catholique Triumph*, 196–203; Stephen Denison, *The New Creature* (1619), 18, 20, 27 (rejecting Roman distinctions between venial and mortal sin and focusing instead on the 'great difference betwixt sinnes of infirmitie whereunto the children of God are subject, and sins of presumption whereunto the wicked are given'); Sir John Warner was convinced by the Roman connection between the evangelical counsels of perfection and Purgatory, Queen's College MS 284, fos. 203ᵛ–4ʳ; the hearing of his converter's discourse about Purgatory was the first thing to awaken in him those 'motives of Change in my Condicion of life', *ibid.*, fo. 203ᵛ.

on this point with the Jovinian heresy in the early Church.[41] Higgons's
perception (as a Catholic) of a 'triple estate of men deceased', those in
heaven, hell and, thirdly, 'in some temporall payn' has a family resemblance
to Leech's quadripartite division of men with some neither saved nor damned
who are temporarily in doubt of their salvation, and therefore must seek
assurance of it.[42] For both Higgons and Leech the agent of change was the
godly search for assurance, the central concern of evangelicals in both Churches.
Anybody could decide that one or other Church was true or false, but,
unless they were regenerate, all evangelicals were agreed, their decision-
making would be irremediably flawed by sin. Their conversion under the
aegis of grace was required first and then they would inevitably adhere to
a true Church with a right faith. Thus the preachers on both sides
distinguished between nominal membership of a Church (true or otherwise)
and life in grace. A decision merely to belong to the Church of England or
the Church of Rome was itself no more than a nominal conversion (although
Catholics in polemic laid greater stress on the importance of visible
membership).[43] John Good was given 'a pure and intire' Catholic education
by his parents but fell away from the Roman Church when he went to
university. This instability in faith he associated with moral depravity. Yet
his resumption of outward Roman faith when he left Oxford did not lead to
any fixity of resolution or correction of his inward nature.[44] As the minister
Richard Kilby argued, all conversion, at base, was evangelical; or rather,
all conversion was unstable unless anchored by grace and discerned in
assurance. He had converted to Rome and become a recusant. For fear he
had occasionally conformed, but his reprobate's heart was hard and where
he 'found any of that religion' he 'was still sutable unto them'. Next he
became enamoured of those he calls puritans 'and in some points was readie
to runne beyond them'. Now he stands amazed 'how fervent' he had been,
'first a Protestant, then a Roman Catholike, afterward a Precisian'; the
lesson is that 'till you bee . . . setled in true godlinesse, it is vaine . . . and

[41] Theophilus Higgons, *Try before you Trust* (Douai, 1609), 63–6; Humphrey Leech, *A Triumph of Truth* (Douai, 1609), 44, 100–1, 105; cf. *idem, Dutifull and Respective Considerations* (St Omer, 1609), 111 which attacks Field over Purgatory as does Higgons's *The First Motive of T. H. Maister of Arts, and lately Minister, to suspect the Integrity of his Religion* (Douai, 1609). Robert Persons's 'Confession of Faith' of July 1580 explaining his change of religion implies that his doctrinal conversion focused heavily on the Jovinian heresy, CRS 39, 36–7; C. Dent, 'Protestants in Elizabethan Oxford' (DPhil. thesis, Oxford, 1980), 420.

[42] Higgons, *First Motive*, 25–6. Higgons cited Augustine to the effect that the prayer of the Church for the deceased is heard 'yet for such onely as (being regenerated in Christ) did neither live so ill, that . . . they be made unworthy of mercy; nor yet so well . . . as that they have no need thereof', *ibid.*, 4; Leech, *Triumph*, 2.

[43] William Hinde, *A Faithfull Remonstrance* (1641), 16; Bell, *Christian Dialogue*, 102.

[44] BL, Lansd. MS 776, fos. 11ᵛ–12ʳ.

dangerous to hammer and meddle with points of religion'. All movement between religion not dictated by grace is likely to be the result of deception.[45] The puritan Robert Bolton fluctuated aimlessly between the Churches of Rome and England (because he was immersed in popish ungodly behaviour) until he perceived himself to be subject to the workings of grace.[46] Similarly William Hinde distinguished between John Bruen's abandonment of popery when he went to university and his subsequent 'more effectual calling'.[47] William Fitch, who reformed his life to the extent of becoming a Capuchin, says in his spiritual autobiography that 'there was nothing els to bee seene in mee, but a superficiall shewe and outward apparance of a carelesse Christian' because he was 'not then a branch of the true vine'.[48] John Dove noted the 'perplexitie, unstayednesse, and trouble of mind' of those whom he regarded as purely formal Protestants, those 'which have renounced that religion [of Rome], and imbraced ours'. Yet their conversion has not been effectual and so, 'lying at the point of death, in the midst of their conflicts and tentations, thinking upon the arguments which are brought on each side', they die 'unresolved'. Worse, they have in their indecision turned papist again, and, like Lot's wife, 'looked backe unto Sodome'.[49] James Wadsworth snr cited Cardinal Pole to the effect that 'one cause of so much heresy in these latter times was in too busily disputing about our faith, before we tooke any care to reforme our life', and that 'it is unlike they will be freed from perverse errors, who do continue their lives in obstinate vices'.[50] Tobias Mathew jnr says that when engaged in conversation with Robert Persons in Rome Persons never urged him 'expressly to any alteration of . . . [his] opinion . . . only that . . . [he] would make the search of true religion' his 'greatest business'. When Persons wrote his 'Memorial' for the re-Catholicising of England he said that though there should be public disputations (to settle doctrinal points once and for all) 'afterwards few Books would be needful on our part, as in truth it were to be wished, that few or none were written in the Vulgar Tongue, against Hereticks: but rather that Books of Devotion, and vertuous Life should enter

[45] Richard Kilby, *The Burthen of a loaden Conscience* (Cambridge, 1616), 8–10; for Kilby, cf. P. Lake, 'Richard Kilby: A Study in Personal Failure', in W. J. Sheils and D. Wood (eds.), *The Ministry: Clerical and Lay* (Studies in Church History 26, Oxford, 1989), 221–35.

[46] J. Morgan, *Godly Learning* (Cambridge, 1986), 31; Robert Bolton, *Mr Boltons Last and Learned Worke of the Foure last Things* (1633), sig. b3ʳ–5ᵛ.

[47] Hinde, *Faithfull Remonstrance*, 15–18, 42.

[48] Brousse, *Life*, sig. Aa8ʳ.

[49] John Dove, *A Perswasion to the English Recusants* (1603), 8.

[50] Wadsworth, *Contrition*, preface, sig. Bᵛ–2ʳ; cf. Wadsworth's letters to Bedell saying that his intention is to be fervent in devotion rather than in polemic, William Bedell, *The Copies of Certaine Letters* (1624), 15, 17.

in their place'.[51] Catholic converts who ascribed their conversions to an exercise of the will were subscribing to an experience of grace which was identical to the one pursued by puritan converts who otherwise seem so different in their emphasis on the primacy of grace and the passivity of the will. William Fitch's conversion was generated by an experimental attitude to grace which had no regard for doctrinal division. He realised that he had been 'delivered by this inspiration, that on my parte I ought to doe my duety, and soe I should trie whether I should bee saved or damned, which whosoever doth hee cannot perish'. He was concerned not so much by the problem of whether he should adhere to the Roman or English Church but that the signs of assurance which he was experiencing should prove to be temporary only, and that he should not persevere. As his evangelical experience started to combine with elements of political and polemical affiliation, he began to express his new sense of assurance through polemical attacks on Protestant doctrines, but the two aspects of his conversion continued to operate separately though now in tandem. One did not subsume the other. Once he had opted for the Church of Rome his main concern was to establish which evangelical degree to pursue – whether to join a religious order and, if so, which one.[52] The severity of his, to all intents and purposes, puritan conversion experience translated into the austerity of the reformed Franciscans.

The evangelical impulse experienced by converts was not, therefore, confined within any doctrinal, far less polemical, formulation, though it might well be expressed in polemical thoughts. That this was so is clearly evident in the disputes in Oxford over grace and conversion which revolved around the Jacobean *cause célèbre* of Humphrey Leech. His ideas, Arminianism *avant la lettre*, have been interpreted as an attack on an English Calvinist consensus about predestination. Historians have seen his polemic as an attempt to make his own radical proto-Arminian ideas seem mainstream at a time when they were clearly not and to label his genuinely mainstream Protestant opponents as a 'faction'. His enemies, like Henry Aglionby, accused him of fronting an anti-Calvinist faction in Oxford.[53] But the ecclesiastical acrobatics which took him from a Calvinist Oxford college to the Society of Jesus were not performed simply because he was a loser in Oxford's factional squabbles. It is impossible to explain the curious circumstances of his change of religion by remarking just that he held a

[51] A. H. Mathew (ed.), *A True Historical Relation of the Conversion of Sir Tobie Matthew* (1904), 33; Robert Persons, ed. E. Gee, *The Jesuit's Memorial for the Intended Reformation of England* (1690), 38–40; for the intention and purpose of Persons's tract, Vatican Archives, Nunziature Diversa 264, fo. 239ʳ.

[52] Brousse, *Life*, sigs. Bb4ᵛ–5ʳ, Dd6ʳ–8ʳ.

[53] Leech, *Triumph*, 63–4.

doctrine of grace which was distasteful to the Protestant establishment. Leech asserted that his conversion was, at first, unrelated to any intention to reject Reformed doctrines of grace, and that his ideas were not inimical to mainstream English Protestantism. He claimed that he delivered the first version of his notorious 'popish' sermon with a 'Protestant' mind.[54] He may have been telling the truth. The emergence of his own evangelical impulses and experiences was certainly not under Roman auspices. Only the aggravated circumstances of its expression inevitably pointed him towards describing his conversion in vitriolic Roman phraseology. Like William Barrett he exacerbated conflict by taking the offensive against his opponents who might otherwise have left him alone.[55] Even Daniel Price conceded that the Christian doctrines of evangelical perfection were extremely fluid. He admitted with a bad grace that when Leech's Calvinist persecutor, John King, listened to the first version of Leech's sermon, he gave 'no signification of dislike conceyved by him against the verity of this doctrine'. Price detects a concession in Leech's tract that what is said there could be delivered in a Protestant (which for Price means Reformed) format.[56] Leech's stated doctrinal position was that works of supererogation are desirable. Men should strive to follow the 'counsayles' of perfection rather than just have regard for the precepts of the Law. He does not deny that decrees of election are immutable. The counsels of evangelical perfection are not meant to affect, far less displace, decrees of election and reprobation. He has no desire to 'shake the certaintie, of anie soules salvation, rightlie builte on gods election'; his aim is only 'to give a caveat to all . . . to dehort us from all sinfull secure presumption of heaven'.[57] One has to separate the polemical statements in his motives tract which follow the standard lines of debate from those things which he says spurred him to consider his standing in grace (as opposed to his standing in the Church of England). It is too crude to describe him just as an anti-Calvinist if by that is meant one who intellectually took up a series of academic propositions about grace to distinguish himself from those who professed a Reformed soteriology.

Leech's consistent subject throughout his Protestant and Roman phases is vows in religion. Protestants like Price did not object to such vows in

---

[54] Questier, 'Phenomenon', 121–3.

[55] Lake, *Moderate Puritans*, 205–6.

[56] Price claims, though there is no way of checking, that Leech's first sermon really was Reformed in tone, and that by the third version words like 'superstition' (as an historical corrupter of evangelical perfection) had replaced words like 'supererogation' in the earlier recensions, Price, *Defence*, 32, 60, 168, 197; Leech, *Triumph*, 3. Leech said that he had moral support even from Calvinists like Ravis, his patron. Price firmly denied all such claims, but it is evident that he means that if Leech did have such friends they did not actively risk supporting his opinions, Price, *Defence*, 243.

[57] Leech, *Triumph*, 34.

themselves. As Hakewill, Benjamin Carier's opponent, wrote, 'wee neither speake nor write against lawfull "Vowes", but the rashnesse of them, and impossibilitie in performing them: Not against "true Virginity"; but the fained shew of it . . . Not against "necessarie Povertie", but the voluntarie choise of it, when more good may be done by possessing and using those meanes God hath sent us'.[58] Price, even in polemic, admits that 'there may be a "verball distinction" of "precepts" and "Counsells"'. What he abhors and detests is 'the maintaining of them, as the workmen of Babell uphold them'.[59] The evangelical structure of conversion was the same. Yet a different perception of human nature meant that Leech and his enemies saw the other's appropriation of grace as flawed. They expressed their enmity through different theological definitions of election and predestination which allowed them to opine that their opponents were wilfully disrupting the divine economy of grace within the Church. 'Counsells tie not all', wrote Price, 'but those only who are better enabled with guifts then others or tied by their vocation to some stricter courses'. In Richard Baxter's words, 'the Resolution and Vow of cleaving unto God in Faith and Holy Obedience, and of renouncing the Flesh, the World, and the Devil, this is for all'.[60] Catholic evangelicals would hardly have disagreed that 'counsels tie not all'; not everyone is required to enter the religious life.[61] They would have consented also, *mutatis mutandis*, to Baxter's dictum that evangelical conversion was in some sense necessary for all the Elect. They simply castigated the Protestant expression of the intense experience of grace by arguing that it relied falsely on an unmerciful God saving and damning without respect to men's works.

Still, the polemic could only partially conceal what all of an evangelical tendency knew affectively to be true: that rival confessional schemes of grace could at best only comment on grace itself. Like all others evangelicals Leech was principally concerned with the problem of the will in conversion; not the academic question of free will, but the more practical problem of how the will might be thought to be capable of stimulation under the effects of

---

58 George Hakewill, *An Answere to a Treatise Written by Dr Carier* (1616), 152; cf. Baxter, *Directions*, 446, objecting to Catholic evangelical vows: 'in unnecessary matters, I had rather you were too backward to Vow. Some will Vow poverty, and some a single Life . . . such Vows as these may be good for some . . . but they are not for all'; Sorlien, *Diary*, 206 reporting a sermon by Henry Parry on the Protestant interpretation of vows in religion.

59 Price, *Defence*, 168–9; cf. R. P. Sorlien (ed.), *The Diary of John Manningham* (Hanover, New Hampshire, 1976), 206.

60 Price, *Defence*, 169; Baxter, *Directions*, 446.

61 Jensen, 'Life', 164. Brousse urged Protestants to consider 'whe[ther] they have any among them comparable to Catholiques in all Christian vertue charitie, humilitie, patience, obedience, modestie, chastitie, contempt of the world and mortification of the flesh', and that 'for concupiscence, whoe seeth not that [in English Protestant religion] it is withheld by noe bridle', Brousse, *Life*, sigs. *8ᵛ, Aa5ʳ⁻ᵛ.

grace.[62] He says that the purpose of the evangelical counsels of perfection is 'to make . . . [our] callinge, and election sure'. This is the shared refrain of all the evangelically inclined in this period. 'Experimental predestinarians' of the Protestant puritan kind as much as the ones considering the religious life in a Roman setting looked to the verse 2 Peter 1: 10: 'give all diligence to make your calling and election sure: for if ye do these things, ye shall never fall'.[63] Through assurance the puritan does not think to fulfil the Covenant by sanctified activity but wants to see whether he is in the Covenant at all. Evidence was found largely in experience. Sanctifying activity did not have to reach a certain level to merit saving grace but was evidence of unmerited Covenantal grace.[64] There was always a certain tension between belief in absolute and double predestination and the quest for assurance, though, as von Rohr shows, intellectually it could be contained within Covenantal thought. Struggle to gain assurance might express itself even in quasi-despairing internal spiritual conflict. But this, in the Elect, as William Harrison's sermon on the death of Katherine Brettergh carefully showed, was to demonstrate the strength of the Covenant and that the Elect could not fall totally and finally.[65]

The 'tension inherent between the emphasis simultaneously placed upon an emotional searching for communion with God . . . and upon the divine sovereignty in election' (as Alistair McGrath describes it) is the same for Humphrey Leech and William Perkins.[66] Of course, in one sense, Leech's tract follows the rules of polemic outlined in chapter 2. He takes a principle on which all are agreed – the need for assurance – and substitutes a sense of assurance which his puritan enemies would not accept. But the historical circumstances of Leech's long-drawn-out conflict with his enemies at Oxford show that his search for assurance was not a voluntaristic excess which derived from a reaction to Calvinist severity. In his evangelical

---

[62] Cf. Sutcliffe, *Unmasking*, 52.

[63] Kendall, *Calvin*, 8; A. McGrath, *Iustitia Dei* (2 vols., Cambridge, 1986), II, 115; von Rohr, *Covenant*, 122; *idem*, 'Covenant and Assurance in Early English Puritanism', *Church History* 34 (1965), 195–203, at pp. 195–7; O. C. Watkins, *The Puritan Experience* (1972), 21–2; Stephen Denison argued that the possibility of finding assurance is a logical guarantee as well as consequence of the Calvinist doctrines of freewill and predestination; otherwise there would be nothing to be assured of, Denison, *New Creature*, 16, 67.

[64] Von Rohr, 'Covenant', *passim*.

[65] William Harrison, *Deaths Advantage Little Regarded* (1612), 14, 81–3. Lancashire Catholics had spitefully put rumours about that she died in despair. Puritans like Stephen Denison argued that internal spiritual conflict was a necessary part of conversion: there will always be a combat 'betweene the flesh and the spirit', 'for there is none truly regenerate, but they have a combat within them', Denison, *New Creature*, 70; cf. Brousse, *Life*, sig. Bb2r, for William Fitch's continual temptations and trials of faith.

[66] McGrath, *Iustitia Dei*, II, 112; Dent argues that Leech's doctrinal definition of evangelical counsels 'had grown out of the same general understanding of election as that of the Calvinist doctors', Dent, 'Protestants', 422.

counsels sermon Leech was describing his conversion before he even considered the question of which particular Church it should be expressed in. As elements of his spiritual experience became absorbed into a very real polemical debate about how the central questions of justification should be phrased and answered, Leech's concern with assurance (which really was mainstream) started to filter out towards the fringes of English Protestant thought. There it began to be picked up by Roman polemical ideas as well as Roman forms of practical spirituality. By a combination of polemical expressions and political pressures he was compelled towards the thought that the Church of England was not a true Church because it restricted his evangelical impulses. People like Leech converted not because of pure doctrinal disagreements but because the 'Calvinist' Church of England did not seem to have a place for their concept of evangelical zeal. His quasi-'puritan' concept of conversion found itself channelled into the Society of Jesus.

Leech was an unusual case because he so clearly broadcast his specific theological concerns in print. But his experience was undoubtedly typical of those who changed religion in this way. John Campion, a trainee seminarist in the 1630s, partly through temporal motives and material misfortune, resolved to 'take some course for the security of . . . [his] soule', but initially he 'dreampt of no other religion' than that of the Church of England. His decision to convert was the result of a perception that 'the church of England had not provided meanes whereby I might effectually put in practice these resolucions' and so he found himself 'wholy unable to doe the least part of what . . . [he] desired'.[67] Even the superficially rather unevangelical Benjamin Carier can be assimilated into this paradigm. Despite his lack of clerical promotion and his unsuccessful career at Court (particularly his failure to break into the moderate Protestant faction around those later to be classed as Arminians), the motives which he voiced during the long period in which he wavered between England and Rome include references to specifically Catholic evangelical concepts of grace and conversion. For him, as much as Leech, Walsingham, Fitch or any of the others, the absence of a clear division in theology (outside polemic) and his belief (retained until quite late) that the Church of England was a true Church, meant that he was confronted with a confusing array of competing positions in religion. He resolved them by leaving England and associating on the Continent first with the Capuchins and then with those spiritual past masters, the Jesuits.[68]

---

[67] CRS 55, 429; Stonyhurst, Collectanea C, fo. 199ᵛ.
[68] C. Dodd, *The Church History of England* (3 vols., Brussels (imprint false, printed at Wolverhampton), 1737–42), II, 508–17; CU Libr., MS Mm 2 23, 29; Balliol MS 270, p. 160; AAW, A XII, 389, 421, XIII, 141–2, 216.

The evangelical converts' reaction against their present ecclesiastical setting was directed against a polemically perceived expression of that Church. The animus which they developed against their Church provided an artificially defined but powerful springboard from which to make a decisive change of life as well as doctrine. Thus William Fitch, addicted to 'transitory pleasures, and the vanities of the worlde', sensed a struggle between his spiritual and carnal wills in the unprofitable setting of a Church where the ministers taught that 'all sinns are mortall . . . by only faith thou maist bee saved', as if the Church of England denied the possibility of assurance altogether (whereas it merely presented one particular definition of it).[69] Protestant converts who abandoned Rome stressed that they had attempted to exercise their evangelical impulses according to the Roman concept of the religious life, but that the Roman setting prevented their effectual conversion.[70]

The similarity of the godly's perception of the practical effects of grace meant that it was possible for those of an evangelical persuasion in either Church to enter into a central evangelical stream of consciousness (from which they might, however, emerge in a different ecclesiastical setting). William Fitch's contemporary biographer says God enlightened him through 'the clouds and foggs of heresye, wherewith his soule was infected' and 'in one moment hee was wholy changed into an other man'; but only after this was he plunged into doubt about Protestant religion. The doubt about which religion he should embrace was simply one of the series of subsequent spiritual conflicts brought about by his experience of grace.[71] The mechanisms which could be used to bring about evangelical change, like Persons's *Christian Directory*, did not irenically ignore polemic. They were simply concerned with a chronological period in grace before polemical differences became significant.[72]

EVANGELICALS AND THE CHURCH

In conclusion, the evangelicals' perception of grace did not slavishly follow polemical formulations of change of religion but still informed perceptions of institutional division between the Churches of England and Rome. The

---

[69] Brousse, *Life*, sig. Bb3ᵛ–4ʳ.
[70] John Nichols, *A Declaration of the Recantation of John Nichols* (1581), sig. Bvʳ.
[71] K. Emery, *Renaissance Dialectic and Renaissance Piety* (New York, 1987), 14; Brousse, *Life*, sig. Aa3ʳ⁻ᵛ.
[72] Jensen observes that the similarity of Catholic devotional techniques devoted towards essentially evangelical ends, defeating the world, the flesh and the Devil, made it potentially attractive to evangelicals who were not members of the Church of Rome, Jensen, 'Life', 150–1, 161–2.

godly tended to see the Church, partly visible and partly invisible, as defined by their understanding of evangelical conversion and apostasy. Thus Daniel Featley, in his preface to the tract by the renegade Ferdinand Texeda, wrote that 'the Church of Christ . . . resembles the Sea, which, what it looseth in one place, it alwaies gaines in another. And therefore let no weake Christian be scandalized at the revolt of so many now a dayes to Popish errors and superstitions'. Apostasy from the Church of England is no slur on it, merely an illustration of the temporary faith of the reprobate. No one should be surprised at 'the Apostacie of seeming Saints, and revolt of outward professors of the truth'.[73] George Abbot, whose chaplain Featley was, had the same thoughts in mind when he told William Trumbull that Benjamin Carier's defection was an irrelevance: 'this doctor for many years hath not been held sound, so that we shall lose nothing by his departure'.[74] Joseph Hall said the same to Roman triumphalists: 'you say, your religion dayly winneth. Brag not of your gaine: you neither need, nor can, if you consider how it gets, and whom'; 'if all our licentious hypocrites were yours, wee should not complaine'.[75] Featley envisaged a 'Jacob's ladder' with individuals on it continually ascending and descending in grace. Archbishop de Dominis's recent defection has been balanced by the conversion of Texeda: 'not to goe farre for instances at this present, for an Italian Apostata, we have a Spanish Convert'.[76]

Movement between the Church of Rome and the Church of England became an aspect of the gathering of the Elect and Reprobate respectively to Zion and Babylon, the working out of God's secret decrees, not just a set of intellectual decisions that one institution had greater doctrinal integrity than another. Witness therefore the contemporary phenomenon of conversion in spite of self. Many claimed that they changed religion as they struggled against the arguments of the side to which they were converting. The brothers John and William Rainolds converted each other out of their respective Churches.[77] Those, like Francis Walsingham and John Pickford,

---

[73] Ferdinand Texeda, *Texeda Retextus* (1623), sig. A3ʳ, A4ʳ.

[74] *HMC Downshire MSS* IV, 193–4. Abbot was delighted at at the conversion of Anthony Clarke, a canon at Ghent: 'they [now] had one come that wold answer D. Carier', AAW, A XII, 486.

[75] Joseph Hall, *The Works of Joseph Hall* (1634), 312.

[76] Texeda, *Texeda Retextus*, sig. A4ʳ.

[77] The sonnet versifying this event was written by William Alabaster, Bodl., Tanner MS 306, fo. 138ʳ. According to John Racster, *A Booke of the Seven Planets* (1598), fo. 43ʳ, Alabaster was 'perverted' 'by meanes of private conference with a certain seminary priest [Thomas Wright], whom in prison he labored to convert'. Cf. other similar contemporary accounts of conversion, George Carleton, trans. William Freake, *The Life of Bernard Gilpin* (1629), 2–4 (for Gilpin's discovery of Protestant truth as he sought to confute Peter Martyr); Godfrey Goodman, ed. J. S. Brewer, *The Court of King James the First* (2 vols., 1839), I, 406.

who say that they were converted by books, state that they had rejected initially those books which converted them.[78] John Copley says that God's providence ensured that he had a view of controversies in religion 'that whilest my studies and labours my purpose and designement was to draw others into the net of Rome, I my selfe was led into the sheepefold wherof Christ in heaven is the chiefe Pastor'.[79] Richard Sheldon likewise noted the effects of providence in this respect: God works on those whom he has 'segregated to himselfe' from all eternity, so that 'often, contrarie to their intended purposes, and designes' he works 'their conversions to him, when they least dreame thereof: yea when they are purposely, and obstinatelie striving against it'.[80] Sir Oliver Manners was converted to Rome by John Gerard who lured him on by getting him to argue *against* Catholicism.[81] The future seminarist Edward Fenton in Dublin was called upon by his Protestant landlady to fend off the attempts of a Catholic to convert her to Rome; the argument veered into the evangelical area of penance and Fenton was ensnared.[82] Edward Laithwait was similarly converted after he travelled to Exeter gaol for the express purpose of dissuading his brother Thomas from the Church of Rome.[83]

This phenomenon was hardly hidden from contemporaries. The regular flow of godly converts forwards and backwards over the boundaries of the institutional Churches could not have told them anything else, though the polemical books did their best to conceal it. Of course, relatively few people left an account of their conversions in terms of an evangelical riot, and there was often little incentive to broadcast them at all. But, each time that this did happen, the conversion narrative tapped into and presented a radical commentary on themes which were common and central to a great deal of mainstream religious discourse. The significance of conversion to and from Rome does not lie in the numbers who tied their evangelical leanings to an ecclesiastical transfer of allegiance but in the very fact that it was possible for contemporaries to exploit the broad topics of grace,

---

[78] Francis Walsingham claims that he read Robert Persons's *Defence of the Censure* only with the intention of 'gathering . . . some absurdities out of it', and that the book threw him into mental turmoil, CRS 54, 170; Walsingham, *Search* (1609), sig. **3r; Carier was said to have begun reading patristic writers with the intention of impugning them, CU Libr., MS Mm 2 23, p. 29; Pickford initially rejected Matthew Kellison's *Survey*, P. Milward, *Religious Controversies of the Jacobean Age* (1978), 138; cf. J. H. Pollen, *Acts of English Martyrs* (1891), 236; William Fitch's first sight of the *Christian Directory* induced in him an unwelcome 'remorse of conscience' and he tried unsuccessfully to put the book out of his mind, Brousse, *Life*, sig. Bb3r.

[79] Copley, *Doctrinall and Morall Observations*, 16; cf. Clancy, 'Papist–Protestant–Puritan', 243, for the similar instance of the ardent Lancashire puritan Sir Cecil Trafford.

[80] Sheldon, *Motives*, sig. ¶3r.

[81] P. Caraman (ed.), *John Gerard* (1951), 185–6.

[82] CRS 54, 232–3.   [83] Foley IV, 630.

election and assurance within the standard forms of ecclesiastical warfare adopted by rivals for control over the English Church. Conversely, the conflict between papists and Protestants, conversions showed, was never merely polemical squabbling (though occasionally made bloody by the political insecurity generated out of the ideology of religious zealots). So evangelical freedom of expression was not constrained by conflict over religion, nor was such conflict toned down by the knowledge that the bitterest opponents shared central evangelical concerns.

For these reasons also this nexus between grace and the Church was a matter of concern for more than a few peculiarly intense clerics. The evangelical understanding of conversion, spiritual turning in religion, informed the division between the Churches of England and Rome, just as movements between the Churches were statements about rival concepts of grace. All changes of religion were a constant source of comment on the regime's stewardship of the Church. Movements in religion, as they affected conformity to the established Church, were of concern to the State. Change of religion was not something which was left for university dons to argue about. The ecclesiastical quarrel between Rome and England meant that several different types of authority, clerical and secular, as well as several different interest groups deprived of authority, were determined to exert an influence over and to appropriate the various processes of conversion. With this in mind, the chapters which follow examine how contemporaries tried to govern and instigate change of religion. How did contemporaries think that true religion could be spread? What was the connection between conformity, dissent and conversion? To what extent did the State's efforts to control movement in religion succeed in making England a Protestant nation?

5

The Church under the law: the regime and the enforcement of conformity

The occasionally shrill arguments of the historians about the pace of Protestantisation after 1560 and the thoroughness with which dissenting conservative (and, later, more overtly Romish) forms of religious belief and observance were reformed have focused very largely on the role of the State's apparatus of enforcement. Could the regime direct and, if necessary, torment intractable people sufficiently to make them convert to some form of Protestantism? Of course, the regime never really stood in the place of the godly evangelists whose task it was to banish the darkness of popery. But, as we have seen, since all types of movement in religion reflected on each other, all fluctuation in religion had a political dimension. So the regime was compelled to consider the ways in which conversion affected ecclesiastical uniformity. Change of religion was not only a private matter for the individual but also a public one over which the authorities could rightly demand some influence. Still, how far might the State's political agenda dictate the opinions of individuals about the Church? Were its own legitimate concerns to change some people's political allegiances successfully combined with inducements for them to alter their religious views? Considerable effort was made by Tudor and Stuart legislators to force people to abandon aspects of their loyalty to the Roman Church. Since recusant Catholicism was not obviously extinguished by force of law, the 'revisionist' historiography of English post-Reformation Catholicism has argued that the State failed in its purpose. But we must consider whether this 'failure' was the result of an early modern government's inability to control religious thought and practice, or whether it was a matter of the regime's policy aims having only a passing acquaintance with the religious programme of the Protestant evangelicals who also wanted to crush popery, but for slightly different reasons.

Did the State require people to become Protestants or merely to conform to the letter of the law? Protestants like William Fulke were dubious about how far the State could compel true religion. If the enforcement of the law meant just the creation of a floating body of church papists, then such 'mere' conformity was very distasteful to the godly.[1] At first glance, the official statutory programme for securing change of religion is only a pale shadow of the plans to instigate godly conversion inspired by competing clerical theologies. The requirement in secular and ecclesiastical law was that all should conform to a minimum standard – attendance at divine service as approved by the State. Weekly attendance there was stipulated by the act of uniformity of 1559. Most subsequent recusancy penalties punished failure to appear regularly in a church. Obviously, other activities were prohibited – for example, hearing the Roman Mass, or procuring it to be said, or being reconciled to Rome or procuring the reconciliation of others. But the unchanging basis of all statutory conformity (sufficient to satisfy secular and ecclesiastical judges alike) was to present oneself, however unwillingly or irreverently, at one's local church.

If the standard of conformity was so low, we may wonder whether forcing the recalcitrant to attend the rituals of the book of common prayer achieved anything at all? A man could appear in a Protestant church at time of divine service while remaining thoroughly Catholic at heart. His alienation from the established Church might even be increased by the pressure to attend a form of worship he disliked. Indeed, conformity enforced by law as part of a battle between Catholics and Protestants might well be seen as counterproductive for the State. As the translator of Persons's *Epistle of the Persecution* wrote in the book's preface (addressed to the privy council),

if your honours shoulde upon terrour bringe any fraile man to conforme him selfe against his conscience, in such externall actes, as you require: yet your wisdomes can not but consider, that he is never the nearer gotten for this, but rather in his harte muche farther of then before, havinge wounded his sowle and conscience upon compulsion, whiche, lyinge grevouse and festeringe with in his breast, must needes often put him in mynde of the injurye receaved, and so more detest the thynge done, then before.[2]

William Allen marvelled that the Protestant authorities should think to derive benefit from compelling Catholics to conform and 'professe that out- wardly, which is knowen they hate in their hartes inwardly', and that it is folly to imagine that such 'othes and statutes do chaunge their [i.e. Catholics'] meanings, though they alter their countenances'.[3]

So, was conformity by those we know to have been in some sense Catholic

[1] William Fulke, *A briefe Confutation, of a Popish Discourse* (1581), fo. 7r; Francis Bunny, *An Answere to a Popish Libell* (Oxford, 1607), 114–15.
[2] Robert Persons, *An Epistle of the Persecution* (Rouen, 1582), 8–9.
[3] William Allen, *An Apologie and True Declaration of the Institution and Endevours of the two English Colleges* (Rheims, 1581), fo. 102v.

anything more than a facade? It seems to be generally agreed that many nonconformists 'relaxed their consciences . . . at regular intervals' during this period, and that prominent 'Catholic' families lapsed into occasional conformity from time to time to avoid the penalties of the law. Several studies have shown that, in those parts of the country where recusancy merged with occasional conformity, mere readiness by recusants to attend church cannot be taken as a sign of changed religious opinion.[4] Aveling calculates that of seventy gentry families in the North Riding of Yorkshire which had Catholic elements, no more than nine had a 'record clear of lapses'. The replies of the students who entered the English College in Rome demonstrate the kaleidoscopic variations in religious opinion among the families even of those who said their religious background was papist.[5] It is arguable, therefore, that just attending the local church was an essentially negative act and had virtually no connection with a person's actual religious beliefs.[6] An archiepiscopal visitation in 1590 reported that Richard Lawson of York 'comes seldom to church and stayeth not when he cometh'.[7] Was Lawson rejecting Romanist dissenting beliefs by such behaviour? Did the State really profit from having a Catholic attend his local church if he made it plain to other parishioners that he thought little of the service or the preacher? The problems occasioned by the severe legal sanctions against recusancy occasioned a heated debate among English Catholics in the 1580s and 1590s about the admissibility of occasional conformity or church papistry. Catholic supporters of occasional conformity (who could marshal casuistically a very good array of arguments for the practice) asserted that of itself attending a Protestant church was an indifferent matter, something

---

[4] V. Burke, 'Catholic Recusants in Elizabethan Worcestershire' (MA thesis, Birmingham, 1972), 308; Davidson, 'Roman Catholicism in Oxfordshire from the Late Elizabethan Period to the Civil War *c.* 1560–1640' (Ph.D thesis, Bristol, 1970),' 101, 235–6; A. Dunbabin, 'Post-Reformation Catholicism in the Parish of Prescot, Lancashire, from the Elizabethan Settlement to the Civil War' (MA thesis, Manchester, 1980), 23–4, 75–6, 77–80.

[5] J. C. H. Aveling, *Northern Catholics* (1966), 190; see also J. T. Cliffe, *The Yorkshire Gentry from the Reformation to the Civil War* (1969), 182; M. C. Questier, 'The Phenomenon of Conversion: Change of Religion to and from Catholicism in England, 1580–1625' (DPhil. thesis, Sussex, 1991), 91–2; M. O'Dwyer, 'Catholic Recusants in Essex *c.* 1580 to *c.* 1600' (MA thesis, London, 1960), 83–4, 93, 96–7, 188; R. B. Manning, 'Catholics and Local Office Holding in Elizabethan Sussex', *BIHR* 35 (1962), 47–61, at pp. 52–3, 60; CRS 54–5, *passim.*

[6] A. Davidson, 'The Recusancy of Ralph Sheldon', *Worcestershire Recusant* 12 (1968), 1–7, at pp. 1–2, 3–4; J. Lister (ed.), *West Riding Sessions Rolls 1597/8–1602* (Yorkshire Archaeological and Topographical Association, Record Series, III, 1888), xxv.

[7] J. C. H. Aveling, *Catholic Recusancy in the City of York 1558–1791* (CRS monograph 2, 1970), 210. Papist preparedness to attend some elements of divine service and not others (particularly preaching) was a source of puritan ire, William Fulke, *A Briefe and plaine Declaration* (1584), 67.

which their Catholic opponents were prepared to admit, though they differed strongly about the circumstances in which it was indifferent.[8]

The theoretical difficulty of what significance we accord to attending church is accompanied by a second, methodological, problem. The probability is that some Catholics who decided to abandon strict recusancy were altering their religious opinions and others were not. How can the historian tell the two sorts apart? The Lancashire Catholic Sir John Southworth who had shown signs of compliance as early as 1568 actively certified his conformity to the authorities in 1587–8. But he was still not trusted and a subsequent search of his house discovered concealed popish books.[9] The casuistry which even the fiercest proponents of strict recusancy could countenance in certain circumstances to allow attendance at heretical services makes it very difficult for us to determine people's opinions by their passage in and out of recusancy.[10] Even those who are known to have made a public recantation of their Romanism did not necessarily surrender their dissident tendencies. During the Interregnum an oath of abjuration was introduced for Catholic conformists. It was a far more serious and sweeping rejection of Catholicism than the oaths which Elizabethan and Jacobean conformists had to take. Yet Lord Petre in May 1652 took this oath before the lord mayor of London to avoid the sequestration of his estates. This leading papist's 'conformity' was made solely to ward off financial ruin; he had no intention of rejecting Rome.[11] The philistine barbarities of the sweeping statements required from those who submitted to the State's procedure for conforming according to law disguise the far more complex religious and political opinions of those who are so often described merely as 'conformists'. The full conversion to a godly expression of the religion of the Church of England by an individual like Sir Thomas Egerton was not a simple or immediate response to the authorities' coercion of him to reject Rome in the 1580s. His official submissions were not actually the points at which he substantially changed religion.[12]

On the other hand, just because there are theoretical and methodological problems here, we cannot dismiss conformity as a dark and obscure area or assume that it was invariably a charade and that conformists' opinions are now indeterminable. Certainly there are limits to what the historian can find

---

[8] P. J. Holmes, *Resistance and Compromise* (Cambridge, 1982), 90–2; A. Walsham, *Church Papists* (1993), 52, 67–8.

[9] PRO, E 368/453, mem. 1a–b; CRS 57, xxxi; CRS 60, 37–41; P. W. Hasler (ed.), *The House of Commons 1558–1603* (3 vols., 1981), III, 423.

[10] Henry Garnet, *An Apology Against the Defence of Schisme* (n.p., 1593), 52–7.

[11] C. Clay, 'The Misfortunes of William, Fourth Lord Petre (1638–1655)', *RH* 11 (1971–2), 87–116, at p. 106. A readiness to take the oath of supremacy was no guarantee that its taker intended to conform, Hasler, *Commons*, I, 28–30.

[12] L. A. Knafla, *Law and Politics in Jacobean England* (Cambridge, 1977), 13.

out. It is virtually impossible to chart accurately the fluctuation in the total numbers of recusants during this period, or the national rise and decline of Catholic sympathies. But this does not mean that we cannot discern from particular conformists what the nature of conformity to the State Church was. And there is a second reason also why conformist abandonment of recusancy is significant. Recusancy was a nexus of political and religious ideas. Dissent in belief could be expressed through the individual's non-compliance with the demands of the State even if not every individual's recusancy represented the same elements or degree of dissent. Committed Protestants did not see recusancy or conformity as administrative categories. Admittedly a person did not become a godly Protestant just by hearing the service in the book of common prayer. (Puritans would have been outraged by precisely such a thought.) But anti-recusancy writers like John Field and Francis Bunny associated conformity to the Church of England with conversion from the apocalyptic Babylon because the outward physical separation from Rome expressed so accurately the inward change analysed by Protestant anti-popery.[13] Even if church attendance was not in itself true religion, the exposition of the attender to godly preaching, the normal instrument of effectual conversion, could turn what William Bradshaw called 'Protestants of state' into 'Protestants of religion'.[14]

In this chapter and the next, I propose to reconsider the seriousness of conformity in religion according to law, particularly in the sense of conforming actively under pressure from the State's apparatuses. Was there a real religious significance for Catholics in the statutory provision for their conformity, and (since conformity legislation without enforcement was a dead letter) could the State enforce it? Finally I discuss the anomalies in the politics of conversion to show why so much could be done to make people change their religion but, nevertheless, the regime could not procure the end of dissenting Catholicism.

CONFORMITY TO THE ESTABLISHED CHURCH: THE
LEGAL POSITION

What evidence is there that the State intended to make Catholics abandon their recusancy in a thoroughgoing fashion? Initially the history of the recusancy statutes seems to demonstrate a certain amount of official back-pedalling. The legislation which was passed in Elizabethan parliaments did not reflect the exact intentions of those who wanted to see recusants submit.

---

[13] John Field, *A Caveat for Parsons Howlet* (1581), sig. Avi^r; Francis Bunny, *Truth and Falshood* (1595), sig. Bb2^v–3^r.
[14] William Bradshaw, *Humble Motives* (n.p., 1601), 14.

Francis Walker has shown that during the formulation of the recusancy bills in 1581 an episcopal party in parliament was trying to get measures accepted which would press recusants first and foremost into submission, but that, in each case, this purpose was frustrated. Political divisions meant that three attempts at a recusancy bill on the bishops' terms came to nothing. The bishops were best placed to force recusants into churches through their own ecclesiastical courts but the successful 1581 bill excluded the bishops from enforcing its penalties. They repeatedly failed to secure legislation which dealt with non-communicants.[15] The draft recusancy bill introduced into the House of Commons in February 1593 would have destroyed recusancy in England since the only way to avoid its dire penalties was open conformity, but it failed because of opposition in the Commons. A less stringent one replaced it.[16] Two further bills in 1601 did not pass, and, in Walker's opinion, the debate on the one which was presented by Sir Francis Hastings 'never really dealt with the basic question how to enforce conformity'.[17]

Still, the Elizabethan recusancy bills which were passed did provide for quite explicit declarations of conformity to be made by recusants. It was not simply a matter of dissenters deciding rather anonymously to start frequenting their local churches again. The submission procedure instituted by the 1581 act (23 Elizabeth I, c.1) was thorough. Its seventh branch laid down that all its sanctions (except those for treason and misprision of treason) could be avoided if the offender

shall before he be thereof indicted, or at his Arrainement or Tryall before Judgement, submit and conforme himselfe before the Bisshop of the Diocese where he shalbe resident, or before the Justices where he shalbe indicted araigned or tried, (haveing not before made like submission at any his Tryall being indicted for his first lyke Offence,).[18]

---

[15] F. X. Walker, 'The Implementation of the Elizabethan Statutes against Recusants 1581–1603' (Ph.D thesis, London, 1961), 121–33; Walsham, *Church Papists*, 87.

[16] Walker, 'Implementation', 344–8; J. E. Neale, *Elizabeth I and her Parliaments* (2 vols., 1953, 1957), II, 280–97.

[17] Walker, 'Implementation', 420.

[18] *The Statutes of the Realm* (11 vols., 1810–28), IV, 658. This branch of the statute clearly envisaged submission being made before conviction. After a conviction the fine of £20 for each month of certified recusancy would be payable whether the recusant decided to forsake recusancy or not, though cf. Bodl., Tanner MS 79, fos. 231^r–3^r. But the 1586/7 recusancy statute (29 Elizabeth I, c.6) levied the fines stipulated by the 1581 act by making penalties of £20 for each month continuous from the date of the first conviction and avoidable only by conformity, proof of legal error or death, and so it provided (in its sixth branch) for conformity to take place after conviction, *Statutes*, IV, 772. The system established by this act whereby the recusant was proclaimed as such at the assizes where he was indicted and then convicted at the next assize hearing was supposed to induce him to conform between the two sets of proceedings, *HMC Salisbury MSS* XVII, 78. The recusant who conformed could escape the accumulative penalty and, through a petition for inclusion

The process by which the recusant obtained a discharge from his status as a convicted recusant was extremely rigorous, in the ecclesiastical as well as the secular sphere. Conformity in all cases of recusancy was based on an appearance before the diocesan bishop. This was itself sufficient if the recusant had not yet been indicted. If recusancy proceedings had reached the indictment stage then the recusant had to submit in open court as well.[19] The conformities pleaded before the exchequer in this period were based in around 5 per cent of cases upon certificates supplied by assize judges rather than bishops, but it seems that an appearance before the bishop was always required at some stage.

In 1593 a specific form of words for a recusant to recite when conforming was laid down in 35 Elizabeth I, c.1 and c.2. In the first statute (directed against 'sectaries') the conformist in the parish church had to

confesse and acknowledge that I have grevouslye offended God in contempnynge her Majesties godlye and laufull Goverment and Aucthoritie, by absenting my selfe from Churche and from hearinge Devyne Service contrarie to the godlye Lawes and Statutes of this Realme, and in usinge and frequentinge disordered and unlauful Conventicles and Assemblies . . . And I am hartely sorye for the same, and do acknowledge and testifye in my Conscience, that noe other person have or ought to have any Power or Aucthoritie over her Majestie; And I doe promysse and proteste, without any dissimulacion . . . that from henceforth I will from tyme to tyme obey and performe her Majesties Lawes and Statutes in repayringe to the Churche.[20]

In the second statute, directed specifically against 'Popishe Recusantes', the conformist had to make a similar protestation about the godly laws of the realm but (in this measure which made provision principally for limiting the recusant's movements to within five miles of his normal place of abode) he acknowledges and testifies in his conscience 'that the Bysshoppe or Sea of Rome hathe not nor oughte to have any Power or Auctoritie over her Majestie', and likewise promises to repair to his church.[21] It might appear odd that such a detailed conformity clause should have been formulated for a five mile act (though the first 1593 act was applicable against all types of sectaries, Catholic and Protestant). But a reconstruction of the history of this legislation shows that the clause was designed for the original bill which never passed, a bill which directed a lethal attack on recusancy (principally

in the Queen's Free and General Pardon (and automatically by 1 James I, c.4), all the outstanding arrears of debt, both of £20 per month and possibly, once his lands were seized by the Crown in lieu of cash payment, the debts which accumulated from the sums levied on his estates to meet the theoretical debts which arose from non-payment of the £20 fine, *Statutes*, IV, 1020; CRS 60, 29; CRS 57, xxvi, though there remains some doubt about this, BL, Add. MS 11574, fo. 388r; *HMC Salisbury MSS* V, 277 (for the position before 1604).

[19] Bodl., Rawl. MS D 1036, fo. 2r–v; cf. Garnet, *Apology*, 9–10.
[20] *Statutes*, IV, 842.
[21] *Statutes*, IV, 845–6; CRS 52, 157.

of the Catholic variety), and specifically stated that such conformity provisions should apply to other recusant penalties and forfeitures in other statutes.[22] Despite the failure of the original bill to pass into law the clause was employed by the bishops when they supervised the conformities of those Catholics convicted under the statutes of the 1580s.[23] The clause is significant in its insistence not only on outward conformity but also that the declaration is made from conscience.[24]

Jacobean legislation was an improvement on Elizabethan statutes in its carrot-and-stick approach to religious tractability. 1 James I, c.4 clarified the rules for inheritance by recusants' heirs (encouraging them therefore to be conformable), though such people had to take publicly the oath of supremacy before recusancy penalties on their inherited estates were lifted.[25] The 'communion clause' of 3 James I, c.4 may not have been as savage as the Commons had desired, but it constrained those who had submitted to receive communion regularly.[26] (Occasional conformists generally drew the line at receiving communion.)[27] Other parts of the 1606 statute actively enforced religious compliance by attacking female recusancy and providing for wardship to be used to isolate from Catholicism the wards who came from Catholic families.[28]

---

[22] House of Lords MSS, Main Papers 1592–3, fos. 12r–13r; for the fate of the original bill, Neale, *Elizabeth*, II, 285–6.

[23] *E.g.*, PRO, E 368/514, mem. 112b. Both statutes directed that each 'Submyssion and Declaracion of Conformytie' should be entered 'into a Booke to be kepte in everie Parishe for that purpose'. The visitation articles of 1622 drawn up by Miles Smith, bishop of Gloucester, enquire about the maintaining of such a register, K. C. Fincham (ed.), *Visitation Articles and Injunctions of the Early Stuart Church*, I (Church of England Record Society, Woodbridge, Suffolk, 1994), 209.

[24] Walker, 'Implementation', 352.

[25] La Rocca suggests that the stipulation of the 1604 act that lessees of sequestrated recusant property should not waste it 'gave the recusant an incentive to recover his property intact if he conformed', J. J. La Rocca, 'James I and his Catholic Subjects, 1606–1612: Some Financial Implications', *RH* 18 (1987), 251–62, at p. 254; cf. CRS 52, 6.

[26] PRO, SP 14/19/27, fos. 40v–1r. All conformists were compelled by it 'once in everie yeere following [their conformity] at the least, [to] receive the blessed Sacrament of the Lordes Supper'. The fines for failure to do this were £20 for the first year, £40 for the second, and £60 for the third and thereafter, *Statutes*, IV, 1071.

[27] E. E. Rose, *Cases of Conscience* (Cambridge, 1975), 6; Walsham, *Church Papists*, 85–9; BL, Harl. MS 1221, fo. 65v. Percival Cockerell of Whitby confessed before the ecclesiastical commissioners in April 1600 that his acquaintance Robert Glover had told him he 'sawe the devell gnawing of the soules of such persons as went to church but chiefly of such as received the communion', BI, HCAB 14, fo. 67r. Nicholas Timperley, who was forced by repeated exchequer inquisitions first into trying to fake his conformity, and finally into the real thing, had, it appears, been an occasional conformist for many years but desperately wished to avoid receiving communion, an essential element of the statutory conformity procedure, PRO, E 134/7 James I/Trinity 3, mm. 3a, 4a, 6a.

[28] M. B. Rowlands, 'Recusant Women 1560–1640', in M. Prior (ed.), *Women in English Society 1580–1800* (1985), 149–80, at p. 155; Walsham, *Church Papists*, 80; W. Notestein,

The central element of the new legislation was the new oath of allegiance.[29] Was it intended just to divide Catholics politically, as its formulators claimed? If so, its introduction into law reduced pressure on recusants to conform in religion. Or did its carefully worded phrasing, in particular its reference to the papal deposing power as a heretical doctrine, have an eye as much to religious conformity as to political allegiance? Historians have differed about the purpose of the oath.[30] But, for all the insistence by the regime that the oath entailed nothing more than a formal assertion of loyalty to the sovereign through a rejection of the papal deposing power, it seems clear enough that it was designed to compel much more than mere temporal allegiance. By exploiting a commonly perceived fault-line between opinions over the origins of the State and the Church (and the relationship between grace and nature) the oath was a direct assault on the papal primacy, and, on one reading at least, was the ideological equivalent of the oath of supremacy.[31] The panic-stricken dismay of many leading Catholic clerical activists when the oath was formulated and

---

The House of Commons 1604–1610 (1971), 149–50; Cliffe, *Yorkshire Gentry*, 184–6; H. E. Bell, *Introduction to the History and Records of the Court of Wards and Liveries* (Cambridge, 1951), 124; cf. also John Gee, *Hold Fast* (1624), sig. A3ᵛ–4ʳ, in his dedication to Sir Robert Naunton, stressing the religious orientation of wards policy. In practice, however, particularly after reforms by Sir Robert Cecil in 1610, most wards would remain with the mother, Bell, *Introduction*, 116–17. Such placements probably never represented anything so advanced as a policy, Aveling, *Northern Catholics*, 224–5; perhaps it was inevitable that central government should really be interested only in using wardship to promote religious conformity principally among the political elite, J. Bossy, *The English Catholic Community 1570–1850* (1975), 162. The quiet demise of measures proposed in 1606 to remove children from Catholic families (with the intention of educating them as Protestants) suggests that such separation was not seen as generally practicable, Notestein, *House*, 156–8. Similar measures had not passed into law in 1593 either, Neale, *Elizabeth*, II, 283–4; LPL, Fairhurst MS 3470, fo. 196ʳ; A. J. Loomie, 'Spain and the English Catholic Exiles 1580–1604' (Ph.D thesis, London, 1957), 310–11; A. C. F. Beales, *Education under Penalty* (1963), 62–3; PRO, SP 14/21/35, fo. 82ʳ⁻ᵛ; cf. *CSPV 1603–7*, 320; cf. SP 14/21/40, 42; *Statutes*, IV, 1081.

29 *Statutes*, IV, 1073–4.
30 K. C. Fincham and P. Lake, 'The Ecclesiastical Policy of King James I', *Journal of British Studies* 24 (1985), 170–206, at pp. 171, 185–6; J. P. Sommerville, 'Jacobean Political Thought and the Controversy over the Oath of Allegiance' (Ph.D thesis, Cambridge, 1981), 16–17, 25; J. V. Gifford, 'The Controversy over the Oath of Allegiance of 1606' (DPhil. thesis, Oxford, 1971), iv; M. Nicholls, *Investigating Gunpowder Plot* (Manchester, 1991), 49; J.C.H. Aveling, *The Catholic Recusants of the West Riding of Yorkshire 1558–1790* (Proceedings of the Leeds Philosophical and Literary Society, Literary and Historical Section, X, part VI, Leeds, 1963), 230–1.
31 Gifford, 'Controversy', chapters 5 and 6, pp. 182–93. The act books of the high commission at York record that in February 1607 John Fletcher appeared in York Castle and was offered the oath of the 'Kings supremacie [*sic*] maid in the last sess[ion] of Parliament', BI, HCAB 15, fo. 25ʳ; George Webbe, *Catalogus Protestantium* (1624), 53; Robert Persons, *The Judgment of a Catholicke English-Man* (St Omer, 1608), 13–16; Stonyhurst, Collectanea P I, fo. 161ᵛ; cf. CRS 68, 80.

enforced and the readiness of renegade Romanist priests to phrase their changes of religion by reference to the oath are vivid illustrations of the sheer political power of the State in drawing religious conformity within the compass of generally accepted notions of political allegiance.[32]

Jacobean legislators' interest in promoting full and rigorous compliance among Catholics did not cease in 1606. In April 1621 a recusancy bill 'for Explanacion of the Lawes against Recusants' was introduced into the Commons. It never passed into law but it dwelt heavily on the minutiae of conformity requirements. Though some of its sections merely repeated measures contained in the 1606 legislation, others tightened up the system for detecting recusants and assessing the values of their estates.[33] Debate during the bill's second reading on 4 May 1621 suggests that MPs wanted to encourage the recusant to conform, but his conformity was to be more thorough. Sir Thomas Posthumous Hoby, a zealous promoter of conformity in the North, argued that episcopal and exchequer fees should be waived for conformists. It was suggested that it was counterproductive 'to bind such as doe Conforme to too greate Solempnity in goeing to the Diocesan'. Sir John Strangeways proposed that the rule in the seventh branch of the 1581 statute should be overturned and 'men that conforme after a relapse maye have ther land againe. He that came at the last howre had reward aswell as they that indured the heat of the daye.'[34] When the bill was discussed in committee on 15 May 1621 the suggested one year's probation before the conforming recusant recovered his land was reduced to three months, but contrary to established practice, 'if any Recusant offer to Conforme . . . hee must presently take the Oathe of Supremacy And make a solemne Protestacion That he doth truly renounce the Supersticions of the Romish Religion'. During the period of probation before he recovered his estates he had to

---

[32] Foley I, 64–5; Gifford, 'Controversy', 61; AAW, A X, 269, XII, 387; Theophilus Higgons, *A Sermon preached at Pauls Crosse* (1611), 50, 54; cf. Foley VII, 1014; John Salkeld, *A Treatise of Angels* (1613), sig. *3r–v; cf. AAW, A XI, 269; Foley V, 854; Richard Sheldon, *Certain General Reasons, proving the Lawfulnesse of the Oath of Allegiance* (1611), bound significantly with Higgons's recantation and William Barclay's *Of the Authoritie of the Pope* (1611); PRO, SP 14/63/18; Richard Sheldon, *The Motives of Richard Sheldon Pr.* (1612), sigs. A2r–v, Bb2r; *idem*, *Christ, on his Throne* (1622), 13; Henry Yaxley, *Morbus et Antidotus* (1630), 8–9, 39–40; John Copley, *Doctrinall and Morall Observations* (1612), 124; M. C. Questier, 'Loyalty, Religion and State Power in Early Modern England: English Romanism and the Jacobean Oath of Allegiance' (forthcoming in *HJ*).

[33] W. Notestein, F. H. Relf and H. Simpson (eds.), *Commons Debates 1621* (7 vols., New Haven, 1935), IV, 214–15; R. Zaller, *The Parliament of 1621* (1971), 132.

[34] Notestein, Relf and Simpson, *Commons Debates*, III, 160, IV, 301, V, 140. A similar point to Strangeway's had been made by Francis Cradock in the 1593 parliament, Hasler, *Commons*, I, 668. For an illustration of the scale of exchequer fees for those seeking discharge from debts, Richard Cholmeley, 'The Memorandum Book of Richard Cholmeley of Brandsby 1602–1623', *North Yorkshire County Record Office Publications* 44 (1988), 145.

frequent 'Sermons and the Communion'.[35] These provisions were to ensure that, as far as outward coercive measures were capable, the conformist should behave like a genuine Protestant. (John Pym wanted non-communicancy to be subject to the same penalties as recusancy.)[36]

CONFORMITY IN PRACTICE

The legislators were determined that when a recusant was compelled to abandon his dissenting ways this should be no mere or gradual lapse into anonymous acquiescence. Active conformity was to be far more than a bureaucratic discharge from a fiscal debt (even if this benefit may have been uppermost in the minds of many recusants who conformed). In practice, the would-be conformist probably signified his new pliability to his bishop first and was directed by him to hear divine service and receive communion in his parish church. The conformer obtained a certificate of his compliance and took it to the bishop. (This was the normal procedure also for recusants in the Church courts.) John Flint, the minister at St Olaf's parish church in London, certified to Bancroft that the recusant John Scudamore had heard divine service, a sermon, and received communion, all of which was testified to by Flint and others whom Bancroft had beforehand 'required to see and observe the same'.[37] The conformer then had to hear divine service in the presence of the bishop himself, and again abjure Roman Catholicism.[38] In this way, statute required that canon law provisions for purging a schismatic/heretical state should be put into effect according to the doctrinal norms of the established Church in England.[39]

---

[35] Notestein, Relf and Simpson, *Commons Debates*, IV, 215, III, 269.

[36] Notestein, Relf and Simpson, *Commons Debates*, III, 160.

[37] PRO, E 368/523, mem. 126a; J. M. Potter, 'The Ecclesiastical Courts in the Diocese of Canterbury 1603–1665' (MPhil. thesis, London, 1973), 111. John Booth, a Staffordshire recusant, had already heard divine service and received communion in his parish church but was ordered by Richard Neile to attend divine service again at Westminster and bring him a certificate to that effect, PRO, E 368/541, mem. 127a–b.

[38] C. W. Foster, *The State of the Church in the Reigns of Elizabeth and James I, as Illustrated by Documents Relating to the Diocese of Lincoln*, I (Lincoln Record Society 23, 1926), xcii; cf. PRO, E 368/535, mem. 116a–b. Very occasionally, the conformer was permitted to submit in his parish immediately after conforming before the bishop, PRO, E 368/541, mem. 130b, but the bishop would not grant his own certificate until the recusant had done this, even if he had already heard divine service in the bishop's presence; cf. PRO, E 368/526, mem. 180b.

[39] J. G. Goodwine, *The Reception of Converts* (Canon Law Studies no. 198, Washington, 1944), 1, stresses that, canonically, in cases of heresy or schism *ad forum externum*, appearance before the bishop was required, *non vero Vicarius Generalis sine mandatis speciali*. Joan Foljambe's conformity certificate says that she appeared before Richard Etkins, Ravis's chaplain, only because Ravis was ill, though she took the oath of allegiance before Ravis on the following day, PRO, E 368/563, mem. 183a. Abjuration of heresy was

Reception of communion broke one of the defining boundaries of church papistry, and frequently the conformity certificate states the conformist has listened to a sermon, something which was recognised as qualitatively different from attendance at a service where no sermon was preached.[40] The recusant might sign a statement of his conformity and intention to continue conformable.[41] (Sometimes he would take the oath of supremacy, and, after 1606, virtually always took the oath of allegiance.) In essence, the full conformity procedure which the lay Catholic had to endure was no different from the one imposed on an apostatising Catholic cleric.[42]

It is slightly surprising that there are, apparently, no contemporary liturgical records of what happened when the recusant came before the bishop to recant. Eighteenth-century sources show that the occasion had considerable liturgical potential. An early-eighteenth-century 'Form for admitting Converts from the Church of Rome' lays down a detailed service for receiving a Catholic into the Church of England. A bishop, or a minister appointed by him, presides. (An alternative form of words is provided for use at the relevant places if the conformer was previously a nonconformist Protestant.) The service incorporates a detailed abjuration of Catholicism which the conformer makes by replying to a series of questions from the bishop or minister. He has to condemn Rome's superstitions and errors as well as acknowledge the Royal Supremacy. The liturgical settings are carefully chosen to emphasise rejection of a false Church and reception into

combined with profession of Christian faith, either in public or in private, according to the nature of the heresy of the convert. If there was a question of notorious error and scandal, the abjuration necessarily had to be made in public, Goodwine, *Reception*, 118–22; cf. Loomie, 'Spain', 136–7, 139–40, showing that Robert Persons and Richard Walpole, in Spain, attempted to have the public ceremony of abjuration omitted in the cases of English prisoners who wanted to renounce Protestantism, in other words, that their cases should be removed from the 'external' to the 'sacramental' forum.

40 For Thomas Wright's dissenting view on listening to Protestant sermons, T. A. Stroud, 'Father Thomas Wright: A Test Case for Toleration', *Biographical Studies* 1 (1951–2), 189–219, at p. 207; Foley IV, 284, 371–4. In February 1612 Richard Smith reported to Rome the scandal of Richard Sheldon and Edward Collier attending 'the sermons in Paules', AAW, A XI, 51. In late 1592 the Warwickshire recusancy commissioners reported that John Arrowsmith made some show of conformity and attended church, 'but when the preacher goeth up to the pulpitt to preache he goeth presentlye, out of the Churche; and saithe he must needes goe out of the Churche; when a knave beginnethe to preache', PRO, SP 12/243/76, fo. 215r; cf. BL, Add. MS 34250, fo. 16r, and *passim*.

41 *CSPD 1627–8*, 289; PRO, E 368/501, mem. 205a, E 368/508, mem. 143b, E 368/509, mem. 116b. Episcopal registers generally do not record recusant conformities, but two exceptions are those of William Chaderton between 1605 and 1607 and Lancelot Andrewes between 1605 and 1609, Foster, *State*, xcii–iii; WSRO, Ep. I/1/8, fo. 53r.

42 BL, Lansd. MS 84, fo. 174r, for the priest Miles Dawson's recantation; PRO, SP 16/73/58.i, for that of the former Jesuit John Jukes.

the sacraments of a true one.[43] Did this happen in the late sixteenth and early seventeenth centuries? George Hakewill in his reply to Carier noted that 'the whole frame of Poperie' is built on the idolatry of the Mass and papal supremacy, and therefore 'in the reformed Churches of France (not without good reason in my judgment) such as forsake the fellowship of the Church of Rome, and betake themselves to their profession, are bound before they bee admitted into their society publikely in the Congregation, as to renounce the errours of that Church in generall, so in speciall, and by name to abjure these two' namely 'the usurped authority of the Bishop of Rome, and the idolatry of the Masse'.[44] But Hakewill does not specifically say that this happened in English churches and cathedrals in his day. There are several records of elaborate rituals being designed for reception of converts from Islam in this period. In *A Recovery from Apostacy* (preached on the occasion of Vincent Jukes's reabsorption into the Church of England after his defection to Islam), William Gouge remarked on the incidence of edifying public recantations since the early Church and claimed that 'this time after time hath beene done in all reformed Churches: And that not onely by such as have returned from Paganisme, Turcisme, and Judaisme, but also from Anabaptisme and Popery'. In the printed version Gouge says that there was a 'solemne, pious, and grave forme of Penance prescribed for admitting . . . [Jukes] againe into the Christian Church'.[45] Of course, those who had professed Islam, or who had become Anabaptists, Familists or Brownists were much easier to visualise as apostates.[46] But while the extant conformity certificates make specific reference only to a public declaration before the bishop and congregation of the conformist's intention to stay conformable to the Church of England, the reason that there is no specific printed format for such recantations from Rome is simply that the forms of the pontifical service required for it rested upon the authority of individual

[43] Bodl., Rawl. MS D 843, fos. 150ʳ–6ᵛ; cf. BL, Add. MS 6482, fos. 65ʳ–72ʳ; LPL, Gibson MS 933, no. 61, recantation ceremony specifically for George Douglas, second earl of Dumbarton.

[44] George Hakewill, *An Answere to a Treatise Written by Dr Carier* (1616), 293. By contrast, Benedict shows that a principal element of Huguenots' recantation of their Protestantism in a formal church ceremony was approach to and reverence of the Host, P. Benedict, *Rouen during the Wars of Religion* (Cambridge, 1981), 129.

[45] William Gouge, *A Recovery from Apostacy* (1639), 19–20, 6; cf. Edward Kellet, *A Returne from Argier* (1628); William Laud, ed. J. Bliss and W. Scott, *Works* (7 vols., Oxford, 1847–60), V, 352, 372–6.

[46] M. Maclure, *The Paul's Cross Sermons, 1534–1642* (Toronto, 1958), 209, 214, 250; E. Cardwell (ed.), *Documentary Annals* (2 vols., Oxford, 1839), I, 361; BL, Lansd. MS 982, fo. 46ʳ. John Woolton, Bishop of Exeter brought twenty Familists to recant their 'vile notions' in Exeter Cathedral, BL, Lansd. MS 33, fo. 29ʳ.

bishops.[47] It is virtually certain that Elizabethan and Jacobean bishops used a Protestant equivalent of the episcopal liturgical ritual in the Roman *Pontifical*.[48] In this ceremony the conforming recusant would therefore make a specific abjuration of Rome as a heretical Church as well as take the oaths laid down by English statute. The State may have required only a political profession of allegiance but the conformist was made to look as if he was making a thorough religious conversion from a heretical to a true Church.

This thoroughgoing religious rejection of Rome was of interest not just to men of the cloth. The State actively assisted its churchmen in their efforts to secure recantations and to put recusants through a punishing course of ecclesiastical submission. Before it discharged a recusant debtor, the exchequer required proof of rigid adherence to all these ecclesiastical elements of conformity. John Martin, a Leicestershire recusant, decided to submit in 1618 (though he claimed that he had been recusant only through infirmity). He received episcopal instructions as to the requirements for submission and he was absolved from excommunication and received communion in his parish church on 27 July 1618 at the direction of Edward Clarke, commissary of the archdeacon of Leicester. Nevertheless, Francis Staresmore JP, who helped to supervise this conformity at the direction of the assize judges at Leicester, reported to Clarke that all this had proved insufficient 'to worke his . . . [Martin's] discharge out of the exchequer without the testimonye and certificate under the Episcopall seall of your office by your selfe because the offence toucheth Church goverment'.[49] It seems that, to satisfy the exchequer barons, in all but exceptional cases the recusant required ecclesiastical certification (generally from a bishop) that he had complied with the Church's conformity requirements. Recusants, when their diocesan bishop was absent from his diocese, might have to make lengthy journeys to conform in front of him before they appeared at the

---

47 W. H. Frere (ed.), *Pontifical Services* (4 vols., Alcuin Club Collections, 3–4, 8–12, 1901–8), I, 1. The recantation liturgy for the second earl of Dumbarton was composed by the archbishop of Canterbury, LPL, Gibson MS 933, no. 61.

48 John White, *A Defence of the Way to the True Church* (1614), 86; John Percy, *A Reply made unto Mr Anthony Wotton and Mr John White* (St Omer, 1612), 34; *Gregorio XIII Pont. Max. Pontificale Romanum ad Omnes Pontificias Caeremonias, quibus nunc utitur sacrosancta R. E. accommodatum* (Venice, 1582), sig. Ddiiii^v–vi^r; *Pontificale Romanum Clementis VIII. Pont. Max. Iussu Restitutum Atque Editum* (Rome, 1595), sigs. Nnnniii^r–Ooooii^r, specifying the intricate symbolic episcopal ritual for reconciliation to the Church of those guilty of heresy and schism, and stressing the driving out of the spirit of heresy, an entirely different ceremony therefore from the one for absolving an excommunicate, sig. Mmmmii^r.

49 PRO, E 368/572, mem. 133^b.

exchequer (though if the absentee bishop was himself in or near London, this presented less difficulty).[50]

Under statute, the conformer had to submit in public at the assizes or quarter sessions. The assize judges (and, after 1604, the justices of the peace at the quarter sessions), would also want to see an ecclesiastical certificate showing that he had gone through all the required stages.[51] According to Henry Garnet, the assize recantation was not a legal poor relation of the submission before the bishop. He referred to the 'ordinary submission which at the Assises divers have pronounced, when they have become conformable, wherin the principall pointes of Catholicke religion are renounced' and that conformists are sometimes with contempt 'like grammer schollers commaunded [by the judges] to repeate againe [their recantation], as not having pronounced it well, or not spoken loud enough'.[52]

---

[50] William Tempest submitted in Oxford and then had to travel to find the bishop of Oxford in London, PRO, E 368/530, mem. 153[a–b]; George Sweeting conformed at the Yorkshire assizes and then before Archbishop Mathew at Ely House in London, though nearly four years separated the two submissions, PRO, E 368/536, mem. 121[a]. The Jesuit annual letters for the Leicestershire District mention a farmer who 'sacrificed his soul to his goods, attended the meetings of the heretics, and even took a long journey to London to obtain absolution from the heretical Bishop of Lincoln', Foley VII, 1123. All of the nine conformists from Chichester diocese during Lancelot Andrewes's tenure had to conform before him in London (at Whitehall, Greenwich or Lambeth) because Andrewes was generally absent from the diocese (except when on visitation), K. C. Fincham, *Prelate as Pastor* (Oxford, 1990), 56–57, 309; PRO, E 368/525, mem. 189[a], E 368/528, mm. 180[a], 211[a], E 368/530, mm. 155[a], 157[a], 167[a], E 368/531, mem. 121[a]; WSRO, Ep. I/1/8, fo. 53[r] (for which reference I am grateful to Kenneth Fincham).

[51] The bishop's certificate might be presented to the assize judges, PRO, E 368/532, mem. 185[a–b] (Richard ap Rees's episcopal certificate presented at the exchequer was originally addressed directly to the assize judges for Denbighshire). Other conformists, though, appeared in the reverse order before judges and bishop, demonstrating that it was the exchequer which really required the episcopal certificate of conformity: PRO, E 368/526, mem. 186[a]; J. Cockburn (ed.), *Calendar of Assize Records: Surrey Indictments: James I* (1982), nos 103–4; PRO, E 368/527, mem. 222[a], E 368/536, mem. 121[a]. It seems that all the secular judges wanted was some proof of conformity satisfying the parliamentary statute. For two Sussex conformists who made public submissions at the assizes – Peter Sandes, J. Cockburn (ed.), *Calendar of Assize Records: Sussex Indictments: James I* (1975), no. 118; WSRO, Ep. I/1/8, fo. 53[r]; PRO, E 368/530, mem. 155[a]; and William Rose, *idem*, *Calendar of Assize Records: Sussex Indictments: James I*, no. 244; PRO, E 368/555, mem. 176[a]. Though there is no episcopal certificate in the memoranda rolls certifying his conformity, Rose had evidently fulfilled the ecclesiastical requirements for submission because he had already attended divine service in London. *Cf.* also PRO, E 368/559, mem. 215[a]: an assize judge at Nottingham in 1615 certified Francis Strellay's conformity (in 1613) when 'the sayd Francis went with us to the publicke Church in Nottingham and there heard prayers and Sermon'; cf. O'Dwyer, 'Catholic Recusants', 188, and for general procedure when submitting at quarter sessions, 96–8; H. Bowler, 'Sir Henry James of Smarden, Kent, and Clerkenwell, Recusant (*c.* 1559–1625)', in A. E. J. Hollaender and W. Kellaway (eds.), *Studies in London History* (1969), 289–313, at pp. 298–301.

[52] Garnet, *Apology*, 9–10.

CONTEMPORARY PERCEPTIONS OF CONFORMITY

To what extent was the conformity promoted by secular and ecclesiastical authorities a serious religious matter for the conformist himself? Its overall significance might be thought to be seriously diminished if recusants regarded statutory conformity as a meaningless charade and Protestants saw no point in refusing the benefits of conformity to those who petitioned to submit according to law irrespective of what they really thought. J. H. Pollen argued that 'presence at Protestant service meant the public acceptance of the new religion. It was the enforced, official, recognized sign that the church-goer accepted the State–Church and rejected the old faith' and in that manner was 'an actual renunciation of Catholicism' and a 'conversion' to Protestantism.[53] Others have been less sure. Pollen was referring to even the most hesitant signs of compliance. La Rocca, thinking of full statutory conformity, writes merely that 'these submissions cannot be entirely discounted' since 'the men and women who conformed were gentry and their acts of conformity, even if only to save their property, had some significance: the offenders had publicly obeyed the Crown even if . . . such acquiescence was not necessarily permanent'.[54]

Did Catholics see the statutory conformity process, however distasteful, just as a means of protecting themselves from Protestant zealots and of recovering property? Men like Sir William Roper and Nicholas Timperley, when threatened with sequestration, were relatively swift to conform. Yet it can be shown from their later behaviour that neither of them abandoned their Catholic beliefs in the least degree.[55] The conformities of wealthy gentry, like the Thatchers and Ashburnhams and Carylls of Sussex, the Lovells of Norfolk and the Thimelbies of Lincolnshire have generally been regarded as religiously motiveless.[56] If submission to the law (even of the variety which went beyond what a casuist could permit) was still regarded as a species of church papistry then the likelihood would be that such conformity, particularly where the principal motive appears to be recovery of property from the Crown's hands, was simply as Aveling describes occasional conformity – a form of estate management.[57] It would become, in fact, a way of protecting and conserving English Catholicism. When

---

[53] J. H. Pollen, 'Recent Studies on Elizabethan Catholic History', *The Month* 117 (1911), 337–51, at p. 343.
[54] La Rocca, 'James I', 257.
[55] La Rocca, 'James I', 257; PRO, E 368/531, mem. 99a–b, E 368/539, mem. 121a–b.
[56] M. J. Urquhart, 'A Sussex Recusant Family', *Dublin Review* 512 (1967), 162–70, at pp. 166–8; cf. PRO, E 368/489, mem. 186a; Foley V, 601; cf. PRO, E 368/494, mem. 43a; CRS 57, xxxii; PRO, E 368/477, mem. 196a.
[57] Aveling, *Northern Catholics*, 266–7.

George Chambers defended his prosecutions of Catholics who technically had conformed in full he stated that he had indicted none but those who are known to be recusants: 'albeit they have brought Certificates of their Conformitie yett are they houlden to be notorious Papists by reason for the most parte their wyves and famylies doe never come to Church; Their Children never christned by any lawfull mynister; And are reported to bee maintayners of Semmynaries and Convicted Papistes in their howses'.[58] The earl of Salisbury was informed in July 1611 that Jane Shelley who had conformed in 1606 had now demised estates in Shropshire to raise money for the Society of Jesus, and that she had remained very much a papist.[59] If compulsion was the exclusive cause of an individual going through what he would inevitably have seen as a charade, his 'conformity' meant nothing in religious terms (perhaps, by association, little enough even in political terms). Where a person conformed because there was no obvious financial alternative, then, while he might stay conformable, this could hardly be a ringing endorsement of the established Church. At best such conformities would be like the 'conversions' of French Huguenots (as analysed by modern historians) in the wake of the 1572 massacre – frequently permanent but essentially a matter of social adjustment.[60] Alexandra Walsham argues that conformity to the satisfaction of the ecclesiastical commissioners (even by those who certified their conformities into the secular courts) was likely to be the adoption of a church papist position rather than a complete rejection of popery. In the absence, she says, of a highly efficient bureaucracy, '"conformity" could be but a temporary expedient, a brief, even unrepeated, response to the harassment of a singularly zealous magistrate or crusading prelate'.[61]

The statute-regulated submission procedure certainly did not go as far as it might have done. A draft bill of 1586 demonstrates what the legislators had considered adding to the statute book. 'An acte for the preservation of the Queenes Majesties moste roiall person' contained draconian measures to ensure full religious conformity. Its preamble stated that recent conspirators against Elizabeth were motivated chiefly by the theological opinion that 'the Church of Rome . . . neither hath erred nor can erre'. The bill would have authorised officials in the provinces to put a specifically doctrinal oath to any person falling under suspicion of disaffection. They would be required to 'acknowledge before the Lorde God of heaven and earth' that the Church

---

[58] PRO, SP 14/51/26, fo. 91ʳ.
[59] PRO, E 368/525, mem. 183ᵏ⁻ˡ; *CSPD 1611–18*, 61.
[60] Benedict, *Rouen*, 128–47; E. Labrousse, 'Conversion dans les Deux Sens', in *La Conversion au XVIIe Siècle* (Centre Méridional de Rencontres sur le XVIIᵉ Siècle, Marseille, 1982), 161–72, at p. 168.
[61] Walsham, *Church Papists*, 74.

of Rome 'is an Antichristian and hereticall Churche, and that it hath erred, and can and doth erre'. They must 'renounce the saide Churche of Rome' and say that they neither owe it obedience 'nor will be directed by it' in matters of faith. The bill tried to ensure that the examinee would not be able to evade subsequent questions as to his opinions if he refused this oath. Among such questions the person could be quizzed as to whether he was a recusant. Refusal to take the oath or affirmation of dangerous views about recusancy or even refusal to answer on this subject brought banishment. Refusal to condemn the authority, political and religious, of the Church of Rome brought an indictment for treason (though all offences in the bill could be purged by submission and 'open profession and protestation that he alloweth holdeth and professeth the true Christian religion publickly taught and professed within this Realme' and by taking the oath he had originally refused). There were heavy financial penalties for officials who did not ensure that the bill's machinery operated properly.[62] The bill never became law. Perhaps it was unworkable. One can hardly imagine all provincial officials showing the level of zeal which it demanded. It is unlikely also that they would have been competent, as the bill assumed, to determine what constituted an 'impertinente' answer to questions about doctrine. But it differs from virtually all other anti-Catholic legislation (proposed or actual) in this period because it tried to compel a clear statement of inward assent to central Protestant tenets. The recusancy legislation on the statute books demanded only that, outwardly, everyone should behave in the same way.

Statutory conformity, however, could not by any stretch of the imagination be seen as a profession purely of political loyalty. It went beyond even what the ecclesiastical commissioners generally demanded (a certified statement of attendance at the individual's parish church). Is it possible to test what those Catholics who conformed actually thought they were doing when they submitted publicly? The problem, of course, is that while a wealth of recorded evidence survives about the actual moment of this species of official conformity – the outward declaration of assent to the ecclesiastical demands of the State – much less is available to the historian about what the individual believed. R. B. Manning suggests that the swearing of the oath of supremacy under pressure 'often did little to change a man's beliefs or alter the course of his action', and that 'it is not the weakness displayed in a difficult moment but rather the pattern of a lifetime that gives the best indication of a man's religious views'.[63] The generality of conformists were not sufficiently prominent to leave adequate records of their beliefs. How are we to enquire what they thought?

---

[62] BL, Lansd. MS 47, no. 33.   [63] Manning, 'Catholics', 47.

One test might be to see whether those who conformed generally remained conformable. The records of the high commission at York and of the recusancy commissioners in the early 1590s show that large numbers fluctuated in and out of vague shows of conformity.[64] It appears that not all of those who certified their conformities to the exchequer refrained permanently from a return to recusancy. In the North Riding of Yorkshire people like the squire James Green, John Constable (the son of the Elizabethan political activist Joseph Constable) and several others seem to have returned to nonconformity, even though in many cases it was only after a long time, and some of these relapses occur in the 1620s and 1630s when the easing of repression of recusancy may have persuaded these people that they were no longer offending the regime by withdrawing from its churches.[65] In a few cases, like that of William Beseley of Skelton, who was persuaded to submit by his father, Edward, the conformity is a matter only of form. He went through a show of attending divine service, and even took the oath of allegiance, but thereafter would not cooperate when the high commission started to prod him in order to see whether he had really meant it.[66] Edward Beseley likewise attended church whenever pressure was put on him to prove himself conformable (though he remained a non-communicant); Edward's brother-in-law, Martin Nelson the seminary priest, apostatised in January 1596, even requesting that he might 'faithfully labour as a Minister, to do good service to god and hir Majestie; and to perswade and reforme such as heretofore he hathe diswaded and seduced'. But, after obtaining a special pardon, he spent the rest of his life working as a an active Catholic cleric in South Wales.[67]

It would be a mistake, though, to assume that all those who submitted

64 J. C. H. Aveling, *Post-Reformation Catholicism in East Yorkshire 1558–1790* (York, 1960), 25; *idem, Northern Catholics*, 146–7.

65 PRO, E 368/493, mem. 206a–b, E 368/528, mem. 210a; cf. J. C. Atkinson, *Quarter Sessions Records* (North Riding Record Society, 1–3, 1884–5), III, 84, 175. Robert Ellerker was fined by the high commission in 1605 though he had conformed before Matthew Hutton in York Minster in 1596, PRO, E 135/12/7, mem. 186a, E 368/493, mem. 89a–c. Robert Gaterd of Melsonby was dealt with similarly, PRO E 368/494, mem. 82a, E 351/595, mem. 2b. Several of those who were compelled to submit by the drive against recusancy in 1616 later relapsed, people like Gregory and Elizabeth Wardell, John and Joan Hogg, Thomas Whitefield and Mariana Tomlin, PRO, E 368/571, mem. 154a–b; cf. Atkinson, *Quarter Sessions*, III, 243–4. Thomas Crathorne of Ness conformed in 1606 when he could no longer dodge the penalties for recusancy. He became non-communicant while his wife remained recusant. He was convicted as a recusant again in 1624 and 1634, CRS 53, 367 n. 98; Aveling, *Northern Catholics*, 268. Thomas Bowes of Angram Grange, Welbury, conformed in 1599 but was reconvicted as a recusant in 1633, PRO, E 368/494, mem. 84a; Aveling, *Northern Catholics*, 274.

66 PRO, E 135/12/7, mm. 305a, 308a; BI, HCAB 15, fos. 134v, 165r, 191r, HCAB 16, fo. 4r.

67 Aveling, *Catholic Recusancy*, 342–3; Anstruther I, 246; BL, Lansd. MS 80, fo. 131r. Robert Nelson (of the same family) conformed in 1606, PRO, E 368/526, mem. 183a–b.

according to the law moved between recusancy and conformity in the same way as those who are generally described as church papists. None of the group of nine recusants who appeared before Lancelot Andrewes as bishop of Chichester was, apparently, ever convicted again. George Meynell, one of only two of his very Catholic family in the North Riding whom we know to have conformed in full, was never subsequently re-convicted.[68] In other cases, statutory conformity took place where previously there had been a stolid resistance to change. Among those listed in the lord treasurer's remembrancer's memoranda rolls from the West Riding of Yorkshire are members of families which Aveling from other evidence describes as strongly recusant – the Walworths, Tankards, Gelstrops, Redmans, Thwaites, Oglethorpes, Hungates, Hamertons and so on.[69]

Are we therefore left unresolved? The answer seems to be that though some recusants did not see statutory conformity at the dictates of Protestant churchmen as a permanent break with their Catholic past, for others it had a seriousness which went far beyond church papistry. Although some recusant conformists were subject to the most pressing of fiscal persuasions, this did not nullify the religious significance of the conformity into which they were forced.[70] The fact that some conformists did not remain conformable should not be taken to mean that they had changed only the appearance of religion rather than the substance of it. Sir Henry James was induced to reject Rome in 1606 not through the weight of the recusancy fines he had been paying but through the shock of the Gunpowder Plot revelations. His decision to conform, far from being a cynical financial manoeuvre, caused him sufficient stress to leave him mentally unbalanced, and his family broke up as he tried to force them to conform as well. His return to recusancy five years later did not mean that he had not abandoned his Catholicism in the intervening years and had merely feigned conformity.[71]

68 PRO, E 368/525, mem. 234a; CRS 56, xiii–xiv.

69 Aveling, *Catholics Recusants*, 223–7.

70 The replies of Thomas Oglethorpe to the questions put to him at the English College in Rome show that his father's conformity was regarded as more than an occasional lapse, BI, HCAB 12, fos. 62r, 68v; Foley III, 148–50, 152, 167; PRO, Stac. Proc. 8/11/12, fo. 1r, although his father's repeated statements of conformity were made primarily to preserve property, especially during the rampage by Bishop John Thornborough's exchequer commission in 1607, BL, Lansd. MS 153, fos. 199r, 260v, as a result of which, apparently, Margaret Oglethorpe of Kellington, part of the Brandsby branch of the family, also conformed, BI, HCAB 15, fo. 37r; PRO, E 368/530, mem. 159a–b.

71 H. Bowler, 'Sir Henry James of Smarden, Kent, and Clerkenwell Recusant (c. 1559–1625', in A. E. J. Hollaender and W. Kellaway (eds.), *Studies in London History* (1969), 289–313, at pp. 301–2, 313. A report from Staffordshire in late 1605 said that William Mountford 'being not at church in half a year before, came to church the very next Sunday after the failing of the said traitors, very solemnly', HMC *Salisbury MSS* XVII, 643; cf. AAW, A VIII, 433.

A significant number of Catholic renegade priests who (unlike Martin Nelson) changed religion permanently had relations who were prepared to conform according to statute, and the suggestion is that the seriousness of conformity in the priests' cases communicates itself by association to that of their relatives. Members of Anthony Tyrrell's family showed themselves willing to submit publicly.[72] Some of John Copley's relations had a conformist slant. Despite his father's exile and financial losses on account of his religious convictions, his mother was content to conform in May 1596. She had sheltered priests after her return to England in 1585 and in 1590 was still described by a hostile Protestant writer as a 'great bigot' but she submitted after years of financial harassment by the exchequer.[73] Francis Barnaby probably did not apostatise in the same sense as Copley, but he went way beyond what the government generally required of a loyalist priest, and he was an enthusiastic supporter of the Jacobean oath of allegiance. His father, with whom he kept in touch and on whom he relied for financial support, conformed according to statute in 1599.[74] The renegade priest John Scudamore of Holme Lacy in Herefordshire had a loyalist father who could be relied on to take action against Catholic recusants. The head of the Kentchurch branch of the family, Thomas Scudamore (who knew the priest John Scudamore well), had conformed according to statute in 1594 and in 1603 assured the authorities of his enthusiastic loyalism when his son, another John Scudamore, became involved in the insane Bye Plot.[75] The renegade cleric Martin Harrington was a member of the Harrington family of Mount St John in Yorkshire. Henry Harrington submitted publicly in 1607; his father William Harrington, Campion's host in 1580, had conformed when arrested for harbouring the Jesuit.[76] The unreliable cleric William Atkinson apostatised

[72] O'Dwyer, 'Catholic Recusants', 84, 188; PRO, E 368/501, mem. 198a.
[73] R. C. Christie (ed.), *Letters of Sir Thomas Copley* (1897), xxxviii–xlii; PRO, E 368/500, mem. 183a. In 1586 her eldest son William had been thought to be 'very tractable' in religion, even though there is no evidence that he submitted formally. Anthony Copley, arch–enemy of the Jesuits, in January 1591 was willing to confer in religion, BL, Lansd. MS 66, fo. 65r.
[74] LPL, Fairhurst MS 2006, fo. 191r; AAW, A XI, 345; PRO, E 368/496, mem. 82a.
[75] Hasler, *Commons*, III, 361; Anstruther I, 304–5; PRO, E 368/505, mem. 122a–b; PRO, SP 14/2/84, SP 14/3/6, 7; *HMC Salisbury MSS* XV, 210, 213–14. Sir James Scudamore, the brother of the priest John Scudamore, shifted in religion sufficiently to be a detector of priests and recusants, M. Foster, 'Thomas Allen of Gloucester Hall, Oxford (1540–1632)', *Oxoniensia* 46 (1981), 99–128, at p. 123.
[76] Aveling, *Catholic Recusancy*, 316–17; Aveling, *Northern Catholics*, 105, 185; PRO, E 368/528, mem. 169a–b; BI, HCAB 15, fo. 48r; PRO, C 231/4, fo. 38v; AAW, A XV, 495, though the extent of Martin Harrington's conformity is not clear. Henry's brother, William Harrington, the seminary priest who was executed in 1594, showed signs of being conformable, for which reason his execution was temporarily respited, Anstruther I, 149–50; *CSPD 1591–4*, 363–4.

openly only in 1602. In June 1597, William Waad had written to Sir Robert Cecil that Atkinson's father had been interrogated and, though a life-long recusant, now 'confesseth with tears that his eyes have now been opened to see the darkness he lived in, and offers his help to apprehend as many as he knows of', as his son subsequently did as well.[77]

Other conformist Catholics are known to have associated closely before submission with clerical renegades. John Seaborne, a Herefordshire gentleman who was of a conformist hue (and formally submitted in 1599 before Herbert Westfaling, bishop of Hereford), was probably influenced in the 1590s by the future renegade priest John Scudamore. Seaborne lived close to Scudamore's family, and Scudamore communicated and even stayed with him.[78] Thomas Bell was chaplain to Miles Gerard at Ince and Bell betrayed him when he abjured Rome in late 1592. Gerard, arrested on Bell's information, in 1593 also recanted in full, and followed this up with a conformity before Bishop Richard Vaughan in Chester Cathedral in 1599 after he was subjected to an exchequer inquisition based on an old recusancy conviction in 1590.[79] It is possible that Gerard's pliability was shaped by Bell's wayward views in his Catholic phase about occasional conformity. At the time of his arrest Gerard was thought by Sir Thomas Egerton to be not ill-affected in religion; his principal crime was to be 'mysledde . . . by his wyffe'.[80] George Sweeting of Ripon conformed finally in 1610, but he had at one time sheltered James Bowland who abjured Roman Catholicism in York Castle in March 1600.[81] Nicholas Langford of Longford in Derbyshire conformed in 1595 (though he presented himself before the exchequer barons only in 1600). Admittedly he had come under huge political and financial pressure for his recusancy in the second half of the 1580s and first half of the 1590s. One wonders, though, whether his eventual submission might not have been influenced by his acquaintance with the perpetually

---

[77] *HMC Salisbury MSS* VII, 264.

[78] *HMC Salisbury MSS* VII, 223–4; CRS 57, 48; *CSPD 1581–90*, 449, though in 1594 Seaborne's wife was reported to have refused a request by John Scudamore for assistance, *CSPD 1591–4*, 408; PRO, E 368/497, mem. 49a–b; cf. PRO, C 231/1, p. 26. In 1601 John Seaborne was being noted, with other Herefordshire Catholic gentry, as part of the earl of Essex's affinity (through marriage links with Sir Gelly Meyrick) and they were said to have relied on the earl to protect them from prosecution for religion, *HMC Salisbury MSS* XI, 107, but Seaborne was not being protected thus in 1599 and had to conform. Seaborne was not prosecuted again as a recusant, though his wife did not show any sign of conformity at all, CRS 60, 122; PRO, SP 14/48/138, fo. 189r.

[79] Anstruther I, 30; *APC* XXIV, 36–7, 110–11; PRO, E 368/497, mem. 55a–b.

[80] BL, Harl. MS 6995, fo. 167r. In the lists of names which Bell gave to the authorities Gerard is classified not as a recusant but as a 'dangerous' individual, implying that he was a church papist, *HMC Salisbury MSS* IV, 241.

[81] BL, Add. MS 34250, fos. 17v, 28v; PRO, E 368/536, mem. 121a. In York Castle in 1600 both Bowland and Sweeting were kept away from the other prisoners, suggesting that both were in compliant mood, though only Bowland publicly conformed at this time.

conforming seminarist Robert Gray (who like Bell held dissenting Catholic opinions about the permissibility of occasional conformity) a celebrant of Mass at Langford's house in Derbyshire.[82] Langford claimed in a letter to Sir Robert Cecil in December 1594 that he had resolved his mind in favour of church attendance by discussion with some of his 'learned friends'.[83] If he had regarded conformity as a matter purely of financial self-preservation he would perhaps not have taken nearly two years to become conformable following the 1592 exchequer inquisition into his property.

Some Catholic clerics, watching from the sidelines in near despair, believed that public submission and abjuration of Rome was more than a charade. Richard Holtby thought conformists were not just cut off from grace but also forced to rely on the good offices of their former per-secutors.[84] This might be construed as clerical pessimism, a tendency to see the worst in lay people's independence of mind. But such sentiments were echoed in optimistic vein by Protestants. The bishops, especially those with evangelical tendencies, were clearly not prepared to rubber-stamp recusant conformities if they thought they were being made solely to recover property. Archbishops Hutton and Mathew frequently referred to receiving parish conformity certificates from 'godly' ministers who, it may be assumed, were not certifying conformities just to help out local Catholics. Sometimes episcopal certificates, theoretically formal documents, explicitly refer to change of religion rather than mere compliance with secular law. Archbishop Mathew certified that Robert Barker, a Yorkshire gentleman, had received communion in his parish church 'for the confirmeinge and streng[t]heninge of his fayth as it becometh the servant of god and a true professor of the gospell of Jesus Christ'. James Montagu, bishop of Bath and Wells, stated that James Taylor has conformed and 'will soe continue as becometh a true Convert' as well as a 'faithfull subject'.[85]

Enthusiasts like Hutton and Mathew did not directly equate evangelical renewal with ceremonial abjuration of Rome. But there was every intention (especially by anti-Romish ecclesiastics) of exploiting such recantations and

---

[82] Hasler, *Commons*, II, 488–9; CRS 57, xx, lxxxiii; *CSPD 1591–4*, 380; PRO, E 368/500, mem. 190a; *HMC Salisbury MSS* V, 277.

[83] *HMC Salisbury MSS* V, 31. Langford's niece and heiress rejected her Catholic background entirely, R. Clark, 'Anglicanism, Recusancy and Dissent in Derbyshire 1603–1730' (DPhil. thesis, Oxford, 1979), 61.

[84] J. Morris (ed.), *The Troubles of our Catholic Forefathers* (3 vols., 1872–7), III, 176–7.

[85] PRO, E 368/532, mem. 183a, E 368/558, mem. 173c. In 1606 George Clark, the minister at Kirkby on Bain, reported to Bishop William Chaderton of George Thimelby that (though he had only five weeks before been assessed by an exchequer inquisition) God had been pleased since Thimelby's 'comyng within my charge to open the dore of his harte and hath endued his understanding with the truth of the gospell', Foster, *State*, xcii; PRO, E 368/525, mem. 172a.

portraying them in at least some sense as an actual conversion. Admittedly there is no clear pattern of recusants of higher status being made to appear for propaganda reasons in public while lower ranking ones were not, something which one would expect if nonconformist Catholicism were thought to be sustained by the gentry.[86] Evidence suggests, all the same, that bishops were determined to exploit the propaganda potential of conforming recusants, particularly those of high status, and not just to demonstrate that they had become loyal subjects. Archbishop Bancroft wrote to the bishops of his province in March 1605 'that the people are commonly carried away by gentlemen recusants . . . so as the winning or punishing of one or two of them is a reclaiming, or a kind of bridling, of many that do depend upon them'.[87] Thomas Barnaby had to hear divine service before Bancroft in Lambeth Palace Chapel and then go through the same process again in front of Hutton in York Cathedral before he could go back down to London and finally present his conformity certificate to the exchequer.[88] Paul Hamerton, another Yorkshire squire, submitted before Hutton on 3 September 1597 and heard divine service in Hutton's private chapel. He was then ordered to hear divine service again (and presumably make a public recantation) on the following day in York Minster.[89] It may be relevant that Joseph Constable, the political malcontent of the 1590s whose original conformity was supposed to have been so influential, had to receive (on his second submission) communion in Archbishop Mathew's presence in public in Cawood parish church (although he had already heard divine service in private in Cawood Castle).[90] Richard Stapleton was by marriage connected

---

[86] Of those who presented their conformity certificates before the exchequer between 1590 and 1625, and for whom clear details exist of where they made their submission before the bishop or his representative, 268 were allowed to appear in the bishop's private chapel (assuming that this is not counted as a 'public' appearance). A further 138 submitted in a parish church at which the bishop was present, generally one near his episcopal residence, and 112 recusants conformed before their bishop in a cathedral church. *Cf.* Sir Francis Hastings, *A Watch–Word* (1598), 77; Bossy, *English Catholic Community*, 175–7; Dunbabin, 'Post-Reformation Catholicism', 66–7; F. H. Pugh, 'Monmouthshire Recusants in the Reigns of Elizabeth I and James I', *South Wales and Monmouth Record Society* 4 (1957), 59–110, at pp. 60–1; Clark, 'Anglicanism', 47–9, 57–8; A. Dures, *English Catholicism 1558–1642* (1983), 58. It is possible that conformists of high status might use their influence to ensure that at least before the bishop they were allowed to submit in private. It was not absolutely necessary for the validity of that part of the conformity that it should be performed in public, just as penance to lift excommunication could be performed privately, Potter, 'Ecclesiastical Courts', 103–4, though statute-based conformity with its ecclesiastical elements could not be commuted in the way that purely ecclesiastical penalties were, Potter, 'Ecclesiastical Courts', 106; Cardwell, *Documentary Annals*, I, 415.

[87] TD IV, xcix.   [88] PRO, E 368/496, mem. 82[d].

[89] PRO, E 368/489, mem. 206[a–b]; cf. the case of Francis Arthington in March 1608, PRO, E 368/530, mem. 164[a].

[90] PRO, E 368/528, mem. 219[a–b].

with the sixth earl of Westmorland's Yorkshire affinity of which Constable had been such a noted leader. Stapleton was compelled by Hutton to receive communion publicly with his wife in York Minster.[91] A few months afterwards, Hutton reported to Burghley that he trusted the submission of Sir William Vavasour in September 1597 (who 'after much and long conference with me, hath yielded to hear divine service and sermons') would 'do much good'. Bishop Richard Vaughan of Chester thought that the 'conversion according to statute' of the squire Edward Langtree in October 1598 was likely to set a suitable example.[92] Thomas Darell of Scotney Castle in Kent does not appear in the lord treasurer's remembrancer's memoranda rolls but his conformity was similarly exploited by George Abbot. The archbishop wrote to a friend in September 1614 that Darell,

a proper gentleman about 24. yeeres of age, and one who hath bene at St Omers, at Doway, and diverse other places in those partes, came unto mee being somewhat prepared before by an honest divine, and after much conference which I had with him, was contented to heare prayers in my Chappell, and afterwards testifyed, that he very well approoved the same. I dismissed him for that time, but tooke his promise, that hee should bee with mee to morrow at Croydon Church, where I told him, that God willing hee should heare mee preache . . . and to morrow I hope publickly to engage him in an Assembly of more then a thousand persons; which I do the rather desire to accomplish, because hee telleth mee that as the greatest part of his fathers kindred are Papists, so there was never any of his mothers kinne or name [including the Gage family of Sussex], which were of our religion.[93]

Kenneth Fincham has demonstrated that those bishops with a common 'evangelical' identity were concerned with preaching and catechising in a way that some of their clerical opponents were not. He sees a radical division between the bishops who perceived their office as a preaching ministry and those who saw themselves as the custodians of order in the Church. The former, generally sharing a Calvinist theology, were committed to evangelisation in a different way from others.[94] Bishops Gervase Babington, Robert Bennett, William James, John Jegon, George Lloyd, James Montagu, Thomas Morton, Henry Parry, Richard Parry, Henry Robinson and Richard Vaughan, and particularly Archbishops Hutton, Mathew and Abbot, all suitable to Fincham's 'evangelical' model, were also notable as episcopal enforcers of recusant conformity. The lord treasurer's remembrancer's memoranda rolls show that many more recusants appeared

---

[91] BL, Lansd. MS 84, fo. 174ʳ.

[92] *HMC Salisbury MSS* VII, 404, VIII, 399.

[93] National Library of Scotland, Advocates MS 33-1-6, xx, fo. 74ʳ (I am very grateful to Kenneth Fincham for supplying the text of this letter); William Berry, *County Genealogies . . . of Sussex* (1830), 165. For the Darell family of Kent, B. Strudwick, 'The Darells of Calehill', *Kent Recusant History* 4 (1980), 89–99.

[94] Fincham, *Prelate*, 82–91, 212–31, 253–76.

in front of Fincham's 'evangelical' prelates to conform than in front of those prelates who are not thus classifiable.[95] For these bishops, evangelisation included making stubborn recusants submit. Of course, the frequency with which recusants appeared before a particular diocesan bishop to conform according to the 1581 statute's requirements depended on which see the bishop occupied (and at what date), how many recusants it contained and how well the secular as well as the diocesan authorities operated there.[96] In addition, bishops like Whitgift were keen to secure conformities but cannot easily be fitted into Fincham's 'evangelical' model. Nevertheless, in all these 'evangelical' prelates' cases corroborative evidence exists to reinforce the impression that they principally were the ones zealously trying to make recusants submit. Robert Bennett, bishop of Hereford, claimed in August 1605 that in his most recent drive against recusants he had made over 200 people conform.[97] Bishop Gervase Babington was zealous not just in his clerical capacity but also as a justice of the peace and recipient of exchequer commissions to sequestrate recusant property.[98] William James used the ecclesiastical commission to drive significant numbers of recusants in Durham and Northumberland into conformity.[99] George Lloyd (whom Fincham classes tentatively as an evangelical) organised mass conformities of Lancashire recusants. In July 1605 he told the earl of Salisbury that he had taken a residence in Lancashire expressly for the purpose of better suppression of popish dissent.[100] Richard Vaughan, Lloyd's predecessor at Chester, boasted that he had made 600 conform in the three years between 1601 and 1604, and made efforts to place the queen's preachers in

---

[95] Questier, 'Phenomenon', 324–6.

[96] For example, William Cotton is generally regarded as having been relatively effective against dissenters in the earlier part of his episcopate, and relatively ineffective in the later part when he became disillusioned with the fight against nonconformity, I. Cassidy, 'The Episcopate of William Cotton, Bishop of Exeter, 1598–1621: With Special Reference to the State of the Clergy and the Administration of the Ecclesiastical Courts' (BLitt. thesis, Oxford, 1963), 11, but though it is known that he was trying hard to secure recusant conformities in the earlier half of his career as bishop of Exeter, *HMC Salisbury MSS* XVIII, 297–8, only two show up in exchequer records; the other eleven conformities certified into the exchequer from Exeter diocese come from his last few years.

[97] *HMC Salisbury MSS* XVII, 360–1, cf. 258–9, 455–6; cf. for general evidence of his anti-Catholic initiatives, CRS 54, 245; Anstruther I, 381–2.

[98] Fincham, *Prelate*, 100; PRO, E 368/531, mem. 98[a–b] (William Cooper's conformity certificate was signed by Babington who confirmed that Cooper had submitted 'personally before me and other Justices of peace at the Quarter Sessions' at Worcester in September 1606. Babington had also been the exchequer commissioner responsible for the three inquisitions into Cooper's property). Babington was active in trying to ensure that recusants were convicted at assize hearings, *HMC Salisbury MSS* XVI, 176–7.

[99] PRO, SP 14/75/1.i; AAW, Anglia IX, no. 2. For his views on the enforcement of conformity, *HMC Salisbury MSS* XIX, 378.

[100] Fincham, *Prelate*, 293; PRO, E 368/571, mem. 142[b]; *HMC Salisbury MSS* XVII, 320.

Lancashire precisely where presentments of recusants in the Church courts and at the assizes showed recusancy to be strongest.[101]

There is no doubt, then, that the formal procedure for conforming was no formality. Though created by statute and regulated in large part by a department of central government, it had a religious as well as a political significance. In theory, at least, Church and State combined to make submission to the law an ecclesiastical as much as a merely legal test. Godly Protestants did not think statutory conformity was simply an anodyne church papistry, and many Catholics seem to have agreed. John Thornborough told Sir Julius Caesar in 1607 that recusants in the North were very willing to attend a local church in order to secure immediate redelivery of their sequestrated goods (common practice in that part of the country). Thornborough said, however, that 'of these not one among five will submit him selfe as law appointeth in the exchequer'. In other words, they then refused to go through the whole statutory conformity procedure (including appearance at divine service in the presence of the bishop). In part this was because 'if they againe revolt after such submission, their penalty is the greater' (because the 1581 statute forbade a recusant from taking financial advantage of a second submission). But, more importantly, they were prepared to attend church (while refusing to conform in full) 'because among the Recusantes they wilbe accounted papistes still'.[102]

The evidence then is that statutory conformity was a world away from church papistry. It was hard and unforgiving. Reabsorption into the established Church came at a price. But a second question now arises. Was the system for compelling genuine conformity actually enforced very widely? Even if the statutes provided for recusants to make a clearly religious rather than just a political profession of conformity, historians have argued that the enforcement of these statutes' penalties for recusancy was not sufficient to drive recusants towards the proposed conformity. K. R. Wark claims that by 1586 recusancy was 'being thought of as a permanent feature of English life' and that 'reformation and conformity were no longer the first consideration'. Aveling suggests that in the North the authorities were seeking a *modus vivendi* as early as 1583, and he doubts whether 'simple . . . extermination' had ever been seriously entertained as a policy at all.[103] Even the 12d fine imposed by the 1559 act of uniformity for failure to attend divine service each week, thought by contemporaries to be a very good way of compelling conformity, was blunted by an inability to enforce

---

[101] CRS 53, 147; *HMC Salisbury MSS* X, 41, 84.

[102] BL, Lansd. MS 153, fo. 267ʳ. Robert Kelway noted similarly that after restoration of goods, they will come 'no more to the Church in a yeare after', *ibid.*, fo. 212ʳ.

[103] K. R. Wark, *Elizabethan Recusancy in Cheshire* (Manchester, 1971), 63; Aveling, *Northern Catholics*, 114–15.

it consistently.[104] The next chapter discusses whether the more complex system evolved in the 1580s for making recusants pliable in religion was undermined by the same difficulties.

[104] James Howell (ed.) *Cottoni Posthuma* (1651), 152–3; Bradshaw, *Humble Motives*, 35; LPL, Tenison MS 663, fo. 50ʳ; *HMC Salisbury MSS* XIX, 378; Aveling, *Catholic Recusancy*, 58, indicating that it was, if levied, a very heavy exaction, though Aveling shows that, in York, the fine was enforced with difficulty; Walker, 'Implementation', 6; Rose, *Cases*, 17; Neale, *Elizabeth*, II, 396–7. The system for enforcing it was tightened up by 3 James I, c.4; CRS 53, 291–2.

'Heresy is dead and policy is the life of religion': State, Church, conversion and conformity

No one has ever suggested that, in this period, statute and judiciary could force all Catholic dissenters to conform within the meaning of the law. It is doubtful whether the Tudor and Stuart authorities ever thought they could compel total conformity (or, indeed, whether any bureaucracy and Church at any time could do this).[1] In any case, it is very difficult to estimate how many people wandered in and out of recusancy, let alone those who changed their religious opinions in some way to deflect the attentions of the authorities. But even if the country could not be Protestantised simply by ordaining that Roman Catholic practices were proscribed, did the State have the capacity to compel, in specific cases, conformity to the degree that it thought was politically necessary and ecclesiastically desirable?

Apart from the clerical renegades, we know of quite a number of lay people who conformed officially at the dictation of the State during this

Chapter title quotation: AAW, A XIII, 631, Edward Bennett to Thomas More, November 1614, referring to the recent tightening up of fiscal policy against Catholic recusants.

[1] J. C. H. Aveling, *Catholic Recusancy in the City of York 1558–1791* (CRS monograph 2, 1970), 58. The central authorities had no intention of proceeding against all those recusants whose convictions were certified to the exchequer by local courts. The fact that the annotation *fiat commissio* appears next to a recusant's name on the Recusant Rolls does not mean that exchequer commissioners assessed his lands immediately, if at all, Aveling, *Northern Catholics*, 131; A. Dunbabin, 'Post-Reformation Catholicism in the Parish of Prescot, Lancashire, from the Elizabethan Settlement to the Civil War' (MA thesis, Manchester, 1980), 20; R. Clark, 'Anglicanism Recusancy and Dissent in Derbyshire 1603–1730' (DPhil. Thesis, Oxford, 1979), 88 (showing that only 20 per cent of the total number of convicted recusants in Derbyshire had any kind of property seized); Pugh suggests that the figure was about 25 per cent for Glamorganshire recusants, F. H. Pugh, 'Glamorgan Recusants 1577–1611: A Selection from the Returns in the Public Record Office', *South Wales and Monmouth Record Society* 3 (1954), 49–72, at p. 51; J. J. La Rocca, 'James I and his Catholic Subjects, 1606–1612: Some Financial Implications', *RH* 18 (1987), 251–62, at p. 256. Recusant historians have argued that pressure to conform was exerted only above a certain social rank, and that those below it were left relatively untouched, J. C. H. Aveling, *Northern Catholics* (1966), 131; M. O'Dwyer, 'Catholic Recusants in Essex *c.* 1580 to *c.* 1600' (MA thesis, London, 1960), 146; V. Burke, 'Catholic Recusants in Elizabethan Worcestershire' (MA thesis, Birmingham, 1972), 217; Dunbabin, 'Post-Reformation Catholicism', 20.

period. There was no national system for recording all such conformities in sixteenth- and seventeenth-century England in the way that there was in eighteenth-century Ireland.[2] English conformists in our period have to be dredged up from several different sources. The State Papers contain records of individuals who had got out of their depth in the politics of religious dissent and established their new political reliability by affirming their acceptance of the State Church.[3] King's Bench records,[4] and quarter sessions and assize rolls contain the names of many conformists. I propose to focus, however, on the source which records more conformities in more detail than any other, the lord treasurer's remembrancer's memoranda rolls, compiled by the institution, the exchequer, which was ultimately responsible for coordinating the pressures to conform exerted (through provincial officials, assize judges and justices of the peace) on those convicted under the recusancy statutes. Of course, those who appeared before the exchequer barons to certify their conformities and obtain a discharge from sequestration of their property were probably only a small fraction of all those who conformed officially before secular and ecclesiastical authorities. The ex-recusant would present himself there only if he had property to recover, or wished to prevent an imminent sequestration (even though, technically, a conformity would not discharge a conviction unless approved and registered by the exchequer court).[5] In 1593 Miles Gerard of Ince, 'conformed himselfe in rell;igion according to the lawes . . . and . . . resorted to the Churche, hearde Devine service and sermons, [and] receaved the Sacrament'. In other words, he went through the full conformity procedure prescribed by statute and canon law. But the conformity which he eventually registered at the exchequer was based on a separate and much later submission before Bishop Richard Vaughan on 27 October 1599.[6] There is no record of his earlier statutory conformity in the exchequer at all. One suspects that this is the

---

2 Under 2 Anne, c.6, it was necessary for *all* conformers to the Church of Ireland to provide proof of their change of religion. About 5,500 conformists registered their submissions under this act between 1703 and 1789, though probably a substantial number of those who conformed did not bother to enrol, E. O'Byrne (ed.), *The Convert Rolls* (Dublin, 1981), vii–xii. Those who wished to be released from the legal disabilities resulting from profession of Catholicism had to register their conformity in the high court of chancery after publicly abjuring specific Catholic doctrinal beliefs (as well as the Jacobite succession) at a public service and obtaining a clerical certificate to that effect.
3 M. C. Questier, 'The Phenomenon of Conversion: Change of Religion to and from Catholicism in England, 1580–1625' (DPhil. thesis, Sussex, 1991), 237.
4 D. M. Clarke, 'Conformity Certificates among the King's Bench Records: A Calendar', *RH* 14 (1977–8), 53–63. It is not exactly clear why conformity certificates should be in the King's Bench records. Possibly it was because cases had been removed into this court through *certiorari* writs or because those who had been recusant for more than twelve months were certified into this court and had then conformed, CRS 57, xxix; CRS 53, 293.
5 *CSPD* 1595–7, 569.
6 *APC* XXIV, 36–7, 110–11; PRO, E 368/497, mem. 55[a–b].

case with many people; their conformities were never recorded in this way.[7] Many others would have conformed before conviction, and likewise their conformities have left no trace. Nevertheless, an investigation into the State's attitude towards, and control over, conformity does not require a complete list of those who conformed but a detailed reliable source to demonstrate how it regulated submission to the established Church. This the memoranda rolls unquestionably are.

PROCEDURAL INEFFICIENCY?

How good was the exchequer at enforcing the undoubtedly 'real' system of conformity which the legislators had devised? The initial impression is that the exchequer was hampered by a number of serious problems (even if they were not completely of its own making). There was always a difficulty in determining who was actually a recusant, and those who were not prepared to indulge in church papistry could still make it hard for the authorities to detect them.[8] There is no doubt that some influential people could escape the legal penalties altogether.[9] But it has often seemed that the effectiveness of

---

[7] Of the people on Richard Heaton's lists of Yorkshire conformists, twenty-six out of sixty-six Elizabethan and nineteen out of thirty Jacobean conformists did not come to register their submissions at Westminster, BL, Lansd. MS 153, fos. 264v–5r. Of the many conformities produced by the activities of an exchequer commission in Northumberland in 1605, only six appear in the lord treasurer's remembrancer's memoranda rolls, *HMC Salisbury MSS* XVII, 427. Many of those who submitted before the ecclesiastical commissions had no financial reason to appear at Westminster, e.g. Mary Ellis of Kidhall, CRS 71, 58; CRS 18, 76; BI, HCAB 12, fos. 43r, 51r, 53r, 146v, 155v, HCAB 16, fos. 327r, 334v; and Marmaduke Watkinson, whom the commissioners certified in October 1615 had conformed 'according to the statute', BI, HCAB 16, fo. 89r. Of the eleven conformists in an Oxfordshire list of recusants drawn up in 1613, none appears in the lord treasurer's remembrancer's memoranda rolls, CRS 60, 211–29. While William Chaderton's Lincoln register contains among its nineteen conformists between 1605 and 1607, C. W. Foster, *The State of the Church in the Reigns of Elizabeth and James I, as Illustrated by Documents Relating to the Diocese of Lincoln*, I (Lincoln Record Society 23, 1926), xcii–iii, thirteen of whose conformities were certified in the exchequer, most of the conformists in the lists sent from the diocese of Durham in 1611 and 1613 by Bishop William James were never thus registered, AAW, Anglia IX, no. 2; PRO, SP 14/75/1.i. Of the twenty-seven conformist North Riding recusants certified to the justices of the peace in October 1616 by Nicholas Lewes, minister of the chapel of Egton, J. C. Atkinson, *Quarter Sessions Records* (North Riding Record Society, 1–3, 1884–5), II, 153, only six appear in the lord treasurer's remembrancer's memoranda rolls. Gerard Salvin of Croxdale made a formal submission in Durham Cathedral to avoid confiscation resulting from a recusancy conviction in 1624, but it was never registered at the exchequer, J. A. Hilton, 'Catholic Recusancy in County Durham, 1559–1625' (MPhil. thesis, Leeds, 1974), 191.

[8] Aveling, *Northern Catholics*, 96–7; P. Tyler, 'The Ecclesiastical Commission for the Province of York 1561–1641' (DPhil. thesis, Oxford, 1965), 288–9; BL, Harl. MS 6849, fo. 277r.

[9] J. C. H. Aveling, 'The Catholic Recusancy of the Yorkshire Fairfaxes', part I, *RH* 3 (1954–6), 69–114, at pp. 88–9.

the whole conformity system was undermined by an unerring tendency to get the wrong people. A sizeable number of conformists presented evidence to the exchequer that they had no Catholic sympathies whatsoever but had temporarily been avoiding their parish churches out of fear of arrest for debt.[10] Others could apparently show that ill-health had kept them away from divine service.[11] Some had not been identified correctly.[12] Some alleged the malice of those who procured their convictions.[13] Fifty-one of the nearly 870 recusants who appeared in the exchequer court to conform between 1590 and 1625 claimed that they had not been properly recusant when they were convicted.

Even if the exchequer could not be expected to take account of the personal circumstances of these people, there is evidence of a certain amount of sheer administrative bungling. If the authorities in York could present for recusancy one of the principal high commission agents whose business was the stamping out of recusancy, it was not surprising that the exchequer could be plagued by bureaucratic mistakes of identification.[14] Thomas Robinson, convicted of recusancy in Yorkshire, claimed that he was convicted in error (and his claim was strongly supported by Archbishop

---

10 E.g. PRO, E 368/479, mem. 140ᵃ, E 368/483, mem. 122ᵃ⁻ᵇ, E 368/552, mem. 132ᵃ. It was a common excuse, BI, HCAB 15, fo. 66ᵛ; J. S. Purvis (ed.), *Tudor Parish Documents of the Diocese of York* (Cambridge, 1948), 93–4; PRO, SP 12/243/76, fo. 212ᵛ.

11 PRO, E 368/539, mem. 279ᵃ⁻ᵇ; Robert Fenwick, convicted for recusancy in Northumberland, brought evidence that he had been resorting to church regularly for twenty years before he was convicted, at which time 'he was so greviouslye wounded that hee was forced to keepe his bedd for manny dayes after', PRO, E 368/558, mem. 193ᵃ; PRO, E 368/590, mem. 92ᵃ, for Henry Smith's assertion of various ailments (including almost total deafness which he said would prevent him from hearing the service anyway). Excuses like these were regularly presented to the ecclesiastical courts, J. M. Potter, 'The Ecclesiastical Courts in the Diocese of Canterbury 1603–1665' (MPhil. thesis, London, 1973), 110; Clark, 'Anglicanism', 33.

12 Richard Cholmeley, 'The Memorandum Book of Richard Cholmeley of Brandsby 1602–1623', *North Yorkshire County Record Office Publications* 44 (1988), 187–9 for a complex attempt to overturn a conviction on the basis of a 'misnomer' (though this case did not involve the exchequer). If the presentments of names (and status) of recusants were insufficiently accurate, then indictments could not be framed against them, *HMC Salisbury MSS* XVI, 177.

13 PRO, E 368/495, mem. 30ᵃ, E 368/568, mem. 114ᵃ. Some Essex justices certified in February 1596 that Mary Smith of Lamarsh was 'excommunicat for not apperinge at the spirituall Courte and duringe the tyme of her said excommunicacion did absent her self from the Churche . . . duringe which tyme one upon mallice (as wee knowe) endited her as a Recusant', PRO, E 368/482, mem. 182ᵃ; cf. Dorothy Burgoyne, another well–documented case of malicious prosecution, PRO, E 368/515, mem. 121ᵇ; CRS 71, 31; CRS 61, 158; PRO, Stac. Proc. 5/K12/15; BL, Lansd. MS 103, fo. 264ʳ. Sir Henry Hastings claimed in his Star Chamber deposition of 26 January 1607 that a recusancy conviction had been procured against him out of malice, PRO, Stac. Proc. 8/55/26, for which reference I am grateful to Richard Cust.

14 Aveling, *Catholic Recusancy*, 233.

Hutton). Ralph Sadler, also of Yorkshire, was a former churchwarden who somehow managed to be convicted of recusancy.[15] Some cases involved former recusants who had been conforming for years (and some had even presented themselves before the exchequer court to verify it). By mistake they had been convicted again and found that their property was being sequestrated for a second time. The 'loathsome and unsavoury smells' of the gaol at Derby probably did not provoke Anthony Fitzherbert of Norbury to an entirely impartial consideration of the relative merits of the Roman and Protestant faiths, but he wrote to the earl of Shrewsbury in May 1591 that he recognised he had been 'misled in points of religion'. He conformed according to statute in mid-1600. He was then reconvicted in April 1605. But Bishop William Overton certified that, nearly fifteen years before, 'upon conference had with learned divines' Fitzherbert had completely reformed himself and had been a dutiful conformist ever since. His present conviction for recusancy was the result of an administrative bungle.[16] Those who appeared twice at the exchequer to conform (though the statute of 1581 expressly forbade that any recusant should take advantage of its submission clause on more than one occasion) had usually been reconvicted in error and had not, in fact, lapsed back into recusancy.[17] Sir Thomas Tildesley reported from Lancashire in 1612 that roving speculators operating by virtue of exchequer commissions were indicting those who 'by the Certificat of the Preachers and Ministers of their severall parishes . . . allwaies both receaved the Sacrament and . . . [were] Conformable', i.e. they were not even non-communicant. Tildesley said that, in other instances, former Lancashire recusants have 'long sithence uppon the yssuing of former Commisons from the exchequer submitted themselves, resorted to the Church, and to this daie do Continue in their due obedience in all respects: Albeit for want of knowledge in the Course of the exchequer, they have not sent in Certificates of their submissions from the Bishopp of the diocese'. They are now being prosecuted, as too are those 'who have pleaded their submissions, have allowances and quietus est', but because 'they goe not through all offices, doe still stand in the schedules to be inquired of [i.e. have their

---

15 PRO, E 368/496, mem. 83ᵃ; PRO, E 368/536, mem. 119ᵃ.

16 John Strype, *Annals of the Reformation* (4 vols., Oxford, 1824), IV, 89–90; PRO, E 368/500, mem. 182ᵃ, E 368/519, mem. 78ᵃ: through the neglect of 'some he putt in trust to retorne a former Certificate had from me nere five yeares past of his Conformitye' he 'standeth in the Chequer as yett of Record as a Recusant'.

17 E.g. PRO, E 368/489, mem. 206ᵃ⁻ᵇ, cf. E 368/526, mem. 223ᵃ (Paul Hamerton who according to the certificate supplied by the vicar of Featherstone had been conforming for the past six years, i.e. almost immediately after his lands were seized in 1589, CRS 71, p. 75). Dislocation of communications within the exchequer did not help, BL, Lansd. MS 153, fos. 266ʳ, 295ʳ, 179ʳ⁻ᵛ; *CSPD 1601–3*, 280.

property assessed and sequestrated]'.[18] In the case of Anne Knowles in Staffordshire, property seizure took place, the Privy Council determined, after she had conformed and been 'reclaimed from Recusancie'.[19] Lady Katherine Copley, convicted of recusancy, conformed in May 1596. When she was assessed by the exchequer commissioners again she simply presented the 1596 conformity certificate to the exchequer court (for a second time) in 1600.[20]

The difficulties of detection were compounded by the fact that, even under the 1581 statute, it was not compulsory to attend one's own parish church once a month. People could legitimately have common prayer in their own houses as long as they frequented the parish church once a quarter, or they could attend other churches.[21] The names which William Chaderton submitted to the Council in 1580 included, among others, 'some [individuals] mistaken and certified by you [Chaderton] not to come to the church, which afterwards have made . . . dew proof to the contrarye – that albeit they doe not at all times repaire to there parishe churches, because of there lawfull absence; yet doe they most comonlie'.[22] Katherine Mariner of Southwick, Hampshire, said that she was presented for recusancy by the churchwardens of Southwick church, but, in the first place, she was unable to attend it since it was in complete disrepair, and, secondly, she had heard divine service elsewhere.[23] Other recusants, like Anthony Joy, could show that they had been attending a different local parish church.[24] Humphrey

---

[18] BL, Lansd. MS 153, fo. 195[r]; PRO, E 368/462, mem. 34[a]: John Norden obtained a certificate confirming his non-recusancy in January 1588 but was convicted in February 1589 and subject to land seizure in June 1590; CRS 71, 127; for the ecclesiastical proceedings against him for recusancy, Canterbury Cathedral Archives and Library, X.2.7, part I, fos. 70[v], 72[r], 76[r], 77[v]; cf. Thomas Barnaby's case, PRO, E 368/496, mem. 83[a-e]. In other instances, those who had given up recusancy but could not afford to certify their conformities to the exchequer also found they were the subject of its attentions, BL, Lansd. MS 153, fo. 295[r]. In April 1608 John Drew of Silverton in Devonshire received a repayment from the exchequer by way of restitution for property seized 'upon misprision and wrong information' of recusancy, even though he had conformed according to the statutory procedure (the only way of purging recusancy indictments unless the recusant could demonstrate actual legal error in the proceedings), PRO, E 368/527, mem. 228[a-b]; PRO, SO 3/4, April 1608; *CSPD 1603–10*, 422.

[19] *APC* XVII, 337; PRO, E 368/476, mem. 142[a-b]; CRS 71, 105; CRS 57, 145–6.

[20] PRO, E 368/483, mem. 121[a-c], E 368/500, mem. 183[a].

[21] *The Statutes of the Realm* (11 vols., 1810–28), IV, 658; PRO, SP 12/147/33, fo. 70[v]; cf. Clark, 'Anglicanism', 7–8.

[22] F. Peck, *Desiderata Curiosa* (2 vols., 1779), I, 98.

[23] PRO, E 368/492, mem. 190[b]; for a similar claim by George White of Sandford, Devonshire, PRO, E 368/555, mem. 200[a]; cf. A. Jessopp, 'Bowthorpe Hall', *Norfolk Archaeology* 8 (1879), 273–81, at p. 276; PRO, SP 12/136/16, fo. 41[v]. The authorities encountered real problems in framing indictments for recusancy, A. Hassell Smith and G. M. Baker (eds.), *The Papers of Nathaniel Bacon of Stiffkey* (2 vols., Norwich, 1979, 1983), II, 237.

[24] PRO, E 368/495, mem. 64[a-b].

Gifford proved his conformity in London but found himself erroneously convicted again in Staffordshire.[25] Some people, notably servants, might run into trouble because they were away from home on official duties.[26] Richard Howland, bishop of Peterborough, certified in July 1598 that Simon Gutteridge had been 'absent from his Parrishe Churche but one daye in the lord Comptons service' (and was convicted of recusancy) but that 'noe man in Northamptonshire is a better Churchman then he and further from Recusancie'.[27] In many cases the exchequer's right hand had no very clear idea what its left hand was doing.

The detection of recusants for exchequer purposes was further obstructed by actual frauds and deceptions whereby the names of recusants were concealed, sometimes even by those who were responsible for their prosecution.[28] There is no doubt that some recusants manipulated the system and went to extraordinary lengths to obstruct the exchequer and local officials.[29] These frauds instigated by recusants to deceive the exchequer were the same as those perpetrated by other classes of people from whom the exchequer hoped to profit.[30]

The exchequer's effectiveness was blunted not just by its myopia but also by the total inflexibility of its procedure for discharging these conformist recusants. The paperwork might easily satisfy the exchequer that some people had been conformable all along but, in all but exceptional cases, they had to go through the tedious, rigorous and expensive conformity process to purge their erroneous convictions. Sir James Altham, an exchequer baron, certified Ralph Sadler's oath that he 'never was recusant in all his lifetyme', but Sadler still had to make an official submission according to law.[31]

One might expect the exchequer's officials to have been good at imposing the swingeing statutory penalties for recusancy, even if they sometimes inflicted them on the wrong people. But the system for enforcing financial sanctions on recusants once they had been detected was plagued by

---

[25] PRO, E 368/534, mem. 57ᵃ; *CSPD 1603–10*, 449.

[26] Aveling, *Northern Catholics*, 97; cf. F. X. Walker, 'The Implementation of the Elizabethan Statutes against Recusants 1581–1603' (Ph.D thesis, London, 1961), 407.

[27] PRO, E 368/493, mem. 188ᵃ. Gutteridge's 'conformity' is one of the rare instances where it appears that the conformist did not have to submit formally.

[28] For the comprehensive accusations by Bishop John Thornborough, BL, Lansd. MS 153, fos. 266ʳ–7ʳ; for Thomas Bell's claims about corrupt practices in Lancashire, AAW, Anglia IX, fo. 108ʳ, cf. fo. 110ʳ; for more general accusations of corrupt dealing by clerks of assize and of the commission of the peace, BL, Cotton MS Titus B III, fo. 79ʳ.

[29] Burke, 'Catholic Recusants', 278–80; J. T. Cliffe, *The Yorkshire Gentry from the Reformation to the Civil War* (1969), 213; BL, Lansd. MS 153, fos. 211ᵛ–12ʳ; HMC *Salisbury MSS* XVII, 193; Thomas Bell, *The Survey of Popery* (1596), 111–12.

[30] BL, Lansd. MS 168, fo. 343ʳ.

[31] PRO, E 368/536, mem. 119ᵃ⁻ᵇ.

procedural drawbacks. Since most recusants could not pay the £20 fine, the only way they could be induced to conform was by seizure of their property. If this did not happen, or was mismanaged, the recusant was under no pressure (from the exchequer) at all. If mistakes were made, the recusant could have the entire process against him voided. A recusant who might otherwise have had to conform could escape.[32] The inquisition into recusant property held at Leeds before Sir Richard Mauleverer and other commissioners on 28 March 1597 was flawed and most of the recusants whose lands were assessed were subsequently discharged before the exchequer court.[33] Heirs of convicted recusants were able, in practice, to recover sequestrated property even though they themselves were recusant.[34] Pressure which might have been exerted on the recusant was frequently relaxed since the person who obtained the grant of the recusant's forfeiture often compounded with the recusant for a sum less than the one at which the exchequer commission had assessed him.[35]

The exchequer's weakest characteristic is generally thought to have been precisely the one by which it was supposed to put fiscal pressure on Catholics convicted of recusancy – namely its inquisitions into their property.[36] It is frequently alleged that corruption and bribery in the provinces meant that commissioners who were ordered to assess recusants' estates returned ludicrously low valuations to the exchequer. Cliffe argues that 'whatever type of [exchequer] commission' was involved (i.e. either to the sheriff and justices of the peace or a private one to other individuals), 'the valuation system was hopelessly inadequate: no proper survey was carried out, lands and goods were frequently concealed and jurymen were often reluctant to be too hard on their recusant neighbours. In the circumstances it is hardly surprising that the rent for the statutory two-thirds

---

[32] For details of the exonerations of recusants before the exchequer other than through submission, see O'Dwyer, 'Catholic Recusants', 219–23, mainly on the grounds of previous (*bona fide*) conveyances of lands sequestrated, CRS 57, xxii–iii, or erroneous assessments by the commissioners and local jury. Robert Kelway complained that commissioners in Northumberland were too ready to 'admit and allow all Conveyaunces that any man could produce in recusantes behalfes', BL, Lansd. MS 153, fo. 214r; Bell, *Survey*, 112; Cliffe, *Yorkshire Gentry*, 212. Copyhold land was exempt from sequestration, CRS 57, xcii, xciv; CRS 71, 164; for an attempt to clear up this problem, see the first extant draft of 35 Elizabeth I, c.2, Walker, 'Implementation', 350–1. The statute 35 Elizabeth I, c.2 does contain a provision that a recusant copyholder's land shall be forfeit to his landlord, but presumably this applies only to the offences in this statute, *Statutes* IV, 844; CRS 52, 124.
[33] PRO, E 368/488–93, *passim*.
[34] D. Shanahan, 'The Family of St Thomas More in Essex 1581–1640', *Essex Recusant* 3 (1961), 71–80, at p. 78.
[35] Cliffe, *Yorkshire Gentry*, 214–16; *CSPD 1591–4*, 159; BL, Lansd. MS 153, fo. 266r–v.
[36] For detail of the way the exchequer's commissions were issued and enforced, see Walker, 'Implementation', 262–3; CRS 57, lxiii, lxxv, lxxxi–iii, xciv, ci, cix; CRS 56, 47.

rarely bore any relation to the true value.'[37] In June 1605 Robert Bennett, bishop of Hereford, complained to the earl of Salisbury that a recent exchequer commission in the county was composed of men 'of the most suspected note' and they empanelled 'a jury like themselves'.[38] George Grant reported to Bishop Tobias Matthew in April 1596 that at an inquisition held to assess the property of Thomas Meynell and Christopher Conyers, Conyers had succeeded in naming the jurors who were supposed to verify the commission's findings.[39] Burke shows further that the Elizabethan exchequer was very tardy in letting recusant property in Worcestershire to Crown tenants (whose leases ensured that the treasury got at least *some* return). In 1603, of forty recusant estates in Worcestershire seized by the exchequer, only six had been leased out.[40]

Finally, even when the cumbersome machinery did swing into action against those whose convictions had filtered through to the central machine at Westminster and who did not have influential friends to protect them, it seems that the administration was utterly vitiated by the mad profiteering scramble of independent speculators and the exchequer's own officers who pulled out all the stops to cash in on this aspect of the Crown's finances.[41] It was agreed that the commissions were potentially of such force that they could crush recusancy, but in practice the sting was taken out of them by corruption.[42] Those who were supposed to be persuading Catholics to capitulate were in practice compounding with them over their debts and raking off substantial sums in the process. The laughable fiasco of recusancy administration was merely one of the horrendous inefficiencies of the Crown's central fiscal machine.[43]

---

[37] Cliffe, *Yorkshire Gentry*, 214; Burke, 'Catholic Recusants', 271–5; CRS 53, pp. 304–5; Tyler, 'Ecclesiastical Commission', 291; Clark; 'Anglicanism', 90–1; S. J. Watts, *From Border to Middle Shire: Northumberland 1586–1625* (Leicester, 1975), 83–4, for the protection of recusants' estates through trusts in the names of conformists. For contemporary assertions that the exchequer's commissions were no match for fraudsters, PRO, SP 12/151/72, fo. 139r; BL, Lansd. MS 153, fos. 100r–2r, 123r, 211v–12r, 214r, 266r–7r; M. C. Questier, 'Sir Henry Spiller, Recusancy, and the Efficiency of the Jacobean Exchequer', *HR* 66 (1993), 251–66, at pp. 252–3.

[38] *HMC Salisbury MSS* XVII, 235. Similar complaints about the probity and efficiency of commissioners had been made by Lord Chief Justice Popham in September 1595, BL, Lansd. MS 79, fo. 95r.

[39] CRS 56, 47–8.

[40] Burke, 'Catholic Recusants', 290–1. For a similar situation in Cheshire and Lancashire in 1590, see K. R. Wark, *Elizabethan Recusancy in Cheshire* (Manchester, 1971), 77.

[41] Questier, 'Sir Henry Spiller', 254–6; PRO, Stac. Proc. 8/11/12.

[42] AAW, Anglia IX, fo. 110v.

[43] G. E. Aylmer, *The King's Servants* (1974), 32; L. M. Hill, *Bench and Bureaucracy* (Cambridge, 1988), 121; M. J. Hawkins, 'The Government: Its Role and its Aims', in C. Russell (ed.), *The Origins of the English Civil War* (1973), 35–65, at pp. 45–6. For evidence that the administrative difficulties experienced in enforcing recusancy fines were virtually identical to those in other types of revenue collection, BL, Lansd. MS 155, fo. 64r–v,

Or so historians have generally thought. There is, of course, more than an element of truth in all these comments about the financial system which was supposed to penalise recusancy. Yet there is a danger that the inevitable inefficiencies in the day-to-day running of a bureaucratic system for enforcing conformity may obscure what that system was capable of doing, and in certain cases certainly did do extremely well. The evidence which seems to show that recusants were under little pressure from the Crown was generated mostly (and none too impartially) from within the system about which such criticism was made.[44] Even if it is true that coercive force against Catholic recusants fluctuated it is simply not true to say that the system could not make life extremely difficult for them if it wanted. As already stated, the lord treasurer's remembrancer's memoranda rolls record nearly 870 people going through an expensive and arduous conformity procedure between 1590 and 1625. Even if that number is not of itself very great, it is, as I have suggested, probably only a small fraction of those who conformed statutorily. The evidence contained in the exchequer's records gives an unparalleled view of how statutory conformity worked. It allows the historian to construct an entirely different account of the capacity of central government and local courts to deal with Catholicism.

First, the system whereby courts certified recusants' names to the exchequer was not abnormally inaccurate.[45] In fact, the secular courts which imposed penalties for recusancy could induce Catholics to conform before they ever had anything to do with the lord treasurer's remembrancer's office.[46] The statutory conformity procedure (after conviction) required recantation at an assize hearing in any case; and some assize judges made efforts to induce conformities there rather than merely impose convictions for not attending Church and leave the rest to the exchequer.[47] Anyway,

---

MS 166, fos. 95^{r-v}, 97^r, 99^{r-v}; C. Russell, *Parliaments and English Politics 1621–1629* (Oxford, 1979), 65 (concerning peculation in administration of wards), 66.

[44] Most of the accusations of double-dealing were made by those who saw a financial profit to be made for themselves as well as the Crown out of their supplanting the officials they criticised, BL, Harl. MS 6849, fo. 277^r; *CSPD 1601–3*, 279–80; Questier, 'Sir Henry Spiller', 254–7.

[45] CRS 57, cii.

[46] Atkinson, *Quarter Sessions*, II, 153–4; PRO, E 368/571, mem. 153^b.

[47] Between 1587 and 1604 only the assizes and higher courts were able to convict for recusancy under the 1581 statute, though on presentations made by the ecclesiastical courts as well as the sessions of the peace. For instances of the manipulation of court procedure to encourage conformity, *HMC Salisbury MSS* XVII, 544; BL, Harl. MS 6995, fo. 58^r; J. Cockburn (ed.), *Calendar of Assize Records: Essex Indictments: Elizabeth I* (1978), no. 3222; cf. PRO, E 368/539, mem. 138^b. In July 1595 John Harpur JP assured Lord Burghley that he 'never kept any recusant from indictment but only in hope to win him to conformity' and had 'conformed all such' as he had 'kept from indicting', though Harpur himself was suspected at the time of Catholic sympathies, *HMC Salisbury MSS* V, 276, 526; P. W. Hasler (ed.), *The House of Commons 1558–1603* (3 vols., 1981), II, 258.

social status and influence were not necessarily any protection. As Alan Dunbabin points out, even in Prescot, a Catholic area, churchwardens proceeded to return gentry in their presentments for recusancy. The famous instance of Sir John Yorke of Nidderdale crossing out the names of his recusant tenants on the list of popishly affected people compiled by George Manson, the minister at Middlemore, was rather an empty gesture; Manson just re-wrote the list and added them in again.[48] Richard Clark shows from the surviving quarter sessions records for Derbyshire that few recusants once indicted subsequently escaped conviction.[49]

The second turn of the screw lay in fines and property seizures. For all the drawbacks of the system which historians have identified, these could exert real coercive influence on Catholic nonconformists. Wark shows that some Cheshire recusants were heavily and systematically penalised by them.[50] Burke demonstrates that over half the conformities he counted in Elizabethan Worcestershire occurred when financial pressure on recusants started to increase.[51] Even if much of the work of detecting and fining recusants was carried out by people who had their own interests at heart as much as the Crown's, this did not *necessarily* reduce the pressure on the recusant.[52] The practices of Thomas Felton, an independent operator who was taken on to increase the yield from recusancy fines, are frequently cited as the epitome of exchequer inefficiency.[53] However, his activities between 1598 and 1602 were seen by contemporaries as a notable burden on the Catholics he prosecuted.[54] The system whereby the Crown was petitioned for grants of recusant property, so open to corrupt manipulation, might

---

[48] Dunbabin, 'Post-Reformation Catholicism', 88; C. Howard, *Sir John Yorke of Nidderdale* (1939), 16–17; Clark, 'Anglicanism', 72–4, argues that the Derbyshire evidence does not allow us to conclude that churchwardens were utterly ineffectual.

[49] Clark, 'Anglicanism', 78.

[50] Wark, *Elizabethan Recusancy*, 120.

[51] V. Burke, 'Submissions of Conformity by Elizabethan Recusants', *Worcestershire Recusant* 21 (1973), 1–7, at p. 4.

[52] CRS 53, 294; J. C. H. Aveling, *The Catholic Recusants of the West Riding of Yorkshire 1558–1790* (Proceedings of the Leeds Philosophical and Literary Society, Literary and Historical Section, X, part VI, Leeds, 1963), 231; CRS 41, 86; cf. CRS 57, xlv, lxxxiii.

[53] Walker, 'Implementation', 378–82.

[54] *CSPD 1598–1601*, 253–4; PRO, SP 46/41, fo 57r; Stonyhurst, Collectanea P II, fo. 444r. Felton's supporters thought he offered value for money, *CSPD 1601–3*, 167, 182–3, 186; cf. PRO, SO 3/5, December 1613, payment to Felton's widow for his service in revenue improvement; BL, Lansd. MS 85, fo. 93r; cf. BL, Royal MS 17 A iv, fo. 4v; *HMC Salisbury MSS* XXIV, 186–7. For a similar instance of entrepreneurial extortion at recusants' expense, see the activities of Charles Grimston in Staffordshire, PRO, E 134/7 James I/Trinity 7, mm. 2a, 4a, 5a, E 368/537, mem. 50a. Grimston was attempting to rig the selection and findings of Staffordshire juries assembled by recusant commissioners.

force recusants to compound financially with all those who had secured such grants.[55]

The rate of conformity increased as greater pressure was exerted on Catholics. La Rocca says that after the Gunpowder Plot when the exchequer should have been cracking down on recusants it signally failed to do so. He suggests that increased repression of recusancy after the Plot 'should be expected [to appear in the records] in 1608 or 1609 but . . . this is not evident in the exchequer records'.[56] In fact, the numbers of conformists after the Plot started to increase sharply in 1606. The surge of conformities in the years 1612–15 supports the claims of the Catholic newsletter writers that repression was particularly effective at this time, and that new attempts were being made to tap recusants as a source of revenue.[57] The pattern of convictions of Derbyshire recusants analysed by Clark describes a sudden escalation just before the Gunpowder Plot lasting until 1608, an increase in 1611 and a brief but unsustained quantum leap in 1613, and then a less dramatic rise again in 1616–17, all which years saw increases in the national rates of conformity.[58]

Let us look again at some of the aspects of the exchequer's procedures in recusancy cases. It is clear that received impressions of inefficiency need to be heavily qualified. Historians have not always recognised the subtle pressures to conform built into the recusancy system. On the surface, it seems illogical that, once a recusant had been convicted and fined (one conviction being sufficient to make him liable under the 1587 statute for the massive £20 per month thereafter), he should be convicted on future occasions, each conviction being estreated to the exchequer and the fine (for the specific but formal period of months of recusancy found by the court) duly noted. Many recusants were regularly re-convicted in this way.[59] This seemingly pointless exercise *was* an extra incentive towards conformity. First, the heirs of recusants were liable for the recusants' accumulated arrears of debts from fines, but only those arising from fines which were as 'of record'. The rule was that if the heir refused to conform there was no way

55 J. Morris (ed.), *The Troubles of our Catholic Forefathers* (3 vols., 1872–7), III, 23; CRS 52, 5, 23; S. R. Gardiner (ed.), *The Fortescue Papers* (Camden Society, second series, 1, 1871), 155–6. Though very few of the recusants who were the subject of royal grants conformed, some, like Sir William Roper, were driven into conformity by the extortionate demands of grantees, La Rocca, 'James I', 257.

56 La Rocca, 'James I', 262, n. 42.

57 Questier, 'Phenomenon', 337 Appendix III, column E; AAW, A XII, 457, 467, XIII, 39, 59, 331, 685, XIV, 14, 39, 291; cf. Clarke, 'Conformity Certificates', 54, for the large number of conformity certificates in King's Bench records in 1614–15.

58 Clark, 'Anglicanism', table 12 (between pp. 74 and 75).

59 Of the recusants who certified their conformity to the exchequer between 1590 and 1625, 168 had been convicted twice, eighty-one three times, and seventy-one on four or more occasions.

he could escape these arrears of debt which had been incurred for the months of recusancy mentioned in the recusant ancestor's indictments.[60] Accumulating convictions alone increased the persuasive pressure on the recusant to conform. Even if the recusant himself had no intention of conforming, his recusant heir would certainly feel threatened. The new convictions also gave the exchequer the opportunity to issue another commission to enquire into the recusants' estates. If he had inherited or acquired further property, this could be seized as well.[61]

Nor were the commissions by which the exchequer assessed recusants' lands and goods a monument to inefficiency. It is not surprising that they were occasionally subject to local coercion, especially considering the sweeping nature of their brief. In April 1609, the recusant Robert Rea had threatened the jury appointed to assess him, and said that if he 'had helpe he would both devide and quarter them the said Jurors'.[62] In practice, though, recusants were extremely vulnerable to exchequer commissions. Some recusants conformed as the inquisition was being held, before their property was seized at all. To them the commission was a very immediate danger. Sir William Selby reported to the earl of Salisbury in September 1605 that he had carried out the commission for enquiring into Northumberland recusants' property directed to himself and Edward Talbot, and 'in that part where my service fell 15 recusants, some gentlemen and gentlewomen . . . were content to submit and conform themselves, who by the appointment of the Commissioners came on Sunday last . . . to my parish church, heard prayers and sermon with due reverence, and made submission according to law'.[63] Nicholas Langford's most valuable Derbyshire manor was subject to assessments in 1593 and 1594. It appears it was seized by the Crown only in Trinity term in 1600. He appeared at the exchequer on 9 June 1600 to certify his conformity. Nevertheless he had not just been sitting idly, waiting to see what the Crown would do. The bishop's certificate which he presented to the barons demonstrates that he had appeared before William Overton to submit in January 1595 and could prove that he had been attending his parish church since November 1594.[64] John Seaborne of

---

[60] CRS 57, xlii; cf. BL, Lansd. MS 171, fo. 324[r], stating that 'nothing should be demanded for the Prince' by the exchequer 'but by matter of Record'. John Milton pointed out that 'wher Recusantes have bin severall tymes convicted and in severall Counties the Clerkes may omitt soome Convictions and make the debts lesse then they are', BL, Lansd. MS 153, fo. 100[v].

[61] For the increased tax burden placed on Richard Cholmeley of Brandsby following his inheritance of Ursula Cholmeley's estates, PRO, E 368/553, mem. 140[a–b]; Cholmeley, 'Memorandum Book of Richard Cholmeley', 76, 86; PRO, E 401/2303 for Cholmeley's additional payments from Michaelmas 1614 onwards.

[62] PRO, E 134/8 James I/Easter 39, mem. 2[a].   [63] HMC Salisbury MSS, XVII, 427.

[64] CRS 71, 106; PRO, E 368/500, mem. 190[a–d].

Sutton in Herefordshire had come to his parish church on 28 August 1599, only three days after an inquisition was taken to assess his property.[65] An analysis of the lord treasurer's remembrancer's memoranda rolls suggests that the principal factor in the submission of the majority of conformists, was the exchequer commission. Out of 624 conformists, 394 submitted under the scrutiny of an exchequer commission within one month of that commission completing an assessment of their land. A further eighty-seven did so within two to six months.[66] A study of the Elizabethan Pells' receipt books among the exchequer records shows that relatively few recusants conformed after a long period of sequestration. They either capitulated quickly when commissions assessed their property, or they had no intention of conforming at all.[67] In 1607 Bishop John Thornborough complained pessimistically that in 1605 'there fell away onely in Yorkshire eight hundreth at once . . . And from that time till now they have daily fallen from us'; but he added 'onely the execucion of the Commission hath lately brought backe to the church almost one hundreth'.[68] In Sussex in late 1610 John Colpes compounded with the agents of the commissioners, but then decided to conform in full. His decision may have been affected by the knowledge that the commission's agents were returning to the county.[69]

It is simplistic to assume that the commissions' findings were invariably inaccurate. It is not correct to say, as Cliffe does, that 'no proper survey was carried out', or that the 'valuation system was hopelessly inadequate'.[70] Valuations during Elizabeth's reign had been shown to contain errors, but at least as early as 1596 orders had been drawn up to do something about faulty assessments. Specific instructions were given in 1603 to commissioners to ensure that their inquisitions should ascertain all the following: the legal tenure of the estate, the manors held by the recusant, all the separate dwellings and pieces of land owned by the recusant and the parish they were in, the names of the people who occupied each property (if it was not occupied by the recusant himself) and the terms on which their leases were held. They were to record the acreage of the land, and, if it was used for agricultural purposes, the type of land.[71] The assessments of each recusant's property in the lord treasurer's remembrancer's memoranda rolls

---

65 PRO, E 368/497, mem. 49b; cf. PRO, E 134/44 Elizabeth I/Hilary 2.
66 This figure includes of course those who claimed to have been conformable already.
67 PRO, E 401/1847–71.
68 BL, Lansd. MS 153, fo. 266v.
69 AAW, A IX, 315, X, 45; PRO, E 368/539, mem. 140a–b.
70 Cliffe, *Yorkshire Gentry*, 214.
71 BL, Lansd. MS 80, fo. 126r–v, for exchequer attempts in 1596 to revalue Yorkshire recusants' estates, which Walker concedes may have had some effect in the cases which he investigated, Walker, 'Implementation', 377–8. Similar instructions were sent to the sheriff of Surrey and Sussex in June 1597, BL, Harl. MS 703, fo. 108r; CRS 57, lxxiii.

are often brief but, in James's reign, they generally incorporate all these elements. These enrolled details are clearly summaries of a much fuller report. Occasionally the memoranda rolls include the entire text of the inquisition (in English) as returned by the commissioners to the exchequer. Land was surveyed with some precision and they aimed at identifying the exact nature of the legal estate which the recusant possessed in it. Individual valuations were put on each farm animal. In cases where household goods were assessed the full inquisition records the contents of each room and cupboard.[72]

Were the inquisitions vitiated because sympathetic neighbours of the recusant sat on the commission's jury and returned a low valuation of his property? This seems unlikely in most cases. The valuation was done by Crown officials under the direction of the sheriff and the commissioners.[73] The commissioners were themselves men of local standing who were appointed by the exchequer barons, so it would be surprising if those sympathetic to recusants were nominated as commissioners.[74] It is highly improbable that commissioners like Bishop Gervase Babington in Worcestershire or the notable crowd of puritans employed on this task in Yorkshire (including Sir Stephen Procter, Sir Thomas Hoby, Sir John Savile and Sir Timothy Whittingham) would have willingly allowed under-valuations to be returned. On the contrary, there is evidence of people like Procter, Thornborough and Hoby making sure that the commission's findings were as hard on the recusant as the law allowed.[75] In October 1605

---

[72] E.g. PRO, E 368/493, mm. 89ᵃ, 200ᵃ, E 368/498, mem. 181ᵃ, E 368/577, mem. 121ᵇ; cf. Morris, *Troubles*, I, 194, 246. For an account of the very precise division of the property, field by field, of Richard Cholmeley of Brandsby by the commissioners who surveyed his estates on 11 April 1614, see PRO, E 368/553, m. 140ᵃ; Cholmeley, 'Memorandum Book of Richard Cholmeley', 76.

[73] CRS 56, 29, 37, 47–9; cf. W. Notestein, F. H. Relf and H. Simpson (eds.), *Commons Debates 1621* (7 vols., New Haven, 1935), IV, 215; CRS 57, lxxv (the separate commission for leasing estates was directly controlled by the lord treasurer's remembrancer's office); PRO, E 101/547/3, accounts of those employed in 1590 in surveying recusants' estates, one of the officials being Alexander King, an exchequer auditor.

[74] CRS 57, lxiii.

[75] CRS 56, xxxi, 57. The 'puritan' inclinations of these people are well known, but note in particular Savile's active participation in dispute with Catholics, BL, Add. MS 34250, fo. 27ᵛ, and his patronage of Yorkshire puritan ministers, J.A. Newton, 'Puritanism in the Diocese of York (excluding Nottinghamshire) 1603–1640' (Ph.D thesis, London, 1955), 263; and the dedication to Procter and Whittingham (as well as Sir Vincent Skinner and Sir Timothy Hutton) of Thomas Bell's *A Christian Dialogue* (1609), sig. A3ʳ–4ʳ, praising their godly labours; for Hoby's enthusiasm in enforcing the law against recusants, G. W. Boddy, 'Players of Interludes in North Yorkshire in the Early Seventeenth Century', *North Yorkshire County Record Office Journal* 3 (1976), 95–130, at p. 109. The wives of Hoby and Thornborough were on good terms, D. M. Meads (ed.), *Diary of Lady Margaret Hoby* (1930), 147, and both Thornborough and Hoby were present at the twentieth of the series of puritan sermons organised by Sir Thomas Cecil in York Castle, BL, Add. MS

Henry Garnet wrote of the rapacity of the commissions and stressed that 'the commissioners in all counties, are the most ernest and base Puritans'.[76]

Aveling suggested that the values put upon recusant property were as formal and meaningless as those given at inquisitions *post mortem*.[77] Inquisition *post mortem* valuations were usually assessments from the past, irrespective of the current value. But recusant inquisition valuations were frequently new. Some recusants undoubtedly attempted to manipulate the process, and some valuations do appear to be low. Yet additional evidence often shows that a low valuation on a particular piece of property is not always an example of a recusant getting off the hook. John Vaughan of Monmouthshire had 140 sheep assessed (for an unstated reason) at a minimal value, but, in the same inquisition, his holdings of grain were estimated to be worth £20.[78] James Hubbard of Norfolk had three manors valued at a total of £5 per annum but in the same inquisition he had other land valued at £204 per annum and moveable goods worth £266 seized.[79] These people were not being assisted by sympathetic neighbours.[80]

The point is, of course, that while rates of taxation may technically be fixed the amount which an individual pays is often anything but a fixed quantity. Particularly in the early modern period virtually all taxation took place by a process of negotiation between taxpayers and the State. Recusancy fines were no different. The penalties to which recusants were subject were fixed by statute, but their liabilities had to be established by

34250, fo. 29[r–v]. Procter cooperated with Whittingham in capturing Catholics at Upsall Castle in August 1609, Howard, *Sir John Yorke*, 15. In April 1606 it was reported that Bancroft tested opinion in the House of Lords whether 'the papists might have a toleration for four years', and Babington 'replied, that it was pity they should be tolerated for seven days', George Roberts (ed.), *Diary of Walter Yonge* (Camden Society, first series, 41, 1848), 6. Henry Ewbank, a prebendary of Durham Cathedral, was named to the exchequer commission for Durham after 1603, PRO, E 368/529, mem. 92[a]; E 368/530, mm. 113[a], 174[a], E 368/532, mm. 86[a], 207[a], E 368/533, mem. 114[a], E 368/543, mem. 244[a], E 368/550, mem. 116 [*bis*][c–d], as, before 1603, was the puritan customs official and priest-hunter Henry Sanderson, PRO, E 368/507, mem. 104[a], E 368/516, mem. 94[a]. Both had been active in the attempt to root out papistry by arresting politically dangerous seminary priests before 1603. The Durham commission invariably included the fearsomely anti-popish William James, both as dean and bishop. In Sussex we find that in the 1590s the recusancy commission was entrusted in part to lawyers and Crown officials, but among the lawyers was the strongly Protestant Thomas Bowyer who had taken a leading role in the high profile prosecution of four seminary priests at Chichester in September 1588 (in particular by presenting an apologia to the jury for the new treason legislation of 1585), PRO, SP 12/217/1; L. J. Ward, 'The Law of Treason in the Reign of Elizabeth I 1558–1588' (Ph.D thesis, Cambridge, 1985), 289 (for which references I am grateful to Peter Lake); Anstruther I, 93–4; PRO, E 368/483, mem. 121[a], E 368/531, mem. 122[a]; R. B. Manning, *Religion and Society in Elizabethan Sussex* (Leicester, 1969), 265.

76 AAW, A VII, 557.   77 CRS 53, 294.
78 PRO, E 368/540, mem. 112[a].   79 PRO, E 368/522, mem. 183[a].
80 Catholic sources assert that a huge assessment placed on George Anne of Frickley in around 1610 was procured through the malice of his neighbours, AAW, A IX, 397.

diligent enquiry into the state of their landed and other possessions. Catholic recusants hardly stood in a favourable position. Nevertheless, the State could not sequestrate what they did not have. Naturally, like all taxpayers, recusants did not welcome the Crown's seizure of their worldly wealth. Those in the provinces whose responsibility it was to assess them said that all manner of tricks were played to make their job more difficult. Recusants not only presented fraudulent deeds of gift and conveyance to the commissioners in an attempt to pass off their land as someone else's; they also exchanged their livestock with that of their neighbours so that the commissioners could not tell which was which. If the commissioners did manage to seize their personal possessions they sometimes rescued them by force of arms; a small pitched battle took place when it was attempted in 1607 to remove farm animals belonging to Sir William Blakiston.[81] But as one scans the wide variety of reasons alleged before the exchequer barons why the Crown should release its grip on particular properties sequestrated under the recusancy statutes – gift, conveyance, marriage settlement and so on, all the way down to mere misidentification – it becomes clear that, while the Crown may occasionally have been defeated by fraud, all we are really seeing is the normal complex state of people's landed property and accompanying tax liabilities, fluid landholding because of purchases, sales and gifts combined with subsisting burdens imposed by various charges and annuities.[82] It was hardly unusual for property to be tied up in this way. In the case of Thomas Meynell of North Kilvington (cited by Aveling as a classic instance of a recusant's ability to flout the system) it seems his claim that a substantial amount of his property was swallowed up in his mother's jointure, annuities to relations and obligations to pay his father's debts, was accepted by the exchequer and was largely correct.[83] (In many cases the plaintiffs before the exchequer were not recusants but other people, recusants' tenants or even the Crown farmer, who argued that they were unjustly burdened with payments imposed on them in error.) Nor was it especially easy to deceive the exchequer barons. Procedural rules ensured that all discharge cases received the scrutiny of the exchequer court. The barons had to be satisfied with the evidence presented to them, and any discharge required the certified assent of the attorney-general as well, in

---

[81] BL, Lansd. MS 153, fos. 266r–7r, 211v–12r, 295r, 108r, 213r.

[82] The valuations recorded in the lord treasurer's remembrancer's memoranda rolls are all given *ultra reprisas*, i.e. minus all ascertained charges on the property, everything from annuities in favour of other people down to poor rate, CRS 57, lxxvii; PRO, E 368/538, mem. 78a; CRS 60, 44; PRO, SO 3/4, June 1608 (a demise to Sir William Ingleby of two-thirds of the estate of William Middleton at a heavily reduced rent for the duration of annuities made by Middleton's father).

[83] Aveling, *Northern Catholics*, 125–7; CRS 56, xxvii–viii.

spite of the criticisms of aggrieved speculators who thought that recusants' petitions for discharge were passed too easily.[84] After 1597 the number of cases where recusants successfully demonstrated to the exchequer that mistakes had been made in the course of the commissions' work was relatively small.

Cases of apparent inefficiency may well be nothing of the kind. Although John Cherington of Edgmond was convicted eight times for recusancy between 1594 and 1607 (when a commission was finally issued for him), and property seizure did not take place until October 1624, the Crown was in fact waiting for him to succeed to the family estates.[85]

The exchequer did not normally extort the full liability at once. The statutory rule was that while two-thirds of landed property were subject to forfeiture to pay off the cumulative arrears of £20 fines, the recusant's entire personal property was similarly forfeit. Hugh Bowler suggests, however, that seizure of goods was progressive, so as to impoverish 'by degrees'.[86] The Crown's agents seized both goods and lands but often in successive inquisitions. The pressure from the later expropriations and a continual official prying into what recusants possessed could persuade an initially stubborn man to submit.[87] Of the 624 individuals in the lord treasurer's remembrancer's memoranda rolls who had their property assessed, 104 were subjected to a second inquisition, thirty-six to a third, eleven to a fourth, and thirteen to five or more.[88] Not all second or subsequent inquisitions produced higher valuations or discovered additional property. Some of these inquisitions were merely speculative and simply returned the same value on land of which the exchequer already had notice. Nevertheless, in seventy-two cases the value of recusants' land returned by the first commission was actually increased by a subsequent one, sometimes very substantially.[89] In forty-five cases the value of goods and chattels was

---

84 PRO, SP 14/40/30, SP 14/80/69, fo. 98ʳ; BL, Lansd. MS 153, fo. 158ʳ; PRO, E 368/521, mem. 29ᵃ⁻ᶜ, SP 14/80/45; cf. J.J. Scarisbrick, 'Cardinal Wolsey and the Common Weal', in E.W. Ives, R. J. Knecht and J. J. Scarisbrick (eds.), *Wealth and Power in Tudor England* (1978), 45–67, at p. 57.

85 CRS 57, ci–ii.

86 CRS 57, xxxiii–xxxiv, lxxx–lxxxii.

87 PRO, E 368/525, mem. 229ᵃ⁻ᶜ.

88 For Catholic statements that recusants were subject to repeated seizures, Foley VII, 990; CRS 54, 105.

89 E.g. Nicholas Reynes of Nottinghamshire (who in 1594 attempted to deceive the high commission into thinking that he was conformable, BI, HCAB 12, fos. 185ᵛ, 208ᵛ, 233ʳ) was subject in 1591 to a valuation of £8 per annum on his landed estate. In 1598, personal property valued at £160 was seized by a second inquisition. He conformed in 1599, PRO, E 368/496, mem. 101ᵃ⁻ᵇ. Nicholas Langford was subject to four separate inquisitions which clearly built up the financial pressure on him by locating additional property and imposing increasingly heavy assessments, PRO, E 368/500, mem. 190ᵃ⁻ᵇ.

increased. Twenty-six of these cases involved recusants whose land values were not increased at the same time. Thus a total of ninety-eight out of the 164 who were assessed more than once were subject to a heavier valuation (let alone simply an additional one) on a subsequent occasion.[90]

Even where a recusant escaped on a technicality, the fiscal authorities in London did not leave it at that. In the case of several of the recusants who were discharged as a result of the disastrously faulty inquisition at Leeds in March 1597, the exchequer moved to reassess them almost immediately.[91] After Thomas Meynell first managed to reduce the amount levied on him he soon found himself under investigation again.[92] The exchequer made efforts to sort out cases where it seemed that the Crown had been deceived. Nicholas Timperley of Hintlesham was convicted of recusancy in 1608. One Captain Thomas Allen obtained a grant in November 1609 of his recusancy from the Crown and then tried to secure the forfeiture of two-thirds of his estate. However, at the commission hearing, Timperley alleged that he had already conformed. In fact, he had arranged for John Pagett, the minister at Hintlesham, to secure fraudulently a certificate of conformity from John Jegon, bishop of Norwich. When Jegon became suspicious the exchequer issued a new commission in May 1609 to ascertain what had actually happened. It took detailed statements from several local witnesses. The findings of this commission in 1609–10 led to the issue of a further commission to sequestrate Timperley's property. As a result, he conformed in full before it even completed its work.[93]

What about other aspects of the recusancy legislation which were designed to push Catholics into uncompromising submission to the established religion, in particular the 'communion clause' of 1606? E. E. Rose thought it had little effect and Walsham suggests that it was a 'paper victory', but there is some evidence that the measure was enforced. Certainly some enthusiastic clerics, like Robert Johnson, archdeacon of Leicester, took to including questions in their visitation articles about conformists'

---

[90] Those who in a second or subsequent inquisition had estates surveyed which had previously escaped the net, or items of personal property taken which had not been seized before or were now being sequestrated for a second time, were experiencing an additional loss.

[91] PRO, E 368/489 mem. 211ᵃ, E 368/496, mem. 82ᵃ (Thomas Barnaby); PRO, E 368/489, mem. 212ᵃ, E 368/495, mem. 49ᵃ⁻ᵇ (Francis Baxter); PRO, E 368/494, mem. 38ᵃ⁻ᵇ, E 368/504, mem 137ᵃ (Frances Bretton); PRO, E 368/493, mem. 206ᵃ (James Green); PRO, E 368/489, mem. 191ᵃ.

[92] Aveling, *Northern Catholics*, 125–7.

[93] *CSPD 1603–10*, 384; PRO, E 368/531, mem. 99ᵃ; PRO, E 134/7 James I/Trinity 3; PRO, E 126/1, fos. 179ᵛ, 214ᵛ; PRO, E 124/8, fo. 68ʳ; PRO, E 368/539, mem. 121ᵃ⁻ᵇ, i.e. not, in the final outcome, as described by G. H. Ryan and L. J. Redstone, *Timperley of Hintlesham* (1931), 53–7.

reception of communion.[94] Most of the people prosecuted under this statutory clause were of high social status. Even if they had no enthusiasm for their original submission, the fact that they could be compelled into an action which went far beyond mere conformity was surely significant.

The determination to inflict heavy financial penalties on religious dissent admittedly was filtered through many different channels, provincial administrators and entrepreneurial middlemen. It is difficult to detect any consistent central policy of targeting strongly recusant areas. Still, it appears from a brief comparison of the strength of recusancy numbers and the incidence of conformity that submission was not occurring merely where recusant Catholicism was weak and isolated. A preliminary study of the geographical spread of the conformities recorded in the lord treasurer's remembrancer's memoranda rolls shows that, at least in parts of the country like the West and North Ridings of Yorkshire, Derbyshire, and in Glamorganshire and Monmouthshire, recusants were being compelled to conform in those areas where many recusants were regularly prosecuted by the several different authorities responsible for dealing with them. Of course, this might be thought to indicate only that wherever recusants were convicted in large enough numbers, some were bound to conform. In Derbyshire the parishes in which detected recusancy was strongest were the ones where prominent conformities of important Catholics occurred, though such conformities do not seem to have markedly reduced the strength of recusancy in those areas. But the fact that people conformed in

---

[94] E. E. Rose, *Cases of Conscience* (Cambridge, 1975), 69; A. Walsham, *Church Papists* (1993), 89; cf. A. Dures, *English Catholicism 1558–1642* (1983), 45. K. C. Fincham (ed.), *Visitation Articles and Injunctions of the Early Stuart Church*, I (Church of England Record Society, Woodbridge, Suffolk, 1994), 124; see also the visitation articles of George Abbot for Gloucester in 1612, Tobias Matthew for York in 1622–3 and Samuel Harsnett for York in 1629, *ibid.*, 105, 67. J. J. La Rocca argues that the measure was ineffective and that if enforcement took place at all it was done by informers, not officers of the Crown, La Rocca, 'James I', 253. Technically this is correct, but much recusant legislation was implemented by third parties, and the agenda books of the king's remembrancer show that those who conformed under the statutory procedure were almost invariably proceeded against speculatively to determine whether they had been communicating as the 1606 statute required. This was done principally by the informers Thomas Whitesander and Henry Sivedale. They had petitioned (evidently successfully) the earl of Salisbury in 1608 (almost immediately after informers were permitted, following an eighteen-year break, to bring *qui tam* actions again in the central courts) to be allowed access to exchequer records in order to undertake this, CRS 57, xvi, xl–xli; PRO, SP 14/40/10; cf. *HMC Salisbury MSS XXIV*, 246; in all such cases in Michaelmas term in 1616, for example, Henry Sivedale is the informer, PRO, E 159/451, *passim*. Analysis of the king's remembrancer records shows that 136 people who had previously certified their conformity to the exchequer were subject to this type of action, though in only nineteen cases was the action taken beyond the initial information, PRO, IND 17063–7. It is not possible to tell from the records whether those against whom prosecutions did not proceed compounded for non-communicancy or had been receiving communion according to the statute.

some places where recusancy was strong and not in others where it was equally entrenched suggests that conformity was the result of official action in specific places rather than a gradual erosion of recusant resistance.[95]

O'Dwyer argues in his study of Essex recusants that 'in practice . . . fines . . . affected only those of the gentry class'.[96] Of course, proportionately there was a heavy gentry representation among conformists. This is not surprising since they were perhaps the principal supporters of the Catholicism at which the recusant statutes were aimed, and their example, resistance or submission, was thought to have a wide impact on Catholic opinion.[97] Perhaps the financial penalties for recusancy were unlikely to hurt the landless labourer. Yet the lord treasurer's remembrancer's memoranda rolls show that conformity induced by recusancy commissions was by no means limited to the gentry. Where it is possible to ascertain the social rank of the exchequer conformists, just over 41 per cent were gentlemen; nearly 43 per cent were described as yeomen or husbandmen. Burke's study of Worcestershire conformities concluded that the law most affected 'those recusants in the middle reaches of the social scale, where the pinch of financial sanctions was most likely to be felt'.[98]

Women were protected from the full force of the recusancy statutes by marital status. It has generally been argued that, by and large, Catholic women were recusant while their husbands with Catholic sympathies

---

[95] Questier, 'Phenomenon', 263–4. E.g., Egton and Grinton, in the North Riding of Yorkshire, were both heavily populated with recusants, PRO, E 135/12/7, mem. 179a; but while many exchequer-certified conformities occurred in the first, PRO, E 368/538, mem. 97a, E 368/571, mem. 153a–b, none are found in the second; cf. Atkinson, *Quarter Sessions*, II, p. vi; Boddy, 'Players', 109. There were similar variations in distribution of conformities in Monmouthshire, many in Llangattock-Vibon-Avell but none in Llanternam, which both experienced regular presentations of large numbers of recusants, F. H. Pugh, 'Monmouthshire Recusants in the Reigns of Elizabeth I and James I', *South Wales and Monmouth Record Society* 4 (1957), 59–110, at p. 65. In the parish of Prescot in Lancashire the conformities of those who submitted at the exchequer are spread very unevenly: between 1598 and 1608 for Parr there were returned 104 recusants none of whom conformed, Sutton had 211 and only three conformities, but Eccleston with 150 had 10 people who conformed statutorily, according to exchequer records, Dunbabin, 'Post-Reformation Catholicism', 42–3; PRO, E 368/524–80. For Derbyshire, Clark, 'Anglicanism', 37–40, 45, 65; PRO, E 368/487, mem. 109a, E 368/500, mm. 182a, 186a, E 368/519, mem. 78a, E 368/527, mem. 190a, E 368/532, mem. 80a, E 368/545, mem. 105a, E 368/563, mem. 183a. These conclusions are tentative only, since the lord treasurer's remembrancer's memoranda rolls do not give a complete picture even of statutory conformity.

[96] O'Dwyer, 'Catholic Recusants', 146.

[97] Peck, *Desiderata*, I, 117.

[98] Burke, 'Submissions', 4. Gentry who conformed were more likely to appear at the exchequer to present conformity certificates since they were the obvious targets for those who were seeking to exploit recusancy's financial potential. The gentry representation among statutory conformists in the lord treasurer's remembrancer's memoranda rolls may therefore be higher than in the total number who submitted according to statute.

conformed to avoid the penalties of the law.[99] The lord treasurer's remembrancer's memoranda rolls show that nearly 10 per cent of those who certified their conformities to the exchequer were either widows or unmarried women. Yet were married women universally exempt from coercion to conform? The effectiveness of statutory provisions in 1593 and 1610 to make husbands liable for their wives' recusancy is not certain. There was no shortage of agitation to put these measures into effect but the political pressure to implement them was never consistent.[100] A conscientious Catholic husband might well abet his wife's nonconformity, but, as Walsham demonstrates, there were several different types of constraint which could be exerted on men with recusant wives, not just imposition of financial penalties but also exclusion from office-holding at all levels.[101] For this reason married women might actually be under more pressure to conform than those who were single.[102] Thirty-two of the 114 women whose conformities were registered in the lord treasurer's remembrancer's office were married. A few male conformists who appeared at the exchequer presented episcopal certificates which show they had come before their diocesan bishop to submit and had brought their wives with them to do the same.[103] There is no doubt at all that many 'schismatic' males connived at

---

[99] Aveling, 'Catholic Recusancy', 69, 83, 88–9; Walsham, *Church Papists*, 79–81.

[100] For the 1593 legislation, CRS 57, xlvi–viii. Despite judicial wavering and general uncertainty about its interpretation, it was occasionally enforced, HMC *Salisbury MSS* VI, 73; Morris, *Troubles*, I, 194; Robert Persons, *The Judgement of a Catholicke English-Man* (St Omer, 1608), 45; *CSPV 1610–13*, 43; 'Annual Letters of the Vice-Province of England' (for 1619), *Letters and Notices* 11 (1876–7), 273–88, at p. 274; and with extreme financial consequences for people like Michael Wentworth of Wolley in Yorkshire, CRS 53, 179; cf. BI, HCAB 15, fo. 66ᵛ; cf. for the 1610 legislation, AAW, A XIV, 531; cf. Bodl., Rawl. MS D 1036, fo. 7ʳ; *Statutes* IV, 1162. Thomas Brome in 1612 and Anthony Champney in 1615 reported to Rome that statutory penalties against husbands with recusant wives were being enforced, AAW, A XI, 47, XIV, 39; AAW A XIV, 305, 327, XV, 259, similar reports from Griffin Floyd, John Frier and William Reyner in 1615–16, and from the Spaniards in 1619, CRS 68, 123, 128; cf. Foley V, 988; and again in 1626, CU Libr., MS Mm IV 38, fo. 12ʳ⁻ᵛ, though apparently with less success; P. Kopperman, *Sir Robert Heath* (Woodbridge, Suffolk, 1989), 95–6.

[101] Walsham, *Church Papists*, 80; Francis Savage, *A Conference betwixt a Mother a devout Recusant, and her Sonne a zealous Protestant* (Cambridge, 1600), 122–3; Andrew Willet, *A Treatise of Salomons Marriage* (1612), 9; cf. Atkinson, *Quarter Sessions*, I, 67 (threat to withhold Richard Beckwith's alehouse licence if his wife refuses to conform).

[102] Dunbabin makes a strong case for this, 'Post-Reformation Catholicism', 37; cf. J. Bossy, *The English Catholic Community 1570–1850* (1975), 153–5; Aveling, *Catholic Recusancy*, 187 (Ann Kitchinman, forcefully dragged to church by her husband), 194 (William Allen who claimed that he could not reform his wife but was evidently willing that the authorities should undertake her reformation).

[103] E.g. PRO, E 368/493, mem. 206ᵃ (James and Mary Green); PRO, E 368/526, mem. 220ᵃ (Everingham and Mary Cressey); Mary Cressey's Fairfax family moved into conformity at about the same time, Aveling, 'Catholic Recusancy', 71; PRO, E 368/536, mem. 121ᵃ (George and Magdalen Sweeting); PRO, E 368/495, mem. 49ᵇ (William and Francis Baxter of Drax, both with their wives). Francis Baxter's wife, daughter to Sir Thomas Lovell of

female recusancy, but pressure, statutory as well as social, militated against female dissidence.

Another perspective on the efficacy of enforcement can be gained from examining the tendering of the Jacobean oath of allegiance. It has been argued already that this oath was on at least one reading a disguised form of the oath of supremacy. This would, however, not have been of much significance if the authorities had not made any attempt to enforce it. Historians think that the oath was not properly enforced at any stage after 1606.[104] It was certainly not meant to be put to everyone who was suspected to have Catholic tendencies, but it was more widely tendered than historians allow. Systematic use of the oath began with the proclamation of 1610 and the accompanying act, 7 James I, c.6.[105] In mid-1610 the archpriest George Birkhead reported to Richard Smith that, following Henri IV's assassination and the new proclamation, 'the prisons are filled againe' and the oath 'is more exacted then ever'; the statute means that 'everie fortnight the Justices are to offer the oath' to selected Catholics.[106] Birkhead's missives between 1610 and 1614 assert that, although there were brief interludes, the exaction of the oath proceeded apace.[107] Despite the archpriest Blackwell's deposition, the papal breves and the deprivation of Catholic clerical supporters of the oath of their priestly faculties, it seemed to Birkhead that the majority of Catholics were being compelled to

---

Harling in Norfolk, came from a family with conformist tendencies, PRO, E 368/560, mem. 148[a]. Ralph Sadler, whose 1609 conformity certificate asserted that he had never properly been recusant, had certified his and his wife's active conformity to the high commission in April 1602, BI, HCAB 14, fo. 222[v].

104 Aveling, *Northern Catholics*, 214–15, 247–8; J. P. Sommerville, 'Jacobean Political Thought and the Controversy over the Oath of Allegiance' (Ph.D thesis, Cambridge, 1981), 73; Aveling, *Catholic Recusants*, 230–1; J. V. Gifford, 'The Controversy over the Oath of Allegiance of 1606' (DPhil. thesis, Oxford, 1971), 69–70; cf. James Howell (ed.), *Cottoni Posthuma* (1651), 154. Financial profit affected official thinking on the oath, *CSPD 1603–10*, 95, but this was the case with much penal legislation. Forfeitures for refusal were absorbed into court patronage and the system of royal grants, Cliffe, *Yorkshire Gentry*, 179; PRO, SO 3/6, August 1614; AAW, A XI, 209; AAW, A XIII, 89.

105 C. J. Ryan, 'The Jacobean Oath of Allegiance and English Lay Catholics', *Catholic Historical Review* 28 (1942), 159–83, at p. 171; T. Birch (ed.), *The Court and Times of James the First* (2 vols., 1848), I, 116–17; La Rocca, 'James I', 254–5; cf. C. H. and J. W. Cooper, *Annals of Cambridge* (5 vols., Cambridge, 1842–1908), III, 35–6. There were some sporadic efforts to enforce the oath before 1610, *CSPD 1603–10*, 425; PRO, SP 14/49/26, fo. 44[r–v].

106 AAW, A IX, 115, 149.

107 AAW, A XI, 194, 213, 217; cf. N. McClure (ed.), *The Letters of John Chamberlain* (2 vols., Philadelphia, 1939), I, 336–7; cf. Atkinson, *Quarter Sessions*, I, 203. In general, the authorities refused to allow the wording of the oath to be varied, and refused also to accept that the oath was simply an affirmation of Bellarmine's understanding of the indirect deposing power, *A Large Examination . . . of M. George Blakwell* (1607), 35, 61.

concede.[108] The pressure was intense in late 1612 and 1613.[109] In 1615 the Jesuits said that Lord Chief Justice Coke had to date summoned 16,000 Catholics to take the oath.[110]

ECCLESIASTICAL JURISDICTION

Was the State's very clear determination to promote thorough rather than mere conformity reflected in the sphere of ecclesiastical justice as well? The diocesan courts and the ecclesiastical penalty of excommunication were not particularly fearsome. Of forty-one recusants excommunicated by Chichester consistory court between October 1600 and October 1601 only one sought absolution and promised to conform. Nor was the seeking of absolution the same as actual conformity. In some areas the secular authorities, on whom the Church courts ultimately relied in order to make the excommunicated person attend, would not cooperate. Catholics sometimes used the fact of their excommunication to avoid church altogether.[111] Walker argues that, for the ecclesiastical courts, recusancy was

---

[108] AAW, A IX, 163, X, 269, 273.

[109] PRO, SP 14/70/9, 51, SP 14/75/44; CRS 68, 10; Stonyhurst, Anglia III, no. 119; CRS 60, 208–10; PRO, SP 14/70/54; AAW, A XII, 486, XIII, 117. In 1612–13 several prominent Catholics compounded to avoid the oath's full penalties, Cliffe, *Yorkshire Gentry*, 178–9; AAW, A XI, 209. For pardons for refusal, PRO, SO 3/5, June 1611 (Lord Montague, cf. AAW, Anglia VIII, no. 32, it was expected that he would have to compound in the sum of £6,000), November 1612 (William Middleton, Richard Townley), July 1613 (John Edwards), December 1613 (Richard Kirkham, Henry Darell, Thomas Aprice), February 1614 (George Talbot); *CSPD 1603–10*, 589; *CSPD 1611–18*, 137 (Edward Morgan, who paid £1,000 for the oath not to be tendered to him again, AAW, A XI, 370). Even on occasions where a family appeared to have escaped the full penalties of the law, e.g. in the case of Sir Henry James, the financial cost of escape could be extremely high, PRO, SO 3/6, March 1614, November 1615; AAW, A XII, 524; H. Bowler, 'Sir Henry James of Smarden, Kent, and Clerkenwell, Recusant (*c.* 1559–1625)', in A. E. J. Hollaender and W. Kellaway (eds.), *Studies in London History* (1969), 269–313, at pp. 307–8.

[110] Foley VII, 1096; AAW, A XII, 523–4, XIII, 59.

[111] Walker, 'Implementation', 403; Wark, *Elizabethan Recusancy*, 85–6 (only one of the fifty-three recusants presented in the visitation of the Chester diocese in 1592 conformed), 116; cf. Clark, 'Anglicanism', 32; R. B. Manning, 'Elizabethan Recusancy Commissions', *HJ* 15 (1972), 23–36, at p. 23; *HMC Salisbury MSS* VI, 266. Recusants were supposed to appear in person to submit, D. Wilkins, *Concilia* (4 vols., 1733–7), IV, 359. Walker's research from a purely recusant perspective is supported by some more general studies of the effectiveness of the diocesan Church courts in this period, R. A. Marchant, *The Church under the Law* (Cambridge, 1969), 204, arguing that visitation was quite ineffectual against recusants; C. Haigh, *Reformation and Resistance in Tudor Lancashire* (Cambridge, 1975), 272, suggests that visitations could detect only minorities, and thus in an area where there were many Catholics, visitation was likely to be ineffective; Purvis, *Tudor Parish Documents*, 36–7; Potter, 'Ecclesiastical Courts', 75–6, citing in Canterbury diocese the large numbers (excommunicated for all types of offences) who never bothered to seek absolution, a picture confirmed by Collinson for Cranbrook, P. Collinson, *The Religion of Protestants* (Oxford, 1982), 214; cf. F. D. Price, 'The Abuses of Excommunication and the Decline of

simply an abuse to be dealt with in the same way as the other misde-
meanours with which those courts were concerned: 'there is no indication
that those curbing it thought that it could be stamped out'.[112]

Protestant clerics always complained about the evil state of the Church's
power to compel Catholics to submit to its demands. Bishop William
Chaderton of Lincoln in August 1605 lamented that the exchequer had a
better knowledge of who was recusant in his diocese than he did. He was
constrained by local refusal to assist his officers.[113] The majority of the
conformities which are recorded in his register were produced by the force
of the exchequer's commissions rather than by the diocesan Church courts.
Were the Church courts really supposed to enforce conformity at all?
Ecclesiastical court hearings could be infused with the zeal of a prelate like
Arthur Lake. Lake preached when notorious offenders appeared in
consistory to do penance there, and he exploited the court as a forum for
projecting his own model of public repentance and conversion (though there
is no evidence that he used it thus for Catholic recusants).[114] Where
recusants were subject to the attentions of both the exchequer and their
diocesan disciplinary machine, the chronology of the action against them
shows that sometimes their decisions to conform were taken because of the
attentions of the consistory court rather than of the secular judges and
bureaucrats.[115] In the archdeaconry of Derby there was a close correlation
after 1603 between those cited for recusancy in visitation *comperta* and
those who appeared in the returns of recusants to the exchequer from the
secular courts. The ecclesiastical courts were at least trying to weaken
recusant resistance. Those presented and excommunicated for mere
absenteeism and the lesser offence of noncommunicancy seem to have learnt
their lesson and made sure that they were not presented again (even if
stubborn recusants refused to comply). So it was papist intransigence rather

---

Ecclesiastical Discipline under Queen Elizabeth', *EHR* 57 (1942), 106–15, at pp. 106–8,
even though Manning, *Religion*, 18–19, argues that Bristol and Gloucester dioceses, the
focus of Price's research, were atypical.

[112] Walker, 'Implementation', 411.
[113] Foster, *State*, lxxxviii–ix.
[114] Arthur Lake, *Sermons* (1629), sigs. Hhhh[r], Iiii3[r], Iiii4[r].
[115] Thus, among the group of recusant conformists who conformed before Lancelot Andrewes
at Chichester between 1605 and 1609, William Coldham showed himself ready to submit
while he was subject to the attentions of the Chichester consistory court without the issue
of an exchequer commission to sequestrate his property, WSRO, Ep. I/17/12, fos. 12[v], 25[r],
45[r], 75[v]; cf. PRO, E 368/531, mem. 121[a]. The conformities of James Thatcher and Hugh
Thornicroft were, apparently, compelled purely by ecclesiastical court proceedings, WSRO,
Ep. II/9/11, fos. 1[r], 31[v], 23[v], 166[v]. I am very grateful to Kenneth Fincham for these
references. See also CRS 53, xcii–iv for Bowler's demonstration that the Wiltshire recusant
John Grove may have submitted because of ecclesiastical coercion.

than futile ecclesiastical justice which was the determining factor.[116] Aveling suggests that in the North the Church courts 'had a nuisance value through repeated summonses and the threat of excommunication', as well as supplying names for the ecclesiastical commissioners.[117] Sir Robert Cotton professed to believe that conformity was more likely to be enforced by the Church courts than the secular ones. He wrote that 'it is hard to free the people of suspition, that new Lawes [evidently referring to the recusancy statutes since 1581] are not rather invented against the particular persons and purses of men, than against their corrupt manners; by force of which reason I am induced to conceive, that the old use of the Church contained in good nurture, and Ecclesiasticall censures, will much more prevaile to muzzle Popery, than any fresh devises whatsoever'.[118]

Bishops and their parish clergy were supposed in person to persuade nonconformists to an actual liking of the established religion. In 1577 the bishops, in conference with privy councillors, agreed upon a tiered structure of conferences about religion to which leading recusants could be subjected before legal sanctions were enforced against them. Detection of recusants ('especiallie such as are of countenance and qualitie, and doe offende in example') was to be followed by an extended period of conference, imprisonment of the obstinate, fines and further conferences with them while they were held in restraint. Only failing that should the oath of supremacy be demanded from them.[119] The privy council regarded such conferring as a permanent episcopal duty (even if performed by delegation) of which bishops should not have to be reminded, and many bishops did engage vigorously in attempts to persuade Catholics from their recusant opinions.[120] In March 1605 Bancroft ordered his bishops 'as much as in you lieth' to put the sixty-sixth of the convocation canons of 1604 into effect: 'no pains may be spared in conferring with the . . . recusants, especially with . . . [those] who are the heads and leaders of the rest'.[121] The ecclesiastical

---

[116] Clark, 'Anglicanism', 31, 34, 71. Clark argues, in addition, that visitation procedures were not, in the Derby archdeaconry, grossly inefficient, *ibid.*, 72–4; cf. M. Ingram, *Church Courts, Sex and Marriage in England, 1570–1640* (Cambridge, 1987), 349.

[117] Aveling, *Northern Catholics*, 147; cf. Ingram, *Church Courts*, 85, 123, 329, 366, which gives a much more positive account of the Church courts' capacity (particularly in the southern province) for enforcing regular attendance from all but the most stubborn recusant minority.

[118] Howell, *Cottoni Posthuma*, 153.

[119] PRO, SP 12/45, fo. 5ᵛ; BL, Cotton MS Titus B III, fo. 69ʳ.

[120] PRO, SP 12/164/2, fo. 2ʳ, SP 12/45, fo. 16ᵛ; E. Cardwell (ed.), *Documentary Annals* (2 vols., Oxford, 1839), I, 401; LPL, Carte Antique et Miscellanee MS CM IV, no. 183, fos. 1ʳ–3ʳ.

[121] TD IV, xcviii: the sixty-sixth canon orders that 'every minister, being a preacher . . . and thought fit by the bishop of the diocese, shall labour diligently with . . . [the recusants in his parish] from time to time, thereby to reclaim them from their errors'. Only if conference

commission at York regularised a system of conferences on bond.[122] Laud's visitation articles for London in 1628 enquired whether preaching ministers regularly tried to reclaim popish recusants by conference.[123] A detailed programme of conferring was enjoined by the convocation canons of 1640.[124] In cases of recusancy the ecclesiastical courts, like the ecclesiastical commissioners, ordered individuals to confer with parish ministers.[125]

Nevertheless, the real basis for successful ecclesiastical compulsion of recusants to submit to the demands of the established Church rested on a combination of clerical and secular authority. The secular backing for excommunication was the writ *de excommunicando capiendo*. It was issued to sheriffs to effect the arrest and imprisonment of contumacious excommunicates when such people were certified to Chancery by their diocesan bishops. In December 1600 Whitgift ordered the bishops of his province to send the names of excommunicates to him and he would deliver them to the lord keeper. In circular letters to the bishops in March 1605 and July 1610 Bancroft urged the recipients to enforce the excommunication procedure properly by availing themselves of the secular arm. Bancroft directed that bishops should select 'two or three of the principallest' contumacious excommunicates, certify their names into Chancery, and he would use his 'utmost endeavour to procure the writ' *de excommunicando capiendo*, and 'take such order as that the same shall be faithfully and speedily served'.[126] Secular reinforcement of church penalties might have the desired effect. Sir Edward Phelips wrote to the earl of Salisbury in September 1609 that 'wee in lancashire at Lent Assizes tooke order that there should be awarded writtes of *Capias* upon Excommunications only against one or two at the most of a parishe of the most obstinate, some whereupon were arrested and amongst divers only one remaines in prison the rest have conformed themselves, which hath occasioned us nowe againe to renew that direction'.[127]

Secular and ecclesiastical powers were brought together principally

fails are the recusants to be denounced publicly according to the stipulations of the sixty-fifth canon. For William Chaderton's attempts to implement this instruction in Lincoln diocese, Foster, *State*, lxxxix; Oliver Ormerod, *The Picture of a Papist* (1606), 2.

[122] Aveling, *Catholic Recusancy*, 55.

[123] William Laud, ed. J. Bliss and W. Scott, *Works* (7 vols., Oxford, 1847–60), V, 402, repeated in his metropolitan visitation of 1635, *ibid.*, 426.

[124] Laud, *Works*, V, 616–17.

[125] Potter, 'Ecclesiastical Courts', 122.

[126] CRS 60, 143; Wilkins, *Concilia*, IV, 363, 410–12; Fincham, *Visitation Articles*, 95. The puritan agitation of the 1580s had included demands for the Church to avail itself of the secular power in enforcing excommunication, A. Peel (ed.), *The Seconde Parte of a Register* (2 vols., Cambridge, 1915), II, 13.

[127] PRO, SP 14/48/25.

through the ecclesiastical commission, based on royal authority and addressed to laymen as well as clerics.[128] In the North the York commission relied up to 1595 very largely on the vigour of its president Henry Hastings, third earl of Huntingdon.[129] But in the exercise of the commission's powers bishops had access to sanctions (imprisonment, fines and so on) which they did not possess in their capacity as a local ordinary. It is not surprising that bishops should have been so enthusiastic for a grant of a commission to their diocese.[130] Ecclesiastical commissioners were not limited to the pains and penalties of imprisonment and fines.[131] They could concentrate on obtaining conformity by attacking the individual's religious beliefs and doubts as well as his pocket and liberty.[132] While the efficiency of the commissions' administration of financial penalties has been seriously doubted,[133] there is quite considerable evidence of a determination by the clerics armed with the commission to force recusants to recant and conform.[134] Financial bonds could be used to remedy the deficiencies of statute, for example to make women conform, to force people to receive communion and to reinforce orders to protestantise recusants' children's

---

[128] I. Cassidy, 'The Episcopate of William Cotton, Bishop of Exeter, 1598–1621: With Special Reference to the State of the Clergy and the Administration of the Ecclesiastical Courts' (BLitt. thesis, Oxford, 1963), 27; Manning, 'Elizabethan Recusancy Commissions', 28.

[129] The York commission personnel coincided with the members of the Council in the North although the regular attenders were archiepiscopal officials and so commission policy might be a reflection of the archbishop's intentions, Newton, 'Puritanism', 67. In Chester the lay personnel outnumbered the clerical, but in Kent, for example, the Elizabethan commission's lay membership fluctuated and its members were eventually drawn heavily from the diocesan church courts, R. B. Manning, 'The Making of a Protestant Aristocracy: The Ecclesiastical Commissioners of the Diocese of Chester, 1550–98', *BIHR* 49 (1976), 60–79, at pp. 60, 64–5; P. Clark, 'The Ecclesiastical Commission at Canterbury: 1572–1603', *Archaeologia Cantiana* 89 (1974), 183–97, at pp. 187–90, a composition typical of most diocesan commissions, K. C. Fincham, *Prelate as Pastor* (Oxford, 1990), 166.

[130] Manning, 'Elizabethan Recusancy Commissions', 24; BL, Lansd. MS 33, fo. 27r; HMC *Salisbury MSS* VI, 266 (Bilson's request for a commission, which will assist him in drawing recusants 'to private and often conference', especially seeing 'how weak ordinary authority is to do any good'), X, 378, XI, 182, XIX, 145; Fincham, *Prelate*, 154–5.

[131] Morris, *Troubles*, III, 156.

[132] Peck, *Desiderata*, I, 97; Aveling, *Catholic Recusancy*, 54–5.

[133] Walker, 'Implementation', 395–6; Aveling, *Northern Catholics*, 134; Tyler, 'Ecclesiastical Commission', 137–9; *CSPD 1598–1601*, 276, for allegations of corruption in the administration of the penalties imposed by the northern commission; cf. CRS 41, 86 for allegations of similar corrupt practices by the pursuivants of the commission for the southern province. Thornborough, however, thought that recusants whom the commission had forced to take bonds were more compliant than others who did not take them, HMC *Salisbury MSS* XIX, 145.

[134] Archbishop John Piers said in May 1590 that many of those imprisoned, 'by God his helpe and conference of learned men . . . have reformed themselves', AAW, A IV, 93.

education.[135] They might contain an obligation to confer with preachers, to compel a spouse to confer, or even to conform by a certain date, and to continue conformable thereafter.[136] Thomas Sleepe and his wife entered into a bond to confer with Richard Bancroft twice a week between February and May 1595.[137] The nagging persistence of repeated proceedings against those who initially were unwilling to comply perhaps undermined their will to resist.[138] Bishop William Cotton of Exeter reported in September 1606 to the earl of Salisbury that the commission had enabled him to reclaim many Romanists as well as stubborn puritan preachers and that in the previous ten days he had brought '8 or 9 recusants to the church'.[139] In June 1615 Bishop William James told Sir Ralph Winwood that in the past the ecclesiastical commission in his diocese had reduced the recusants there from 700 to 400 (though now they have started to increase again).[140]

The determination to compel recusants to enter into conferences with specified Protestant ministers indicates that the commission wanted to induce a thoroughgoing conformity. As a Catholic commentator observed, 'the high commissioners troble even those that satisfie the statute' (to the extent of paying recusancy fines).[141] The authorities, it seems, were aware of the political and psychological elements in voluntary discussion. Time to

---

[135] Cliffe, *Yorkshire Gentry*, 175–6; Aveling, *Northern Catholics*, 90, 147; BI, HCAB 11, fo. 332ᵛ, HCAB 16, fo. 41ᵛ; cf. PRO, SP 14/58/97, fos. 182ᵛ–3ʳ; cf. William Fulke, A *briefe Confutation, of a Popish Discourse* (1581), fos. 18ᵛ–19ʳ, emphasising that the commissioners did not enquire just whether the person before them has attended church.

[136] E.g. LPL, Carte Antique et Miscellanee MS CM IV, no. 23; PRO, E 135/12/2, fo. 2ʳ; LPL, Carte Antique et Miscellanee MS CM IV, no. 42; PRO, E 135/12/7, fo. 19ʳ. The statutory bond in 23 Elizabeth I, c.1 to be taken from those who had been recusant for more than twelve months for their 'good behaviour' could be interpreted as a bond to conform rather than one merely to keep the peace, but in general it was read in the second rather than the first sense, Aveling, *Northern Catholics*, 138–9.

[137] PRO, E 135/12/2, fos. 6ʳ (*bis*) and 7ʳ; cf. CRS 60, 48–9; for recusants' official conformity reinforced by bonds to continue it, PRO, E 368/510, mem. 152ª (Thomas Alcock, imprisoned in the Marshalsea, submitted and was bound by Whitgift in the sum of £100 for his 'repayre and resortinge from tyme to tyme unto the Churche to the heareinge of devine service according to the law and to make certificate thereof the first Courte day of the terme then next followinge and soe from thence forth the first or second Courte day in every Terme for the space of one whole yeare'); PRO, E 368/522, mem. 191ª, E 368/495, mem. 49ᵇ (a condition of William Baxter's conformity at York was that he certified his and his family's continued acquiescence, from time to time, to Archbishop Hutton). Bancroft arranged to confer with Tobias Mathew jnr twice a week, A. H. Mathew (ed.), *A True Historical Relation of the Conversion of Sir Tobie Matthew* (1904), 63.

[138] CRS 56, xxxii–iii, for the continuous attention of the York commission to Thomas Meynell. After fifteen years of recusancy Meynell was still being enjoined to confer with a minister and the indefatigable Archbishop Tobias Mathew was trying to lend him Protestant books to read, *ibid.*, xxx; Morris, *Troubles*, I, 246, III, 456.

[139] Cassidy, 'Episcopate', 29.

[140] PRO, SP 14/80/116; cf. AAW, Anglia IX, no. 2; PRO SP 14/75/1.i; cf. Matthew Hutton's report from Durham in January 1593, PRO, SP 12/244/8.

[141] AAW, A X, 169; BI, HCAB 15, fo. 139ᵛ.

conform gradually might be welcome to some who could not envisage a straight move from one communion to the other.[142] In some cases agreement to confer signified no intention whatever of submitting,[143] but in others it may well have been a prelude to conformity, an easier way of making an otherwise unjustifiable transfer of ecclesiastical and religious allegiance. Between June 1591 and October 1592 Dorothy Swaile of North Stainley was coerced by all the means available to the commission towards conferring with Protestant ministers, and the pressure applied eventually produced a conformity certificate from her.[144] Of the 58 recusants imprisoned in and around London who were examined in 1593 by order of the privy council only one offered to conform, but, having promised to submit, he asked to confer in religion with, among others, the dean of Westminster.[145] In May 1621 Margaret Spence appeared before the York commissioners, said she desired to confer, was placed on bond to do so, and afterwards came to prayers in York Minster and conformed to the satisfaction of the commission.[146] Zealous Romanists regarded conferences as a distinct threat to the constancy of leading Catholics. They saw a willingness to discuss matters of faith with a Protestant minister on his terms (rather than by way of polemical argument) as a step towards conformity. While priests might confer because the conference would seem, on account of their learning, to be a disputation, unlearned laymen might not because their action would look like submission and could possibly affect their faith.[147] People like the puritan Francis Bunny, regularly named as a conferrer by the York commission, saw it as an important part of the Protestant evangelical onslaught on popery.[148] Some recusants appear to have submitted because

---

[142] Savage, *Conference*, 104; B. N. de Luna, *Jonson's Romish Plot* (Oxford, 1967), 135; cf. E. H. Dickerman, 'The Conversion of Henry IV: "Paris is well worth a Mass" in Psychological Perspective', *Catholic Historical Review* 63 (1977), 1–13, at p. 11.

[143] Burke, 'Catholic Recusants', 206; Walker, 'Implementation', 83–4; BL, Lansd. MS 72, fo. 118v. Thomas Pickering of Crosby Ravensworth in Westmorland had allowed Henry Robinson, Bishop of Carlisle, to think that he was potentially conformable as far back as December 1599 but he conformed only in August 1606 following the exchequer's seizure of his property in October 1605, *CSPD 1598–1601*, 362; *HMC Salisbury MSS* XI, 164–5; PRO, E 368/553, mem. 145a.

[144] BI, HCAB 11, fos. 348v, 357r, HCAB 12, fos. 8v, 15r, 80v, although it seems she may have been presented again as a recusant in January 1609, HCAB 15, fo. 211r.

[145] CRS 60, 46.

[146] BI, HCAB 16, fo. 272r.

[147] Robert Charnock, *A Reply to a Notorious Libell* (1603), 70; Stonyhurst, Collectanea P II, fo. 464r; cf. P. J. Holmes, *Resistance and Compromise* (Cambridge, 1982), 198–9; Henry Garnet, *An Apology against the Defence of Schisme* (n.p., 1593), 68–9; J. C. H. Aveling, 'Some Cases Pertaining to England', in G. T. Bradley (ed.), *Yorkshire Catholics* (Leeds Diocesan Archives Occasional Publications no. 1, Darlington, 1985), 15–25, at p. 21; Aveling, *Catholic Recusancy*, 50, 73–4.

[148] Francis Bunny, *Truth and Falshood* (1595), sigs. Aa3v, Bb2r.

of the attentions of the ecclesiastical commissioners even though they certified their conformities to the exchequer eventually.[149]

Of course, no one would deny that the ecclesiastical commission had its problems. Aveling argued that although at certain dates the York commission functioned efficiently enough the only time when the commission induced a respectable number of conformities was a very short period in the early 1580s. Moreover, these successes resulted from proceeding against waverers rather than convinced Catholics. He judges that 'from the court records, conferences only rarely brought about conformity'.[150] (Certainly Thomas Sleepe and his wife, subjected to so much official attention by the commission in London, presented themselves not once, let alone the stipulated twenty-six times, to discuss religion with Bancroft!)[151] Sir John Southworth would not respond to any amount of badgering by the ecclesiastical commission but eventually succumbed to secular recusancy fines.[152] In any case, the extension of ecclesiastical commissions to

---

[149] Morris, *Troubles*, III, 176, for Richard Holtby's citation of northerners who conformed after conference, including Henry Blenkinsop who had submitted by May 1594, PRO, E 368/479, mem. 143[a]. Holtby claimed that it was the ecclesiastical commission's badgering (Blenkinsop had been put under bond and imprisoned by the commission in November 1593, BI, HCAB 12, fo. 143[v]) rather than the 1591 exchequer assessment of his property, which was not very high, which finally brought him down; also (possibly) Robert Ward who conformed at the York assizes in 1598 but had reportedly conformed five years before the inquisition into his property, PRO, E 368/493, mem. 191[a-b]. (However, at this time in the North, these recusants were under intense political pressure, and this, rather than discussions with preachers, may have influenced their conformity.) Cf. the cases of Ralph Hodgson, BI, HCAB 13, fos. 72[v], 95[v]; PRO, E 368/526, mem. 209[a]; Stephen Vaughan, *CSPD 1591–4*, 245, PRO, E 368/474, mem. 124[a]; John Hotham, PRO, E 135/12/7, mem. 189[a], E 368/527, mem. 181[a]. William Lascelles was convicted in 1605 and conformed in October 1607. There is no evidence of an inquisition into his property and the conformity certificate which he presented to the exchequer was signed by three ecclesiastical commissioners. He had been subject to the ecclesiastical commission's attention from March to June 1607, PRO, E 368/528, mem. 188[a-b]; BI, HCAB 15, fos. 35[v], 44[v], 61[r]. Anthony Wild was subjected to an ecclesiastical commission fine at the direction of John Thornborough who supervised his conformity, PRO, E 368/528, mem. 176[a-b], E 135/12/7, mem. 304[a]; BI, HCAB 15, fo. 70[v]. William Walworth may have been brought to a conformable state by the ecclesiastical commission before he was subject to an exchequer inquisition, PRO, E 135/12/7, mem. 304[a]; BI, HCAB 12, fo. 81[r]; PRO, E 368/492, mem. 186[a].

[150] J. C. H. Aveling, *Post-Reformation Catholicism in East Yorkshire 1558–1790* (York, 1960), 24–5; idem, *Northern Catholics*, 215, 146–7; cf. Walker, 'Implementation', 391–3; Tyler, 'Ecclesiastical Commission', chapter 4, esp. pp. 258–61; Fincham, *Prelate*, 167–8; cf. Wark, *Elizabethan Recusancy*, 34–5.

[151] PRO, E 135/12/2, fo. 6[r] (*bis*).

[152] BL, Lansd. MS 11, fo. 136[r]; PRO, E 368/453, mem. 1[a-b]; Hasler, *Commons*, III, 423; cf. the similar case of Ursula Dawney: conference with a preacher had no effect until the arrival of two exchequer inquisitions (in 1596 and 1597), CRS 53, 23–4; PRO, E 368/493, mem. 208[a].

the individual dioceses was severely restricted by lay parliamentary hostility.[153] But, as with the exchequer, it was not really a matter of the high commission compelling all those it dealt with to conform. The point was that, through it, the State could sometimes compel a conformity to the established Church which was more than a secular formality.

So, in spite of the drawbacks of the recusancy statutes and the unreliability of some of the authorities responsible for prosecuting Catholic nonconformists, the machinery for enforcing conformity evidently had teeth. Conformity could be loaded with a considerable weight of religious symbolism. It often went far beyond church papistry, as both Protestants and refractory Catholics were well aware. Furthermore, just as the conformity ritual combined religious and political elements, so secular and ecclesiastical powers could cooperate extremely effectively in the bringing of recusants to the point of submission. The encouragement to conform to which Catholics were subjected in this period varied considerably from time to time, but the system for extorting it was never a dead letter nor a purely administrative procedure, even though its administration, from a godly Protestant's viewpoint, sometimes fell short of the ideal. When the political and religious concerns of all the Protestant authorities were in alignment, then it was possible for them to force many Catholics, as far as the system allowed, into a serious profession of allegiance to the Church of England which went beyond the purely political aspects of temporal allegiance.

CONFLICT BETWEEN CHURCH AND STATE: RELIGION AND POLITICS IN THE ENFORCEMENT OF CONFORMITY

Why then did the late Tudor and early Stuart State not produce a more thoroughly conformist or even 'Protestant' country? One answer is that even if, for a time, the late Elizabethan regime did make serious efforts to repress dissent, after 1603 the authorities turned a more benign face towards Catholics. Certainly, after James's accession, nonconformist Catholicism was not as pressing a political problem as before 1603. On its own, however, this does not suffice as an explanation. The Jacobean State did try hard at times to repress particular elements of Roman Catholicism in England. The answer is more complex. It lies in an appreciation of the different, even antagonistic, motives of the separate authorities which wanted to bring about conformity to the established religion in England.

---

153 Fincham, *Prelate*, 155; L. A. Knafla, *Law and Politics in Jacobean England* (Cambridge, 1977), 138–40.

As we have seen, statute-conformity was both religious and political. Politically, the focus tended to be on the rejection of the jurisdictional implications of papal supremacy and affirmation of the royal one. In religion, conformity was principally an affirmation of the Church of England as an ecclesiastical institution which sponsored a particular form of Protestant religion and a rejection of aspects of the Roman version of Christianity. It was inevitable that some in authority would see some elements of conformity as more important than others. The secular functionaries of the State naturally considered uniformity as it was a political necessity. Those who saw Rome primarily as a political threat were interested in theological affirmation of the Church of England as good political propaganda. This is not to say that politicians did not care what Catholics believed, or that Protestant churchmen were interested only in the theological state of mind of conformists. Politics and religion were always intertwined in the endorsement of the established Church. The privy council, from time to time, showed itself active in driving Catholics to profess some form of Protestantism.[154] But when it came to regulating conformity, and especially to deciding how hard it was to be enforced, then Protestants started to disagree over its application.

Of course, while religious and political sources of conflict were firmly in alignment, as they were in the 1580s and early 1590s (the period which saw the principal Catholic works of political resistance theory, and active Romanist scheming to undermine the regime), then those Protestants with different conformity agendas could cooperate with each other in pursuing harmoniously what looked like a single objective – uniformity in religion. From 1580, when the influx of seminary priests was inevitably equated with the objectives of the most heavily politicised and belligerent section of the Catholic exiles, the political effort to secure the recantations of seminarists was intensified, and it coincided perfectly with the theological polemic against the evils of popery. Even those like the somewhat inadequate seminarists Lawrence Caddey, Edward Osborne and John Nichols suddenly found themselves the focus of official attention. William Allen warned that the Elizabethan government proceeded both by the 'writing and preaching of the Sect-maisters' and the authority of the 'Civil Magistrate', but made

---

[154] For privy council interest in securing and assuring the conformity of specific individuals, *APC* VIII, 314, 327–8, IX, 17, 41, 46, 75, 93, 224, X, 310–13, 327, 333, 359–60, 372–3, XI, 15, 47–8, 103, 166, 204, XII, 167–8, 169, 170, 200, 271, 301, 338, 346, 362, XIII, 203, 223–4, 265, 285–6, 408–10, XVI, 228–9, XXII, 454, XXIII, 126–7, 198, 227, 341–2, 355–6, 368, XXIV, 36–7, 110–11, 454–5, XXV, 50–1, XXVII, 85, 209, XXIX, 184–5.

more political capital out of publicising the recantations of Catholic renegades.[155] Several priests said that the devilish conspiracies to invade the country had provoked their conversions to Protestantism, and others implicitly based their changes of religion upon their own latent loyalist political tendencies.[156] The seminarist John Hart was brought after his arrest to confer with the Oxford puritan John Rainolds. Their discussions were printed in 1584.[157] Hart appears to make no theological concessions in the hundreds of pages of dispute, something at which Catholics rejoiced.[158] But the exercise was taken by Protestants as a sign that he had denied part of the current Roman position, and the book was regarded as one which affirmed the Protestant establishment.[159] This was because he could plausibly be thought to have rejected the deposing power, direct and indirect.[160] The council wrote to the bishop of Norwich after he had persuaded Thomas Lovell to conform, and ordered that Lovell should be 'released upon his promise and subscription of his newe conformitie, without bande, that yt maie appeare to the worlde that he is willingly converted and not coacte [coerced]'.[161] The council expected waverers to draw lessons from the conformities of men of high status.[162] Renegades were also used as persuaders. Thomas Clarke preached in London while Thomas Bell was sent back to the North to proselytise there, and he took part in disputations against the Jesuit Henry Walpole in York. William Hardesty tried to deliver a Protestant sermon to the Catholic prisoners in York Castle just as John Nichols had been used to preach to Catholics in the Tower. Miles Dawson was similarly engaged to persuade prisoners at York away from their

[155] William Allen, *A True Report of the late Apprehension and Imprisonnement of John Nicols* (Rheims, 1583), sig. Aii^r–iii^r.
[156] E.g. *The Recantations as they were severallie pronounced by Wylliam Tedder and Anthony Tyrrell* (1588), 9; Richard Sheldon, *The Motives of Richard Sheldon Pr.* (1612), sig. Bb2^r; Henry Yaxley, *Morbus et Antidotus* (1630), 39–40; cf. John Copley, *Doctrinall and Morall Observations* (1612), 124.
[157] John Rainolds, *The Summe of the Conference* (1584).
[158] R. M. Kingdon (ed.), *The Execution of Justice* (New York, 1965), 74. Later he did in fact temporarily apostatise, though he then withdrew his offer, Morris, *Troubles*, II, 30.
[159] BI, HCAB 12, fo. 83^r; Francis Walsingham, *A Search Made into Matters of Religion* (St Omer, 1609), 3.
[160] Sir Francis Hastings, *An Apologie or Defence of the Watch-word* (1600), 170; Daniel Price, *The Defence of Truth* (Oxford, 1610), 65, 361–2.
[161] *APC* X, 333. The bishop was ordered also to see that he remained conformable. Cf. *APC* XXII, 454.
[162] *APC* XXVII, 85.

Catholic opinions.[163] Paul's Cross recantation sermons were frequently attended by privy council members.[164]

Still, in the 1580s and early 1590s one senses that recanting priests were valued for more than their new views about justification. In fact, they were probably more useful to secular politicians as spies and informers than as rhetorical persuaders to Protestantism. Thomas Bell revealed the structure of Lancashire Catholicism to his interrogators. The confessions of other renegades were employed by the authorities to break down the resistance of Catholics who were convened before them.[165] The extraordinary Richard Baines was used by the English government as an infiltrator at the seminary in Rheims in the early 1580s.[166] Clarke, Hardesty and Major were all employed as priest-hunters.[167] Most renegades betrayed former

[163] Foley III, 762; J. E. Bailey, 'Thomas Bell', *Notes and Queries*, sixth series, 2 (1880), 429–31, at p. 430; Strype, *Annals*, IV, 210–11; John Nichols, *A Declaration of the Recantation of John Nichols* (1581); G. Anstruther, 'A Missing Martyr Pamphlet', *London Recusant* 5 (1975), 67–74, at p. 70, showing that Nichols's example was used by the judges at Everard Hanse's trial to get Hanse to recant; *HMC Salisbury MSS* VI, 339, VII, 404. Obviously converts to Protestantism continued to be useful as propaganda, and much was made of them, even of the unreliable Leonard Rountree at York in 1613, PRO, SP 14/88/53; AAW, A XII, 467, 523. But confrontations between renegades and Catholics retreated somewhat into a more private setting. In August 1607 Sir George Snigge told the earl of Salisbury that he had used the renegade Peter Chambers to challenge two recusants and see whether their opinions might be changed, *HMC Salisbury MSS* XIX, 213. In March 1607 John Scudamore was employed by Bancroft in an attempt to persuade Robert Drury and William Davies to take the oath of allegiance, Vatican Archives, Borghese MS III. 43. de. fos. 88ʳ–9ᵛ.

[164] The earl of Leicester with other councillors went to Nichols's Tower sermon in order to give it credit, CRS 4, 7, 9.

[165] Morris, *Troubles*, III, 175. W. F. Rea, 'The Authorship of "News from Spayne and Holland" and its Bearing on the Genuineness of the Confessions of the Blessed Henry Walpole, SJ', *Biographical Studies* 1 (1951–2), 220–30, suggests that Walpole's confessions contained in the State Papers were partly concocted by the secular authorities in order to confront other Catholics with them.

[166] For Richard Baines, see C. B. Kuriyama, 'Marlowe's Nemesis: The Identity of Richard Baines', in K. Friedenreich *et al.* (ed.), *'A Poet and Filthy Play-Maker': New Essays on Christopher Marlowe* (New York, 1988), 343–60, at pp. 347–8, and now principally, R. Kendall, 'Richard Baines and Christopher Marlowe's Milieu', *English Literary Renaissance* 24 (1994), 507–52, in which Kendall establishes the connection between Marlowe's and Baines's opinions and sets out the exact chronology of Baines's spying activities.

[167] Questier, 'Phenomenon', 162. The secular authorities made use also of those who left the seminaries without completing their clerical training. In January 1591, Thomas Pawlin was expelled from Rheims, returned to England and betrayed many Catholics, also professing himself, according to Robert Fisher, a Protestant, CRS 51, 251. Three renegades from Valladolid cooperated in Mark Barkworth's prosecution, CRS 30, 35–6; A. J. Loomie, 'Spain and the English Catholic Exiles 1580–1604' (Ph.D thesis, London, 1957), 316–21. In 1597 an ex-seminarist Lawrence Bright living near Hastings in Sussex betrayed two seminarists, Loomie, 'Spain', 274. William Jessopp returned from Seville in October 1600 after five years at that seminary, and took the oath of supremacy, *HMC Salisbury MSS* X, 340–2, 378. Robert Griffith, en route to the Seville seminary in 1600, apostatised and returned to

colleagues. John Hart wrote to Sir Francis Walsingham in December 1581 that the intelligence which he might pass on about Catholics 'wil better serve for the setting forth of that true cause in deede which your honour . . . doth so mightily defend. I meane the religion this day professed in . . . England. For as for my bare yelding and conforming of my selfe which I have promised . . . though it may doe some good thereunto by gyving others of my profession example to do the lyke, yet that thing is not of such importance as this which hytherto I have spoken of' (i.e. intelligence gathering).[168] Anthony Tyrrell, who supplied reams of information (of doubtful veracity) about Catholic plotting, claimed in one of his penitent moments that after his arrest in 1586 he requested that he might have conference with a Protestant cleric, attend church and receive the Protestant communion, but all of this was refused 'so long as ther was any meanes for . . . [him] to prosecute the catholickes'.[169]

After around 1595, though Catholics remained politically active, the former connection between religious conversion and political loyalty clearly started to disintegrate. The appellant controversy demonstrated that loyalism was compatible with profession of Roman Catholicism. Subsequently, the renegade priests Richard Sheldon and John Salkeld were of more interest to the secular authorities, and notably to James, because of their opinions about the oath of allegiance. Even in the North, where belligerent papistry was more of a problem, weakness set in when State and Church, secular and clerical concerns, came adrift – principally in the divisions between Matthew Hutton and Sir Thomas Cecil, and then later, between Bishop Thornborough and Lord Sheffield. Hutton dissented from Sir Thomas Cecil's policy of compelling the Catholics in York Castle to listen to puritan sermons, and Cecil's very secular attitude towards public conformity must have enraged the evangelical archbishop. Sheffield, on the secular grounds of good order, attacked Thornborough's over-enthusiasm for prosecuting recusants.[170]

It would be a mistake, though, to deduce from all this that there was simply a growing rift between those with a Protestant theological training, and those without. It is not as straightforward as saying that politicians

---

England, *HMC Salisbury MSS* X, 144, XI, 182. Douai produced the renegades Edward Biller and John Fawether (who informed against Robert Watkinson) in March 1602, and also Alexander Capell in July 1611, *HMC Salisbury MSS* XII, 87–8, CRS 10, 36, 335; CRS 11, 567–70; Anstruther I, 372; cf. BL, Harl. MS 360, fo. 36ʳ; AAW, A VII, no. 37; PRO, SP 14/65/13, fo. 24ʳ; Anstruther II, 229 (suggesting that Capell's accurate information led to the arrest of Peter Nanconan).

168 PRO, SP 12/150/80, fos. 148ᵛ–9ʳ.
169 BL, Lansd. MS 51, fo. 156ᵛ.
170 BL, Add. MS 34250, fos. 19ᵛ–20ᵛ; *HMC Salisbury MSS* XIX, 274; Aveling, *Catholic Recusancy*, 50.

thought in a secular way, and clerics concerned themselves with purely religious issues. It was more a matter of the role which particular individuals in authority played in enforcing conformity, their 'ethos'. All officially wanted to see Catholics conform within the meaning of the law. But the way in which they pursued it varied depending on what their job was in the apparatus of the State or its Church.

Let us look briefly, by way of illustration, at the regime's administrators, the civil servants who implemented policy once it had been formulated. They were capable of bringing heavy financial pressure to bear on recusants in line with government policy towards nonconformist Catholicism. But even if the original purpose of the recusant statutes was to compel conformity, as Burke and Rose argue,[171] the administrative concerns of those in charge of their enforcement gradually started to take precedence. As late as 1597, Lord Burghley might tell those in the provinces who were responsible for prosecuting recusants that 'the well executing of the . . . [exchequer] Commissions in some Counties hath of late brought many of them to submission and Conformitie which is more desired then any [financial] Benefitte of the service and is the onely ende of the Statute'.[172] But the exchequer's officials were not churchmen, nor even, primarily, politicians. Recusancy inevitably had a financial significance among those bureaucrats whose duty it was to penalise it. After 1603 there was a running battle between proponents of different ways of administering the recusants' fines and sequestrated property, with both sides saying that their method would produce more revenue for the Crown.[173] In addition, convicted recusants became useful as a supply of grants for James's courtiers.[174] After a grant had been made of recusants' estates, conformity was an irritating spoke in the wheels of the patronage system.[175] When John Thornborough had run into a brick wall in his efforts to proceed indiscriminately and rigorously against Yorkshire recusants, the earl of Salisbury curtly informed him that if he had been permitted to act against 'those that were in speach with the kings servants' (that is, recusants negotiating with royal grantees of their forfeitures), their grants would not have been worth 'sixpence'.[176]

---

[171] Burke, 'Submissions', 1; Rose, *Cases*, 45–7; cf. PRO, SP 12/127/6.
[172] BL, Harl. MS 703, fo. 108ʳ.   [173] Questier, 'Sir Henry Spiller', *passim*.
[174] Even the 1604 statutory measure designed to damage powerful and wealthy recusants by allowing the Crown to take two-thirds of their estates rather than settling for the (in their cases much smaller) fine of £20 per month soon became part of the system of compounding and grants of forfeitures so that its potential effect was never realised, PRO, SO 3/3, January–March 1607 (Michael Hare, Sir John Arundell, Sir John Talbot, Edward Morgan), July 1607 (John Sayer).
[175] *HMC Salisbury MSS*, XIX, 434–5; cf. PRO, SP 14/14/66, fo. 141ʳ; cf. CRS 56, xxxii–iv.
[176] PRO, SP 14/15/105, fo. 169ᵛ; cf. BL, Lansd. MS 153, fo. 162ʳ, for Sir Julius Caesar's direction to the same effect.

It has often been thought anomalous that the exchequer clerk in the lord treasurer's remembrancer's office with responsibility by around 1602 for the administration of all recusant financial business at Westminster, Henry Spiller, was at the centre of a Catholic network, and himself probably held Catholic religious opinions. The puritan attacks on him in successive Jacobean parliaments give the impression that he was being criticised as a popish sympathiser who was trying to protect recusants.[177] But even if Spiller was no evangelical Protestant, the exchequer was very much a puritan enclave, with officials and judges like Sir Vincent Skinner, Sir Julius Caesar, Sir George Snigge, Sir John Savile, Sir Thomas Fanshaw, Sir Thomas Fleming and others, and Spiller's colleagues evidently did not judge see him in the same light as his enraged parliamentary enemies.[178]

The point was that the exchequer operated as a bureaucratic institution. It was not an arm of the Church. Like other branches of government it safe-guarded the Crown's interests, but in the exchequer's case those interests were financial ones. Spiller always successfully deflected the accusations of his opponents by showing that his 'lenient' proposals for dealing with recusants were fiscally rational.[179] The unsuccessful schemes concocted towards the end of Elizabeth's reign to use semi-independent agents to locate and lease out recusant property had, from a bureaucratic point of view, not worked well, even though they undoubtedly increased pressure on Catholics to conform.[180] Spiller and others who saw their principal objective as the sound management of the Crown's financial resources decided to change the way the recusancy system was administered. They wished to guarantee the flow of income from recusancy by ensuring that recusant Catholics were subject only to moderate demands upon their estates.

This did not mean that exchequer powers to enquire into recusant property were suddenly curtailed. Catholic newsletter writers were reporting in late 1613 and early 1614 that commissions *ad melius inquirendum* were being sent out against even those Catholics who had already availed them-selves of the benefits of a compounding commission. George Birkhead thought they would 'never cease till poore catholiques be utterly beggered'.

---

177 Questier, 'Sir Henry Spiller', 254–7.
178 Hasler, *Commons*, III, 350–1, 412–13, 390–1, II, 105–6; Hill, *Bench*, 4, 14; N. Tyacke, *Anti-Calvinists* (Oxford, 1990), 132, 137; Matthew Sutcliffe, *The Examination and Confutation of a certain scurrilous Treatise entituled, The Survey of the newe Religion* (1606), sig. A2r; cf. also Sir William Periam, Hasler, *Commons*, III, 209; ARSJ, Angl. 31/I, fo. 247r (for the report in December 1603 that Periam objected to relaxing judicial measures against recusancy).
179 BL, Lansd. MS 153, fo. 107r; PRO, SP 14/80/69; Notestein, Relf and Simpson, *Commons Debates* IV, 101.
180 *CSPD 1601–3*, 279–80; CRS 57, lxxvi.

The commission was accompanied by a letter from Sir Julius Caesar commanding 'enquirye of there landes, and that everye acre of theire lande should bee valued at the highest note and the number and value thearof bee returned'.[181] Particularly after the failure of the 1610 parliament to deliver a satisfactory solution to the Crown's financial problems, all possible sources of income were being more rigorously exploited, and recusancy was one of them.

Spiller advised nevertheless (and in practice the Pells receipt books show his advice was frequently followed) that inquisitions should not be repeated, nor should lands and goods be sequestrated together. Both measures were ultimately counterproductive since in the long run they would cause recusants to conform and the Crown would lose money. Moderation in pressing the Crown's demands would be an incentive for them to continue paying.[182] Spiller's professional responsibilities meant that he was more likely to stamp out the chaos caused in the system by people like John Thornborough than he was to stamp out Catholicism, whatever his own religious opinions were.[183]

Naturally, Spiller's enemies claimed to be horrified at the laxity they detected in the handling of exchequer business concerned with Catholics, though they virtually conceded much of his argument by phrasing their complaints largely in fiscal terms. (They said they would raise money for the

---

[181] AAW, A XII, 443, 467, XIII, 39.

[182] BL, Lansd. MS 153, fo. 116ʳ. Though the 1606 statute (3 James I, c.4) forbade the leasing of recusant lands back to recusants or to their use, this was effectively overridden by Lord Chief Baron Fleming and the earl of Dorset, *Statutes* IV, 1073; BL, Lansd. MS 153, fo. 240ʳ. A 1608 memorandum in the State Papers which contains a paragraph advising that the law against Catholics should be enforced specifically so as to obtain conformities has that paragraph struck out, PRO, SP 14/37/76, fo. 156ᵛ. Spiller thought the exchequer ought always to allow debtors to compound where it could not easily secure full payment. Commissions with power to compound for recusant debts were issued periodically, PRO, E 368/519, mem. 2ᵃ⁻ᶜ; BL, Lansd. MS 153, fo. 304ʳ; PRO, SP 14/50/63, fos. 104ᵛ⁻5ʳ; PRO, SP 14/115/32, fo. 43ʳ. This was in line with the exchequer's compounding policy for other types of debt at this time, BL, Add. MS 36767, fos. 66ʳ, 80ʳ, 182ʳ.

[183] Spiller could show that, though the exchequer commission on which Thornborough had been a prominent member had raised larger sums than previous commissions, many of the recusants whose estates the commission had sequestrated had subsequently submitted or obtained discharges on other grounds, BL, Lansd. MS 153, fos. 199ʳ–207ʳ, 253ʳ–61ʳ; PRO, E 368/526, mm. 209ᵃ, 216ᵃ, 222ᵃ, 223ᵃ, E 368/527, mm. 184ᵃ⁻ᵇ, 195ᵃ, E 368/528, mm. 166ᵃ, 169ᵃ, 176ᵃ, 189ᵃ, 193ᵃ, 210ᵃ, E 368/529, mem. 51ᵃ, E 368/530, mm. 151ᵃ, 166ᵃ, E 368/532, mm. 82ᵃ, 128ᵃ, 139ᵃ, 140ᵃ, 183ᵃ, 188ᵃ. Cf. Spiller's objections to the activities of George Chambers, whose 'service' in Herefordshire in 1609 may have been the cause of a high rate of conformity there in 1610–11, BL, Lansd. MS 153, fo. 64ʳ; PRO, E 368/538–45. Cf. also PRO, E 134/41 Elizabeth I/Trinity 9, E 368/489, mem. 208ᵃ, E 134/7 James I/Trinity 7, E 134/8 James I/Easter 39, E 368/537, mem. 50ᵃ, for evidence of the havoc caused by Andrew Morgan and Charles Grimston in Monmouthshire and Staffordshire respectively.

Crown where Spiller had failed.)[184] But it would be wrong to ascribe such complaints by people like John Thornborough either to a simple religious horror at the increase of recusancy or merely to a cynical determination to profit from this aspect of legislation against religious dissent. They just took a different approach towards papists. Thornborough and his ilk were interested in a blunt enforcement of the law against papists rather than bureaucratic rationality and fiscal common sense. They were motivated neither principally by financial concerns, like the officers in the exchequer, nor purely by religious concerns, like the evangelical churchmen who agonised over the spiritual welfare of recusants' souls. (Thornborough, though a churchman, was definitely not an evangelical.) Recusant-hunters of Thornborough's stamp wished to enforce the law's penalties against a large number of Catholics and did not want such penalties to be merely a small tax on a few wealthy ones. Lord Sheffield wrote in 1607 to Salisbury that Thornborough, the 'unholy' bishop, preferred prosecuting recusants to performing his proper episcopal functions and had not preached 'above once or twice in this whole year'.[185] He showed virtually no interest in the doctrinal issues over which, in his presence, the Catholic laymen in York Castle in 1599–1600 disputed with Yorkshire puritan ministers.[186] But Thornborough and his agents still saw themselves as promoters of conformity, and this conformity they viewed with an essentially political cast of mind. One gets a sense of this from the tracts which Thornborough published in 1604 and 1605 about the proposed union with Scotland. He compares political with religious schism: schism 'renteth the Seamlesse Coat of Christ, both in the Church and in the Civil State'. God governs believers 'by one holy law, and uniteth them in the same faith . . . that hereby the gods on earth, whom he hath placed to rule over many and divers kingdoms upon earth, might learne by the same lawes in things humane, and same religion in matters divine, to preserve Weale publike, and Christian Societie among men'. At the debates with the recusants at York, Thornborough challenged not their doctrinal beliefs but their resistance to established authority. In one of his few serious interventions there he accused the recusant spokesman, William Stillington, not of doctrinal error, but of schism.[187] It was not that Thornborough had no interest in religious conformity. The lord

---

[184] Spiller's opponents had a point when they argued that recusants like Thomas Meynell and Richard Cholmeley *could* pay much more, BL, Lansd. MS 153, fo. 127r. They were also right that diminishing the prospect of profit for middlemen in the recusancy business would reduce incentives to locate and prosecute recusants, BL, Lansd. MS 153, fo. 102r.

[185] *HMC Salisbury MSS* XIX, 274.

[186] Questier, 'Sir Henry Spiller', 264–5; BL, Add. MS 34250, fo. 30v.

[187] John Thornborough, *The Joiefull and Blessed Reuniting* (Oxford, 1605), 11, 77; *idem, A Discourse* (1604), 28–9; B. Galloway, *The Union of England and Scotland 1603–1608* (Edinburgh, 1986), 31, 33; BL, Add. MS 34250, fo. 13v.

treasurer's remembrancer's memoranda rolls show that he, with puritan commissioners like Hoby and Procter, personally supervised recusants' public submissions.[188] But his concept of conformity tended to serve his concept of political order.

The regime could extort a high degree of compliance from those to whom it turned its attentions; and the agents whom it entrusted with the task were not a collection of weak, corrupt and cynical servants of an inefficient and inadequate early modern State. The trouble was that the Church and the State could view conformity in religion differently. Their interests might coincide from time to time, notably in moments of extreme political crisis when Catholic religious dissent could be seen as part and parcel of radical and violent political schemes. But at other times the tendency was for the State's perception of conformity to drift apart from the one entertained by evangelical churchmen. Paradoxically the very act of enforcement by the State then had the effect of promoting conformity as a political necessity rather than a religious one.

Of course, clergy were also trying to persuade dissenters to conform to the established Church, a quasi-political profession of allegiance, and some churchmen held positions of authority in the State which made them responsible for enforcing the law against Romanists. With clerics like Thornborough, political conformity seems to have been more important than religious conversion. But those whose identity was primarily clerical, especially if they were evangelical Protestants, could not easily visualise their concept of conversion as coterminous with obedience to the State. This perhaps explains the constant tension between the alternate optimism and pessimism of leading puritan evangelicals, between belief in the efficacy of evangelisation and its apparent failure to bring about conversion. There was always a difficulty in extending a change which took place principally in the sphere of religion to a forum which was essentially political.

The number of Catholics who were brought by the State from an attachment to papistry to an explicit recantation of their Romishness and a sincere profession of Protestantism, the avowed aim of so many preachers, may never have been very great, certainly not enough to say that by this means post-Reformation English Catholicism was likely to be extinguished. But too often the historians who have charted this 'failure' have blamed basic legislative and administrative incapacity, as if all that was required was a

---

[188] Fincham, *Prelate*, 90; PRO, E 368/528, mem. 176ᵃ⁻ᵇ, E 368/536, mem. 21ᵃ; cf. J. Lister (ed.), *West Riding Sessions Rolls 1597/8–1602* (Yorkshire Archaeological and Topographical Association, Record Series, III, 1888), 52. Thornborough conferred with recusants like Elizabeth Darcy of York, BI, HCAB 15, fo. 77ᵛ. For Thornborough's enthusiasm for converting recusants when he was bishop of Worcester, and his supervision of the conversion of the ex-Jesuit John Jukes, *CSPD 1628–9*, 277, 289.

more effective central bureaucracy at Westminster or more powerful ecclesiastical commissions in the provinces. The statutes, we are told, were unworkable, and those who operated them, either through sympathy with Catholics or corrupt practices for financial gain, had no intention of putting them into full effect. However, this is a serious misreading. As is clearly illustrated by the examples of individual recusants who were compelled into conformity, the State and its Church were quite capable of forcing some Catholics into a submission to the Church of England which was no mere formality. The root cause of the problem was that some churchmen and secular politicians entertained different ideas about change of religion. The virtue of the recusancy legislation was that it identified a specific and visible offence which turned a principal element of the requirements made of the English Catholic laity by their clergy into a crime. But for the State's purposes there was really no need to go beyond it into the actual beliefs of those who were prosecuted for it. The State was quite satisfied with extorting from Catholics a capitulation which was only a fraction of the wider concept of what it meant to convert or even the Protestant evangelical concept of what it meant to forsake Babylon. The State's political rhetoric of unity was not the Reformed evangelical rhetoric of grace and renewal. Persuasions to change religion could hardly be contained within the boundaries of statute-conformity. (Likewise, Catholic proselytising was never just a matter of inducing people to become recusants.) To illustrate this I propose in chapter 7 to examine how contemporaries persuaded each other to change religion.

7

'The common people still retain a scent of the Roman perfume': conversion and the proselytiser

We have seen, then, that the law *could* compel dissenters to conform. Sometimes those who conformed seem to have gone beyond the bounds of mere conformity afterwards to show themselves as godly Protestants. But the law could not by itself evangelise. It did not even set out to penalise doctrinal dissent, only specific legal offences like recusancy. Protestant evangelicals did not imagine that true religion would come through prosecuting a relatively insignificant number of papistical malcontents. In fact, those to be evangelised were not only or even mainly the ideologically hostile Romanist or conservative elements in society but all the ungodly, irrespective of their opinions (though all the ungodly could be envisaged as to some extent popish). The problem is that, because historians have tended to identify post-Reformation English Catholicism almost entirely with recusancy and associated offences, there has been a tendency to connect Romish and Protestant evangelisation with persuasion to take up or abandon recusancy. Rival clergy are deemed to have failed or succeeded purely on the basis of their track record in persuading the unresolved either to become recusants or to conform.

It is the intention of this final chapter to draw together the threads which previous chapters have explored by examining what the proselytisers, those who tried to induce changes of religion, did. Many were indeed interested in conformity and nonconformity, upholding or defeating the statutes which insisted on minimal compliance with religion as established by law in England. They engaged in a forceful polemical battle to put their point across. But the polemic which argued that people ought to change from one ecclesiastical institution to another, and the statutes which tried to force them to do this, remained very much in the foothills of evangelisation. They did not encompass the full range of meanings of conversion with which contemporaries were familiar. What then did the proselytisers aim at? Did

Chapter title quotation: James Howell (ed.), *Cottoni Posthuma* (1651), 146.

they all work in the same way, and were the divisions between them caused exclusively by opposing ecclesiastical allegiances?

Clerical activists on both sides certainly paid a great deal of attention to the enforcement or obstruction of the law. Evangelicals who trusted to the power of the Word thought that the Word could be spread with the assistance of the secular power. As Francis Savage said, the magistrate 'doth not compell to faith, but to the meanes whereby God useth to give faith, namely, to hearing: for faith commeth by hearing'.[1] When Edward Gee, at an assize sermon, fulminated against the 'wilfull Recusants', it was not so much because of pernicious doctrines which they held, but because they 'will not once come to the Temple . . . nor once heare the Word preached . . . that they might be converted unto Christ'. They are 'like the deafe Adder, which clappeth one of his eares close unto the ground, and with his twining tayle stoppeth the other, that hee may not heare the voice of the Charmer, charme he never so wisely'.[2] Godly Protestants could therefore allow conformity promoted by force as well as persuasion. The first facilitated the second. People could legitimately be forced to give attention to the ordinary means of salvation, the Word preached (providing always that a godly ministry existed to preach the Word). Josias Nichols could 'avow, that no papist' let alone atheist or wicked man 'hath anie joy, to live where there is a good teacher: but that eather they are brought home by repentance, and become notable Christians, or els they shifte from such places as men with soare eies do flie the lighte of the bright shining sunne'.[3] Grace worked on the stony hearts of the unconverted as they listened to the promises of Christ in Scripture expounded through the art of the godly divine. William Harrison observed that Augustine approved of stringent imperial decrees on right religion. By the fear of it, 'not onely some few persons, but likewise many whole cities, who formerly had bene Donatists, became right Catholikes'. Harrison thought that 'if our lawes might be duely executed' then 'within a while, we should drawe most of the people to due conformitie'.[4] Even the most basic, potentially barbaric, measures to break down the corrupt Catholic structure which protected false religion could ultimately promote

---

[1] Francis Savage, *A Conference betwixt a Mother a devout Recusant, and her Sonne a zealous Protestant* (Cambridge, 1600), 111–12; see also Gabriel Powel, *A Refutation of an Epistle Apologeticall* (1605), 66.

[2] Edward Gee, *Two Sermons* (1620), sig. D3^r.

[3] Josias Nichols, *The Plea of the Innocent* (n.p., 1602), 225–6; cf. J. Morgan, *Godly Learning* (Cambridge, 1986), 81, 84.

[4] William Harrison, *The Difference of Hearers* (1614), sig. A7^v. Harrison's view was echoed by Dean Tobias Mathew, see 'Two Sermons, hitherto unpublished, of Dr Tobie Mathew, when Dean of Durham in 1591, afterwards Archbishop of York', *Christian Observer* (1847), 603–18, 664–75, 722–34, 776–90, at pp. 672–3. See also Francis Bunny, *An Answere to a Popish Libell* (Oxford, 1607), 23.

godly Protestantism. William Bradshaw thought the operation of the law was vital in turning those whom he calls 'Papists of state' into 'Protestants of state'. Proper enforcement of the oath of supremacy would crush Catholic resistance: 'their hope being taken a way, I make no doubt but their practise will end'.[5] It might at least break down their resistance to hearing the Gospel. James I seems to have favoured a combination of persuasion and compulsion, but thought that consciences should not ultimately be forced.[6]

Protestants like Harrison did not want the protection of the law for Protestant doctrine and practice just to induce a uniformity which would keep Romanist alternatives out. They undoubtedly wanted to restrict their opponents' opportunity to disseminate their brand of religion. (They would have agreed with Robert Persons's sentiment that 'if Dame Eva had not presumed to heare the serpent talke, she had not beene beguiled'.)[7] But Harrison's call for persecution was more a response of despair than an optimistic hope that repression could produce a godly Church. 'All their bookes have bene answered, all their dispersed pamphlets confuted, and many disputations have bene graunted them' and yet they still remain. The 'execution of the lawe against the enemies of the faith' is all that is left.[8] Evangelicals like Matthew Hutton showed a reluctance to employ the full force of secular authority to compel conformity. Despite his avowed enmity towards popery he consistently displayed a moderate attitude towards recusant Catholics themselves.[9] He objected to the compulsion exerted on recusants by Sir Thomas Cecil when they were brought by force to listen to the series of puritan sermons in York Castle in 1599–1600 (though Hutton was pressured into preaching one of them himself).[10] In the puritan scheme of conversion, as von Rohr puts it, 'neither divine coercion not human coercion will do'. Only thus could the concept of relative freedom of the will be maintained.[11]

In the eyes of contemporary proselytisers, change of religion between the Churches of England and Rome, as institutions, was part of true conversion. But, for more enthusiastic Protestants, institutions were in themselves no

---

[5] William Bradshaw, *Humble Motives* (n.p., 1601), 6–7, 11.

[6] *CSPV 1619–21, 581*.

[7] William Fulke, *A briefe Confutation, of a Popish Discourse* (1581), fo. 12ʳ.

[8] Harrison, *Difference*, sig. A7ᵛ.

[9] BL, Lansd. MS 85, fo. 12ʳ, MS 84, fo. 236ʳ; CRS 5, 219; LPL, Tenison MS 655, fo. 93ʳ; J. Raine (ed.), *The Correspondence of Dr Matthew Hutton* (Surtees Society, 17, 1843), 147; cf. P. Lake, 'Matthew Hutton: a Puritan Bishop?', *History* 64 (1979), 182–204, at pp. 190–1, 198–9; *HMC Salisbury MSS* VII, 230; *Borders 1595–1603*, 344; J. C. H. Aveling, *Catholic Recusancy in the City of York 1558–1791* (CRS monograph 2, 1970), 50; idem, *Northern Catholics* (1966), 114. Hutton took a moderate line when conferring with Richard Stapleton in 1597, *APC* XXVII, 85.

[10] BL, Add. MS 34250, fos. 19ᵛ–20ᵛ; cf. Raine, *Correspondence*, 156.

[11] J. von Rohr, *The Covenant of Grace in Puritan Thought* (Atlanta, Georgia, 1986), 140–1.

grounds for assurance of grace, certainly not, in some Protestants' opinion, the insufficiently reformed Church of England.[12] The abuses in the ministry are the reason, wrote George Gifford, that there 'should be so many, which being borne since the Gospell was restored in this land, are [now] so zealously addicted unto Popery'. Inadequate ministers may 'cry out against Popery, and proclaime utter defiance in speech' but their conduct is such 'that for every one which they convert to the Gospell, they cause an hundred to revolt'.[13] Josias Nichols said that where adequate ministers were placed, it was 'well knowen . . . how manie thousands of people, have ben instructed and made verie faithfull subjectes' while the absence of such clergy is the cause of 'encrease of Papistes'.[14]

So, to explore the form and force of contemporary proselytising as it was an issue between the Church of England and the Church of Rome we must focus primarily on the intersection and antagonism between evangelising and the establishment.

PROTESTANTS, CATHOLICS AND PROSELYTISING

Even puritans thought that evangelisation could be promoted through the forum provided by the institutional Church. There would not have been much point, otherwise, in puritan agitation for reform of the ministry. Particularly in the early part of this period puritan interests could be symbiotically reconciled with those of the regime which saw toleration of their excesses within the State Church as a means of attacking residual Romanism. Virtually all of the Protestant polemic in the early 1580s against the Romanist drive for widespread recusancy was produced by puritans.[15] In the North, where the political threat from popery was perceived to be greater, allowances, financial and political, were made for the creation of a godly ministry to quell Romanist dissent. Preachers were placed strategically in Catholic areas.[16] Aggressive puritans were tolerable there, even to the

---

12 William Fulke, *A Briefe and plaine Declaration* (1584), 48–9, 60–1; Dudley Fenner, *A Counter-Poyson* (1584), 63, 72–3, 78–9; John Penry, *An Humble Motion* (n.p., 1590), sig. H[r-v]; George Gifford, *A Briefe Discourse* (1598), sig. Aii[v]–iii[r]; P. Lake, *Moderate Puritans and the Elizabethan Church* (Cambridge, 1982), 25; for which reason puritans militated against mere conformity, C. Cross (ed.), *The Letters of Sir Francis Hastings, 1544–1609* (Frome, 1969), 104; P. Collinson, *The Religion of Protestants* (Oxford, 1982), 199–200.
13 George Gifford, *A Dialogue betweene a Papist and a Protestant* (1599), sig. A3[r].
14 Nichols, *Plea*, 171–2.
15 P. Milward, *Religious Controversies of the Elizabethan Age* (1977), 50–9. I owe this point to Peter Lake.
16 E. Axon, 'The King's Preachers in Lancashire, 1599–1845', *Transactions of the Lancashire and Cheshire Antiquarian Society* 66 (1944), 67–104, at p. 70; M. H. Curtis, 'The Trials of a Puritan in Jacobean Lancashire', in C. R. Cole and M. E. Moody (eds.), *The Dissenting Tradition* (Ohio, 1975), 78–99, at pp. 87–8; HMC *Salisbury MSS* X, 41; PRO, SP

extent of nonconformity, for their anti-popish example.[17] Conflict over the mechanisms of Church government did not preclude godly evangelising within the Church or drive preaching and lectures into clandestine extra-ecclesial forms.[18] The formation of a preaching ministry based on the diocesan parish structure was supplemented by the foundation of lecture-ships. They were seen as an effective weapon against Romanism as much as against spiritual slothfulness.[19]

Beyond the sermon, what did the Protestant evangeliser do when he came directly into contact with those he thought needed converting? There were a number of institutionalised methods of persuasion on which he could rely, principally to deal with those whose religious errors revolved around a belief that the Church of Rome represented the true Church. Persuasion through preaching extended also to persuasion through conference. For bishops like Hutton, Mathew, Gervase Babington and Thomas Morton it was a form of evangelisation.[20] All clergy had a duty, expressed in the sixty-sixth canon

14/121/68. A scheme similar to the one in Lancashire was suggested by Lord Eure for Wales, PRO, SP 14/48/121, fo. 163ᵛ; CRS 56, xxxii–iii, for the placement of John Bramhall at South Kilvington. Bramhall may have had puritan elements in his past, J. A. Newton, 'Puritanism in the Diocese of York (excluding Nottinghamshire) 1603–1640' (Ph.D thesis, London, 1955), 285, and was certainly an enthusiastic polemicist. He was used by the high commission to confer with papists, John Bramhall, *Works* (Dublin, 1676), 623–4; PRO, E 135/13/1, fo. 67ʳ, E 135/13/4, fos. 29ʳ, 39ʳ, 43ʳ, 65ʳ. Several Yorkshire puritan clerics were involved in the refounding of Ripon Minster in 1604, an institution 'which had an explicitly anti-Catholic reference', Newton, 'Puritanism', 285–6, and a high proportion of the conformities registered at the exchequer from the West Riding came from Ripon, M. C. Questier, 'The Phenomenon of Conversion: Change of Religion to and from Catholicism in England, 1580–1625' (DPhil. thesis, Sussex, 1991), 331.

[17] BL, Lansd. MS 25, fo. 63ᵛ, MS 43, fo. 17ʳ; P. Collinson, *The Elizabethan Puritan Movement* (Oxford, 1967), 202, 210 (pointing out that Elizabeth's ban on prophesyings did not extend to the northern province); R. C. Richardson, *Puritanism in north-west England* (Manchester, 1972), 154, 159; Newton, 'Puritanism', 275; cf. R. Clark, 'Anglicanism, Recusancy and Dissent in Derbyshire 1603–1730' (DPhil. thesis, Oxford, 1979), 108–9; K. C. Fincham, *Prelate as Pastor* (Oxford, 1990), 221–2, 229–30. The deployment of godly preaching ministers may have had the desired effect in some places. Newton argued that there was very little overlap in Yorkshire between detected recusancy and an active puritan preaching ministry. For example, in the Cleveland and Bulmer deaneries there was, by Newton's definition, little puritanism but considerable Catholic recusancy, while the reverse was the case in the deaneries of Pontefract, Craven and Doncaster, Newton, 'Puritanism', 274–80 (though Ainsty and Harthill contained both).

[18] Collinson, *Religion of Protestants*, 136–40.

[19] P. Seaver, *The Puritan Lectureships* (Stanford, California, 1970), 112–13.

[20] J. C. Atkinson, *Quarter Sessions Records* (North Riding Record Society, 1–3, 1884–5), I, 6; Aveling, *Catholic Recusancy*, 183; BI, HCAB 14, fos. 150ʳ, 197ᵛ; cf. CU Libr., MS Mm 1 45, p. 380; Savage, *Conference*, sig. ¶2ʳ, implying that Savage's establishment in religion was assisted by Babington's effectual persuasions, as will understand all those who have heard Babington's 'publike exhortations or private conferences'; T. W. Jones (ed.), *A True Relation of the Life and Death of William Bedell* (Camden Society, second series, 4, 1872), 22; J. H. Pollen, *Acts of English Martyrs* (1891), 294; A. Davidson, 'Roman Catholicism in

of 1604, to engage Catholics in this way. Admittedly, records of conference at the bidding of the high commission have a bureaucratic and rather formal aspect. Nor do the forfeited bonds of recusant Catholics who were not sufficiently intimidated to confer instil confidence that conferring did much good. The bevies of clerical disputants assigned to deal with prominent religious deviants do not seem generally to have succeeded.[21] But puritans in particular were convinced that, as an extension of the godly preaching ministry, conferences in religion were effective.[22] The really enthusiastic Yorkshire clerical conferrers were puritan clerics.[23] Private conference allowed more scope for persuasive latitude and moderation than the public declarations of a sermon. Puritans who subscribed to an apocalyptic interpretation of Rome and set an absolute gulf between true religion and popery sometimes tried to persuade papists by being conciliatory rather than antagonistic and by emphasising the institutional virtues of the Church of England. If Francis Bunny's *Short Answer to the Reasons* (why northern popish recusants refuse to come to church) is anything to go by, the papist would have spent more time talking to him about conscience and the nature of a true sacrament than the apocalyptic division between the Churches of England and Rome.[24]

Beyond conferring was the somewhat less aggressive technique of catechising, a preventive medicine against the danger of popery coming in through ignorance.[25] Sir Robert Cotton thought that catechising rather than enforcing attendance at church was what counted. The reason popery subsists is that 'the formall obedience of coming to Church hath been more expected, than the instruction of private families'.[26] Catechism is a necessary

Oxfordshire from the Late Elizabethan Period to the Civil War *c.* 1580–1640' (Ph.D thesis, Bristol, 1970), 535.

[21] Francis Walsingham, *A Search Made into Matters of Religion* (St Omer, 1609), 39–74; A. H. Mathew (ed.), *A True Historical Relation of the Conversion of Sir Tobie Matthew* (1904), 63–4; Story and Gardner, *Sonnets*, xiv–xv; R. C. Bald, *John Donne* (Oxford, 1970), 69. B. N. de Luna suggests that conferences with prominent clerics were mainly for show, B. N. de Luna, *Jonson's Romish Plot* (Oxford, 1967), 135.

[22] John White, *The Way to the True Church* (1616), sig. a5ᵛ.

[23] Newton, 'Puritanism', 288; cf. J. Morris (ed.), *The Troubles of our Catholic Forefathers* (3 vols., 1872–7), III, 308–9, 314.

[24] Bunny was used as a conferrer by the Durham ecclesiastical commission, PRO, SP 12/262/25.i, fo. 58ᵛ, E 135/12/2, mem. 6ª; cf. Bunny, *Answere*, 14. Newton detects a vein of moderation even in the Yorkshire puritan clerics' anti-Romish books, not a sign of irenicism of course but designed all the same to attract rather than to alienate, Newton, 'Puritanism', 288-90.

[25] Joseph Hall, *The Olde Religion* (1628), sig. †ʳ–†2ᵛ.

[26] Howell, *Cottoni Posthuma*, 146–8; cf. Richard Kilby, *The Burthen of a loaden Conscience* (Cambridge, 1616), 90–1; Gervase Babington, *Workes* (1615), sig. Sss3ᵛ; Robert Abbot, *The Danger of Popery* (1625), 36; I. Green, '"For Children in Yeeres and Children in Understanding": The Emergence of the English Catechism under Elizabeth and the Early Stuarts', *JEH* 37 (1986), 397–425, at p. 414.

preparation for preaching, and a more broad-minded activity than merely instructing people about Rome's errors. Even catechisms relying heavily upon a Calvinist understanding of grace and double predestination and the most zealous concept of evangelical conversion might not be explicitly directed against papistry.[27] Still, Robert Abbot argued that 'the Papists have confessed that all the grounde wee have gotten of them is by catechisme'.[28]

In a necessarily restricted and clandestine manner, Catholic proselytisers used some of these techniques of persuasion as well. Their polemic filtered from print into catechesis.[29] One surviving manuscript delineating how the 'priests are to use their catechisme, prescribed by the seminarists for instructynge and reconcilynge', is based squarely on the visibility theme in Catholic polemic.[30] The appearance of manuscript variants of popular tracts like Richard Bristow's *Briefe Treatise* or Thomas Wright's *Certaine Articles* suggests that such books or parts of them were copied out in order formally to challenge in disputation the Protestant opinions of particular individuals.[31]

When conformists submitted to the Church of England, the procedure governing their submission was largely dictated by canon law, as the previous chapter demonstrated. After conversion away from Protestant opinions, a similar process of reconciliation was required by the Roman Church to absolve sacramentally the individual from heresy and schism.[32] Canon law demanded that exterior heresy or schism should be purged *in*

---

[27] E.g. William Gouge, *A Short Catechisme* (1631); William Perkins, *The Foundation of Christian Religion* (1633); Edward Elton, *A Forme of Catechising* (1634); Stephen Egerton, *A Briefe Method of Catechizing* (1631); Stephen Denison, *A Compendious Catechisme* (1632). P. F. Jensen, 'The Life of Faith in the Teaching of Elizabethan Protestants' (DPhil. thesis, Oxford, 1979), 174f., and *passim*, charts the dozens of unofficial Elizabethan catechisms, and shows that the popular ones were all by puritans.

[28] Abbot, *Danger*, 36.

[29] Catholic dissidents who were prevented by law from disputing publicly relied on the written word, CRS 41, 141; Foley VII, 1076; F. A. Youngs jnr, 'Definitions of Treason in an Elizabethan Proclamation', *HJ* 14 (1971), 675–91, at pp. 678–9; CRS 73, 125.

[30] Bodl., Rawl. MS D 853, fos. 20ʳ–1ʳ; cf. White, *Way*, sig. c7ʳ⁻ᵛ.

[31] William Fulke, *Two Treatises* (1577), sig. *iiiᵛ; Oliver Carter, *An Answere* (1579), sig. ¶4ʳ; John Knewstub, *An Aunsweare unto certaine Assertions, tending to maintaine the Church of Rome to bee the true and Catholique church* (1579), sig. *3ᵛ–4ʳ; Richard Woodcock, *A Godly and Learned Answer* (1608), sig. A2ʳ⁻ᵛ; Edward Bulkeley, *An Apologie for Religion* (1602); White, *Way*, sig. d7ᵛ.

[32] Accounts of reconciliations in Italy, France and Spain describe elaborate procedure for the reception of Englishmen there into the Catholic Church, PRO, SP 12/149/84, fo. 190ʳ; T. F. Knox (ed.), *The Letters and Memorials of William Cardinal Allen* (1882), 96; James Wadsworth jnr, *The English Spanish Pilgrime* (1629), 3, though cf. B. Camm, 'An Apostate at St Omers, 1618–1622', *The Month* 94 (1899), 163–70, at p. 165; A. J. Loomie, 'Religion and Elizabethan Commerce with Spain', *Catholic Historical Review* 50 (1964–5), 27–51, at p. 36; CRS 9, 118; PRO, SP 14/49/72, fo. 113ʳ.

foro externo, in public, generally before the diocesan bishop.[33] In England all aspects of Romanist proselytisation were usually hidden and normal rules concerning public purgation of notorious error were suspended. Absolution took place therefore through the operation of sacramental confession by priests with special faculties for this purpose.[34] Roman exercise of spiritual power in confession was not just the mechanism by which reconciliation took place. It also made a statement about the nature of repentance in true conversion.[35] Catholic assertions about the power of sacramental confession were thought to have a persuasive influence on people to join the Roman communion in order to avail themselves of this channel of grace. Claims about the spiritual power of the Roman Church in this sphere extended to exorcism as well. The casting out of devils permitted Catholic clerics to join an attack on Protestant heresy with an assertion of their exclusive stewardship of grace. John White latched onto the passage in the Roman rite for reconciling a heretic or schismatic which seemed to him to imply a ceremony of exorcism, namely the bishop's exhortation 'Exorcizo te, immunde spiritus, per Deum Patrem omnipotentem, et per Jesum Christum filium eius, et per Spiritum sanctum, ut recedas ab hoc famulo Dei'. 'Their hatred against us is such', commented White, that they 'hold us to be "possessed" (not simply seduced, but even possessed by the divell:) and thereupon, when any of us revolteth to the Papacy, and is reconciled to them, they have an order to exorcize the partie.'[36] There was certainly a connection between exorcism and conversion in contemporaries' minds. The more that the opposing religion was seen as an anti-religion (rather than merely a separate doctrinal system) the more sense it made to connect it with the Devil, as much as the world and the flesh. Anthony Tyrrell, in his intense experience of conversion and apostasy, started to worry that he was being possessed by the devils in whose expulsion from the bodies of others he had

33 J. G. Goodwine, *The Reception of Converts* (Canon Law Studies no. 198, Washington, 1944), 1, 120, 154–7; J. C. H. Aveling, 'Some Cases Pertaining to England', in G. T. Bradley (ed.), *Yorkshire Catholics* (Leeds Diocesan Archives Occasional Publications no. 1, Darlington, 1985), 15–25, at p. 25.

34 PRO, SP 12/192/46.i, fo. 75^{r-v}, SP 12/238/126.iv, fo. 189^r, SP 12/235/72, fo. 141^r. An oath might be required by the absolver from the heretic that he will not lapse back into heresy, CRS 67, 37; cf. Goodwine, *Reception*, 122; Aveling, 'Some Cases', 21.

35 M. Bernos, 'Confession et Conversion', in *La Conversion au XVIIe Siècle* (Centre Méridional de Rencontres sur le XVIIe Siècle, Marseille, 1982), 283–93, at p. 293, arguing that in the seventeenth century 'confession sincère et conversion profonde étaient indissolublement liées'; CRS 67, 94; PRO, SP 12/144/48, John Parker's declaration in December 1580 that he was initially persuaded of the truth of Roman claims by hearing a crypto-Catholic minister preach on the necessity of auricular confession; PRO, SP 14/7/30, fo. 64^r; Davidson, 'Roman Catholicism', 496–7.

36 *Pontificale Romanum Clementis VIII. Pont. Max. Iussu Restitutum Atque Editum* (Rome, 1595), 649; White, *Way*, sig. c2^v; idem, *A Defence of the Way to the True Church* (1614), 86.

assisted William Weston SJ. When he decided to reject Rome in 1588, his recantation sermons harped on the expulsion of the unclean spirit in Matthew 12: 43–5.[37] Weston's exorcisms, in which the expelled devils made it clear that they had Protestant tendencies, were supposed to have converted large numbers of spectators.[38]

How was evangelical grace thought to combine with shifts in ecclesiastical allegiance when clerics proselytised? The tendency of the 'revisionist' historians of the later English Reformation has been to argue that they were kept separate. Certainly, any intention the seminarist clergy may have had to exercise their clerical function as purveyors of grace was divided from an intention to turn Protestants into Catholics. They swiftly abandoned the connection between their clerical role and implementing any sort of ecclesiastical religious change at all. They subsided into a seigneurial torpor and willingly allowed themselves to be tied to people of gentry status who required domestic chaplains, not an evangelical ministry.[39] Revisionist historians point to the seminarists' determination to concentrate their attentions on those they called 'schismatics', people of a 'church papist' persuasion, Catholic in all but name, and ignore those whom they called 'heretics', people who were in some measure convinced Protestants (though even the seminarist ministry to church papists was so inadequate that the country was eventually de-Romanised by default). Practical considerations rapidly crushed any initial intention there may have been to release the evangelical tendencies (if any) of the incoming seminary-trained clerics. Protestant evangelism is seen by revisionists as similarly restricted and

---

[37] Morris, *Troubles*, II, 433–4; CRS 52, 134; Anthony Tyrrell, *A Fruitfull Sermon* (1589), sig. Bii[v]. Catholics argued that successful Roman exorcisms were proof that Rome is the true Church because only the true Church has the power of exorcism, John Colleton, *A Supplication to the Kings most excellent Majestie* (n.p., 1604), 44–5; cf. Jacques Brousse, *The Life of the Reverend Fa. Angel of Joyeuse* (Douai, 1623), sig. Cc[v]. When Anthony Copley was interrogated in August 1603 about the details of the Bye Plot he said William Watson had proposed to persuade James of the truth of the Roman religion *inter alia* by the 'exorcisme of some possessed person by either partie', PRO, SP 14/3/7.i, fo. 11[v]. Shortly afterwards we find Sir Thomas Cornwallis reporting that the banishment of two priests 'taken . . . at Court' was delayed because certain people thought they might be able to free from demonic possession a 'gentleman of the court', Bodl., Tanner MS 75, fo. 11[r].

[38] P. Caraman (ed.), *William Weston* (1955), 27, 30. In Harsnett's rendering, Anne Smith said that it was a 'common thing amongst them [the Catholics], to give out words, as though Protestants were all possessed', Samuel Harsnett, *A Declaration of egregious Popish Impostures* (1603), 245; cf. Richard Baddeley, *The Boy of Bilson* (1622), 51; D. P. Walker, *Unclean Spirits* (1981), 4, showing that, in France, exorcisms were used to 'convert, or at least to confute, the Huguenots'.

[39] C. Haigh, 'From Monopoly to Minority: Catholicism in Early Modern England', *TRHS*, fifth series, 31 (1981), 129–47, at pp. 136, 146–7; *idem*, 'The Continuity of Catholicism in the English Reformation', *P&P* 93 (1981), 37–69, at p. 59, and *passim*.

unsuccessful. It created a small godly minority, fearfully zealous and equally unpopular. It did not turn England into a Protestant nation.[40]

But this perception relies upon an artificial regimentation of terms used in conversion discourse ('schismatic', 'heretic', 'church papist', 'Protestant' and so on) which, as we have seen in chapters 3 and 4, those terms cannot easily bear, and which contemporaries would have found odd. When Catholics referred to 'schismatics' they were not invariably thinking of an ideologically coherent party of people who held to a developed concept of occasional conformity. Such words *could* refer to a grade of ecclesiastical allegiance but they also contained a reference to a state of grace (or lack of it) in the person to whom they were applied. In the same way, the concept of popery allowed for a fluid association of anti-Romanism with the characteristics of true religion and the practice of evangelical imperatives far beyond the narrow confines of social 'puritanism' of the kind which Christopher Haigh describes. It is impossible to interpret accurately what different clerical activists were trying to do unless one keeps these multiple definitions in mind.[41]

The revisionist model of religion and politics in post-Reformation England creates more problems than it solves. In it we are confronted with a country full of people who are in some way Catholic or Protestant but which is nevertheless etherised by religious indifferentism (if the complaints of the preachers are taken literally). Then, in spite of this torpor (a combination of backwardness and provincialism), we have to account for immense friction over questions of religion between irreconcilable groups which clearly extended beyond the narrow confines of the Court, high politics and the universities.

The revisionist argument concedes that there was a battle for religious allegiances in progress but ignores the complex contemporary spectrum of conversion which informed it. The political sense of persuading individuals to change their religion (and profess loyalty to a different Church), and the religious sense (progress in grace) were never separate in the minds of contemporary clerical proselytisers. In the peculiar circumstances of the later English Reformation the political and religious elements of conversion moved in tandem but retained their separate characters. Thus the struggle to evangelise was never just a matter of squashing the opposing party's will to resist. Persuading someone to become a Catholic was not just a matter of convincing them that they should not be a Protestant (and vice versa).

---

[40] C. Haigh, 'The Church of England, the Catholics and the People', in C. Haigh (ed.), *The Reign of Elizabeth I* (1984), 195–219.

[41] J. T. Cliffe, *The Yorkshire Gentry from the Reformation to the Civil War* (1969), 193; C. Haigh, 'The Fall of a Church or the Rise of a Sect? Post-Reformation Catholicism in England', *HJ* 21 (1978), 182–6, at p. 184.

JESUITS, PURITANS AND RIVAL EVANGELISMS

To illustrate this, let us look at the artistry of those proselytisers on each side who were generally regarded as being the most extreme in their religious profession. The Jesuits' enthusiasm as persuaders accounted in large part for Protestant unease at their activities. What exactly did they do? Obviously, they wrote polemic, and they followed up their writing wherever possible by disputing verbally along similar lines with any Protestant willing to engage them.[42] The proselytising disputations in which Catholic clerics took on Protestant ones, either in the prisons, or semi-publicly at times of relative toleration, were generally fronted by Jesuits.[43] The Jesuits, though, did not think polemic was adequate of itself to induce true conversion nor did they understand proselytising primarily as a polemical exercise.[44] Disagreements over doctrine were designed merely to open proceedings. Disputation of some kind *was* generally necessary. (John Gerard entered into argument with all his converts.) But the Jesuit method for instructing and reconciling envisages that little actual debate will take place. The rubric of one Jesuit set of rules for fishing directs 'what soever you [the proselytiser] ask of him [the intended proselyte] awnswer it your self if you perceave he cannot lest he be confounded with his own ignoraunce and so alienated from conferringe with you'. It asks the proselyte where he thinks the Protestants' Church was before Luther, but then proceeds to work through fundamentals, Creation, Incarnation and so on, much more in a catechetical than a polemical manner.[45] Another manual, 'How to proceede with heretickes in their conversion', follows the rules established by polemicists and suggests that the proselytiser should 'prove the falsitie of heresie' by using 'generall motyves and reasons which are more evident and accommodate to all mens

[42] P. Milward, *Religious Controversies of the Jacobean Age* (1978), 143–7; Questier, 'Phenomenon', 65–8; Robert Crowley, *An Aunswer to sixe Reasons, that Thomas Pownde . . . required to be aunswered* (1581), sig. Aii[r]; White, *Way*, sig. d7[v]; Bodl., Jones MS 53, no. 3, Rawl. MS D 853, fo. 22[r-v].

[43] Milward, *Religious Controversies of the Jacobean Age*, 220–2; Daniel Featley, *The Fisher Catched in his owne Net* (1623); BL, Add. MS 28640, fo. 113[r]; George Roberts (ed.), *Diary of Walter Yonge* (Camden Society, first series, 41, 1848), 63; George Walker, *The Summe of a Disputation* (1624). Paul Spence, the Marian cleric and seminarist who disputed with Robert Abbot in Worcester Castle in the early 1590s, was said to be a stooge for the Jesuits, Robert Abbot, *A Mirrour of Popish Subtilties* (1594), sig. A4[v]–*[v]; PRO, SP 14/14/40, fo. 95[r].

[44] Robert Persons, *A Review of Ten Publike Disputations* (St Omer, 1604), 19–20; Walsingham, *Search* (1609), 481–2; J. W. O'Malley, *The First Jesuits* (Cambridge, Massachusetts, 1993), 70–1; Caro, 'William Alabaster: Rhetor, Meditator, Devotional Poet', *RH* 19 (1988), 62–79, 155–70, at p. 66.

[45] Bodl., Rawl. MS D 853, fo. 20[v]; cf. Bodl., Rawl. MS D 853, fos. 22[r]–3[r], Jones MS 53, fo. 220[v], for similar approaches, demonstrating that the proselytiser's aim should not be primarily to start a high-powered academic debate.

capacitie', and then it concentrates on catechising: 'beinge resolved in their faith theie must be instructed in thinges which are of obligation to be beleved'.[46]

The principal document which sets out the Jesuit approach to proselytisation in England is the manuscript instruction written by George Gilbert in 1583 (a distillation of the method employed by Campion and Persons).[47] It tells the missioner that he will encounter four sorts of people. The first is the reliable Catholic. His house can be used as a place to preach to his relations, friends and dependants whether they are Catholic or not. Then there are three other classes to be approached – those people whom Gilbert's instruction terms 'heretics', 'schismatics' and 'lukewarm Catholics'. Where it is possible to discern a real circumspection in dealing with 'heretics' is in doubts expressed about the small return obtained by disputing with them about doctrine alone. The Gilbert manuscript says that 'the heretical spirit is so much given to pride that few of them are converted by argument'; success is likely with them only if the priest can find some means 'whereby to make them more inclined to humility and submission, such as the consideration of their own worth, contempt of the world and such-like thoughts', and that, in their case, 'more fruit is gained from sermons giving advice for the direction of one's life, for the saving of one's soul and from other such-like meditations, than from those on subjects of dispute and controversy, which are more likely to stir up contention than to bring about amendment of life and conversion'.[48]

Jesuits probably did concentrate more intensely on 'schismatics' than on 'heretics', but not in the revisionist sense of directing their ministrations towards those who were basically Romanist already because it was more practical and required less effort. If they preferred to sift the souls of 'schismatics' it was not because such people were invariably occasional conformists, orthodox Catholics except to the extent that they conformed out of fear. Of course, Jesuits conceded that schism might be, *inter alia*, merely a 'separation of them that thinke the same thing'. Henry Garnet, it is true, warned against schismatic separation from Rome because it could lead eventually to a whole-hearted approval of the rites of the Church of England. And John Gerard did indeed say of some whom he called

---

[46] Bodl., Jones MS 53, fo. 235^{r-v}.

[47] CRS 39, 331–40.

[48] CRS 39, 334, 336. Persons said that, when dealing with a heretic, it is best 'never to dispute with him in publick as neer as may be, for that heresy is pride and wil not yield before others', and that 'when there is difficulty and much obstinacy in the partie the best way is to desist from urging of controversy and rather talke of matters of devotion', Stonyhurst, Collectanea P I, fo. 204^v. Cf. similar rules drawn up, apparently by Persons himself, for Jesuits operating in England, ARSJ, Angl. 156/II fos. 167^r–168^r (a reference which I owe to Thomas McCoog).

schismatics that they were Catholics by conviction, clearly distinguished from heretics.[49] But 'conversion' of a schismatic in the language of a Jesuit cleric like Gerard does not refer just to formal reconciliation to Rome.[50] For Jesuit evangelicals 'heresy' was merely a misdirected intellectual persuasion while 'schism' tended to signify a state of spiritual torpor (though the two could easily be associated). They were more interested in conversion as regeneration of the will, an experiment in grace to see whether the man separated from the Church of Rome might throw off his schismatic state and become a zealous professor of true religion.

For the Jesuits, evangelical renovation went as far beyond the simple profession of a formal allegiance to an institutional Church as it did for the godly puritan. Schismatics required as much converting as heretics in this respect, probably more. Robert Persons distinguished between formal reconciliation to Rome, virtually an administrative process, and 'sound Reconciliation', which generally produces 'a sure and constant Christian afterwards'. Persons says that Reconciliation 'as well in these Men [schismatics], as in all others that shall return [to the Roman communion] . . . whether they have been Hereticks or no, ought to be made with great attention and deliberation'.[51] The conversion of 'heretics' simply includes an additional dimension where the individual at some stage rejects Reformed doctrines.[52] In Gerard's terminology, 'schism' could refer just as easily to a state of disinterestedness or spiritual laziness as to a formal dislocation from the Roman Church.[53]

The effectual stages of the conversions of the Jesuit Edmund Neville and the Jesuit-minded Tobias Mathew jnr began with considerations not of polemical doctrine but of Lent, and Lenten observance. They discovered that the path to Rome lay first through the regeneration of the will by grace, not, primarily, through the re-orientation of the mind by disputation. Mathew was convinced in Rome, by Robert Persons's persuasions, of the truth of Roman doctrines. This, however, was merely an intellectual

---

[49] Fulke, *Briefe Confutation*, fo. 20ʳ; Henry Garnet, *An Apology against the Defence of Schisme* (n.p., 1593), 117–18; *idem, A Treatise of Christian Renunciation* (n.p., 1593), 168, where Garnet says of Thomas Bell (against whose doctrines of occasional conformity Garnet is writing) that his becoming a Protestant has shown 'how neare this point of doctrine [of occasional conformity] in Gods judgement is unto flatte heresy and Atheisme'. Robert Jones reported to Richard Blount that some of those who have accepted the ex-Jesuit Thomas Wright's arguments about church attendance 'have swallowed the supremacy without scruple', Foley IV, 374; P. Caraman (ed.), *John Gerard* (1951), 161, 174.

[50] Cf. Haigh, 'Continuity', 56.

[51] Robert Persons, ed. E. Gee, *The Jesuit's Memorial for the Intended Reformation of England* (1690), 31; cf. Stonyhurst, Collectanea P II, fo. 420ʳ.

[52] Persons, *Jesuit's Memorial*, 35–6, 38–40.

[53] Caraman, *John Gerard*, 174.

persuasion. He returned to Florence and frequented 'plays, and worse places'. But then Carnival ends, Lent begins, and by frequenting sermons instead (preached by a Jesuit) though only out of curiosity, 'it pleased his Divine Majesty to alter the object of . . . [his] eyes, which till then had wandered throughout the corners of the world'.[54]

There is hardly a source concerned with the Society which does not manifestly illustrate that the Jesuits' proselytising was at least as much a communication of their own evangelical ethos as a mechanical catechising of the ignorant or badgering of the educated into the paths of the extremely artificial contemporary polemical formulations of the Roman faith. Their persuasions that the Roman Church was the true Church in which salvation was possible were shot through with their perception of themselves as an order of clerks regular, dedicated to defeating the world, the flesh and the Devil. The Society's proselytisers were concerned with the generality of sin as much as with heresy. Their converts not only recanted Protestantism but made general confessions, which Jesuits envisaged as part of a process of evangelical change.[55] John Floyd wrote of the Protestants killed in the Blackfriars disaster of October 1623, 'may we not . . . hope of the conversion of these that came spontaneously to this sermon' (at Hunsdon House), and died in an exercise of piety where they had gathered 'to sorrow for their sinnes', even though they had not formally expressed allegiance to Rome.[56]

The Spiritual Exercises of Ignatius Loyola were the foundation of virtually all Jesuit proselytising. They were not, of course, used simply to induce people to abandon doctrinal Protestantism. As John O'Malley says, they are clearly meant to be given to 'believing Catholics'.[57] But their purpose is the re-orientation of self and turning in religion which is at the centre of every evangelical change, and they often provided a vehicle for the evangelical stage of conversion of an individual in a state of flux between the Churches of England and Rome. Francis Walsingham's Jesuit converter pushed him towards the first week of the Exercises as soon as it was clear that he had shaken himself free of an intellectual attachment to Protestant doctrinal formulae.[58] John Gerard in particular exploited the Exercises to assist conversion in this sense.[59] The Jesuit proselytising tract entitled 'How to proceede with heretickes in their conversion' says that Protestants might

54 CRS 54, 172; A. H. Mathew (ed.), *A True Historical Relation of the Conversion of Sir Tobie Matthew* (1904), 35.
55 A. Lynn Martin, *The Jesuit Mind* (Ithaca, 1988), 13, 88–9; Bernos, 'Confession'.
56 John Floyd, *A Word of Comfort* (St Omer, 1623), 49.
57 O'Malley, *First Jesuits*, 37–9, 42.
58 Walsingham, *Search* (1609), 505–7; Questier, 'Phenomenon', 105–6.
59 Caraman, *John Gerard*, 184.

be dealt with first in doctrinal matters but 'secondlie theie muste have some cheife motives gyven them to move them to hartie sorrow for their synns' and 'to such as cann reade maie be given the cheife points of the exercise of the first weeke drawen into einglishe for that purpose'.[60]

English Jesuits would have violently rejected modern historians' arguments that the range of their proselytising was limited. Robert Persons wrote that by the zeal and industry of the Jesuits 'many a separation is made between good and bad, many a heat enkindled in Christian hartes, where deadly cold occupied the place before . . . many an heathen and heretique made Christian, many a frostie catholique made a hoat recusant, many a vitious lyver made observant, many a careles and earthly mynd stirred up to apprehend and think of eternitie'.[61] If their intended proselyte wallowed in the thought that the Church of England provided a safe way to salvation and could not be dislodged from this belief by polemical reasoning, they might even first ground their arguments in assertions of the general need for grace and regeneration, and then the convert would gradually be made aware that the Church of Rome was the best, in fact the only, Church in which this was possible. Conversion in the first sense ultimately necessitated conversion in the second sense. Gerard planned to convert the heretical Grace Fortescue by stirring up her will into an appreciation of the Catholic model of evangelical activity, the way of perfection, and persuade her that it could not be found 'in a false religion where no account' is taken of it.[62] Jesuit spirituality, though, was not confined to the later stages of a shift of allegiance to Rome. It could be exploited heavily before the doctrinal stage was over, sometimes even before it commenced.[63]

---

[60] Bodl., Jones MS 53, fos. 236ʳ–7ʳ.

[61] Robert Persons, *A Temperate Ward-Word* (Antwerp, 1599), 66.

[62] Caraman, *John Gerard*, 161–2. The Jesuit annual letter for 1614 says that it 'is more difficult to uproot evil habits, especially when strengthened by lapse of time, than to get people to unlearn heresy', Foley VII, 1056–7; cf. Sir Kenelm Digby, *A Discourse* (Amsterdam, 1652), 6, where Digby argues that a thorough conversion, attended with difficulty, ensures 'vigorous progresse' afterwards, and spiritual strength to resist 'new stormes'.

[63] The evangelical impulse could arise at any stage. The initial stimulus for Charles Yelverton's conversion was partly evangelical; only subsequently did he buy a manual of controversies, Foley I, 145; John Greaves began to reflect 'upon the state of . . . [his] past life' and then found he 'had reason to suspect the truth of . . . [his] opinions', Foley IV, 407–8. But cf. Nicholas Hart who experiences a conversion from a vicious life even after he has become a recusant, Foley I, 167; or, similarly, Henry Chadderton who is convinced of the truth of Catholicism by reading polemic but refuses to embrace Catholicism until he is persuaded thereto by Thomas Pounde who criticises the 'vanities of this world', Foley III, 547; and Henry Lanman, who was convinced only as far as recusancy by reading the Catholic 'Challenge' polemicists John Rastell and Thomas Harding but was converted fully when he read Jerome Platus's book on the religious life (an English edition of which appeared in 1632), Foley I, 176.

John Gerard, a man of immense subtlety and guile, got results by placing his arguments in an evangelical passage from the flesh to the spirit. He inveigled Sir Oliver Manners into meeting him over a game of cards, but as the game proceeded Gerard began to turn the focus of conversation from the worldly pursuit of the card game to a discussion of religion. He evoked in Manners an evangelical reorientation which led him towards the Society.[64] Gerard assisted his persuasion of individuals by preparing them for conversion with doctrinal argument while he was dressed as a layman. He then reappeared clad in full Jesuit apparel, establishing his Roman identity and representing visibly through his altered clothing the alteration from the life of sin to the life of grace.[65]

Jesuit techniques of persuasion owed as much to psychology as to theology. The Gilbert manuscript specifically instructs the proselytiser to proceed by inducing a particular mood, and to render the intended convert liable to evangelical suggestion without even hinting at Rome's doctrinal authority. He should 'make use of certain methods and of times that are propitious – as for instance, if he should see him in a fit of melancholy or desolation of soul, he will then be able, under the pretext of consoling him', to tell him that 'the soul of man is often in desolation because, sharing as it does in the divine nature, it cannot be contented and find rest in these things below' telling him also 'of the causes which have led souls to damnation'. The Jesuit proselytiser is looking to trigger the onset of grace (if necessary through an outwardly cynical exploitation of periods of depression and melancholy). 'The evening, after the Ave Maria, is the time most apt to make a man receptive and adopt a reflective mood, because then there is quietness everywhere and repose; the world appears to be deserted and lonely . . . the adornments and pleasures of the daytime are in abeyance, and the sun has fled to other regions, and the earth has been clothed in darkness, the image of death and the end of the world.'[66] William Fitch's conversion, instigated by reading the Protestant version of Persons's *Christian Directory*, is portrayed as entering on its most dramatic phases on two separate days in

---

[64] Caraman, *John Gerard*, 185–6.
[65] Caraman, *John Gerard*, 20–1. For similar Capuchin exploitation of apparel, BL, Harl. MS 3888, fo. 31ᵛ; Brousse, *Life*, sig. Gg6ᵛ; *CSPD 1598–1601*, 398; N. McClure (ed.), *The Letters of John Chamberlain* (2 vols., Philadelphia, 1939), I, 90; T. Birch (ed.), *The Court and Times of Charles I* (2 vols., 1848), II, 302–3 (Cyprien de Gamache describes a 'gentleman whose obstinacy and false zeal rendered him remarkable [even] among the Puritans or Calvinists', but, when he encountered Henrietta Maria's Capuchins who had recently been allowed to resume their full religious habit, he 'reflected long upon the gravity of their demeanour, [and] the poverty of their dress' and was suddenly convinced that 'these men were the real professors of religion'.
[66] CRS 39, 334–5.

the evening, during which time he was clearly in a state of melancholia. This was the natural moment for an evangelical proselytiser to strike.[67]

Only in the crudest sense were the Jesuits an army of propagandists who might either succeed or fail in 'signing up' large numbers of otherwise passive laymen. The wild enthusiasm which was evident in the Catholic estimates of the numbers reconciled in the early 1580s after the Campion–Persons mission[68] was never a reference to the type of proselytising which evangelical missioners carried out when they were approaching specific individuals.

The Jesuits therefore saw proselytising as extending far beyond recusancy. Protestant evangelicals also regarded mere conformity as, at most, the first step in evangelisation. If mere conformity meant church papistry then it was a positive danger (if left untreated). Most Protestants militated against popery in some shape or form, but the puritan tendency was to see popery as akin to man's natural state of corruption. Man's corrupt state leads him to embrace the excesses of the Church of Rome, which, as Peter Lake has so comprehensively demonstrated, could be seen as an anti-religion, an inversion or mirror image of all true religion.[69] For Daniel Price, papistry was a doctrinal form of Epicureanism. Henry Holland claimed that more people were converted to papistry by books of Italian love songs than by the theological books sent from Louvain.[70] Conversion from Romishness is not a matter of changing formal profession of a few doctrines. William Bradshaw perceived two basic principles at work in the Church, one of corruption, the other of regeneration. Corruption works at all levels to produce 'Papists of religion', while grace draws the Elect from their imperfect state to become 'Protestants of religion'.[71] The fact that converts from Rome abandon their recusancy is merely one proof of their inward change.[72] On this reading, a bland uniformity (whether through occasional conformity or not) is the last thing a godly cleric wants to see. Although

---

[67] Brousse, *Life*, sigs. Bb6ᵛ–7ʳ, Cc4ᵛ; see also the circumstances of the puritan conversion experience of Edmund Staunton, Samuel Clarke, *The Lives of Sundry Eminent Persons in this Later Age* (1683), sig. Xʳ, 'being one Evening at Prayer all alone in the dark'; cf. J. Gennings, *The Life and Death of Mr Edmund Geninges* (St Omer, 1614), 99.

[68] Foley III, 667, 669; T. F. Knox (ed.), *The Letters and Memorials of William Cardinal Allen* (1882), 236; J. E. Paul, 'The Hampshire Recusants in the Reign of Elizabeth I with some Reference to the Problem of Church Papists' (Ph.D thesis, Southampton, 1958), 84, 308.

[69] P. Lake, 'Anti-popery: The Structure of a Prejudice', in R. Cust and A. Hughes (eds.), *Conflict in Early Stuart England* (1989), 72–106.

[70] Daniel Price, *Recusants Conversion* (Oxford, 1608), 10; Richard Greenham, ed. Henry Holland, *Workes* (second edition, 1599), sig. A4ᵛ.

[71] Bradshaw, *Humble Motives*, 11–12.

[72] Price, *Recusants Conversion*, 30.

failure to achieve a general conformity on one level defeats the spread of the Gospel, the phenomenon of dissent from true religion is not necessarily an evil thing. Thus William Harrison wrote of the 'difference of hearers' and of distinct kinds of faith. The apparent inability of a preacher to persuade effectually may simply be a reflection of God's will.[73] Bradshaw thought that State Protestants were much of a kind with State papists; they simply had a different political bias. Protestants of religion can only become so by being 'inwardly and effectually called'.[74] Measures taken by secular or ecclesiastical authority can of themselves create, at most, a mass of 'Protestants of state', out of whom 'Protestants of religion' may be drawn. The 'indifferent' in the puritans' scheme of things are in the same position as the slothful schismatics about whom the Jesuits complained.[75] In George Gifford's *Briefe Discourse*, set out in dialogue form, Atheos, one of its characters, is not actually a recusant Roman Catholic, but from self-satisfied ignorance he says Romish things.

Like the Jesuits, evangelical godly Protestants did, at times, map patterns of grace onto patterns of church-going. Francis Bunny's anti-recusancy polemic, focusing on the exercise of conscience, implies an identification of Elect and Reprobate with church-goers and recusants respectively. Bunny does not explicitly say that recusancy leads to moral degeneration, but it is clearly implied. Church-going and desire for instruction in faith are aligned with the signs of sanctification which may be expected from the elect individual, regenerate in grace. Their new conversation is witness to a conversion which is more than a simple adjustment of ecclesiastical loyalties. The decision of a recusant to abandon his recusancy and attend church takes on an evangelical significance.[76] Still, mere alteration of opinion was not enough. As Richard Baxter said, if no more than 'evil professions' and 'outward practices' are changed, then 'you are wicked still'. Said Baxter, 'it's one thing to turn from loose prophane Opinions, to strict Opinions; and think the Godly are indeed in the right, and that their case and way is safest, and best: and its another thing to be made One of them in Newness and Spirituality of heart', because 'a lively Faith differs much from Opinion'.[77] The Protestant evangelical concept of conversion meant

---

73 Harrison, *Difference*, sig. F^{r–v}, and *passim*.
74 Bradshaw, *Humble Motives*, 14.
75 Gifford, *Briefe Discourse*, sig. Aii^v–iii^r.
76 Francis Bunny, *Truth and Falshood* (1595), sigs. Aa8^r, Bb2^r–3^r; cf. Thomas Bell, *Thomas Bels Motives* (Cambridge, 1593), 9.
77 Richard Baxter, *Directions and Persuasions to a Sound Conversion* (1683), 230–1; cf. James Wadsworth snr, *The Contrition of a Protestant Preacher* (St Omer, 1615), sig. B2^r, opining that those not subject to grace 'may talke of opinions in religion; but seldome shall you see any fruites of their religion, more then opinion and table-talke'.

ultimately that any absolute identification of ecclesiastical and evangelical conversion was made principally for propaganda reasons.

The greater the evangelical zeal of the proselytiser, the more likely it was that the association of godly conversion with rigid patterns of institutional change would begin to fall apart. I do not wish to fall into the trap of saying that evangelicals on each side had identical aims. One should not underestimate the reality of the polemical division between Jesuits and puritans with their extreme expressions of Catholic and Protestant faith. Still, it is nonsense to talk about rival evangelisms as if proselytising was simply an extension of politics, and so aimed to create politically defined ecclesiastical groups. When Edmund Bunny produced his puritan edition of Persons's *Christian Directory* it was not just to prevent readers thinking that it was an exclusively Roman work, or that Rome was the natural focus for latent evangelicals, but because godly Protestants approved the aims of that book, though they censured Persons's Roman terminology. William Fitch, whose conversion to Rome began in earnest when he read Bunny's edition of Persons's book, is one instance of what other evidence indicates may have been a common phenomenon. The evangelical proselytisers on either side were drawing their concept of conversion from an area of theology and spirituality which was of common concern to Protestants and Catholics. Although contemporary evangelicals were divided by their disagreements about the mechanisms by which grace infiltrated into man's corrupt nature, they were together (though not through any spirit of moderation) in their consensus that the experience of conversion was an arousal of the will under the influence of grace, and this was principally what they were seeking to instigate in their proselytes. They did this rather than base their rhetorical persuasions exclusively on the stark and off-putting monotony of polemical doctrinal arguments. The way to or from Rome was then opened up through an evangelical consciousness which was equally alluring to zealots of both sides, Protestants and Catholics. It is evident from records like the 'Responsa Scholarum' of the English College in Rome that there was a direct path from the condition which contemporary Catholics described as 'heretical' to Rome through the evangelical state of conversion which Catholic evangelical proselytisers aimed to induce.[78]

---

[78] Between 1598 and 1640, of the seminarists who left an account of their religious background at the English College in Rome, 124 were ordained and professed as Jesuits. Of these forty-nine said that they had been formerly heretical and give the names of those who converted them. Two-thirds say that where a priest was involved it was a Jesuit as opposed to a secular, CRS 54–5, *passim*; cf. Questier, 'Phenomenon', 102. Of the twelve Roman seminarists who entered the Society but died before ordination, four were formerly 'heretical' and six 'schismatic'.

BELONGING TO THE CHURCH

All proselytisers persuaded their converts to belong to 'the Church'. There were several rival polemical definitions of the Church and so it was not surprising that 'belonging to the Church' for some clergy might be loaded with emphases which other clergy would not want to acknowledge so readily. But since 'belonging to the Church' comprehended, potentially, much more than a quasi-political profession of allegiance to either the Church of Rome or the Church of England, divisions over what it meant and how it was to be effected arose not just between Catholics and Protestants but also between those who were more and less evangelical on each side. There were tensions among Catholic clerics about the way in which the true Church as an expression of grace should be described as visible, infallible and so on, just as there were disagreements among Protestant clergy on these issues; and this was expressed in their antagonistic attitudes to conversion. In fact, when religious division occurred over zeal rather than doctrinal probity, rivalry and conflict was less between Catholic and Protestant evangelisms than between those in each Church who were more and less enthusiastic about conversion and its potential speed and intensity. The Jesuits (with their alienation from aspects of the Tridentine emphasis on the primacy of the ecclesiastical structures of the institutional Church) entertained an idea of conversion which resembled the one held by English Protestants who adhered to more uncompromising doctrines of grace, and who played down the extent to which the institutional Church was necessary for grace to be efficacious. Hostility to such people was likely to arise from those in both Churches who saw elements of that type of activity as being in conflict with the structure, purpose and potential of the institutional Church, its hierarchies and authority. Sir Francis Bacon, in his 'Advertisement' against puritan demands in the Church of England wrote that he had heard 'some [puritan] sermons of mortification, which I think (with very good meaning) they have preached out of their own experience and exercise, and things [which] in private counsels [are] not unmeet; but surely no sound conceits, much like to Persons's *Resolution* [the *Christian Directory*] . . . apt to breed in men . . . weak opinions and perplexed despairs'.[79]

Protestant churchmen who all agreed that papists should relax their allegiance to Rome dissented among themselves about how conformity was to be promoted because they viewed differently the nature of effectual conversion. Lancelot Andrewes's court sermon in February 1620 on

---

[79] J. Spedding, R. L. Ellis and D. D. Heath (eds.), *The Works of Francis Bacon* (14 vols., 1858–74), VIII, 92–3.

conversion and repentance represented the relationship between the will and the intellect in a light which might have alerted other Protestants to his hostility to their theology of grace.[80] This antagonism is very evident in the divisions among Protestants over papists' abjuration of Rome. The tendency of most Catholic clerical defectors to portray their conversions as departure from the apocalyptic Babylon, thus intensifying the link between regeneration by grace with movement between institutional Churches, irritated some more moderate Protestant churchmen. This was because apocalyptic expressions of change of religion damaged the Church of England's institutional claims against Rome by questioning the integrity of its institutional structure as a positive expression and channel of grace. Conversion from Rome depicted as departure from Babylon undermined concepts of succession and validity of orders to which moderate Protestant clerics subscribed and implied doctrines of grace, election and predestination to which they were opposed. Richard Carpenter, who abandoned Rome around 1635, was instructed by Archbishop Laud that in his recantation sermon he 'must not speak revengefully or ungratefully against the church of Rome'.[81] William Bray, Laud's chaplain, refused to license a new edition of the motives tract by the lay ex-papist Sir Anthony Hungerford because of its 'harsh phrases'.[82] For churchmen like the Laudians, conversion from Rome had to be made from a corrupt but true element of the Church to a reformed branch of it. Laud said that a man ought to 'hate the corruption which depraves religion, and to run from it; but from no part of religion itself'. Laud's apparent moderation over conversion, that 'a man is apt to think he can never run far enough from that which he once begins to hate', masks a theological perspective on conversion which was quite unacceptable to his godly enemies.[83] It is significant that several prominent Caroline Catholic renegades slated or worked against Laud.[84] Those who converted

---

[80] Lancelot Andrewes, *XCVI Sermons* (1629), 205, 207: though he disclaims 'the false imputation cast on us' that repentance consists merely of 'amendment of life', he casts a potentially threatening aspersion on the Reformed stress on the passivity of the will in repentance. He caricatures the concept of conversion belonging to those whom he felt would caricature his own views: 'by some, our conversion is conceived to be a turning of the braine only (by doting to[o] much on the word *resipiscere*) as a matter meerly mentall'.

[81] Anstruther II, 46: Carpenter later preached an anti-popery sermon, presumably apocalyptic in tone, provoking Laud to tell him 'you had better have stayed where you were than to have done as you have done', though cf. LPL, Carte Antique et Miscellanee MS 943, p. 729; A. Milton, 'The Laudians and the Church of Rome c. 1625–1640' (Ph.D thesis, Cambridge, 1989), 142–3.

[82] T. B. and T. J. Howell (eds.), *A Complete Collection of State Trials* (34 vols., 1816–28), IV, 507; Davidson, 'Roman Catholicism', 540–1.

[83] William Laud, ed. J. Bliss and W. Scott, *Works* (7 vols., Oxford, 1847–60), II, pp. xv–xvi.

[84] Howell and Howell, *State Trials*, IV, 547; C. M. Hibbard, *Charles I and the Popish Plot* (North Carolina, 1983), 110, 113–14; Thomas Gage, *A New Survey* (1655), 205–12; John Browne, *A Discovery of the Notorious Proceedings of William Laud* (1641).

to the Church of England but refused to interpret their conversion as a departure from Babylon, aroused the wrath of less moderate Protestants. De Dominis infuriated George Abbot in this way, though he did not avail himself ultimately of the support of proto-Arminians which might have sustained his position in the Church of England.[85] William Alabaster, whose conversion away from Rome appeared distinctly suspect to some Protestants, was associated with Richard Neile. Oliver Cromwell noted in parliament in 1629 that Neile had refused permission for Alabaster's sermons, regarded by some as crypto-Catholic, to be answered.[86]

Antagonistic perceptions of grace actually influenced the enforcement of conformity. Protestant churchmen of all persuasions tried to cajole Catholics towards the Church of England, but they did it in different ways.[87] Just as 'puritans' in McGee's model regarded the 'Anglican' way of conversion as too lax and uncomprehending of the rigours of appropriating grace in effectual conversion, so it seemed to some Protestants that others were too ready to admit papists into the Church of England without adequate tests and safeguards. This criticism came from a different understanding of grace and repentance. Thomas Cartwright thought that ex-Catholics ought to be prevented from conforming officially until they had 'purged themselves of suspicion of Popery'. Such a view contrasted with that of Richard Hooker who thought that it was wrong to quench the 'feeble smoke of conformity' of those who might subsequently embrace the Church of England more whole-heartedly.[88] Some Protestant clerics appeared vulnerable to their opponents on precisely this score. In June 1614 Richard Neile was accused in the Commons of providing in return for a bribe a false certificate of conformity for a recusant, Francis Lovett. It was

---

[85] Bodl., Tanner MS 73A, fo. 138ʳ; cf. his more extreme statements which appeared in the initial account of his motivation, Marc'Antonio de Dominis, *Marcus Antonius de Dominis . . . Suae Profectionis* (1616), 34.

[86] A. W. Foster, 'A Biography of Archbishop Richard Neile (1562–1640)' (DPhil. thesis, Oxford, 1978), 156. James Montagu voiced openly his suspicion that Alabaster would eventually relapse, McClure, *Letters*, I, 568; AAW, A XIV, 117.

[87] It would not be true to say that only evangelicals like Hutton and Mathew were interested in converting papists. Both Bancroft and John Overall conferred with prominent converts to Catholicism in order to make them return to the Church of England. Thomas Bilson and Henry Cotton were keen to force Catholic recusants into submission rather than just cooperate in subjecting them to financial penalties for their recusancy, *HMC Salisbury MSS* VI, 265–6; CRS 57, xciv. Richard Montagu's polemical works of the mid-1620s were inspired initially by disputes with papists, G. Ornsby (ed.), *The Correspondence of John Cosin* (2 vols., Surtees Society, 52, 55, 1868, 1872), I, 32–3. Laud at his trial gave a detailed account of the Romanists he had persuaded to change religion, Laud, *Works*, IV, 62–6.

[88] J. Lister (ed.), *West Riding Sessions Rolls 1597/8–1602* (Yorkshire Archaeological and Topographical Association, Record Series, 3, 1888), xxiv; cf. William Gouge, *A Recovery from Apostacy* (1639), 21.

alleged that Lovett had not been made to take the oaths of allegiance and supremacy, or to receive communion.[89] There is plenty of evidence to show that moderate clerics, and later those whose names were linked to an 'Arminian' theology of grace, did approach the problem of proselytisation differently from the more 'Reformed', 'evangelical' or 'puritan' English clergy. Bancroft set various divines to work on Francis Walsingham. Though at one stage he was sent to see George Downame, he was also confronted with William Covell who employed notably moderate arguments to convert him.[90] Lancelot Andrewes was seen to object to harsher anti-Catholic measures, and he also was thought to confer with Catholics in a suspiciously moderate way (in order to persuade them).[91] Both Tobias Mathew jnr and William Alabaster discussed religion with Andrewes. Mathew said Andrewes told him that 'in England no one learned man, except Dr Fulke, had declared that there was no necessity of a continual visibility in the Church', and also that 'the English Protestant Catholic Church, and the Roman Catholic Church' were 'one and the same Church of Christ, forasmuch as he might conceive the fundamental points of faith'.[92] Laud said at his trial that calling the Pope Antichrist never converted an 'understanding Papist'.[93] His persuasions exercised on Sir Kenelm Digby show that he believed irenicism would prove more attractive to Romanists (of the type he would like to see in the Church of England).[94] Among the allegations brought against John Cosin in Durham in 1628 was the assertion that he, 'perswading a papist to come to church, said that the body of Christ was substantially and really in the sacrament: and shewing him the new service-book intended for Scotland, he said it was all one with theirs of the Romish Church'.[95] Some godly Protestants would not have approved of the advice which was offered to Elizabeth Cary at Durham House.[96] In the debates in 1623 held for the benefit of the countess of Buckingham, the disputants, Laud, Francis White and John Williams, were selected (and Daniel Featley passed over) in part because of the moderate reasoning which

---

[89] Foster, 'Biography', 126–7; T. L. Moir, *The Addled Parliament of 1614* (Oxford, 1958), 134–6; M. Jansson (ed.), *Proceedings in Parliament 1614* (Philadelphia, 1988), 406, 410–14. The evidence for Neile's dereliction of duty over Lovett's conformity is ambiguous, but Neile was thought in the 1621 parliament to have opposed the introduction of more stringent recusancy legislation, *CSPD 1619–23*, 225.

[90] Walsingham, *Search* (1609), 63–74, 39–43.

[91] *HMC Rutland MSS* I, 420; Caraman, *William Weston*, 128–9.

[92] Mathew, *True Historical Relation*, 99–100.

[93] Howell, *State Trials*, IV, 525.

[94] Laud, *Works*, VI, 447–55.

[95] W. H. D. Longstaffe (ed.), *The Acts of the High Commission Court within the Diocese of Durham* (Surtees Society, 34, 1858), 230.

[96] R. Simpson (ed.), *The Lady Falkland* (1861), 10–11.

they would employ.[97] Richard Montagu's anti-Roman polemic was sufficiently un-Reformed to prompt the 'Calvinist' backlash against him. John Bramhall, placed in South Kilvington in the North Riding of Yorkshire, an area where much influence could be exercised on non-conformist Catholics, was active during 1623 in disputing with Catholic clergy. Although he made as much of his triumph in disputation as any puritan might, his approach to proselytisation may have set him apart from some of the clergy who had taken on themselves the task of converting papists in that part of the world.[98]

The arguments which these moderates used (whether they focused directly on grace and repentance or not) were unwelcome to less moderate Protestants because they seemed to obscure the nature of true conversion. Laud wrote that, at his trial, after he had given an account of the converts he had made from the Church of Rome, Thomas Hoyle said 'it was a very strange conversion that . . . [Laud] was like to make of them'.[99] Though William Prynne said that scarcely any bishop could lay claim to having 'converted one papist' to Protestantism, the argument was not about numbers.[100] Laud's enemies thought that his understanding of leaving the Church of Rome was not sufficiently aligned with what they perceived as evangelical change of religion. Laudian laxity over admission to the Church of England brought up all their collective animus about a non-preaching ministry and mere conformity. William Gouge in 1639 remarked that the 'ancient Discipline of the Church about receiving such as had Apostatised from her, into her bosome againe, was more austere, then now it is'; in the early Church 'they suffered none, that had once renounced the Christian Faith to be received as members of the Church, unlesse they gave good evidences of their true repentance, and that by their deepe humiliation, free confession, and willing subjection to such satisfactions as the Church should enjoyne'.[101]

CONVERSION AND DEATH

Proselytisation (in the sense of directing a spoken persuasion at a specific individual) was something which generally occurred in private, and has left few records. Nevertheless, extraordinary circumstances and occasions sometimes flung the proselytisers and their methods into the public gaze, and then

---

[97] T. H. Wadkins, 'The Percy–"Fisher" Controversies and the Ecclesiastical Politics of Jacobean Anti-Catholicism, 1622–1625', *Church History* 57 (1988), 153–69; John Hacket, *Scrinia Reserata* (1693), I, 42, 172.
[98] Bramhall, *Works*, sig. f², 623–4; CRS 56, xxxii.
[99] Laud, *Works*, IV, 65.
[100] Laud, *Works*, IV, 62.   [101] Gouge, *Recovery*, 19–20.

the anomalies of regarding them according to a strict Roman–Reformed model of division became plain for all to see.

Unanimity among evangelicals and their extreme disdain for those whom they regarded as insufficiently intense came out into the open in the Church's ministry to the dying. Illness and considerations of death were generally seen as powerful persuasive factors impelling people to consider whether they belonged to the true Church.[102] The zealous on both sides were determined both to assist and to exploit them. Those who more urgently wanted to stimulate the moment of regeneration focused (almost paradoxically) upon the danger of deferring one's conversion until the final moments. George Gifford makes his disputant Atheos say 'what would ye have more then this, at the last to call for mercie . . . I pray God I may have time to repent in the end', all of which his puritan antagonist Zelotes considers to be the road to hell.[103] William Harrison wrote 'in the time of our life and of our health we be scarse able . . . to begin serious repentance: but much more unable and unfit shall wee bee in the time of sicknesse and death'.[104] It was folly to defer one's conversion because death might steal upon one unawares, leaving time only for the most cursory of repentances, perhaps not even that. This was no way to gain the godly assurance which evangelicals saw as the necessary accompaniment to election and vocation. English Jesuits censured those who hesitated to become fully recusant, not so much for quasi-political disloyalty to the cause but rather because they associated recusancy with that permanent separation of the godly from the wicked which Protestant and Catholic evangelicals took to be a sign of

---

[102] Illness stimulated the high-profile clerical conversions of John Nichols, Benjamin Carier, Theodore Price and Thomas Vane, John Nichols, *A Declaration of the Recantation of John Nichols* (1581), sig. Biiiiᵛ; Benjamin Carier, *A Treatise* (Brussels, 1614), 7; George Hakewill, *An Answere to a Treatise Written by Dr Carier* (1616), sig. d3ᵛ; C. Dodd, *The Church History of England* (3 vols., Brussels (impring false, printed at Wolverhampton), 1737–42), II, 510, 517; William Prynne, *The Popish Royall Favourite* (1643), 70; G. Albion, *Charles I and the Court of Rome* (Louvain, 1935), 197; Birch, *Court and Times of Charles I*, II, 335; Thomas Vane, *A Lost Sheep Returned Home* (Paris, 1649). Illness figured also in the conversions of Everard Hanse and John Blackfan, Anthony Munday, *A breefe Aunswer made unto two seditious Pamphlets* (1582), sig. Cvʳ⁻ᵛ; Foley II, 625; also in the cases of laymen, like Pickering Wotton and (possibly) Sir Francis Cottington, L. P. Smith (ed.), *The Life and Letters of Sir Henry Wotton* (2 vols., Oxford, 1907), II, 482–1; Wadsworth, *The English Spanish Pilgrime*, 2–3; M. J. Havran, *Caroline Courtier* (1973), 77. See also George Fisher, *The Bishop of London his Legacy* (St Omer, 1623); Daniel Featley, *The Fisher Catched in his owne Net* (1623), 1; N. N., *An Epistle of a Catholike Young Gentleman* (Douai (imprint false, printed secretly in England), 1623), 7. For both Protestants and Catholics it had a providential character in that it encouraged the Elect towards evangelical regeneration in spite of themselves, see, e.g. the cases of John Good and Sir John Warner, BL, Lansd. MS 776, fos. 12ᵛ, 47ʳ⁻ᵛ; Queen's College MS 284, fo. 204ᵛ.

[103] Gifford, *Briefe discourse*, 107.

[104] William Harrison, *Deaths Advantage Little Regarded* (1612), 39.

effectual change in religion and the work of saving grace.[105] The Jesuit Richard Holtby warned to the 'terror of such as defer their conversion, and abuse the time God hath granted them . . . let them consider how few there be that have grace to come home in time, perhaps two amongst a thousand'.[106] Those who wanted (within whichever doctrinal scheme) to see clear evidence of assurance of saving grace (and perseverance in it), also wanted to shift the effectual moment of conversion forward through life as far as possible.

Of course, at the moment of death, it was impolitic to worry people by denouncing their folly in deferring conversion for so long, and necessary, even profitable for propaganda purposes, to induce a sudden, effectual and explosive conversion experience in the dying man. Nowhere was this more evident than when condemned felons came within reach of a particular type of cleric who saw them as fertile ground for experiments in grace.[107] On the scaffold, an alternative pulpit, a direct connection could be made between regeneration and true and false religion. Catholic clerics who operated in the prisons tried not just to convert the targeted felon in an evangelical sense but also to make him adopt as a sign of his new sense of election a Roman ecclesiastical allegiance, both of which things he was urged to declare in the recognised valedictory form of the 'last dying speech'. Catholic priests who were executed in the company of other criminals evangelised them and converted them from both sin and Protestantism. In Worcester gaol the attention of the Jesuit Edward Oldcorne was attracted by a condemned 'Calvinist' criminal. The felon took a delightfully simplistic solace in a Calvinist scheme of grace and assurance and, indeed, thought himself assured of his salvation in a Calvinist sense. Oldcorne soon disillusioned him and 'with the effectual assistance of God's grace, he wrought this man's mind not only to a constant belief of the Catholic faith, but to a fervent profession also of the same, and a public demonstration of a perfect conversion'. Like the most effective of puritan ministers, Oldcorne 'made good proof in this one patient how great dexterity and skill he had in the curing of diseased souls'.[108] A thief convicted at the same assizes as the priests John Amias and Robert Dalby, repented the sins of his past life and, sharing their scaffold, 'behaved with such constancy, that he refused to pray with the heretical ministers'.[109] The Benedictine John Roberts had

---

[105] Morris, *Troubles*, II, 114–15.
[106] Morris, *Troubles*, III, 119.
[107] For a broader treatment of this topic, see P. Lake and M. C. Questier, 'Agency, Appropriation and Rhetoric under the Gallows: Puritans, Romanists and the State in Early Modern England' (forthcoming in *P&P*).
[108] Foley IV, 238–40.
[109] Pollen, *Acts*, 331.

apparently not had the opportunity to work on the felons who were hanged with him, but the moment he stood in the cart underneath the crossbeam he immediately exhorted them to consider their spiritual state and their hopes of salvation, attainable, naturally, only in the Church of Rome.[110] Alban Roe converted two felons actually at Tyburn in early 1642 who 'were observed to make signs of sorrow and repentance; and when they were asked by the Calvinist minister to sing a Psalm after the Puritan manner, they turned away their faces'.[111]

Condemned felons were of interest to an evangelical Catholic cleric even when he did not have the opportunity of being executed with them.[112] At the end of April 1610 Peter Lambert, a mercenary soldier, was hanged for killing one Hamden 'a Low-countrie Lieutenant'. Lambert had not been noted previously for good character or religious zeal but shortly before he was indicted he was approached in Newgate by a Catholic priest. This cleric 'framed him in the Popish Moold, so that according to the summe of his Learning, he dyed . . . a professed Papist'. The Jesuits exulted over this triumph. Five years later it was still being cited by the priest John Ainsworth as a notable victory.[113] Ainsworth, an inflammatory proselytiser with Jesuit links, himself converted two notorious murderers in Newgate, John Heydon (apparently a former servant of Sir Robert Cecil) and George Stringar. They were first converted to Roman Catholicism by a formal and lengthy disputation. This aspect of their conversion was followed by sacramental confession and absolution. Heydon argued about doctrine with two royal chaplains, and made a public profession of his Catholicism before dying. It was reported in April 1615 that Ainsworth had written a letter (seen by James I) in which he said that he worked actively to ensure that 'all the fellons that were executed might turne Papistes, and that going from the prison and at the Gallowes they should with a lowd voyce crye out, All Catholicks pray for us'.[114] In 1622 Walter Yonge reported that a felon who was condemned at the assizes which began at Exeter on 11 March 'was dealt withal in prison' by John Sweet, 'and made an instrument to disgrace our religion'. The felon had a confession of faith on him at his death which he never delivered, but it contained an account of his conversion, and a

[110] AAW, A IX, 343; Pollen, *Acts*, 163.
[111] Pollen, *Acts*, 342.
[112] J. Gerard, 'Contributions towards a Life of Father Henry Garnet SJ', part IV, *The Month* 91 (1898), 366; CRS 5, 208, 293, 389.
[113] McClure, *Letters*, I, 298 (I am grateful to Michael Bowman for this reference); PRO, SP 14/53/107, fo. 157ᵛ; Foley VII, 1014; AAW, A XIV, 211.
[114] Anstruther II, 3; AAW, A XIV, 210–11; PRO, SP 14/80/84, fo. 125ʳ. Benjamin Norton wrote to the clergy agent in January 1615 that a report of various 'malefacters' publicly declaring themselves Catholic as they were taken to Tyburn was 'the beste newes I hearde [in] a greate whiles', AAW, A XIV, 32.

statement that 'the motive which did persuade him to popery was that the clergy of England were men of unsanctified lives', clearly an element of Sweet's regular polemical anti-Protestant canon.[115]

Protestants were equal to the challenge. Thomas Fitzherbert wrote in 1602 that in a recent pamphlet (dealing with the Essex rebellion) which noted Sir Christopher Blount's protestation that he died a Catholic, 'some foolish minister . . . foysted in an aparenthesis, signifying that he dyed not such a Catholyk, but that he hoped to be saved by the merits of Christs passion, not ascribing his salvation to his owne workes'.[116] Some Protestants spent as much time proselytising in the prisons as Catholics did. Henry Goodcole, an active visitor of prisons, wrote up and had printed his spiritual conquests. He recorded that one Francis Robinson, sentenced to die for forging the Great Seal, had been led into evil ways by a Romanist. This man, called Morgan, 'shewed the fruites of his Religion, to bring by his wicked device, the body of this Gentleman to his destruction, and (had not God in his great mercy prevented the same)' would have 'destroyed . . . his soule also, for he went the right way thereunto, by crafty seducing of him to become a Papist'. Execution was temporarily respited by Sir Henry Montagu, the lord chief justice, to allow Goodcole to work on Robinson for his thorough repentance in a suitably Protestant context.[117] When John Roberts was executed, the Protestant minister who was present retaliated against Roberts's proselytising speech by organising the condemned felons in the second cart to drown Roberts's words by singing hymns made up from the 'Psalms according to the fashion of Geneva'.[118]

The emphasis on felons rejecting one Church or the other at the prompting of Catholic and Protestant ministers might suggest that these occasions had a purely polemical Romanist–Protestant significance. But it is clear that this type of ministry was virtually an evangelical preserve, and that the evangelicals had more in common with each other than the polemicising of execution speeches implies. In that they were concerned with doing down the clergy of an opposing Church they really wanted to show not that their enemies were doctrinally inadequate but to display the nature of true conversion and to oppose against it a mass of ungodly beliefs and practices which Protestant zealots would lump together as popery and Roman ones would see as the product of heresy and schism.

---

[115] Roberts, *Diary*, 54.

[116] Thomas Fitzherbert, *A Defence of the Catholyke Cause* (Antwerp, 1602), fo. 64ʳ.

[117] Henry Goodcole, *A True Declaration of the happy Conversion, Contrition, and Christian Preparation of Francis Robinson* (1618), sigs. A3ʳ⁻ᵛ, Bʳ, B3ʳ, C3ʳ. The puritan Thomas Tregoss in the 1660s exploited his imprisonments to make conversions among the prisoners in the common gaol at Launceston and then at Bodmin, Clarke, *Lives*, sig. Pʳ⁻ᵛ.

[118] AAW, A IX, 343.

The Catholic clerics who proselytised in the prisons and around the scaffold were drawn very heavily from the religious orders, or if they were secular clerics, they had close associations with them.[119] The evangelical concerns of the regulars translated well into this type of ministry. Mark Barkworth took the habit of the Order of St Benedict shortly before execution and appeared clothed as such on the scaffold.[120] At execution, John Roberts, the Benedictine, stressed his monastic profession by saying that he was of the same religion as St Augustine of Canterbury.[121] The most dramatic sign of evangelical conversion imaginable for a Roman Catholic, the taking of the vows of a religious order, Barkworth and Roberts physically associated with their deaths through their apparel, thus demonstrating for their audience their own godly assurance of their election and standing in grace, and displaying simultaneously a polemical expression of it in distinctively Romanist terms.

There was a perennial Jesuit interest in converting felons on the scaffold, but there is no secular clergy equivalent to the long lists of such conversions recorded in the Jesuit annual letters. The secular priest John Jackson objected strongly to the 'blind zeall' which had led an evangelically inclined secular to secure and publicise the conversion of Lord Sanquhair, executed for murder in 1612.[122] The most explicit descriptions of the penal system as an agent of providence, sorting out those predestined to salvation, came from Jesuits.[123] In 1620 there was published a translation by Tobias Mathew jnr, the Jesuit-inclined son of the archbishop of York, of a long Italian 'murder tract' (written by a Jesuit, Giuseppe Biondo). It dealt with

---

[119] Among the religious, one finds William Fitch, John Gerard, William Wright, William Whittingham, John Percy and Thomas Worsley, BL, Harl. MS 3888, fos. 30ᵛ, 31ᵛ; Caraman, *John Gerard, passim*; Foley II, 282–4, 556, VII, 1099, 1098. For instances of the secular clerics who had connections with the religious, John Pibush and Roger Dickenson, Anstruther I, 274–5; Pollen, *Acts*, 87–8. Thomas Laithwait who was imprisoned in Exeter gaol withdrew from the common gaol to practise an ascetic lifestyle, Foley IV, 632–5. Thomas Maxfield, an energetic proselytiser in the Gatehouse prison, had a Jesuit confessor there, CRS 3, 35–6. The militant proselytisers John Ainsworth and George Fisher had links with the religious orders, AAW, A VII, 37; Anstruther II, 2–3, 102–9; AAW, A XII, 523; John Gee, *The Foot out of the Snare* (fourth edition, 1624), sigs. P3ʳ–R3ᵛ: 'if hee [Fisher] bee not already a Jesuite by obligation and profession, yet he is Jesuitable, and fit to receive that lawrel Garland', sig. Qʳ.

[120] Anstruther I, 21–2, cf. 105, II, 128–9.

[121] AAW, A IX, 343.

[122] AAW, A XI, 565.

[123] Morris, *Troubles*, II, 124–7: William Weston recounts the fate of a boatman who was convicted unjustly of a crime in which he was an unwitting accomplice. Weston describes his subsequent arrest and execution as God ordering 'all things to work for the good of His elect' because this temporal calamity forced him to consider the state of his soul, and by the operation of a priest in prison, he converted to Catholicism. Like other carefully instructed converts he refused to receive the Protestant communion before death and declared his Catholicism on the scaffold, showing himself to be 'a vessel of eternal predestination'.

the crimes, apprehension, repentance and death of an Italian nobleman. It was produced on the Jesuit press at St Omers, and the Annual Letter for 1624 records that the tract was used by a Jesuit to convert a condemned man who was prevailed upon, at his execution, to make 'a public recantation of the Calvinistic heresy, which exceedingly enraged an heretical minister who was present'.[124]

On the other side, the Protestant clerics who most enthusiastically attended the progress of the condemned from trial to execution were those like Francis Bunny, Henry Goodcole and William Perkins – all puritan evangelicals.[125] Samuel Clarke reports of William Perkins that 'his manner was to go with the Prisoners to the place of execution when they were condemned' and cites as an example of his extraordinary success his interruption of the proceedings in the case of a felon in whom he perceived a suitable 'dejection of spirit'; he brought the man down off the ladder, and by 'effectual praier' and depiction of the eternal punishment due by God's justice for sin, 'brought him low enough, even to hell gates', but then 'proceeded to the second part of his Praier, and therein to shew him the Lords [*sic*] Jesus', thus triggering the evangelical conversion which Perkins sought, and producing an 'inward consolation' which the condemned man 'gave such expression of . . . to the beholders as made them lift up their hands, and prais God to see such a blessed change in him'.[126] Such Protestants might see the scaffold conversion as a satisfactory demonstration of the workings of grace in a way that less evangelical Protestants might not.

If the clerical interest in scaffold conversions was not principally directed towards defining the boundaries between opposing institutional Churches, then it is likely that any real divisions over conversion in this sphere would appear not so much between Catholics and Protestants as between those who were evangelicals and those who were not, a much less clearly defined politico-ecclesiastical distinction. The analysis which the condemned felon presented for the delectation of the spectators – a fall from grace and good life (which might in some cases lead to apostasy from the true Church) followed by a return to grace (and the true Church) – was a vivid depiction

---

124 Giuseppe Biondo, *A Relation of the Death, of . . . Troilo Savelli* (St Omer, 1620); Foley VII, 1104.

125 B. Camm, *The Lives of the English Martyrs* (2 vols., 1904–5), II, 615, 629; cf. *The Life, Confession and Heartie Repentance of Francis Cartwright* (1621), sigs. D^{r-v}, E2^v (a reference I owe to Peter Lake).

126 Samuel Clarke, *The Marrow of Ecclesiastical Historie* (1650), 417–18. Perkins's interest in this type of evangelising is suggested also in the image of the two prisoners in *A Reformed Catholicke* (Cambridge, 1598), 17–18. For instances of English Catholic clerics behaving in a similar fashion abroad, Stonyhurst Anglia IV, no. 1; *CSPV 1610–13*, 100; AAW, A XIII, 665–6; *CSPV 1613–15*, 265, 275.

of the evangelicals' central concerns. In this regard, the Tyburn gallows was probably a better pulpit than Paul's Cross. Clerics who were politically, and in a sense, theologically, poles apart, had a common aim in this type of evangelisation. What better way for evangelical Christianity to operate than by public conversions (supervised by the ministers of the Church) and on what better stage than a scaffold? As Richard Baxter wrote, 'though I would have no ostentation of Conversion, nothing done rashly in publick, nor without the advice of a faithful Minister beforehand: yet with these Cautions, I must say, that it's a shame that we hear no more in publick of the Conversion of Sinners. As Baptism is to be in publick, that the Congregation may witness your engagement . . . so the solemn renewing of the same Covenant by Repentance after a Wicked Life, should ordinarily be in publick, to give warning to others to avoid the Sin, and to give God the Honour . . . and to satisfie them of our Repentance, that they may have Communion with us'.[127] Baxter did not have public executions in mind, merely open confessions, but the suitability of the scaffold for them is obvious.

Thus did the scaffold assist public proselytising. And even when the clerics of one or other Church were rejected publicly, all evangelicals might still think the purposes of grace were well served. On one level, for example, the Catholics who denounced Protestant heresy from the scaffold were making as much of a mockery of the system of ideological and ecclesiastical control which their deaths were supposed to legitimise as the ordinary felons who shocked godly contemporaries by refusing the suggestions of attendant Protestant clerics that they should show signs of repentance for their crimes.[128] But even for Protestant evangelical clerics such people were as satisfactory a sight, in a sense, as those who repented dutifully. God was distinguishing, via the platform provided by the civil law, between the saved and the damned. Those who did not repent were those who were not called effectually, the Reprobate, the ones who, as all Reformed Protestants stressed, were still responsible for their fate even though they had not been elected to salvation. In fact, if a man was reprobate, or even seemed so, it was highly undesirable that he should seem to repent partially or even be given the opportunity. The 'prayers of the wicked man which doth not

---

[127] Baxter, *Directions*, 448; cf. Gouge, *Recovery*, 19–20; Catholic evangelicals' conversation and carriage at death converted their auditors, CRS 52, 242; cf. Harrison, *Deaths Advantage*, sig. M6r. As O'Malley points out, for the Jesuits, 'ministry to persons in danger of death extended far beyond administering the sacraments to them'; on the Continent they concentrated on their ministry to the condemned in the same way, though in a less polemical manner, as in England, O'Malley, *First Jesuits*, 174–8.

[128] J. Sharpe, ' "Last Dying Speeches": Religion, Ideology and Public Execution in Seventeenth-Century England', *P&P* 107 (1985), 144–67, at pp. 154–5.

repent, and therefore hath not the true faith . . . are no prayers before God, although he crie loude', said George Gifford, and it was extremely unsatisfactory, thought the evangelicals, that godly doctrines of repentance should be watered down by a belief that token or partial grief would do. Of an Arian heretic executed at Norwich, Richard Greenham wrote that 'a little before he should bee executed, [he] afforded a few whorish teares, asking whether he might be saved in Christ or no' but only in order to draw what he considered a doctrinally inadequate reply which he then scorned all the more. Greenham remarked, 'Oh how good a thing had it been not to have cast this pretious stone to this swine?' Richard Sheldon wrote that Ravaillac, after the murder of Henri IV 'did seem to make some shew of repentance at his end: in so villanous a sort, (as before God his repentance was as bad as the deed it self)'.[129] The Romanist equivalent was the refusal of the condemned man to join the Church of Rome and openly declare himself a Catholic. This interpretation relied on the Roman polemical concept of the visible Church standing in opposition to an artificially perceived invisible Protestant one, but, in soteriological terms, it was identical to the puritan version of repentance, or the lack of it, on the scaffold.

To confirm these subtle variations in views of conversion and assurance we need look no further than the prisons where different clerics enjoyed remarkable freedom to exercise their ministries relatively unhindered.[130] Both sides used the prisons for their propaganda activities. Romish priests preached in prisons. They even distributed their books through them. The authorities replied with sermons and disputations at which Catholic prisoners were compelled to attend, and by exploiting political divisions among Catholic prisoners, notably over the Jacobean oath of allegiance.[131]

---

129 Gifford, *Briefe Discourse*, 111; Greenham, *Workes*, 253; Richard Sheldon, *The Motives of Richard Sheldon Pr.* (1612), sig. Dd^{r-v}.

130 BL, Lansd. MS 38, fo. 212^r, MS 56, fo. 14^r; *CSPV 1617–19*, 241; *CSPV 1619–21*, 90, 464. Prisons were the obvious places for confession, which included, of course, sacramental reconciling to Rome from schism as well as heresy, CRS 68, 30; CRS 54, 98, 249–50, 265–6; *HMC Salisbury MSS* VI, 312–13; Caraman, *John Gerard*, 79. Evangelicals like Margaret Clitherow saw prisons as substitutes for religious houses. In prison she 'planted in her heart a perfect contempt of the world', Morris, *Troubles*, III, 370; cf. CRS 4, 79; *HMC Salisbury MSS*, XI, 363–4; Pollen, *Acts*, 276; BL, Harl. MS 286, fo. 97^r; PRO, SP 12/195/114, fo. 194^v; McClure, *Letters*, I, 90.

131 *CSPD 1581–90*, 46, 50, 54; CRS 73, 176; BL, Add. MS 34250; P. J. Holmes, *Resistance and Compromise* (Cambridge, 1982), 183–4; CRS 4, 9; John Keltridge, *Two Godlie and learned Sermons* (1581); William Fulke, *A True Reporte of a Conference* (1581); PRO, SP 12/168/1. For efforts to exploit prisoners' political quarrels, W. K. L. Webb, 'Thomas Preston OSB, alias Roger Widdrington (1567–1640)', *Biographical Studies* 2 (1953–4), 216–69, at p. 236; AAW, A X, 125; Anstruther I, 206. Birkhead said to the clergy agent in Rome in November 1613 that 'the Clinck [prison] is visited with many' and there was a surge of support in favour of Thomas Preston and his loyalist stance, AAW, A XII, 443.

Recantations were frequently staged by the authorities in the prisons where they would have a considerable political impact on Catholics. Men like John Nichols, Anthony Major, William Hardesty, Miles Dawson, Thomas Bell and James Bowland were directed to proselytise, preach or recant in front of Catholic prisoners.[132]

The prisons also presented the Catholic evangelicals and establishment-men with the problem of how they should live in the absence of an established Church where they had their own clearly separated spheres of activity. The question of what their 'conversation' in prison should be like would reflect their differing theological attitudes to evangelical conversion. The first notable manifestation of such conflict was the conflagration at Wisbech Castle in the 1590s. The 'Wisbech Stirs' were partly the result of factional struggle over who would succeed to Cardinal Allen's influence over English Catholic affairs.[133] But they were caused also by the infiltration of regular elements into the life of secular priests. The party led by Christopher Bagshaw wanted to live in a secular house of clergy; William Weston SJ wanted to live in something which was rather too similar to a monastery. A hostile account of Bagshaw said that 'if any priests [in Wisbech Castle] sought to procure greater modesty or holiness in their lives, he [Bagshaw] was then wont to speak of them as Puritans, Precisians, Genevans'.[134]

CONVERSION, EVANGELISATION, SUCCESS AND FAILURE

The complex interaction between politics and religion in contemporaries' understanding of conversion was therefore displayed in contemporary proselytising. Perhaps a revision is required of the way that historians have discussed the extent to which England 'became' a Protestant, or at least a non-Catholic, country after the Elizabethan settlement. An almost exclusively political historiography of change of religion has, in practice, meant that political issues, like allegiance, and the numbers of people who could be regarded as in some sense committed to supporting one ecclesiastical institution against another, have been allowed to obscure the essence

---

[132] CRS 4, 9, 11; Foley III, 762; *HMC Salisbury MSS* VI, 339, VII, 404; J. E. Bailey, 'Thomas Bell', *Notes and Queries*, sixth series, 2 (1880), 429–31, at p. 430; BL, Add. MS 34250, fos. 28ᵛ, 67ʳ.

[133] CRS 51, introduction.

[134] CRS 51, 330. William Fitch, the Capuchin, made his prison 'a Cloistre for the austeritie of his profession', Brousse, *Life*, sig. Hh2ʳ. It is perhaps significant that it was John Colleton, an anti-Jesuit but a priest who had tried his vocation with the Carthusians in the 1570s, who took violent exception towards the low standards of behaviour of certain secular priests in the Clink in 1613, Anstruther I, 83; AAW, A XIV, 471: Colleton objected to the scandals occasioned by their modes of dress and frequenting of plays; they retaliated by having his day-release privileges stopped.

of what conversion and change of religion meant in this period, and much confusion has resulted. Historians have found evidence which points in both directions on virtually all the currently controverted points about Catholicisation and Protestantisation – that both large and small numbers of people were persuaded to turn Catholic or Protestant; that this was done either by evangelism or by gradual assimilation as either one side or the other was seen to be abandoning the mass of the population; that Catholic seminary priests were either a success or a failure; that they were either well or badly equipped to revivify Roman Catholicism in England; that Protestant godly ministers were popular or unpopular, and, like their Catholic opponents, either successful or unsuccessful in their proselytising. The implication is surely that the prevailing historical model into which stray elements of information have been fitted is wrong because it relies on an artificially restricted concept of how change of religion took place. It has been argued here that a model of religious change must reflect the entire contemporary perception of what conversion meant. Contemporaries could not easily imagine conversion in just the political or the ecclesiastical or the intellectual or the evangelical sense. It is certainly a misreading to visualise opposing clerical groups, through their proselytising, trying to create parties of people who could be defined as either 'Catholics' or 'Protestants' merely on a political basis. Not that politics was not seen as important for the progress of religion. The whole thrust of this book has been to show that different political and religious ideas about change of religion gave an immediacy to each other, and to conversion generally, which they otherwise would not have had. But the fact that specific political and religious interests might temporarily be in alignment, that clerics might well want to exploit political issues like the succession, toleration and so on, did not mean that clerics envisaged proselytisation as simply persuading people to support one ecclesiastical body against another. Secular politicians might well find clerics useful as propagandists, especially when religion was a matter of extreme political concern (because people defined their political loyalties partly by their religious beliefs). But the people who proselytised with the greatest enthusiasm, the ones for whom an intense concept of conversion was really important, regarded themselves not primarily as agents (or enemies) of the State or its established Church, but as emissaries of grace, whatever their particular doctrinal beliefs about how grace worked. The political conflict over who belonged to which Church could not then be forced into simplistic and absolute politico-ecclesiastical categories.

Quite obviously, no amount of proselytising towards or away from Rome was going to change the settlement of religion in England. But our perception of the way that contemporaries thought an individual could be persuaded to change religion still tells us something about the state of religion in England more generally. The recent revisionist tendency has been to measure Protestantisation in England by referring to aspects of post-Reformation English Catholicism, or rather of indigenous conservative thought and practice in Church matters. In the revisionist model a middle-way non-Catholicism emerged from a conservative strain of English religion because the religious *engagés* on either side were such a disaster. Christopher Haigh has argued that puritan proselytising was as ineffective (because unpopular) as the seminarist revival was unsuccessful (because inefficient). Without the active enforcement of the law, says Haigh citing William Harrison and John White, the Gospel was nothing. But he equates William Harrison's lament at the want of 'good hearing' exclusively with despair at cultural decadence, as if Harrison regarded it as a problem to be remedied by a change in social and political attitudes.[135] But John White, whose *Defence* Haigh cites as an indicator that all was not well for puritans in Lancashire, said also in that book that in parts of Lancashire 'where the word hath bene more frequent', preaching 'yeelds at this day, and long hath done, as many, and as sound professors of the truth, as any part of our kingdome. And in the backwardest part thereof, many people have joyfully received the truth, and acknowledged the errors, wherein the guile of Seminaries have holden them.'[136] Was the condition of the godly ministry on his mind rather than quotas of recusants and church-goers? Was he thinking principally of the effects of grace on the unregenerate rather than the social cachet of godly religion? Very possibly sermonising was not always popular with the majority, but one suspects that the preachers themselves might have become rather suspicious if they had been faced with an apparent uniform enthusiasm for what they said about godly and ungodly, separation, and difference of hearers. Likewise, it is too simplistic to read post-Reformation English Catholicism as either a success or failure by reference to an essentially social concept of continuity and geographical distribution of its clergy. This book has tried to show that the revisionist approach to religious change, the treatment of the topic on only one level, falls far short of explaining the complexities of how people became Catholics and Protestants during this period.

---

[135] C. Haigh, 'Puritan Evangelism in the Reign of Elizabeth I', *EHR* 92 (1977), 30–58, at pp. 46–7, 56–7.
[136] White, *Defence*, 96.

8

Conclusion

In this book I have argued that the overt superstructure of flux between ecclesiastical bodies, particularly as it is familiar to historians from polemical texts, has a tendency to be deceptive. The fact that there was a very potent political element in many conversions, and that conversion to and from Rome was easily assimilable into a number of different factional struggles, should not be allowed to disguise another fact – namely that conversion between Churches was not politically and polemically bounded. 'Bywayes of pollicy', thought William Bedell, 'doe more ordinarily conduct the changes of Religion' than conscience does, 'yt being as the corruption of our nature no otherwise to love the very Truth then as it may comport with our owne affayres'.[1] But even Bedell's evocation here of the conflict between truth and policy, grace and nature, shows that he recognised the complex relationship between religious and political motivation when people altered their perception of the true faith and their practice of it. The rhetorical and polemical devices which were used to set forth the evils of Romish popery or Protestant heresy were also the mechanisms for expressing and instigating types of conversion which did not rely exclusively on an institutional division between particular churches.

Movement between Churches was invested on one level with a polemical underpinning. Sometimes it seems from the converts' accounts of their changes of opinion that the entire conversion process was instigated by doubts and worries derived from polemical texts. Certainly they expressed the resolution of such doubts in polemical terms, using the violent language of controversialists to say why they had not stayed as they were. But conversion, even between the hostile ecclesiastical institutions of the Churches of England and Rome, did not occur solely or even mainly within polemic's terms of reference. It had a tendency to move outside those terms when people probed the experience of sin and grace, searched out regeneration by experimenting with grace upon nature, and, indeed, made almost a

---

[1] BL, Lansd. MS 90, fo. 109r.

virtue of instability in their opinions and affections, putting into practice the urge to progress in grace by moving about over all sorts of boundaries, moral and ethical, religious in the broadest sense, and also, in the curious English circumstances of a divided Church, over ecclesiastical boundaries as well, an exciting, innovative and occasionally violent manner of feeling regenerate and advertising widely one's opinions about conversion as a Christian imperative.

In these circumstances, what may initially have come as a surprise to the reader, namely that there should be so much ecclesiastical conversion to as well as from Rome (when, as Diarmaid MacCulloch rightly tells us, the Protestant English Reformation can be regarded as a 'howling success',[2] and when flexibility in religion was not generally seen as a virtue at this time), makes perfect sense. Conversion, then, is a key to the debates over Protestantisation, particularly as it figures in the revisionist-dominated discourse about changes in English religion during the Reformation. By eschewing the path of number-crunching and counting of attenders at church, and positing instead the existence of a more complex model of flux in religion than revisionists have allowed, I have suggested that the perception of an absolute, virtually institutionalised division between Protestant and Catholic concerns is misleading – in the same way as some historians are now arguing that the debate over divisions among Protestants between the Reformation and the Civil War is vitiated by a too ready adoption of stark binary divisions between Calvinism and Arminianism, or Anglicanism and Puritanism.[3] In fact, this study suggests, there was in this period no such thing as a unitary English Catholicism at all. In that there was an 'English Catholicism' it was a series of dissident oppositional expressions of religious motive (linked by a common reliance on Rome). Movements to and from it can be comprehended as aspects of the wider experience of grace which Reformation and Counter-Reformation polemical and spiritual discourses were keen to exploit and disseminate.

But where does this leave the question of the State and religion (and particularly the State as the guarantor of true religion), the second principal topic which this book has tried to address? The State had a very visible vested interest in controlling conversion, partly as a means of sustaining and propagandising its own Protestant character, and partly from the sheer political necessity of compelling practical conformity to the religion established by law. Historians have generally viewed the State as the natural Protestant bulwark against Romanist infiltration. But traditional histories of the period have lurched uncomfortably between seeing the State as virtually

---

[2] D. MacCulloch, 'The Impact of the English Reformation', *HJ* 38 (1995), 151–3, at p. 152.
[3] P. Lake, 'Calvinism and the English Church, 1570–1635', *P&P* 114 (1987), 32–76, *passim*.

totalitarian in its violent and intolerant response to religious dissent, and (particularly in the case of the 'Catholic' issue) utterly incapable of enforcing its wishes even in relatively minor matters like securing attendance at church by a small number of dissenters. Another surprising conclusion of this study, then, has been that several of the agencies which were principally concerned with securing conformity as prescribed by law (the Church courts, the ecclesiastical commissions and exchequer) seem to have been extremely efficient in performing their allotted tasks. Although many of the records relating to State-sponsored conformity are lost, it is clear that the depiction by previous generations of historians of a regime blundering about, failing to secure Protestant conformity as much by its own bureaucratic inadequacies as by a failure of political will, and thus incapable of controlling movement between competing ecclesiastical allegiances, can no longer be allowed. So, then, how do we explain the eminently clear fact that while only a small proportion of the population ever actively dissented in matters of religious practice, the possibility of change of religion away from Protestant norms, religious thought and culture, never vanished and sometimes loomed very large? The answer, I have suggested, is that while the State was very efficient at enforcing religious conformity with respect to its bureaucratic structure, it did not regard itself as in the business of securing unity in religion – or rather that it visualised its role in guaranteeing uniformity as severely limited, however grandiloquent the frequently rehearsed claims for the royal supremacy. (There was an essential truth in the Elizabethan refrain that the State prosecuted Catholics for treason not religion.) Of itself the State was concerned to guard against only limited elements of English Romanism, and only when English Catholics could be clearly identified with a threat to political stability. This curious self-limitation of the State's regulation of religion sits easily with what may be deduced also from the books of polemic and the converts' accounts of their changes of religion, namely that there were distinct ambiguities in the multiple layers of opposition between different aspects of Catholic and Protestant allegiances in England. The complexity of conversion, as I have tried to describe it, arose from and illustrates to us these ambiguities, and particularly the way in which they could be used rhetorically and polemically in a country where there were several different explanations for the otherwise obvious fact that people were not all of one religion.

All in all, a study of conversion tells us that instability was as much a defining characteristic of English religion in this unsettled period as the placid acquiescent conformity for which some historians have argued, or, as others have it, a stubborn conservative adherence to the values and practice of the past in opposition to Protestant novelty (even if we do not positively know that large numbers of people actually wavered in what they perceived as their religious profession). During this time, within the apparently rigid constraints of doctrinal formulation and political loyalism, flux in religion was the norm rather than the exception in religious experience, actually expected rather than regarded with astonishment. Confessional polemical conflict itself undermined certainty and questioned uniformity. In 1608 Anthony Wotton asked, 'Do we not find in daily experience, that as flint and steele stricken together bring forth fire: so truth is, as it were, beaten out by disputation?'[4] Yes, but not merely in the sense of establishing a polemical body of 'truth' as a binary inversion of its false opposite, a single standard for intellectual reference. Change of religion was the visible index of the complexities of religious experience in this period. It allows us to see how the outwardly staid and unyielding divisions between groups of religious *engagés* were related to the wider evangelical purposes which these people entertained. And change of religion was also part of the negotiation over conformity between the State and the amorphous body of Catholic dissent, a conformity which several interested parties tried to influence and gloss according to their own understanding of its significance. Conversion, in its many forms, provides, therefore, a means of determining how the political and religious elements of entrenched Catholic and Protestant positions fell into place in the confrontation between these two starkly opposed but also frequently aligned concepts of Christianity. For this reason, the individual conversions which the historian is able to trace during this period tell him not just why these unstable people wavered in their profession of religion but more widely how the Reformation in England may be interpreted as a conflict between Catholic and Protestant ideas and practice.

---

[4] Anthony Wotton, *A Trial of the Romish Clergies Title to the Church* (1608), 13.

BIBLIOGRAPHY

MANUSCRIPT SOURCES

BALLIOL COLLEGE, OXFORD

MS 270   Treatise by Benjamin Carier

BODLEIAN LIBRARY, OXFORD

Jones Manuscript
53   Casuistry treatises and proselytisation manuals

Rawlinson Manuscripts
C 167   Theological opinions on the doctrine of Christ's descent into Hell
D 47   Letter-book of Daniel Featley
D 399   Miscellanea
D 843   Recantation liturgy
D 853   Miscellanea
D 1036   Decision of the judges on points of law concerning recusancy
D 1331   Theological commonplace book of William Sancroft snr

Tanner Manuscripts
73A   Letter of Thomas Goad
75   Correspondence of William Bedell; letter of Thomas Cornwallis
77   Miscellanea
79   Commission for discharging recusants
303   Narrative of the York House Conference
306   Sonnet of William Alabaster

BORTHWICK INSTITUTE, YORK

HCAB 11–17   High Commission Act Books, 1585–1631

BRITISH LIBRARY, LONDON

Additional Manuscripts
6842   Recantation liturgy for use in the Church of Ireland
11574   Papers of Sir Julius Caesar

28640	Letter of J. F. concerning disputation between John Percy and Daniel Featley
34250	Narrative of the sermons in York Castle, 1599–1600
36767	Papers of Sir Julius Caesar
39828	Papers of Sir Thomas Tresham

Cotton Manuscript

| Titus B III | Reports on recusants |

Harleian Manuscripts

286	Report on Romish practises in Newgate prison
360	Report of proposed prison disputation, 1606
703	Proceedings of Sussex recusancy commissions
1221	Character of a Church Papist
3888	'Evangelicall Fruict of the Seraphicall Franciscan Order'
6849	Memorandum concerning the conduct of recusancy business
6995	Papers of Lord Keeper Puckering

Lansdowne Manuscripts

1–122	Papers of Sir William Cecil
123–74	Papers of Sir Julius Caesar
776	Conversion narrative of John Good
982	Bishop Kennett's collections

Royal Manuscript

| 17 A iv | Report of Thomas Felton on his Crown service: 'A Vew of the lawes statuts and courses held by the late Queene Elizabeth against Popish Recusants' |

CAMBRIDGE UNIVERSITY LIBRARY

Mm 1 44	Miscellanea
Mm 1 45	Miscellanea
Mm 2 23	Miscellanea
Mm IV 38	Miscellanea

CANTERBURY CATHEDRAL ARCHIVES AND LIBRARY

| X.2.7, pt 1 | Archdeacon's Court, *Comperta* and *Detecta*, 1584–91 |

CHRIST CHURCH COLLEGE, OXFORD

| MS xii b 48–9 | Disbursement books 1604–5 |

HOUSE OF LORDS RECORD OFFICE, LONDON

Main Papers 1592–3

LAMBETH PALACE LIBRARY, LONDON

Carte Antique et Miscellanee
CM IV   High commission recognisances
MS 943   Papers of William Laud

Fairhurst Manuscripts
2006   Papers concerning the archpriest controversy
2014   Miscellanea
3470   Miscellanea

Gibson Manuscript
933   Recantation liturgy for second earl of Dumbarton

Tenison Manuscripts
655   Papers of Anthony Bacon
663   Miscellanea

MAGDALEN COLLEGE, OXFORD

MS 281   Letter of James Wadsworth jnr

NATIONAL LIBRARY OF SCOTLAND, EDINBURGH

Advocates Manuscript
33-1-66 xx   Letter of George Abbot

PUBLIC RECORD OFFICE, LONDON

C 231/1–4   Crown Office docquet books
E 101/547/3   Accounts of exchequer surveyors of recusants' estates, 1590
E 123–6   Exchequer Decrees and Orders, Elizabeth I–James I
E 134   Depositions before exchequer commissions
E 135/12–13   Recognisances taken and fines and penalties imposed by commissioners for ecclesiastical causes
E 159/451   King's remembrancer's memoranda roll, 1616
E 351/595–6   Receiver's accounts for ecclesiastical fines
E 368/450–595   Lord Treasurer's remembrancer's memoranda rolls, Elizabeth I–James I
E 401/1860–2311 Pells receipt books, Elizabeth I and James I
IND 17063–7   King's Remembrancer's agenda books, James I
SO 3/1–7   Signet Office docquet books, Elizabeth I–James I
SP 12   State Papers domestic, Elizabeth I
SP 14   State Papers domestic, James I
SP 16   State Papers domestic, Charles I
SP46/41–2   Exchequer correspondence
SP46/63   Letter of Benjamin Carier
SP77/8   Letter of Thomas Worthington
Stac. Proc. 5   Star Chamber cases, Elizabeth I
Stac. Proc. 8   Star Chamber cases, James I

THE QUEEN'S COLLEGE, OXFORD

MS 284   Conversion narrative of Sir John Warner

SAINT ALBAN'S COLLEGE, VALLADOLID

(transcriptions at Archives of Society of Jesus, Farm Street, London)
Series II, leg. 1–2   Letters of Robert Persons

SOCIETY OF JESUS, ARCHIVES, ROME

(transcriptions at Archives of Society of Jesus, Farm Street, London)
ARSJ, Angl. 31/I   Newsletter from England, 1603
ARSJ, Angl. 156/II   Instructions for members of the Society of Jesus living in
                     England

STONYHURST COLLEGE

Anglia I–VII   Jesuit letters and papers
Collectanea C   Transcriptions of Jesuit correspondence
Collectanea P I–II   Transcriptions of Jesuit correspondence

VATICAN ARCHIVES

(transcriptions at Archives of Society of Jesus, Farm Street, London)

Borghese Manuscript
III 43   Newsletter 1607

Nunziature Diversa
264   Robert Persons's answer to Charles Paget, 1598

WEST SUSSEX RECORD OFFICE, CHICHESTER

Diocese and Archdeaconry of Chichester
Ep. I/1/8   Episcopal register, 1596–1675
Ep. I/17/12   Detection book
Ep. II/9/11   Detection book

WESTMINSTER CATHEDRAL, ARCHIVES OF THE ARCHDIOCESE

A Series I–XXXII   Correspondence of the secular clergy and miscellanea
Anglia VIII–IX   Miscellanea
OB I–III   Archive of the Old Brotherhood of the English Secular
                     Clergy

PRINTED WORKS

PRIMARY SOURCES

Unless otherwise indicated the place of publication is London.

Abbot, George, *The Reasons which Doctour Hill hath Brought* (Oxford, 1604).

Abbot, Robert, *The Danger of Popery* (1625).

Abbot, Robert, *A Mirrour of Popish Subtilties* (1594).

Abernethie, Thomas, *Abjuration of Poperie* (Edinburgh, 1638).

Alabaster, William, *Apparatus in Revelationem Jesu Christi* (Antwerp, 1607).

Allen, William, *An Apologie and True Declaration of the Institution and Endevours of the two English Colleges* (Rheims, 1581).

    A True Report of the late Apprehension and Imprisonnement of John Nicols (Rheims, 1583).

Anderson, Patrick, *The Ground of the Catholike and Roman Religion* (St Omer, 1623).

Anderton, Lawrence, *The Triple Cord* (St Omer, 1634).

Andrewes, Lancelot, *Tortura Torti* (1609).

    XCVI Sermons (1629).

'Annual Letters of the Vice-Province of England' (for 1619), *Letters and Notices* 11 (1876–7), 273–88.

An Antiquodlibet (Middelburg, 1602).

Atkinson, J. C., *Quarter Sessions Records* (North Riding Record Society, 1–3, 1884–5).

Babington, Gervase, *Workes* (1615).

Baddeley, Richard, *The Boy of Bilson* (1622).

Bancroft, Richard, *A Survay of the Pretended Holy Discipline* (1593).

Barclay, William, *Of the Authoritie of the Pope* (1611).

Barlow, William, *An Answer to a Catholike English-Man* (1609).

Baxter, Richard, *Directions and Persuasions to a Sound Conversion* (1683).

Bedell, William, *The Copies of Certaine Letters* (1624).

Bedford, Thomas, *Luthers Predecessours* (1624).

Bell, Thomas, *The Anatomie of Popish Tyrannie* (1603).

    The Catholique Triumph (1610).

    A Christian Dialogue (1609).

    The Downefall of Poperie (1604).

    The Golden Ballance of Tryall (1603).

    The Jesuites Antepast (1608).

    The Survey of Popery (1596).

    Thomas Bels Motives (Cambridge, 1593).

Berington, Joseph (ed.), *The Memoirs of Gregorio Panzani* (Birmingham, 1793).

Birch, T. (ed.), *The Court and Times of Charles I* (2 vols., 1848).

    The Court and Times of James the First (2 vols, 1848).

Biondo, Giuseppe, *A Relation of the Death, of . . . Troilo Savelli* (St Omer, 1620).

Bolton, Robert, *Mr Boltons Last and Learned Worke of the Foure last Things* (1633).

Bradshaw, William, *Humble Motives* (n.p., 1601).

Bramhall, John, *Works* (Dublin, 1676).

Brereley, John (*vere* James Anderton), *The Apologie of the Romane Church* (n.p., 1604).

The Protestants Apologie for the Roman Church (St Omer, 1608).

Sainct Austines Religion (np, 1620).

Bristow, Richard, *A Briefe Treatise of diverse plaine and sure Wayes to finde out the Truthe* (Antwerp, 1574).

Demaundes to bee proponed of Catholickes to the Heretickes (Antwerp, 1576).

A Reply to Fulke (Louvain, 1580).

Broughton, Richard, *A Booke Intituled: The English Protestants Recantation* (Douai, 1617).

The First Part of Protestants Proofes (n.p., 1607).

Protestants Demonstrations (Douai, 1615).

Brousse, Jacques, *The Life of the Reverend Fa. Angel of Joyeuse* (Douai, 1623).

Browne, John, *A Discovery of the Notorious Proceedings of William Laud* (1641).

Bulkeley, Edward, *An Apologie for Religion* (1602).

Bunny, Edmund, *A Booke of Christian Exercise* (1585).

Bunny, Francis, *An Answere to a Popish Libell* (Oxford, 1607).

A Short Answer to the Reasons (1595).

Truth and Falshood (1595).

Campion, Edmund, *Campian Englished: Or a Translation of the Ten Reasons* (n.p., 1632).

Caraman, P. (ed.), *John Gerard* (1951).

William Weston (1955).

Cardwell, E. (ed.), *Documentary Annals* (2 vols., Oxford, 1839).

Carier, Benjamin, *A Copy of a Letter* (n.p., 1615).

A Treatise (Brussels, 1614).

Carleton, George, *Directions to Know the True Church* (1615).

trans. William Freake, *The Life of Bernard Gilpin* (1629).

Carter, Oliver, *An Answere* (1579).

Champney, Anthony, *A Manual of Controversies* (Paris, 1614).

Charnock, Robert, *A Reply to a Notorious Libell* (1603).

Cholmeley, Richard, 'The Memorandum Book of Richard Cholmeley of Brandsby 1602–1623', *North Yorkshire County Record Office Publications* 44 (1988).

Christie, R. C. (ed.), *Letters of Sir Thomas Copley* (1897).

Clarke, Anthony, *The Defence of the Honor of God* (Paris (imprint false, printed secretly in England), 1621).

Clarke, Samuel, *The Lives of Sundry Eminent Persons in this Later Age* (1683).

The Marrow of Ecclesiastical Historie (1650).

Clarke, Thomas, *The Recantation of Thomas Clarke* (1594).

Colleton, John, *A Supplication to the Kings most excellent Majestie* (n.p., 1604).

Cooke, Alexander, *Saint Austins Religion* (1625).

The Copies of certaine Discourses (Rouen (imprint false, printed in London), 1601).

Copley, Anthony, *Another Letter of Mr A. C. to his dis-jesuited Kinseman* (1602).

Copley, John, *Doctrinall and Morall Observations* (1612).

Cranfield, N., and Fincham, K. C. (eds.), 'John Howson's Answers . . . ', *Camden Miscellany* XXIX (Camden Society, fourth series, 34, 1987), 319–41.

Cressy, Hugh-Paulin de, *Exomologesis* (Paris, 1653).

Crompton, William, *Saint Austins Summes* (1625).

Cross, C. (ed.), *The Letters of Sir Francis Hastings, 1544–1609* (Frome, 1969).

Crowley, Robert, *An Aunswer to six Reasons, that Thomas Pownde . . . required to be aunswered* (1581).

A breefe Discourse, concerning those foure usuall Notes, whereby Christes Catholique Church is knowen (1581).

Denison, John, *The Sinne against the Holy Ghost Plainly Described* (1611).

Denison, Stephen, *A Compendious Catechisme* (1632).

The New Creature (1619).

Digby, Sir Kenelm, *A Conference* (Paris, 1638).

A Discourse (Amsterdam, 1652).

Dillingham, Francis, *A Disswasive from Poperie* (Cambridge, 1599).

Dodd, C., *The Church History of England* (3 vols., Brussels (imprint false, printed at Wolverhampton), 1737–42).

Dominis, Marc'Antonio de, ed. and transl. Thomas Goad, *A Declaration of the Reasons* (Edinburgh, 1617).

M. Antonius de Dominis Archbishop of Spalato, Declares the cause of his Returne (St Omer, 1623).

Marcus Antonius de Dominis . . . Suae Profectionis (1616).

Dove, John, *The Conversion of Salomon* (1613).

A Perswasion to the English Recusants (1603).

Edwards, F. (ed.), *The Elizabethan Jesuits* (1981).

Egerton, Stephen, *A Briefe Method of Catechizing* (1631).

Elton, Edward, *A Forme of Catechising* (1634).

Featley, Daniel, *Cygnea Cantio* (1629).

The Fisher Catched in his owne Net (1623).

Fenner, Dudley, *An Answere unto the Confutation of John Nichols his Recantation* (1583).

A Counter-Poyson (1584).

Field, John, *A Caveat for Parsons Howlet* (1581).

Finch, Richard, *The Knowledge or Appearance of the Church* (1590).

Fincham, K. C. (ed.), *Visitation Articles and Injunctions of the Early Stuart Church*, I (Church of England Record Society, Woodbridge, Suffolk, 1994).

Fisher, George, *The Bishop of London his Legacy* (St Omer, 1623).

Fitzherbert, Thomas, *A Defence of the Catholyke Cause* (Antwerp, 1602).

Floyd, John, *A Word of Comfort* (St Omer, 1623).

Frere, W. H. (ed.), *Pontifical Services* (4 vols., Alcuin Club Collections, 3–4, 8–12, 1901–8).

Fulke, William, *A briefe Confutation, of a Popish Discourse* (1581).

A Briefe and plaine Declaration (1584).

A Confutation of a Popishe and sclaunderous Libelle (1571).

A Retentive, to stay good Christians, in true Faith and Religion, against the Motives of Richard Bristow (1580).

A True Reporte of a Conference (1581).

Two Treatises (1577).

Gage, Thomas, *A New Survey* (1655).

The Tyranny of Satan (1642).

Gardiner, S. R. (ed.), *The Fortescue Papers* (Camden Society, second series, 1, 1871).

Garnet, Henry, *An Apology against the Defence of Schisme* (n.p., 1593).

A Treatise of Christian Renunciation (n.p., 1593).

Gee, Edward, *Two Sermons* (1620).

Gee, John, *The Foot out of the Snare* (fourth edition, 1624).

Hold Fast (1624).

Gennings, John, *The Life and Death of Mr Edmund Geninges* (St Omer, 1614).
Gifford, George, *A Briefe Discourse* (1598).
A Dialogue betweene a Papist and a Protestant (1599).
Goodcole, Henry, *A True Declaration of the happy Conversion, Contrition, and Christian Preparation of Francis Robinson* (1618).
Goodman, Godfrey, ed. J. S. Brewer, *The Court of King James the First* (2 vols., 1839).
Gordon, James, *A Summary of Controversies* (n.p., 1618).
Gouge, William, *A Recovery from Apostacy* (1639).
A Short Catechisme (1631).
Greenham, Richard, ed. Henry Holland, *Workes* (second edition, 1599).
Gregorio XIII Pont. Max. Pontificale Romanum ad Omnes Pontificias Caeremonias, quibus nunc utitur sacrosancta R. E. accommodatum (Venice, 1582).
Hacket, John, *Scrinia Reserata* (1693).
Hakewill, George *An Answere to a Treatise Written by Dr Carier* (1616).
Hall, Joseph, *The Olde Religion* (1628).
The Works of Joseph Hall (1634).
Harding, John, *A Recantation Sermon* (1620).
Harington, Sir John, *A Briefe View of the State of the Church of England* (1653).
Harrison, William, *Deaths Advantage Little Regarded* (1612).
The Difference of Hearers (1614).
Harsnet, Samuel, *A Declaration of egregious Popish Impostures* (1603).
Hastings, Sir Francis, *An Apologie or Defence of the Watch-word* (1600).
A Watch-Word (1598).
Hide, Thomas, *A Consolatorie Epistle* (Louvain (imprint false, printed at East Ham), 1580).
Higgons, Theophilus, *The Apology of Theophilus Higgons lately Minister, now Catholique* (Rouen, 1609).
A Briefe Consideration of Mans Iniquitie, and Gods Justice (1608).
The First Motive of T. H. Maister of Arts, and lately Minister, to suspect the Integrity of his Religion (Douai, 1609).
Mystical Babylon (1624).
A Sermon preached at Pauls Crosse (1611).
Try before you Trust (Douai, 1609).
Hinde, William, *A Faithfull Remonstrance* (1641).
Hoby, Sir Edward, *A Letter to Mr T. H. Late Minister* (1609).
Howell, James (ed.), *Cottoni Posthuma* (1651).
Hughes, P. L., and Larkin, J. F., *Tudor Royal Proclamations* (2 vols., New Haven, 1964, 1969).
Hungerford, Anthony, *The Advise* (1639).
Hutton, Luke, *Luke Huttons Lamentation* (1596).
Jansson, M. (ed.), *Proceedings in Parliament 1614* (Philadelphia, 1988).
Jones, T. W. (ed.), *A True Relation of the Life and Death of William Bedell* (Camden Society, second series, 4, 1872).
Keepe your Text (n.p., 1619).
Kellet, Edward, *A Returne from Argier* (1628).
Kellison, Matthew *A Survey of the New Religion* (Douai, 1605).
Keltridge, John, *Two Godlie and learned Sermons* (1581).
Kennedy, W. P. M. (ed.), *Elizabethan Episcopal Administration* (3 vols., Alcuin Club, 25–7, 1924).

Kilby, Richard, *The Burthen of a loaden Conscience* (Cambridge, 1616).

Kilby, Richard, *A Sermon* (Oxford, 1613).

Kingdon, R. M. (ed.), *The Execution of Justice* (New York, 1965).

Knewstub, John, *An Aunsweare unto certaine Assertions, tending to maintaine the Church of Rome to bee the true and Catholique Church* (1579).

Knox, T. F. (ed.), *The First and Second Diaries of the English College, Douay* (1878).

The Letters and Memorials of William Cardinal Allen (1882).

Lake, Arthur, *Sermons* (1629).

A Large Examination . . . of M. George Blakwell (1607).

Laud, William, ed. J. Bliss and W. Scott, *Works* (7 vols., Oxford, 1847–60).

Law, T. G., *The Archpriest Controversy* (2 vols., Camden Society, second series, 56, 58, 1896, 1898).

Leech, Humphrey, *Dutifull and Respective Considerations* (St Omer, 1609).

A Triumph of Truth (Douai, 1609).

The Life, Confession and Heartie Repentance of Francis Cartwright (1621).

Lister, J. (ed.), *West Riding Sessions Rolls 1597/8–1602* (Yorkshire Archaeological and Topographical Association, Record Series, 3, 1888).

Longstaffe, W. H. D. (ed.), *The Acts of the High Commission Court within the Diocese of Durham* (Surtees Society, 34, 1858).

McClure, N. (ed.), *The Letters of John Chamberlain* (2 vols., Philadelphia, 1939).

Martin, Gregory, *A Treatise of Schisme* (Douai (imprint false, printed in London), 1578).

Mathew, A. H. (ed.), *A True Historical Relation of the Conversion of Sir Tobie Matthew* (1904).

Mathew jnr, Tobias, *The Confessions* (St Omer, 1620).

Meads, D. M. (ed.), *Diary of Lady Margaret Hoby* (1930).

Meredyth, John, *The Sinne of Blasphemie* (1622).

Montagu, Richard, *Appello Caesarem* (1625).

Mornay, Philippe de, *A Notable Treatise of the Church* (1579).

Morris, J. (ed.), *The Troubles of our Catholic Forefathers* (3 vols., 1872–7).

Morton, Thomas, *A Catholike Appeale* (1609).

A Direct Answer unto the Scandalous Exceptions, which Theophilus Higgons hath lately objected against D. Morton (1609).

Munday, Anthony, *A breefe Aunswer made unto two seditious Pamphlets* (1582).

Musgrave, Christopher, *Musgraves Motives* (1621).

N. N., *An Epistle of a Catholike Young Gentleman* (Douai (imprint false, printed secretly in England), 1623).

O. N., *An Apology of English Arminianisme* (St Omer, 1634).

Neile, Richard, *M. Ant. de Dnis. Archbishop of Spalato, his Shiftings in Religion* (1624).

Newman, J. H., ed. I. T. Ker, *An Essay in Aid of a Grammar of Assent* (Oxford, 1985).

Nichols, John, *A Declaration of the Recantation of John Nichols* (1581).

Nichols, Josias, *The Plea of the Innocent* (n.p., 1602).

Norris, Sylvester, *An Appendix to the Antidote* (St Omer, 1621).

The Guide of Faith (St Omer, 1621).

A True Report of the Private Colloquy betweene M. Smith, aliâs Norrice, and M. Walker (St Omer, 1624).

Notestein, W., Relf, F. H., and Simpson, H. (eds.), *Commons Debates 1621* (7 vols., New Haven, 1935).

O'Byrne, E. (ed.), *The Convert Rolls* (Dublin, 1981).

Ormerod, Oliver, *The Picture of a Papist* (1606).

Ornsby, G. (ed.), *The Correspondence of John Cosin* (2 vols., Surtees Society, 52, 55, 1868, 1872).

Owen, Lewis, *The Running Register* (1626).

Peck, F., *Desiderata Curiosa* (2 vols., 1779).

Peel, A. (ed.), *The Seconde Parte of a Register* (2 vols., Cambridge, 1915).

Penry, John, *An Humble Motion* (n.p., 1590).

Percy, John, *A Catalogue of divers visible Professors* (St Omer, 1614).

　　A Reply made unto Mr Anthony Wotton and Mr John White (St Omer, 1612).

　　A Treatise of Faith (n.p., 1605).

　　A Treatise of Faith (St Omer, 1614).

Perkins, William, *The Foundation of Christian Religion* (1633).

　　A Reformed Catholike (Cambridge, 1598).

Persons, Robert, *An Answere to the Fifth Part of Reportes* (St Omer, 1606).

　　A Briefe Apologie (Antwerp, 1601).

　　A Briefe Censure (n.p., 1581).

　　A Christian Directorie Guiding Men to their Salvation (Rouen, 1585).

　　A Defence of the Censure (Rouen, 1582).

　　A Discoverie of J. Nichols (1581).

　　An Epistle of the Persecution (Rouen, 1582).

　　The First Booke of the Christian Exercise (Rouen, 1582).

　　ed. E. Gee, *The Jesuit's Memorial, for the Intended Reformation of England* (1690).

　　The Judgment of a Catholicke English-Man (St Omer, 1608).

　　A Manifestation (Antwerp, 1602).

　　'Of the Life and Martyrdom of Father Edmond Campian', *Letters and Notices* 11 (1876–7), 219–42, 308–39, and 12 (1878), 1–68.

　　A Review of Ten Publike Disputations (St Omer, 1604).

　　A Temperate Ward-Word (Antwerp, 1599).

　　A Treatise of Three Conversions (3 vols., n.p., 1603–4).

　　The Warn-word (Antwerp, 1602).

Pickford, John, *The Safegarde from Ship-wracke* (Douai, 1618).

Platus, Jerome, *The Happines of a Religious State* (Rouen, 1632).

Pontificale Romanum Clementis VIII. Pont. Max. Iussu Restitutum Atque Editum (Rome, 1595).

Powel, Gabriel, *The Catholikes Supplication* (1603).

　　A Refutation of an Epistle Apologeticall (1605).

Preston, Thomas, *Apologia Cardinalis Bellarmini* (1611).

Price, Daniel, *The Defence of Truth* (Oxford, 1610).

　　Recusants Conversion (Oxford, 1608).

Prynne, William, *The Popish Royall Favourite* (1643).

Racster, John, *A Booke of the Seven Planets* (1598).

Raine, J. (ed.), *The Correspondence of Dr Matthew Hutton* (Surtees Society, 17, 1843).

Rainolds, John, *The Summe of the Conference* (1584).

Rainolds, William, *A Refutation of Sundry Reprehensions* (Paris, 1583).

Ramsay, Andrew, *A Warning to Come out of Babylon* (Edinburgh, 1638).

The Recantations as they were severallie pronounced by Wylliam Tedder and Anthony Tyrrell (1588).

Roberts, George (ed.), *Diary of Walter Yonge* (Camden Society, first series, 41, 1848).

Rogers, Timothy, *The Roman-Catharist* (1621).

Sacharles, John Nicholas y, *The Reformed Spaniard* (1623).

Salkeld, John, *A Treatise of Angels* (1613).

Sander, Nicholas, *Doctissimi Viri Nicolai Sanderi, de Origine ac Progressu Schismatis Anglicani, Liber* (Rheims,1585).

Savage, Francis, *A Conference betwixt a Mother a devout Recusant, and her Sonne a zealous Protestant* (Cambridge, 1600).

Sawyer, E., (ed.), *Memorials of Affairs of State* (3 vols., 1725).

Sharpe, James, *The Triall of the Protestant Private Spirit* (St Omer, 1630).

Sheldon, Richard, *Certain General Reasons, proving the Lawfulnesse of the Oath of Allegiance* (1611).

Christ, on his Throne (1622).

The First Sermon of R. Sheldon Priest, after his Conversion from the Romish Church (1612).

The Motives of Richard Sheldon Pr. (1612).

A Sermon Preached At Pauls Crosse (1625).

A Survey of the Miracles of the Church of Rome, proving them to be Antichristian (1616).

Sibbes, Richard, ed. A. B. Grosart, *The Complete Works of Richard Sibbes* (7 vols., Edinburgh, 1862–4).

Simpson, R. (ed.), *The Lady Falkland* (1861).

Smith, A. Hassell, and Baker, G. M. (eds.), *The Papers of Nathaniel Bacon of Stiffkey* (2 vols., Norwich, 1979, 1983).

Smith, L. P. (ed.), *The Life and Letters of Sir Henry Wotton* (2 vols., Oxford, 1907).

Smith, Richard, *An Answer to Thomas Bels late Challeng* (Douai, 1605).

Of the Author and Substance of the Protestant Church and Religion (St Omer, 1621).

A Conference of the Catholike and Protestant Doctrine with the expresse words of Holie Scripture (Douai, 1631).

The Prudentiall Ballance of Religion (St Omer, 1609).

Smith, Samuel, *The Admirable Convert* (1632).

Sorlien, R. P. (ed.), *The Diary of John Manningham* (Hanover, New Hampshire, 1976).

Spedding, J., Ellis, R. L. and Heath, D. D. (eds.), *The Works of Francis Bacon* (14 vols., 1858–74).

The Statutes of the Realm (11 vols., 1810–28).

Story, G. M. and Gardner, H. (eds.), *The Sonnets of William Alabaster* (1959).

Sutcliffe, Matthew, *The Examination and Confutation of a certain scurrilous Treatise entituled, The Survey of the newe Religion* (1606).

The Subversion of Robert Parsons (1606).

The Unmasking of a Masse-monger (1626).

Sweet, John, *Monsigr Fate Voi* (St Omer, 1617).

Swynnerton, John, *A Christian Love-Letter* (1606).

Tait, J. (ed.), *Lancashire Quarter Session Records* (Chetham Society, new series, 77, Manchester 1917).

Texeda, Ferdinand, *Scrutamini Scripturas* (1624).
  Texeda Retextus (1623).
Thornborough, John, *A Discourse* (1604).
  The Joiefull and Blessed Reuniting (Oxford, 1605).
Traske, John, *The Power of Preaching* (1623).
'Two Sermons, hitherto unpublished, of Dr Tobie Mathew, when Dean of Durham in 1591, afterwards Archbishop of York', *Christian Observer* (1847), 603–18, 664–75, 722–34, 776–90.
Tyrrell, Anthony, *A Fruitfull Sermon* (1589).
Ussher, James, *A Briefe Declaration of the Universalitie of the Church of Christ* (1624).
Vane, Thomas, *A Lost Sheep Returned Home* (Paris, 1649).
C. W., *A Summarie of Controversies* (n.p., 1616).
Wadsworth jnr, James, *The English Spanish Pilgrime* (1629).
Wadsworth snr, James, *The Contrition of a Protestant Preacher* (St Omer, 1615).
Walker, George, *Fishers Folly Unfolded* (1624).
  The Summe of a Disputation (1624).
Walsingham, Francis, *A Search Made into Matters of Religion* (St Omer, 1609).
  A Search Made into Matters of Religion (second edition, St Omer, 1615).
Walton, Izaak, *Reliquiae Wottoniae* (1685).
Watson, William, *A Decacordon of Ten Quodlibeticall Questions* (1602).
Webbe, George, *Catalogus Protestantium* (1624).
Weston, Edward, *The Repaire of Honour* (Bruges (imprint false, printed at St Omer), 1624).
  The Trial of Christian Truth (Douai, 1614).
Whately, William, *The New Birth* (1618).
White, John, *A Defence of the Way to the True Church* (1614).
  The Way to the True Church (1616).
Wilkins, D., *Concilia* (4 vols., 1733–7).
Willet, Andrew, *An Antilogie or Counterplea* (1603).
  Synopsis Papismi (1600).
  A Treatise of Salomons Marriage (1612).
Woodcock, Richard, *A Godly and Learned Answer* (1608).
Woodward, Philip, *Bels Trial Examined* (Rouen (imprint false, printed at Douai), 1608).
  The Dolefull Knell, of Thomas Bell (Rouen (imprint false, printed at Douai), 1607).
Worthington, Thomas, *An Anker of Christian Doctrine* (Douai, 1622).
  A Relation of Sixtene Martyrs (Douai, 1601).
  Whyte Dyed Black (n.p., 1615).
Wotton, Anthony, *Runne from Rome* (1624).
  A Trial of the Romish Clergies Title to the Church (1608).
Wright, Thomas, *Certaine Articles or Forcible Reasons* (Antwerp, (imprint false, printed secretly in England), 1600).
Wright, William, *A Discovery of Certaine Notorious Shifts, Evasions, and Untruthes uttered by M. John White Minister* (St Omer, 1614).
  A Treatise of the Church (St Omer, 1616).
Yaxley, Henry, *Morbus et Antidotus* (1630).

SECONDARY SOURCES

Albion, G., *Charles I and the Court of Rome* (Louvain, 1935).

Allison, A. F., 'The Writings of Fr Henry Garnet, SJ (1555–1606)', *Biographical Studies* 1 (1951–2), 7–21.

Anstruther, G., 'A Missing Martyr Pamphlet', *London Recusant* 5 (1975), 67–74.

Armogathe, J.-R., 'De l'Art de Penser comme Art de Persuader', in *La Conversion au XVIIᵉ Siècle* (Centre Méridional de Rencontres sur le XVIIᵉ Siècle, Marseille, 1982), 29–41.

Armstrong, B. G., *Calvinism and the Amyraut Heresy* (Madison, 1969).

Aveling, J. C. H., *Catholic Recusancy in the City of York 1558–1791* (CRS monograph 2, 1970).

'The Catholic Recusancy of the Yorkshire Fairfaxes', part I, *RH* 3 (1954–6), 69–114.

The Catholic Recusants of the West Riding of Yorkshire 1558–1790 (Proceedings of the Leeds Philosophical and Literary Society, Literary and Historical Section, 10, part VI, Leeds, 1963).

'The English Clergy, Catholic and Protestant, in the 16th and 17th Centuries', in J. C. H. Aveling, D. M. Loades, H. R. McAdoo and W. Haase, *Rome and the Anglicans* (Berlin, 1982).

The Handle and the Axe (1976).

Northern Catholics (1966).

Post-Reformation Catholicism in East Yorkshire 1558–1790 (York, 1960).

'Some Cases Pertaining to England', in G. T. Bradley (ed.), *Yorkshire Catholics* (Leeds Diocesan Archives Occasional Publications no. 1, Darlington, 1985), 15–25.

Axon, E., 'The King's Preachers in Lancashire, 1599–1845', *Transactions of the Lancashire and Cheshire Antiquarian Society* 66 (1944), 67–104.

Aylmer, G. E., *The King's Servants* (1974).

Bailey, J. E., 'Thomas Bell', *Notes and Queries*, sixth series, 2 (1880), 429–31.

Baillie, J., *Baptism and Conversion* (1964).

Bald, R. C., *John Donne* (Oxford, 1970).

Beales, A. C. F., *Education under Penalty* (1963).

Bell, H. E., *Introduction to the History and Records of the Court of Wards and Liveries* (Cambridge, 1951).

Bellenger, D. A., *English and Welsh Priests 1558–1800* (Bath, 1984).

Benedict, P., *Rouen during the Wars of Religion* (Cambridge, 1981).

Bernos, M., 'Confession et Conversion', in *La Conversion au XVIIᵉ Siècle* (Centre Méridional de Rencontres sur le XVIIᵉ Siècle, Marseille, 1982), 283–93.

Berry, William, *County Genealogies . . . of Sussex* (1830).

Boddy, G. W., 'Players of Interludes in North Yorkshire in the Early Seventeenth Century', *North Yorkshire County Record Office Journal* 3 (1976), 95–130.

Booty, J. E., *John Jewel as Apologist of the Church of England* (1963).

Bossy, J., 'A Propos of Henry Constable', *RH* 6 (1961–2), 228–37.

The English Catholic Community 1570–1850 (1975).

Bowler, H., 'Sir Henry James of Smarden, Kent, and Clerkenwell, Recusant (*c.* 1559–1625)', in A. E. J. Hollaender and W. Kellaway (eds.), *Studies in London History* (1969), 289–313.

Brandon, O., *Christianity from Within* (1965).

Breen, Q., 'John Calvin and the Rhetorical Tradition', *Church History* 26 (1957), 3–21.

Burke, V., 'Submissions of Conformity by Elizabethan Recusants', *Worcestershire Recusant* 21 (1973), 1–7.

Camm, B., 'An Apostate at St Omers, 1618–1622', *The Month* 94 (1899), 163–70.
The Lives of the English Martyrs (2 vols., 1904–5).

Caro, R. V., 'William Alabaster: Rhetor, Meditator, Devotional Poet', *RH* 19 (1988), 62–79, 155–70.

A Catholic Dictionary of Theology (3 vols., 1962–71).

Citron, B., *New Birth* (Edinburgh, 1951).

Clancy, T. H., 'Papist–Protestant–Puritan: English Religious Taxonomy 1565–1665', *RH* 13 (1975–6), 227–53.
'Priestly Perseverance in the Old Society of Jesus: the Case of England', *RH* 19 (1988–9), 286–312.

Clark, P., 'The Ecclesiastical Commission at Canterbury: 1572–1603', *Archaeologia Cantiana* 89 (1974), 183–97.

Clarke, D. M., 'Conformity Certificates among the King's Bench Records: A Calendar', *RH* 14 (1977–8), 53–63.

Clay, C., 'The Misfortunes of William, Fourth Lord Petre (1638–1655)', *RH* 11 (1971–2), 87–116.

Cliffe, J. T., *The Yorkshire Gentry from the Reformation to the Civil War* (1969).

Clifton, R., 'Fear of Popery', in C. Russell (ed.), *The Origins of the English Civil War* (1973), 144–67.

Cockburn, J. (ed.), *Calendar of Assize Records: Essex Indictments: Elizabeth I* (1978).
Calendar of Assize Records: Surrey Indictments: James I (1982).
Calendar of Assize Records: Sussex Indictments: James I (1975).

Cohen, C. L., *God's Caress* (New York, 1986).
'Two Biblical Models of Conversion: An Example of Puritan Hermeneutics', *Church History* 57 (1988), 182–96.

Collinson, P., *The Elizabethan Puritan Movement* (Oxford, 1967).
A Mirror of Elizabethan Puritanism: The Life and Letters of 'Godly Master Dering', Friends of Dr Williams's Library Seventeenth Lecture 1963 (1964).
The Religion of Protestants (Oxford, 1982).

Cooper, C. H., and Cooper, J. W., *Annals of Cambridge* (5 vols., Cambridge, 1842–1908).

Curtis, M. H., 'The Alienated Intellectuals of Early Stuart England', *P&P* 23 (1962), 25–43.
'The Trials of a Puritan in Jacobean Lancashire', in C. R. Cole and M. E. Moody (eds.), *The Dissenting Tradition* (Ohio, 1975), 78–99.

Davidson, A., 'The Recusancy of Ralph Sheldon', *Worcestershire Recusant* 12 (1968), 1–7.

Dent, C., *Protestant Reformers in Elizabethan Oxford* (Oxford, 1983).

Devlin, C., 'An Unwilling Apostate: The Case of Anthony Tyrrell', *The Month* new series 6 (1951), 346–58.

Dickerman, E. H., 'The Conversion of Henry IV: "Paris is well worth a Mass" in Psychological Perspective', *Catholic Historical Review* 63 (1977), 1–13.

Dodaro, R., and Questier, M. C., 'Strategies in Jacobean Polemic: The Use and Abuse of St Augustine in English Theological Controversy', *JEH* 44 (1993), 432–49.

Donagan, B., 'The York House Conference Revisited: Laymen, Calvinism and Arminianism', *HR* 64 (1991), 312–30.

Dumonceux, P., 'Conversion, Convertir, Etude Comparative d'après les Lexicographes du XVIIᵉ Siècle', in *La Conversion au XVIIᵉ Siècle* (Centre Méridional de Rencontres sur le XVIIᵉ Siècle, Marseille, 1982), 7–15.

Dures, A., *English Catholicism 1558–1642* (1983).

Ellul, J., *Propaganda* (New York, 1969).

Emery, K., *Renaissance Dialectic and Renaissance Piety* (New York, 1987).

Fincham, K. C., *Prelate as Pastor* (Oxford, 1990).

Fincham, K. C. and Lake, P., 'The Ecclesiastical Policy of King James I', *Journal of British Studies* 24 (1985), 170–206.

Flynn, D., 'Donne's Catholicism', *RH* 13 (1975–6), 1–17, 178–95.

'Irony in Donne's *Biathanatos* and *Pseudo-Martyr*', *RH* 12 (1973–4), 49–69.

Foster, C. W., *The State of the Church in the Reigns of Elizabeth and James I, as Illustrated by Documents Relating to the Diocese of Lincoln*, I (Lincoln Record Society 23, 1926).

Foster, J., *Alumni Oxonienses: The Members of the University of Oxford, 1500–1714* (4 vols., 1891–2).

Foster, M., 'Thomas Allen of Gloucester Hall, Oxford (1540–1632)', *Oxoniensia* 46 (1981), 99–128.

Galloway, G., *The Union of England and Scotland, 1603–1608* (Edinburgh, 1986).

Gerard, J., 'Contributions towards a Life of Father Henry Garnet SJ', part IV, *The Month* 91 (1898).

Goodwine, J. G., *The Reception of Converts* (Canon Law Studies no. 198, Washington, 1944).

Green, I., 'Career Prospects and Clerical Conformity in the Early Stuart Church', *P&P* 90 (1981), 71–115.

' "For Children in Yeeres and Children in Understanding": The Emergence of the English Catechism under Elizabeth and the Early Stuarts', *JEH* 37 (1986), 397–425.

Guibert, J. de, *The Jesuits: Their Spiritual Doctrine and Practice* (St Louis, 1972).

Haigh, C., 'The Church of England, the Catholics and the People', in C. Haigh (ed.), *The Reign of Elizabeth I* (1984), 195–219.

'The Continuity of Catholicism in the English Reformation', *P&P* 93 (1981), 37–69.

'The Fall of a Church or the Rise of a Sect? Post-Reformation Catholicism in England', *HJ* 21 (1978), 182–6.

'From Monopoly to Minority: Catholicism in Early Modern England', *TRHS*, fifth series, 31 (1981), 129–47.

'Puritan Evangelism in the Reign of Elizabeth I', *EHR* 92 (1977), 30–58.

Reformation and Resistance in Tudor Lancashire (Cambridge, 1975).

Hambrick-Stowe, C. E., *The Practice of Piety* (North Carolina, 1982).

Harran, M. J., *Luther on Conversion* (1983).

Hasler, P. W. (ed.), *The House of Commons 1558–1603* (3 vols., 1981).

Havran, M. J., *Caroline Courtier* (1973).

Hawkins, M. J., 'The Government: Its Role and its Aims', in C. Russell (ed.), *The Origins of the English Civil War* (1973), 35–65.

Hibbard, C. M., *Charles I and the Popish Plot* (North Carolina, 1983).

Hill, L. M., *Bench and Bureaucracy* (Cambridge, 1988).

Hogan, E. (ed.), *Words of Comfort* (Dublin, 1881).

Holmes, P. J., *Resistance and Compromise* (Cambridge, 1982).

Houliston, V., 'Why Robert Persons would not be Pacified', in T. M. McCoog and J. A. Munitiz (eds.), *The Reckoned Expense: Edmund Campion and the Early English Jesuits* (1996).

Howard, C., *Sir John Yorke of Nidderdale* (1939).

Howell, T. B., and Howell, T. J. (eds.), *A Complete Collection of State Trials* (34 vols., 1816–28).

Howell, W. S., *Logic and Rhetoric in England, 1500–1700* (New York, 1956).

Hughes, P., *Theology of the English Reformers* (1965).

Ingram, M., *Church Courts, Sex and Marriage in England, 1570–1640* (Cambridge, 1987).

Jessopp, A., 'Bowthorpe Hall', *Norfolk Archaeology* 8 (1879), 273–81.

Kendall, R., 'Richard Baines and Christopher Marlowe's Milieu', *English Literary Renaissance* 24 (1994), 507–52.

Kendall, R. T., *Calvin and English Calvinism to 1649* (Oxford, 1979).

Kenny, A., 'A Martyr Manqué: The Early Life of Anthony Tyrrell', *Clergy Review* 42 (1957), 651–8.

Knafla, L. A., *Law and Politics in Jacobean England* (Cambridge, 1977).

Kopperman, P., *Sir Robert Heath* (Woodbridge, Suffolk, 1989).

Kuriyama, C. B., 'Marlowe's Nemesis: The Identity of Richard Baines', in K. Friedenreich *et al.* (eds.), *'A Poet and Filthy Play-Maker': New Essays on Christopher Marlowe* (New York, 1988), 343–60.

Labrousse, E., 'Conversion dans les Deux Sens', in *La Conversion au XVIIᵉ Siècle* (Centre Méridional de Rencontres sur le XVIIᵉ Siècle, Marseille, 1982), 161–72.

Lake, P., 'Anti-popery: The Structure of a Prejudice', in R. Cust and A. Hughes (eds.), *Conflict in Early Stuart England* (1989), 72–106.

'Calvinism and the English Church, 1570–1635', *P&P* 114 (1987), 32–76.

'Matthew Hutton: a Puritan Bishop?', *History* 64 (1979), 182–204.

Moderate Puritans and the Elizabethan Church (Cambridge, 1982).

'Richard Kilby: A Study in Personal Failure', in W. J. Sheils and D. Wood (eds.), *The Ministry: Clerical and Lay* (Studies in Church History 26, Oxford, 1989), 221–35.

'The Significance of the Elizabethan Identification of the Pope as Antichrist', *JEH* 31 (1980), 161–78.

Lake, P. and Questier, M. C., 'Agency, Appropriation and Rhetoric under the Gallows: Puritans, Romanists and the State in Early Modern England' (forthcoming in *P&P*).

La Rocca, J. J., 'James I and his Catholic Subjects, 1606–1612: Some Financial Implications', *RH* 18 (1987), 251–62.

Loomie, A. J., 'Religion and Elizabethan Commerce with Spain', *Catholic Historical Review* 50 (1964–5), 27–51.

Luna, B. N. de, *Jonson's Romish Plot* (Oxford, 1967).

MacCulloch, D., 'The Impact of the English Reformation', *HJ* 38 (1995), 151–3.

MacDougall, H. A., *Racial Myth in English History* (Hanover, New Hampshire, 1982).

McGee, J. S., 'Conversion and the Imitation of Christ in Anglican and Puritan Writing', *JBS* 15 (1976), 21–39.

The Godly Man in Stuart England (1976).

McGrath, A., *Iustitia Dei* (2 vols., Cambridge, 1986).

The Intellectual Origins of the European Reformation (Oxford, 1987).

Maclure, M., *The Paul's Cross Sermons, 1534–1642* (Toronto, 1958).

Malcolm, N., *De Dominis (1560–1624)* (1984).

Manning, R. B., 'Catholics and Local Office Holding in Elizabethan Sussex', *BIHR* 35 (1962), 47–61.

'Elizabethan Recusancy Commissions', *HJ* 15 (1972), 23–36.

'The Making of a Protestant Aristocracy: The Ecclesiastical Commissioners of the Diocese of Chester, 1550–98', *BIHR* 49 (1976), 60–79.

Religion and Society in Elizabethan Sussex (Leicester, 1969).

Marchant, R. A., *The Church under the Law* (Cambridge, 1969).

Martin, A. Lynn, *The Jesuit Mind* (Ithaca, 1988).

Milton, A., *Catholic and Reformed* (Cambridge, 1995).

'The Church of England, Rome, and the True Church: The Demise of a Jacobean Consensus', in K. C. Fincham (ed.), *The Early Stuart Church, 1603–1642* (1993), 187–210.

Milward, P., *Religious Controversies of the Elizabethan Age* (1977).

Religious Controversies of the Jacobean Age (1978).

Moir, T. L., *The Addled Parliament of 1614* (Oxford, 1958).

Morgan, J., *Godly Learning* (Cambridge, 1986).

Neale, J. E., *Elizabeth I and her Parliaments* (2 vols., 1953, 1957).

New Catholic Encyclopaedia (17 vols., Washington, 1967–78).

Nicholls, M., *Investigating Gunpowder Plot* (Manchester, 1991).

Notestein, W., *The House of Commons 1604–1610* (1971).

Nugent, D., *Ecumenism in the Age of the Reformation* (Cambridge, Massachusetts, 1974).

O'Malley, J. W., *The First Jesuits* (Cambridge, Massachusetts, 1993).

Orr, R. R., *Reason and Authority* (Oxford, 1967).

Pattison, M., *Isaac Casaubon* (1875).

Peters, R., 'Some Catholic Opinions of King James VI and I', *RH* 10 (1968–9), 292–303.

Pettit, N., *The Heart Prepared* (New Haven, 1966).

Pollen, J. H., *Acts of English Martyrs* (1891).

The Institution of the Archpriest Blackwell (1916).

'Recent Studies on Elizabethan Catholic History', *The Month* 117 (1911), 337–51.

Price, F. D., 'The Abuses of Excommunication and the Decline of Ecclesiastical Discipline under Queen Elizabeth', *EHR* 57 (1942), 106–15.

Pritchard, A., *Catholic Loyalism in Elizabethan England* (1979).

Pugh, F. H., 'Glamorgan Recusants 1577–1611: A Selection from the Returns in the Public Record Office', *South Wales and Monmouth Record Society* 3 (1954), 49–72.

'Monmouthshire Recusants in the Reigns of Elizabeth I and James I', *South Wales and Monmouth Record Society* 4 (1957), 59–110.

Purvis, J. S. (ed.), *Tudor Parish Documents of the Diocese of York* (Cambridge, 1948).

Questier, M. C., 'Crypto-Catholicism, Anti-Calvinism and Conversion at the Jacobean Court: The Enigma of Benjamin Carier', *JEH* 47 (1996), 45–64.

'John Gee, Archbishop Abbot, and the Use of Converts from Rome in Jacobean Anti-Catholicism', *RH* 24 (1993), 347–60.

'Loyalty, Religion and State Power in Early Modern England: English Romanism and the Jacobean Oath of Allegiance' (forthcoming in *HJ*).

'Sir Henry Spiller, Recusancy and the Efficiency of the Jacobean Exchequer', *HR* 66 (1993), 251–66.

Rea, W. F., 'The Authorship of "News from Spayne and Holland" and its Bearing on the Genuineness of the Confessions of the Blessed Henry Walpole, SJ', *Biographical Studies* 1 (1951–2), 220–30.

Richardson, A., and Bowden, J. (eds.), *The Westminster Dictionary of Christian Theology* (Philadelphia, 1983).

Richardson, R. C., *Puritanism in north-west England* (Manchester, 1972).

Rohr, J. von, 'Covenant and Assurance in Early English Puritanism', *Church History* 34 (1965), 195–203.

The Covenant of Grace in Puritan Thought (Atlanta, Georgia, 1986).

Rose, E. E., *Cases of Conscience* (Cambridge, 1975).

Rowlands, M. B., 'Recusant Women 1560–1640', in M. Prior (ed.), *Women in English Society 1580–1800* (1985), 149–80.

Russell, C., *Parliaments and English Politics 1621–1629* (Oxford, 1979).

'The Parliamentary Career of John Pym, 1621–1629', in C. Russell, *Unrevolutionary England, 1603–1642* (1990), 205–28.

Ryan, C. J., 'The Jacobean Oath of Allegiance and English Lay Catholics', *Catholic Historical Review* 28 (1942), 159–83.

Ryan, G. H., and Redstone, L. J., *Timperley of Hintlesham* (1931).

Sanctis, S. de, *Religious Conversion* (1927).

Scarisbrick, J. J., 'Cardinal Wolsey and the Common Weal', in E. W. Ives, R. J. Knecht and J. J. Scarisbrick (eds.), *Wealth and Power in Tudor England* (1978), 45–67.

Seaver, P., *The Puritan Lectureships* (Stanford, California, 1970).

Shanahan, D., 'The Family of St Thomas More in Essex 1581–1640', *Essex Recusant* 3 (1961), 71–80.

Sharpe, J., ' "Last Dying Speeches": Religion, Ideology and Public Execution in Seventeenth–Century England', *P&P* 107 (1985), 144–67.

Simpson, R., *Edmund Campion* (1896).

Skinner, Q., 'The Principles and Practice of Opposition: The Case of Bolingbroke versus Walpole' in N. McKendrick (ed.), *Historical Perspectives* (1974), 93–128.

Solé, J., *Le Débat entre Protestants et Catholiques Français de 1598 à 1685* (4 vols., Lille, 1985).

Stebbing, L. S., *A Modern Introduction to Logic* (New York, 1961).

Stroud, T. A., 'Father Thomas Wright: A Test Case for Toleration', *Biographical Studies* 1 (1951–2), 189–219.

Strudwick, B., 'The Darells of Calehill', *Kent Recusant History* 4 (1980), 89–99.

Strype, John, *Annals of the Reformation* (4 vols., Oxford, 1824).

The Life and Acts of John Whitgift (3 vols., Oxford, 1822).

Tavard, G. H., *Holy Writ or Holy Church* (1959).

Tighe, W. J., 'Herbert Croft's Repulse', *BIHR* 58 (1985), 106–9.

Tyacke, N., *Anti-Calvinists* (Oxford, 1990).

Urquhart, M. J., 'A Sussex Recusant Family', *Dublin Review* 512 (1967), 162–70.

Wadkins, T. H., 'The Percy-"Fisher" Controversies and the Ecclesiastical Politics of Jacobean Anti-Catholicism, 1622–1625', *Church History* 57 (1988), 153–69.

Walker, D. P., *Unclean Spirits* (1981).

Wallace, D. D., 'Puritan and Anglican: The Interpretation of Christ's Descent into Hell in Elizabethan Theology', *Archiv für Reformationsgeschichte* 69 (1978), 248–86.

Puritans and Predestination (North Carolina, 1982).

Walsham, A., *Church Papists* (1993).

Wark, K. R., *Elizabethan Recusancy in Cheshire* (Manchester, 1971).

Watkins, O. C., *The Puritan Experience* (1972).

Watts, S. J., *From Border to Middle Shire: Northumberland 1586–1625* (Leicester, 1975).

Webb, W. K. L., 'Thomas Preston OSB, alias Roger Widdrington (1567–1640)', *Biographical Studies* 2 (1953–4), 216–69.

White, H. C., *English Devotional Literature [Prose] 1600–1640* (New York, 1966).

Wickes, G., 'Henry Constable, Poet and Courtier, 1562–1613', *Biographical Studies* 2 (1953–4), 272–300.

Williams, M. E., *The Venerable English College, Rome* (1979).

Youngs jnr, F. A., 'Definitions of Treason in an Elizabethan Proclamation', *HJ* 14 (1971), 675–91.

Zaller, R., *The Parliament of 1621* (1971).

UNPUBLISHED THESES

Burke, V., 'Catholic Recusants in Elizabethan Worcestershire' (M.A thesis, Birmingham, 1972).

Cassidy, I., 'The Episcopate of William Cotton, Bishop of Exeter, 1598–1621: With Special Reference to the State of the Clergy and the Administration of the Ecclesiastical Courts' (BLitt. thesis, Oxford, 1963).

Clark, R., 'Anglicanism, Recusancy and Dissent in Derbyshire 1603–1730' (DPhil. thesis, Oxford, 1979).

Davidson, A., 'Roman Catholicism in Oxfordshire from the Late Elizabethan Period to the Civil War *c.* 1580–1640' (Ph.D thesis, Bristol, 1970).

Dent, C., 'Protestants in Elizabethan Oxford' (DPhil. thesis, Oxford, 1980).

Dunbabin, A., 'Post-Reformation Catholicism in the Parish of Prescot, Lancashire, from the Elizabethan Settlement to the Civil War' (MA thesis, Manchester, 1980).

Foster, A. W., 'A Biography of Archbishop Richard Neile (1562–1640)' (DPhil. thesis, Oxford, 1978).

Gifford, J. V., 'The Controversy over the Oath of Allegiance of 1606' (DPhil. thesis, Oxford, 1971).

Hilton, J. A., 'Catholic Recusancy in County Durham, 1559–1625' (MPhil. thesis, Leeds, 1974).

Jensen, P. F., 'The Life of Faith in the Teaching of Elizabethan Protestants' (DPhil. thesis, Oxford, 1979).

Loomie, A. J., 'Spain and the English Catholic Exiles 1580–1604' (Ph.D thesis, London, 1957).

Marcombe, D., 'The Dean and Chapter of Durham, 1558–1603' (Ph.D thesis, Durham, 1973).

Milton, A., 'The Laudians and the Church of Rome *c.* 1625–1640' (Ph. D. thesis, Cambridge, 1989).

Newton, J. A., 'Puritanism in the Diocese of York (excluding Nottinghamshire) 1603–1640' (Ph.D thesis, London, 1955).

O'Dwyer, M., 'Catholic Recusants in Essex *c.* 1580 to *c.* 1600' (MA thesis, London, 1960).

Paul, J. E., 'The Hampshire Recusants in the Reign of Elizabeth I with some Reference to the Problem of Church Papists' (Ph.D thesis, Southampton, 1958).

Potter, J. M., 'The Ecclesiastical Courts in the Diocese of Canterbury 1603–1665' (MPhil. thesis, London, 1973).

Questier, M. C., 'The Phenomenon of Conversion: Change of Religion to and from Catholicism in England, 1580–1625' (DPhil. thesis, Sussex, 1991).

Sommerville, J. P., 'Jacobean Political Thought and the Controversy over the Oath of Allegiance' (Ph.D thesis, Cambridge, 1981).

Tyler, P., 'The Ecclesiastical Commission for the Province of York 1561–1641' (DPhil. thesis, Oxford, 1965).

Walker, F. X., 'The Implementation of the Elizabethan Statutes against Recusants 1581–1603' (Ph.D thesis, London, 1961).

Ward, L. J., 'The Law of Treason in the Reign of Elizabeth I 1558–1588' (Ph.D thesis, Cambridge, 1985).

INDEX

Cambridge Studies in Early Modern British History

Titles in the series